Coyote
Warrior

Coyote Warrior

ONE MAN, THREE TRIBES,
AND THE TRIAL THAT FORGED A NATION

Paul VanDevelder

Little, Brown and Company
NEW YORK BOSTON

Little, Brown and Company
Time Warner Book Group
1271 Avenue of the Americas, New York, NY 10020
Visit our Web site at www.twbookmark.com

FIRST EDITION

Maps designed by Jeffrey Ward

Library of Congress Cataloging-in-Publication Data

VanDevelder, Paul.
    Coyote warrior : one man, three tribes, and the trial that forged a nation /
Paul VanDevelder. — 1st ed.
        p.   cm.
Includes bibliographical references and index.
    ISBN 0-316-89689-6
    1. Three Affiliated Tribes — History.   2. Indians of North America — North Dakota —
Government policy.   3. Indians of North America — North Dakota — Relocation.
4. Indians of North America — North Dakota — Legal status, laws, etc.   5. Indians,
Treatment of — North Dakota — Garrison Dam.   6. Dams — Law and legislation —
North Dakota — Garrison Dam.   7. Trials — United States.   8. Garrison Dam (N.D.) —
Environmental aspects.   9. Garrison Dam (N.D.) — Social aspects.   10. United States —
Social policy.   11. United States — Race relations.   12. United States — Politics and
government.   I. Title.

E78.N4V35   2004
323.1197'0784 — dc22   2003026614

10   9   8   7   6   5   4   3   2   1

Q-FF

Book design by Fearn Cutler de Vicq
Printed in the United States of America

for the dancers
gone and yet to come

Contents

꙾

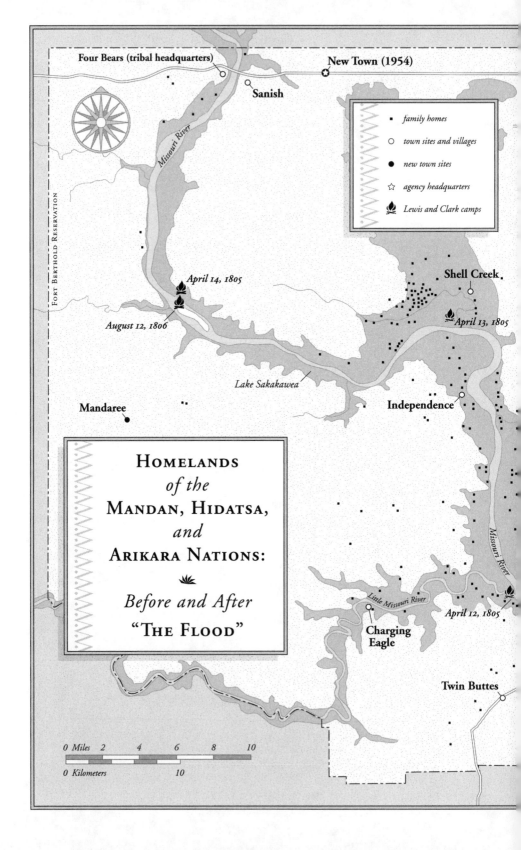

Four Bears (tribal headquarters)

New Town (1954)

Sanish

Legend

- ▪ family homes
- ○ town sites and villages
- ● new town sites
- ☆ agency headquarters
- 🔥 Lewis and Clark camps

FORT BERTHOLD RESERVATION

Missouri River

Shell Creek

April 14, 1805

August 12, 1806

🔥 *April 13, 1805*

Lake Sakakawea

Mandaree

Independence

HOMELANDS
of the
MANDAN, HIDATSA,
and
ARIKARA NATIONS:

Before and After
"THE FLOOD"

Missouri River

Little Missouri River

🔥 *April 12, 1805*

Charging
Eagle

Twin Buttes

0 Miles   2   4   6   8   10

0 Kilometers   10

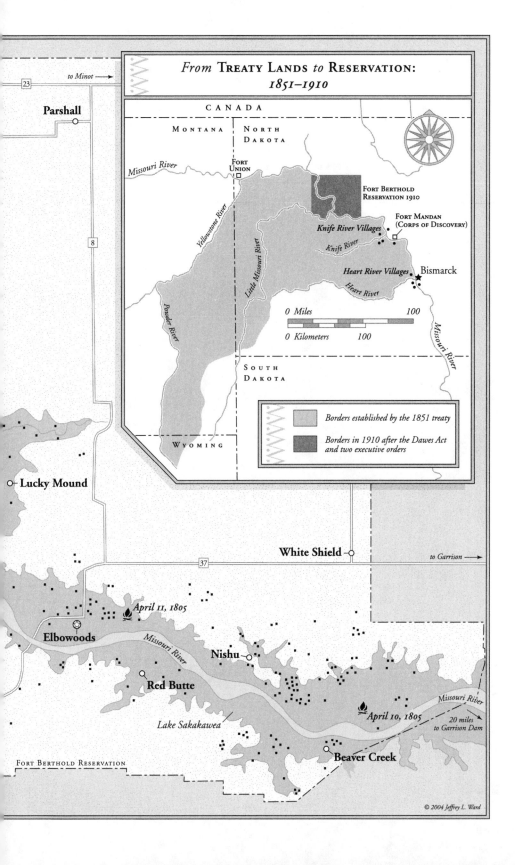

From Treaty Lands to Reservation: 1851–1910

CANADA

MONTANA   NORTH DAKOTA

Missouri River

FORT UNION

FORT BERTHOLD RESERVATION 1910

FORT MANDAN (CORPS OF DISCOVERY)

Knife River Villages

Knife River

Yellowstone River

Little Missouri River

Heart River Villages

Bismarck

Heart River

Powder River

Missouri River

0 Miles   100

0 Kilometers   100

SOUTH DAKOTA

WYOMING

Borders established by the 1851 treaty

Borders in 1910 after the Dawes Act and two executive orders

to Minot →

23

Parshall

8

Lucky Mound

White Shield

to Garrison →

37

April 11, 1805

Elbowoods

Missouri River

Nishu

Red Butte

Lake Sakakawea

April 10, 1805

Missouri River

20 miles to Garrison Dam

FORT BERTHOLD RESERVATION

Beaver Creek

© 2004 Jeffrey L. Ward

"He who learns must suffer. And even in our sleep
pain that cannot forget falls drop by drop
upon the heart, and in our own despair,
against our will, comes wisdom to
us by the awful grace of God."

AESCHYLUS

coyote: a mythical, spiritual, or human being living on the geographic and social fringe of a community, whose role within that community is to use humor, shock, cunning, and surprise to assist individuals in "waking up," and to prevent the community from developing self-destructive modes of behavior

warrior: a protector of the people, a high distinction earned through fidelity to truth, common sense, physical and mental prowess, and personal integrity

Coyote
Warrior

Introduction

***

We are a comet without a tail, streaking across the desert at one hundred five miles per hour in a rented Buick. The Mojave, a vast and silvery landscape, slipstreams by in a whisper. Ours are the only headlights we have seen for many miles. Tom Goldtooth, the national director of the Indigenous Environmental Network, glows like a Buddha in the dash lights.

"A black guy, an Indian, and a white guy arrive at the pearly gates," he begins. "Saint Peter says, 'Welcome to heaven. This is your lucky day. You get to pick the heaven of your dreams.' So the black guy goes first. 'I want to be in heaven with lots of brothers and sisters and great music.' Saint Peter says, 'No problem, that's exactly what you'll find behind door number one.' Next, the Indian steps up. 'What do you want heaven to be?' The old Indian doesn't hesitate. 'I want heaven to have beautiful mountain streams and deep forests and plenty of food to eat.' Saint Peter says, 'No problem, Chief, that's exactly what you'll find behind door number three.' Then the white guy steps up and Saint Peter says, 'What do you want heaven to look like?' And the white guy says, 'Where did that Indian go?'"

Ever since Hernán Cortés waded ashore in Mexico in 1519, white guys in funny hats have been asking, "Where did that Indian go?" For Goldtooth, this question carries as much freight today as it did five centuries ago. Indians comprise less than 1 percent of the population, yet they own 40 percent of the nation's coal reserves. Indians also own 65 percent of the uranium reserves in the United States, untold ounces of gold, silver, cadmium, and manganese, and billions of board feet of timber, all still in the ground or standing on the stump. They own oil, billions of cubic feet of natural gas, and an unopened treasure chest of copper and zinc. They guard the door to 20 percent of the nation's freshwater and millions of acres of pristine real estate. A recent commentary in *Forbes* magazine observed: "Now, at a time when the United

States seems to be running out of practically everything, Indian reservations constitute one of the least-known repositories of natural resources on the continent." They might have added, "and the largest."

The pressure on tribal governments to begin selling off these resources has never been greater. State and federal politicians, industrial tycoons, and international mineral conglomerates are not easily discouraged. In their world every commodity has a price. But a new generation of Indian leaders has arisen. These coyote warriors, as they are known, have resisted the seductions of the global marketplace. To that end, the coyotes have declared much of Indian Country off-limits to mineral and resource development. From the hardwood forests of Wisconsin to the panoramic mesas of the Southwest, Indian Country's crystalline rivers and virgin forests, its gold-bearing hills and fresh, clean air, are not for sale.

In the late 1980s many young Native American biologists, hydrologists, atmospheric chemists, and lawyers began returning to their reservations of origin and reconnecting with their ancestral traditions. Foremost among those traditions was the Sacred Trust, or what the Sioux call *wouncage,* the guiding ethic of conducting the life of the individual and the tribe in a state of reverence and balance with the natural world. For many throughout the indigenous world, *wouncage* is the enlightened state of living in harmony and balance with the "great mysterious."

Back on the res, these young leaders banded together to find new economic and political solutions to long-standing ailments. More often than not, that meant working independently of tribal institutions with vested interests in the status quo. The coyote warriors were soon to learn that their interests had not been served either by tribal institutions or by the federal agencies assigned by Congress to safeguard tribal resources. The long-overdue accounting of a century of thievery and malfeasance finally came to a boil in August 1999. Ruling from his federal district court in Washington, D.C., Judge Royce Lamberth found the federal government guilty of swindling thousand of Indians out of $10 billion in mineral royalties, a practice that went unchecked for more than a century. Reliable information from government ledgers was such a scarce commodity throughout the three-year trial that Judge Lamberth has since cited two secretaries of the interior with contempt for bureaucratic foot-dragging and repeated failures to produce subpoenaed evidence. Any figure the court settled on, said the Price Waterhouse accountants who crunched the numbers, should be viewed as a gift to the thief from his victims. When the government appealed the decision in August

2002, attorneys for the plaintiffs estimated the true value of the missing funds at $50 billion.

About ten years earlier, a young Navajo biologist named Lori Goodman stunned the mainstream environmental community when her grassroots coalition, Diné CARE, succeeded in halting the construction of a nuclear-waste incinerator at Dilkon, Arizona. For two years, Goodman and her loyal volunteers went from hogan to hogan, patiently building their case against their tribal leaders and the federal government. This was new. Until then, native political activists had been viewed in the mainstream as a ragtag group of marginalized hotheads. In the 1970s members of AIM, the American Indian Movement, were persecuted and jailed along with militant Black Panthers and more radical revolutionaries in the SDS, Students for a Democratic Society. After these tumultuous years, AIM fizzled for want of effective leadership. Its leaders could force a siege at Wounded Knee, but they could not organize a car wash if their bail bondsman was holding the hose. Goodman's Diné CARE was a bold departure. When the contest of rhetoric and wills was finally put to Navajo voters, the U.S. Department of Energy (DOE) waved a white flag, and the tribal chairman was sent to federal prison for embezzlement.

Demonstrating a familiarity with "the real world," Goodman and Diné CARE were victorious at Dilkon, signaling a maturing of tactics and organization — proof that the coyotes were a force to be reckoned with. In order to capitalize on the publicity that followed, visionaries such as Goodman, Winona LaDuke, Gail Small, and Walt Bressette formed the Indigenous Environmental Network, a group dedicated to carrying the work to the 100 million acres of Indian Country that stretched from the tropics to the tundra. When Goldtooth opened the IEN for business in the spring of 1990, the greatest challenge was deciding where to begin. Like the cavalry of another century, the machinery of the industrialized world was camped out on every horizon. By the mid-1990s, the IEN had evolved into an international cyber network connecting Inuit coyotes to their counterparts in Minnesota, Panama, Nigeria, and New Zealand.

"In the old days we used bows and arrows to protect our land, our families, our resources," Goldtooth recently told one of his many audiences. "But that wasn't very effective, so a hundred years later we exchanged our bows and arrows for science and law. Science and law, combined with sovereignty, work much better. They can be very persuasive."

Dateline: Isleta, New Mexico. As the city of Albuquerque grew by leaps and bounds in the 1990s, the Rio Grande became so foul with untreated sewage that the Isleta Pueblo tribe's young governor, Verna Teller, had no choice but to challenge the city. With help from the federal Environmental Protection Agency, Teller invoked a little-known provision in the federal Clean Water Act to assert her tribe's right to establish its own water-quality standards. The city of Albuquerque filed suit to prevent the Isleta standards from taking force. The city lost. In the final appeal to the U.S. Supreme Court in 1998, the tribe's right to establish its own water-quality standards was upheld. From Maine to California, dozens of tribes have since followed the Isleta's lead.

Dateline: Hanford, Washington. Visionary architect William McDonough met with a team of DOE engineers to explore long-term storage solutions for nuclear waste. While in Hanford, he was invited to attend a powwow hosted by the nearby Yakima tribe. Over dinner the tribal chairman inquired about the nature of the project. McDonough explained that his team was looking for a fail-safe way to tell people ten thousand years from now that the nuclear waste at Hanford was extremely dangerous. "That's what all this is about?" said the chairman. "Don't worry, we'll tell them."

⋇

Whether at Isleta, Hanford, Dilkon, or a dozen other hot spots, the particulars in these cases are window dressing that often conceal much larger issues. Strip away the clams and oysters, remove the copper, gold, and fishing rods, and what lurks behind the details are battles over self-determination and cultural survival, the ownership of natural resources, and the challenge of living in fidelity with the promises and contracts of generations long gone.

In the decade or so since their victory at Dilkon, the coyotes have won dozens of landmark courtroom battles by successfully coupling science with the law. When combined, these seemingly disparate disciplines have forged for the coyotes a powerful new weapon in the defense of treaty-protected rights and resources. In the difficult and often discouraging process of erecting those defenses, they have also learned that politics and economics are simply weather, the thunderstorm in the foreground. Law, on the other hand, is the ground beneath their feet. The new social contract presumes that the courts will steer them toward reckonings with the shoals of principle that few politicians have the courage, or vision, to navigate.

Dateline: Missoula, Montana. It is late winter, 2000, and a federal commission convened by the Army Corps of Engineers has come to this railroad and logging town of seventy thousand citizens to find out what people think about salmon, the Snake River dams, and the economic future of this vast region of the American outback. Missoula is one of ten stops for the commission. At every venue thus far they have drawn angry, standing-room-only crowds. Apart and alone, a man with short cropped hair and penetrating black eyes sits quietly at the back of the room. With his legs crossed, fingertips pressed together, he measures the milling crowd. Mandan attorney and law professor Raymond Cross finds himself at the center of the national debate over how to rescue twelve endangered stocks of native salmon, and the tribal people who have depended on that resource for millennia, from extinction. Born fifty-two years earlier in the village of Elbowoods, North Dakota, he has made a longer journey than anyone else has to get here. Raymond Cross knows that there are distances across the American landscape that cannot be measured in miles.

But Raymond Cross's story does not begin with that journey, or even with his birth in 1948 — the youngest of ten children born to tribal chairman Martin Cross and his wife, Dorothy, the daughter of Norwegian homesteaders. It begins in October of 1804, at the mouth of the Knife River, in what is known today as central North Dakota. Here, Raymond Cross's ancestors welcomed Captains Meriwether Lewis and William Clark, the leaders of Thomas Jefferson's Corps of Discovery, to the five Mandan and Hidatsa Villages. This constellation of semipermanent enclaves sat at the hub of a trade network connecting the Cree of Nova Scotia, in the far northeast, to the Pueblo and Comanche of the desert southwest. Dozens of European traders, entrepreneurs, and explorers preceded Jefferson's Corps of Discovery to the Mandan Villages at the Heart and Knife Rivers, some by as much as eighty years. The first American expedition was in fact the last chapter in the Age of Exploration of the Upper Missouri and the American West.

In his seminal work, *Lewis and Clark Among the Indians,* historian James Rhonda observed that the Americans were sailing out of their depth as they approached the Knife River. "The simplistic diplomatic model Lewis and Clark brought with them sought to reduce the highly complex social and economic structure of intertribal relations . . . into one of childlike servility to the Great White Fathers, a model that served neither the Indians nor the whites in future dealings." Yet the Mandan set aside their doubts about the Americans. They saw them safely through the winter of 1805 and helped them prepare for the journey ahead. "No set of men that ever I associated with have better hearts than the Mandan," wrote the artist George Catlin, when he lived among the Mandan in the 1830s, "and no man in any country keeps his word, and guards his honor, more closely."

From the moment of "first contact," the Cross family story is spun from the same thread that binds together the larger story of the Mandan, Hidatsa, and Arikara people. Across the next two centuries, their tragedies and triumphs would lay bare the cultural and legal paradoxes that were already at work, shaping the America we live in today. Conflicts and contradictions built into the nation's foundational charter would lead inevitably to a legal high noon in the final decade of the twentieth century. When that day arrived, Raymond Cross would be standing at its center.

In the twelfth century, the Mandan people were establishing their first permanent settlements on the Upper Missouri River. Simultaneously, the Papal See was asserting its "divine prerogative" to send crusading armies to the Holy Lands in order to confiscate land from Muslim "heathens and infidels." These papal prerogatives were formally incorporated into canon law by Popes Innocent III and IV, and would continue to evolve through discovery-era Spain, through the Elizabethan and Jacobean courts in England, and, finally, through the U.S. Supreme Court — becoming Chief Justice John Marshall's reckoning with the Doctrine of Discovery, and its offspring, *eminent domain.*

This was the evolutionary lineage of the laws that Congress would invoke midway through the twentieth century to forcibly remove the Mandan, Hidatsa, and Arikara people from their homelands of prehistory to make way for a giant dam at the Mandan Bluffs on the Upper Missouri River. While the tribes claimed an absolute right to protect their ancestral lands from being inundated by the dam, the Republic of the United States asserted a countervailing prerogative to trump the tribes' aboriginal title by claiming a superior right — under *eminent domain* — to take that land away. Twice threatened with extinction in the previous two centuries, the descendants of the tribes that saved Lewis and Clark were once again face-to-face with their own demise. The ensuing struggle for survival would span five decades.

"How these paradoxes play out in real people's lives is not simply a story about Indians," says Raymond Cross. "It is the story of America, about all of us. How we resolve those great paradoxes is our own Age of Discovery, one that asks all Americans, 'After the storms, who are we?' "

On the Yellowstone, 2003

CHAPTER I

Heart of the World

ﺀ

"The white man does not understand the Indian for the reason that he does not understand America. The roots of the tree of his life have not yet grasped the rock and the soil. He is still troubled with primitive fears. In the Indian the spirit of the land is still vested. Men must be formed of the dust of their forefather's bones."

STANDING BEAR, OGLALA

For twenty years after the spaceships landed in the pintail tulies and gooseberry woods on the floodplain, downstream from Elbowoods, Phyllis Old Dog Cross was afraid to look at the moon. A lifetime later, on a June evening in 2002, an unexpected glimpse of the prairie moonrise still sends shivers up her spine. She laughs self-consciously, then turns away and settles into a ladder-back chair at the kitchen table. The opening in the wall beside the table seems less like a window than a picture frame, one that corrals an intimidating sweep of purple sky and a bright yellow coin, balanced edgewise on a bruised horizon. Cowlicked and wind-scoured, the silver swells of storied landscape framed by this window have sustained members of the Cross family for dozens of generations. At the end of a life spent in other places, Phyllis has come back to the only home she has ever known.

"My memories of that night are very evocative, like a smell that reminds you of your mother's kitchen," she says. "I was only eight years old, but before it was over I knew that nothing would ever be the same for us."

At seventy-two, Phyllis's short gray hair and high forehead frame the clear, darting eyes of a teenage girl. The muscular deterioration brought on by Parkinson's disease is advancing slowly, but things she took for granted ten years ago, such as getting in and out of her car and walking down the street to her sister Marilyn's house, require a cane and extra effort. She lives alone in a modest frame house on the outskirts of Parshall, a small community with one stoplight and eight hundred residents, farmers and ranchers mostly, perched at the edge of the world in central North Dakota. Her home is a comfortable, solidly built refuge from extremes of prairie weather. A lifetime of mementos and souvenirs surround her in every room. There were the years in the Carter White House working for mental-health legislation, the 1981 Wonder Woman of the Year Award, and her career with the Air Force as a flight nurse and with the Department of the Interior as a pioneering mental-health specialist. Despite the familiarity of local landmarks such as grain silos and cemeteries, Phyllis has been away so long that sometimes she feels like she is trespassing in her own memories.

At the center of those memories lies the broad, meandering valley of the Upper Missouri River. Where the valley begins upstream, the river shakes itself free from the high, sunbaked bluffs and sandstone pillars of the badlands, then bends southward after being joined by the Yellowstone for the long run to the sea. When Phyllis was a little girl, the alluvial valley of the Upper Missouri River was a lush, thickly wooded floodplain that snaked its way across the continent some four to eight hundred feet below the surrounding grasslands of the Great Plains. In central North Dakota — at the middle of this green, four-mile-wide belt of terraced woodlands and open meadows — was the village of Elbowoods and the small house where Phyllis lived with her mother and father, Dorothy and Martin Cross, and her nine brothers and sisters. The house sat at the edge of a dense woodland of maple trees, live oaks, and Russian olives, an unfenced wilderness that was home to white-tailed deer and sparrow hawks, badgers, black bears, rabbits, meadowlarks, bull snakes, and whooping cranes. There, just a five-minute walk from the shallow back eddies in the river where Phyllis learned to swim as a little girl, her mother and father raised cows and chickens, pigs and goats, and grew vegetable gardens and crops of grain on 160 acres of the richest bottomland in North America.

Phyllis is the oldest of the four girls and six boys, their ages spanning eighteen years. Raymond, the youngest, was born in 1948, a year after Phyllis left home. With so many chores around the ranch, and so many little brothers and sisters, Phyllis became the third adult in the Cross household on her sixth birthday. Clustered around the edges of the family portrait are aunts and uncles, and all the far-flung cousins and secondhand relations who played supporting roles in a cast of hundreds. She flips through the pages of a scrapbook. "If you live long enough, your head turns into your own private ghost town."

Phyllis's fear of the moon began on an ordinary school night at her childhood home in Elbowoods. It was an autumn evening, with the usual routine of dinner and dishes, homework afterward, then early to bed. As she and her mother finished up in the kitchen that evening, her father, Martin, fiddled with the dials on the small cherrywood radio in the living room. He tuned the frequency dial to KFYR, a station in Bismarck, hoping to pick up CBS's *Mercury Theater on the Air.* Back then, the radio's antenna was nothing more than a bare copper wire strung from a window sash at the house to the steel frame of the windmill out by the barn. Slung beneath the prairie sky, this was their ear to the world beyond the horizon, one that captured everything from basketball games and cowboy crooners to New York City jazz clubs. But that evening, instead of the familiar radio drama, Martin and 9 million other people suddenly found themselves listening to a live, eyewitness report of spaceships landing in a small town in New Jersey. Orson Welles's dramatization of H. G. Wells's novella *The War of the Worlds* had just begun.

It was October 30, 1938, the night the twenty-three-year-old theatrical wunderkind would become a household name. The radio drama, staged as a breaking news flash of an alien invasion, instantly spread terror across the nation. The panic that swept through the Cross household would visit thousands of other homes from Boston to San Francisco. In the CBS studio in New York, however, Welles and his cast were completely oblivious to the chaos being unleashed in towns and cities across America. In fact, prior to going on the air the cast found the script so dull that they asked for a last-minute replacement. None was available, so once the drama began, the cast's lingering doubts about the script charged their on-air performances with a heightened air of realism. Ten minutes into the show, a squad of New York City police stormed into the CBS sound studios with revolvers drawn. Out in the great beyond, from Manhattan to Elbowoods, an estimated 2 million Americans were frantically planning their escapes from the invasion.

"My memory of that night starts with my mom and dad running around the house like a couple of crazy people," says Phyllis. "To this day I can hear Orson Welles's voice describing the spaceships flying across the face of the moon as they came in for a landing. There was no doubt in my mind that they would be in Elbowoods in minutes."

⅍

The house where Martin and Dorothy Cross raised their ten children sat in a copse of trees on the northeast side of a cottonwood lane. Rutted to ankle-deep dust by horseshoes and steel-rimmed wagon wheels, the country road disappeared over low-lying hills on its way up the Missouri River from Elbowoods to the village of Lucky Mound. The house itself, a thirty-by-forty-foot rectangle, was a modern abode by the standards of the day. It was built by Phyllis's grandfather Old Dog, a Hidatsa tribal chief and judge who managed to complete it just months before he died in April 1928. When Old Dog's twenty-two-year-old bachelor son, Martin Cross, courted and married Dorothy Bartel, a Norwegian girl from the nearby village of Van Hook, on September 2, 1928, the house became the son's by right and custom.

The young couple's home lacked any sort of newfangled amenities, such as a washing machine or telephone, but for Grandfather Old Dog, frame construction was a bold step into the modern era. Until then, the revered chief had spent his entire life living in traditional, dome-shaped earth lodges and log cabins. The new house allotted each of the Cross family members a hundred feet of space. Typical of most homes built on the Great Plains by do-it-yourself carpenters, this was a practical, no-frills single-story structure. Beneath the hipped roof were three small bedrooms, a living room, a kitchen, and a screened-in porch that doubled as an extra bedroom during warm weather. The Cross house owed its longevity less to mastery of trade by the builders than to the holding power of galvanized nails and the miracle of tar paper. Without tar paper, barbed wire, and the centrifugal pump — the holy trinity of American ingenuity at the turn of the twentieth century — the central highlands of the North American continent might well have remained an unfenced sea of grass.

The tallest order for any house on the Great Plains was keeping out the weather. Temperatures in Elbowoods could range from sixty below in February to a hundred and ten above in August. Old newspapers were stuffed into the voids between siding and lath. Tongue-and-groove floors in the kitchen and living room were covered with rolled linoleum to cut down on drafts from the root cellar. Windows let light and summer breezes into every room, a dramatic improvement from the shadowy interiors of traditional earth lodges, but this was the extent of the home's architectural luxuries. There was no plumbing or electricity, no central heating, and no closets in the bedrooms. During the winter months, a coal stove squatted in the middle of the living-room floor, consuming fuel around the clock. Beside the radio and Martin's overstuffed easy chair, a plain coffee table sat on an oval-shaped rag rug. A narrow corridor connected the living room to the kitchen, where the family ate its meals. Here were the simple necessities: a cast-iron wood stove that vented into a chimney; a table and chairs; and a hand pump that drew water from a well beneath the house.

"My mom baked bread in that oven at least four days a week," remembers Phyllis. "She chopped the wood and cooked three meals a day for twelve people on that stove. She canned enough food to get us through the winter, and when the temperature dropped to fifty below, we'd get that stove so hot it glowed like a cherry. Why that house didn't burn down I will never know."

When things got too hot in the kitchen in the summertime, a door was propped open onto the back porch. Beyond the porch was the requisite menagerie of outbuildings: a barn and an outhouse; the tack shed with harnesses, saddles, and bridles for Martin's small herd of horses; and chicken coops, whose occupants helped fertilize a two-acre garden that started at the clotheslines and kept on going until Dorothy Cross ran out of energy. At that very spot lay an invisible boundary to another world. Beyond Dorothy Cross's garden there was nothing but open prairie until the outskirts of Minot, sixty miles north. But neither Minot nor Bismarck conjured images of actual places in the young minds of Phyllis and her siblings. "Whatever was out there, beyond Elbowoods, was a big blank."

A half-mile walk from the Cross's front steps was the small town of Elbowoods. The town itself was a simple, right-angled grid of pretty tree-lined streets laid out around a central square on the cardinal points of the compass. A team of government surveyors had picked the site in the early 1890s. It sat at a bend in the Missouri River, about eighty free-flowing water miles upstream from the state capital at Bismarck. Most years, when the river behaved itself and stayed within its banks, the town sat high and dry on an elevated bench of land that overlooked a fertile hundred-year floodplain. As it had for centuries, the river dictated the terms of life for the valley's widely scattered residents. The only thing predictable about the Big Muddy, as locals called the river, was its unpredictability.

Within rock-throwing distance of the town's main square were Simon's and Twilling's general stores, a courthouse, a clump of official-looking Indian agency buildings, the sheriff's house and jail, and the agency-run boarding school. When Phyllis was a teenager, the boarding school was home to more than 250 children for nine months of the year. There were electric lights in the dorms, central heating in the classrooms, flush toilets, and running water that poured from taps. Down the street from the main square was a state-of-the-art hospital and outpatient clinic. Built by the federal government in 1929, this facility was staffed year-round with a doctor and three nurses. It had eighteen beds, six cribs, a surgical center, and a new ambulance. News of local emergencies could be transmitted to the outside world on a Western Union telegraph key at the agency office, which also boasted the only telephone between Elbowoods and Parshall, thirty miles to the north. For the two thousand members of the Mandan, Hidatsa, and Arikara nations, Elbowoods was the heart of the world.

⋇

The War of the Worlds broadcast quickly transformed an ordinary school night into a frightful drama. Phyllis's father told everybody in the household to dress in his or her warmest clothes and to meet him at the truck. Then he raced out of the house to tell his sisters, Alice and Lucy, who lived in a small house out by the barn. The two youngest children, Forrest and Marilyn, were both with Dorothy in the kitchen. Phyllis collected the babies, one under each arm, and quickly bundled them up in coats and blankets on the living-room floor. While Phyllis was helping her little brothers, Bucky and Crusoe, into their coats, Dorothy was frantically packing food and filling water jugs from the hand pump in the kitchen.

"That's when I heard the news reporter describing more spaceships landing, and I was instantly terrified," says Phyllis. With baby Forrest on her hip and sister Marilyn holding her hand, Phyllis pushed Bucky and Crusoe out the door ahead of her and led them through the dark toward the waiting truck.

In a crisis, Martin Cross was the guy you wanted making the important decisions. At six foot four, 220 pounds, the former rodeo cowboy was physically self-assured and tougher than a fence post. Having spent years at an Indian boarding school in Wahpeton, South Dakota, and several more following the rodeo circuit, Martin had a reputation for being a man of the world, a guy who could think under pressure. But in the haste of the moment that night, he had gotten a step ahead of himself. The car battery, which also powered the cherrywood radio in the living room, was still in the house. As his wife, sisters, and five children all huddled under blankets in the back of the truck, he cursed a blue streak and raced back into the house to fetch the battery.

Squeezed between her two aunts and pinned beneath her little sister, Phyllis held her breath as precious minutes slipped by. Lying under the starlit sky, she fully expected lights from spaceships to begin appearing over the treetops. She was certain that this was their only chance to get away. What were her friends doing? What was happening at the school, in the dorms? Had they heard about the aliens? As her aunts chattered anxiously in their native Hidatsa, Phyllis fretted over what was taking her father so long. Then, a yellow lantern flame ignited in the front room and threw her father's shadow across the wall. Finally, the front door opened. After descending the front steps, Martin Cross paused for a moment with his hands on his hips, gazing quietly at the sky.

"He walked back to the truck and said it was all a big hoax. There were no martians. No spaceships. I'd never seen my father look so angry, so defeated."

Martin Cross had been humbled by invisible forces that originated far beyond his reckoning. Phyllis does not remember him ever laughing again, not freely or joyfully the way he had before that night. He took the hoax personally, as though he was somehow at fault for his own innocence, for the limitations built into a life on the bottomlands of the Upper Missouri River, a life that allowed him to be toyed with like a child and shamed in front of his wife and children. After that night, says Phyllis, the family never talked about it again, not across the supper table in Dorothy Cross's kitchen, not until they were adults, many years later.

"As we now know, a war of the worlds is exactly what was in store for us that night," says Phyllis. "It was coming soon enough, but it wouldn't be little green men in spaceships. It'd be the Army engineers."

⚜

Back when Phyllis was a little girl, Old State Road Number Eight connected the small, thriving farming communities of Parshall and Elbowoods. Each village was laid out by surveyors along about the turn of the twentieth century, and each sat at the center of a vast green disk, with fifty-mile views in any direction. From cradle to grave, many citizens of both villages lived their entire lives without ever venturing beyond the visible boundaries of that circle. Most residents of Parshall were the descendants of blond, blue-eyed stoics who emigrated to America from Scandinavia. They were a stouthearted people of few words and deep Christian faith, utilitarian men and women who were willing to endure extremes of physical and psychological isolation in order to transform the wild North American grasslands into a Garden of

Eden. Their closest neighbors, in Elbowoods, lived in tidy, well-kept houses on pretty elm-shaded streets. These were the descendants of the once powerful Mandan, Hidatsa, and Arikara nations, a tribal people who had been farming the fertile bottomlands of the Upper Missouri River for nearly a thousand years. Ever since the two villages were built, boundaries laid down by treaties, railroads, and government surveyors had kept the homesteaders of Parshall and the tribes of Elbowoods in semi-isolated worlds, thirty miles apart.

To early residents of Elbowoods like Chief Old Dog, the transformation of the buffalo commons known as the Great Plains into half a million square miles of fenced wheat fields seemed to have happened overnight. To the homesteaders who supplied the strong arms and backs to build those fences and bust the virgin sod, this overnight transformation took the better part of a century. Turning the High Plains into a Garden of Eden was a far larger endeavor than most immigrants imagined. As wave after wave of immigrants made the Atlantic crossing in the closing years of the nineteenth century, America's seaboards teemed with growing cities, squalid neighborhoods of newly arrived immigrants, and industrial centers that hissed and belched beside every deepwater port. By contrast, beyond the Ohio Valley and the Mississippi River, the defining feature of America's wide-open middle was its imperious silence. Faced with meager prospects in their own densely populated homelands, Scandinavian farmers and tradesmen clamored to redeem the promise of free land on America's Great Plains. Thousands of emigrants exchanged life savings for one-way tickets to this place where milk and honey were said to flow in rivers. The arduous journey across an ocean, and half a continent, often took months. What awaited them when they stepped off the train was a silent, semi-arid landscape, one that would punish the weak, humble the strong, and take pity on neither.

To the dismay of many, the journey was the easy part. Once they arrived, there was no time to rest or celebrate. In their first months on the plains, in the Dakotas, Minnesota, Nebraska, or Iowa, homesteaders faced a daunting onslaught of elements. Fierce heat, ferocious winds, and frigid, subarctic winters tested the fortitude of the strongest among them. Only three out of ten would endure the loneliness and grueling physical hardships of the first withering years. In time, most of those who drifted away would melt back into the ethnic enclaves of America's industrial cities. Bit by bit, the few who stuck it out built unassuming little worlds in towns like Parshall. From central Minnesota to the Rocky Mountain front, one shelter-belted community looked much like another, with a rail spur and grain silos, wide streets, and modest, freshly painted houses with groomed lawns and potted geraniums arranged just so on porch steps. Everything they bought, built, or invented was an installment in advance on future prosperity, an eventuality they took to be as inevitable as the wind, the silence, and the wrath of the Almighty.

When the state finally got around to paving Old Number Eight in the late 1960s, Main Street in Parshall boasted a bank and a movie house, a bowling alley and grocery store, three churches, eight grain silos at the south end of town, a high school with a track and a football field at the north end, an airport with half a dozen tie-downs, a Ford dealer, a kidney-shaped public swimming pool with a diving board and a wading pool for toddlers, and a nine-hole golf course. The shared values that rooted its two thousand residents to the earth had survived the journey from the old country. Foremost among these were discipline, sacrifice, and an unswerving fidelity to God, neighbor, and country. Payment for life's sundry necessities, from quilting needles to canning jars and John Deere's eight-bottom plow, were made with the cash from the cookie jar. There was no greater sin than going to meet your Maker with a basket of unpaid bills.

Like their newly arrived neighbors from northern Europe, the citizens of Elbowoods cultivated the same fields and lived in the same villages for hundreds of years. They built things with a view to posterity. The Mandan in particular were famed throughout the pre-Columbian Americas as masters of horticulture and trade. At the peak of their material wealth, perhaps early in the eighteenth century, the cluster of nine Mandan Villages at the mouth of the Heart River, in what today is central North Dakota, was home to more than fourteen thousand people. Two centuries before the first French voyageurs established commercial ties with the tribes, the Heart River Villages were the commercial hub of a trade and distribution network that linked the Aztec and Toltec cultures of Mesoamerica to the Cree of northern Quebec. Comanche of the Southwest brought Arab stallions and Spanish knives to trade with Hudson Bay Assiniboin, who bartered English flintlocks, gunpowder, and textiles. By the early seventeenth century, French explorers on the Gulf Coast were well aware of the great trading bazaar at the Heart River from stories they heard while mapping the Lower Mississippi. At about the time Benjamin Franklin was born in the small seaside village of Boston, the Spanish horse culture was meeting the English gun culture three miles west of a hilltop where Norwegian immigrants would build the North Dakota state capitol in Bismarck two hundred years later.

When the French explorer Sieur de La Vérendrye finally made his way to the Mandan Villages in November of 1738, he was heartened to discover that the Mandan's reputation as skilled diplomats was well deserved. This, combined with reports from the Assiniboin that the Mandan had blue eyes and fair hair, bolstered the legend that the Mandan people were not Indians at all. Their hair and eyes suggested that they were the long-lost descendants of the famous Welshman Prince Modoc, the beloved eleventh-century ruler who sailed over the western horizon with two boatloads of loyal subjects, never to be heard from again. After meeting the Mandan, La Vérendrye was skeptical about the legend but was nevertheless impressed when he found the Mandan trading goods manufactured in England, France, and Spain. Upon his return to Montreal, La Vérendrye reported to his Paris benefactors that the Mandan leaders promoted their people's well-being through diplomacy and trade, rather than the familiar tactics of war and conquest. In his opinion, establishing a commercial partnership with these Indians would be required of any European monarch hopeful of exploiting the untapped wealth of the western lands.

Two generations later, Thomas Jefferson drew the same conclusion. Nearly seventy years after La Vérendrye's visit to the Mandan Villages at the Heart River, the grandparents of Elbowoods' first citizens would greet two young American captains, Meriwether Lewis and William Clark, when they stepped ashore from their pirogue at the mouth of the Knife River. While tribal societies on the Missouri River were well acquainted with European traders, this would be the Mandan's first encounter with the Americans. The timing of their arrival could not have been more fortuitous. Winter would come early that year. Within weeks the High Plains were covered with snow. By late November, Captain Clark complained in his daily log that his thermometer had stopped working at forty-five below zero. Arctic conditions would linger over the Great Plains for the next five months.

The people of the Mandan and Hidatsa tribes that Lewis and Clark encountered at the Knife River Villages had lived in close proximity to one another for hundreds of years. Generations of intermarriage and shared customs had formed a highly complex matrilineal society of clan-based, semisedentary farmers, hunters, and gatherers. Unlike their nomadic cousins, the Sioux and Assiniboin, these agrarian societies built semipermanent villages of domed-shaped earth lodges inside palisaded walls and protective moats. A single village was commonly home to a thousand or more inhabitants. Between forty and fifty feet in diameter, each earth lodge housed as many as twenty-five family members, though the average was closer to fifteen. Each family had its own hunters and warriors, and the women of the clan were the owners of both the lodge and the family gardens. Apart from the clan's ceremonial medicine bundles, these dwellings were a clan's principal material asset, and were passed from mother to daughter.

After the women, children, and elders had finished the harvest, crops were dried and stored in cache pits, or underground larders that were usually accessible from inside the lodge. Typically, these bottle-shaped pits were ten feet deep and four feet wide. At the onset of winter, they would be filled to the top with dried corn, squash, beans, wild turnips, and dried berries harvested from the plentiful bushes and trees that grew along the river and low-lying hills. Cache pits held enough food to last the tribe through two poor harvests. To the good fortune of the Americans, it was these surplus stores that kept the fifty members of the Corps of Discovery from starvation through the lean winter months of 1805.

Asking for little in return, the Mandan and Hidatsa people shared with the American explorers their lodges and hearths, their winter feasts, and the sexual hospitality of their wives and daughters. Sexual favors could be traded as freely as food for hard-to-obtain European trade goods such as ironware, textiles, and prized glass beads, but at the same time sexual relations with newly arrived strangers were an integral element of native hospitality. A woman's sexuality was regarded as the surest method for transferring mystical powers from one male to another, from an accomplished warrior of great valor to a young husband striving to win the esteem of his elders on the field of battle, or in the hunt.

Leading historians of colonial-era exploration Harry Fritz and James Rhonda agree that the Village Indians played the decisive role in the eventual success of the Lewis and Clark expedition. Had Jefferson's emissaries been turned back by the hostile Teton, or had they been trapped by winter near the Yellowstone, they would likely have perished from cold and starvation that first winter. As they passed the long winter nights camped in their makeshift fort near the bend in the river that the Indians called Elbowoods, the Mandan and Hidatsa leaders prepared them for the obstacles they would encounter on their journey west. It was here, too, that the captains secured the services of a guide and translator to accompany them from the Knife to the "shining mountains" of the Rockies. She was a congenial fourteen-year-old girl named Bird Woman who lived with her sister and their French husband among the powerful Prairie Chicken clan in the largest of the three Hidatsa villages. Captured as a nine-year-old girl in a battle with the Shoshones, Bird Woman was adopted into the Hidatsa tribe by a young warrior named Cherry Necklace. The captains knew her by her Indian name, which they transcribed into their journals as Sakakawea.

Phyllis Old Dog Cross and her nine brothers and sisters are the great-great-grandchildren of Cherry Necklace. Back when they were kids, Old State Road Number Eight was little more than a wheel-rutted, bone-rattling "farm-to-market" washboard of a road. Like everything else in their world, Number Eight seemed to both originate and end in Elbowoods. To the south it went to the town of Halliday, and to the north, Parshall, but a sudden spell of bad weather could keep people from going anywhere. "Our life in Elbowoods was very much like it was for our ancestors at the Knife River," says Phyllis. Life's necessities were readily available out the back door, in the woods along the river, or just down the road, in town. They farmed the rich bottomlands, hunted game, and gathered food that grew wild in the hills and along the river. And just as it had been for their ancestors on the Knife and Heart Rivers, the village was still the social hub for the people of the three tribes. Forty generations of their ancestors had lived in villages in this valley. They still owned half a million acres of land straddling the river — land they possessed in perpetuity by virtue of aboriginal title that was formally recognized by the federal government at the Treaty of Horse Creek in 1851. When the Cross children were growing up, tribal members lived in nine villages that were strung out along sixty miles of river bottom like widely spaced emeralds on a silver thread.

"Our views of how the world worked were pretty much shaped by the complexities, the nuances, the social pathologies, good and bad, of small-town relationships," says Phyllis. "Like any close family, my friends in Parshall today are as familiar to me as they are mysterious. The world beyond the horizon can go to hell in a handbasket overnight. When the sun comes up in the morning, the roosters will crow, and those people will still be here."

᙮

As the Mandan people were slowly making their way up the Missouri Valley in the eleventh century, feudal Europe was languishing in a long medieval night. Thanks to extensive trade routes and favorable climate, horticulture flourished during this period throughout the Americas. Across the ocean, however, famine and disease held Europe in a death grip that kept political and social evolution in a state of arrested development. Living conditions in feudal Europe were wretched. Disease and famine ravaged the continent for centuries. For a time in the Middle Ages, widespread drought and crop failures popularized the custom of cannibalism, a practice that became pandemic across France, Scandinavia, and Germany. As Pope Urban II was convening knights and clergy at the Council of Clermont to launch the First Crusade against the infidel "Saracens" in the Holy Lands, the Aztec and Inca cultures, with their courts and theaters, their farms and extended networks of communication, were approaching their apex of cultural development. Centuries of favorable climate and material well-being helped to propagate a pre-Columbian population in the Americas that is now believed to have exceeded 100 million people.

Sometime around the beginning of the second millennium, leaders of the Mandan society made a providential decision to push out of the increasingly crowded central lowlands of the Mississippi River Valley and turn the corner up the Missouri. The search for a new homeland could not have begun at a more auspicious time. From the outset, favorable climate followed this Siouan-speaking subgroup on their two-thousand-mile migration up the river. The weather was optimum for their gardens, and the network of trade routes that awaited them along the way on the Middle and Upper Missouri had been worn into the soil of the High Plains by thousands of years of foot traffic.

Combined, these conditions gave the Mandan a degree of social and economic stability that they could count on from one year to the next. Professor W. Raymond Wood, the leading archaeological authority on prehistoric Village Indian culture, notes that the Mandan picked the best possible time to begin their migration. Already the Mandan were developing their own varieties of corn from seed that they acquired from the Aztecs. Through cross-pollination, they developed exotic varieties that would ripen in just seventy days. From gardens grown by the Mandan and similar agrarian societies, corn, squash, beans, and potatoes became the staple foods for people throughout the Americas. Busy trade networks also brought the inevitable exchange of religious rites and ceremonies with distant peoples such as the Hopi and the Pueblo. Over centuries, their shared cosmologies had contributed to the evolution of highly complex societies.

Unknown to each other, the Mandan and the Arikara were approaching the Middle Missouri River Valley from opposite directions at about the same time. The Arikara, a Caddo subgroup and close relatives of the Pawnee, wandered east off the plains of modern-day Nebraska as the Mandan approached from the wooded region of the central lowlands, in modern-day Iowa. Several centuries after the Mandan and Arikara met on the Central Missouri, the Hidatsa began migrating toward the river from the north. In the mid-1500s, they finally met up with the two tribes of Village Indians near the Heart River, in modern-day North Dakota.

After the Hidatsa established their first villages upstream from the Mandan in the sixteenth century, a dispute between the Hidatsa leaders split the tribe into two factions. One group elected to remain at the Knife while the other continued to migrate west, finally settling by the Tongue and Powder Rivers at the base of the Bighorn Mountains. These people called themselves the Children of the Long-Beaked Bird and continue to maintain close relations with their Hidatsa relatives to this day. After fur traders arrived in the late 1830s and built a trading post on the Bighorn River, the Children of the Long-Beaked Bird would be known more simply as the Crow.

The continent's central lowlands rise gradually from the Mississippi River Valley as they approach the foothills of the Rockies. Once the lowland ecosystem crosses the Hundredth meridian, its humid woodlands are suddenly transformed into the arid highlands of the Great Plains. There, annual precipitation drops to a meager fifteen inches, and often less. Sedimentary formations, alluvial soils, and unbroken grasslands take over as the continent's shelf begins to climb several feet per mile. At its high point at the base of the Rocky Mountains, the continental plate bulges a mile above sea level. Despite the great geologic diversity found within this million-square-mile region, the Great Plains are regarded by scientists as a contiguous unit defined by uniform climate, geology, and similar flora and fauna. When the glaciers receded at the end of the last ice age, approximately sixteen thousand years ago, a rich but thin blanket of topsoil began building a thin mantle of nutrients that were held in place against the scouring winds by sixty species of native grass. For thousands of years, the most prominent features of this million square miles of North American landscape were wind and grass, silence, and sky.

The Mandan quickly learned how to exploit this shift in topography. To the west, the Rocky Mountains diverted massive weather systems onto the central highlands from the Arctic and the Gulf of Mexico. Here, converging cells of unstable energy often spawned violent weather and produced extreme swings in temperature. By building their villages on the sheltered bottomlands along the river, the Mandan had effectively remained in the ecological environment of the central lowlands as they journeyed upstream. This narrow geologic niche, with its rich alluvial soils and heavy timber, acted as a two-thousand-mile extension of the central-lowland ecology they had known on the Mississippi.

Through numerous seminomadic intermediaries, the Mandan traded seed stock with farmers of the Gulf Coast, the Southwest, and Mesoamerica. Little could they imagine how their horticultural and trading success would one day impact the larger world. The Dutch and English transplanted to Africa corn gathered from Indian gardens in the Americas. The effect of migrating seed was miraculous and immediate. A thousand-year decline in Africa's human population reversed itself in less than a decade. By the twenty-first century, more than half of the crops grown commercially around the world — from potatoes and peppers to corn and countless varieties of squash — had originated from pre-Columbian tribal horticulture in the western hemisphere, from gardens cultivated in thousands of villages like Elbowoods.

Then, midway through the fifteenth century, weather patterns shifted and the neo-Atlantic period that had favored the Mandan for centuries suddenly gave way to a "Little Ice Age." The radical change in weather would continue to govern climate in the northern hemisphere for the next four hundred years. By then, the Mandan had consolidated their hold on the Upper Missouri and were rapidly expanding their trade networks, despite the sudden change in climate. Across the ocean, meanwhile, two centuries of crusading had left the royal houses of Europe in complete disarray.

In hopes of bringing order to the political chaos, a meeting of the kings' ministers, known as the Council of Constance, was convened in 1414 to decide the thorny issue of papal succession. Perhaps at no time in history had the question of succession carried more importance. Portugal's King Duarte had suddenly upended the balance of power in Europe by capturing and subjugating the African port city of Ceuta, opposite Gibraltar, to Portuguese authority. Duarte's boldness inevitably drew the Spanish crown into the hunt for new lands. Since the two Iberian kings could not be trusted to resolve their differences, the rest of Europe looked to the newly installed pope, Eugenius IV, to assert his authority and reestablish order among the crown heads in the Holy Roman Empire. Eugenius IV seized the opportunity and issued a papal bull that consolidated his autocratic control over the unruly monarchs.

The new pope's decrees reestablished the Vatican as the dominant political force in the Holy Roman Empire. With the discovery era now well under way in Africa, it would not be long before the Spanish conquistadors were wading ashore on Caribbean beaches. Intent on winning converts to the faith, Eugenius IV and his successors made them agents of the Vatican and declared them free to do as they wished with native "heathens and infidels" that resisted conversion to Christianity. Bolstered by two centuries of experience in the Crusades, the popes could easily defend the legality of their sixteenth-century dictums. The Vatican's discovery-era conquests in the New World could be justified by citing laws created by twelfth-century popes to take possession of foreign lands held by "heathens and infidels."

After scholastic philosophers of Renaissance Spain tailored the crusading-era edicts to fit into international law, Spanish conquistadors such as Cortés and Pizarro were essentially free to rape, pillage, and plunder at will in the name of exacting tribute for the Vatican and winning converts to Christendom. If citizens of the Aztec and Inca empires refused to take the holy sacrament of Christian baptism, they would suffer the consequences. Crusading-era law had now landed on the shores of the Americas.

These laws, which began as "theocratically derived prerogatives" in medieval Europe, advanced and retreated by fits and starts — from the Vatican to the royal courts of European monarchs; through historic debates in the great ecclesiastical universities of Spain; in and out of Elizabethan courts; to fiercely contested debates in the small village of Philadelphia in 1787, where the founders of the American republic gathered to decide how the new nation would be governed. Less than a century after the U.S. Constitution was adopted by the original thirteen states, discovery-era laws would be alchemized by the U.S. Supreme Court as the Doctrine of Discovery, and by congressional lawmakers as the doctrines of "manifest destiny" and "eminent domain."

In his groundbreaking work on the origins of federal Indian law, *The American Indian in Western Legal Thought,* legal historian Robert A. Williams Jr. concludes that the adoption of these doctrines by the young American republic "preserved the legacy of 1,000 years of European racism and colonialism directed against non-Western peoples. The Doctrine of Discovery's underlying medievally derived ideology — that normatively divergent 'savage' peoples could be denied rights and status equal to those accorded to the civilized nations of Europe — had become an integral part of the fabric of United States federal Indian law."

⚜

On a busy day, the smooth, shoulderless two-lane ribbon of asphalt of Old State Road Number Eight may carry a dozen cars an hour. This is durum and milling wheat country, as far as the eyes can see. Heading south out of Parshall, population 940 and falling, Number Eight passes Barbara's Steakhouse and the Redwood Cafe, the Food Pride grocery store, a single white sedan parked in front of the Parshall Farmers Union office, and finally, a cluster of whitewashed grain silos straddling the Soo Line railroad tracks at the south end of town. After rumbling over tracks, veering around the small nine-hole golf course and a landing strip for crop dusters, Number Eight resumes its straight-line course between telephone poles and fence posts for nearly thirty miles. This is High Plains landscape at its horizontal, hypnotic finest. They say you can drive for days out here without touching the steering wheel or taking your foot off the gas. There's the sun and the horizon, the road bisecting a million acres of wheat, then blue sky and white clouds. As the wheat fields pass in a blur, the windshield of Phyllis's late-model Chevrolet minivan looks like a picture framing a piece of eternity.

"Back when we were kids," says her brother Bucky from the backseat, "you had to choose between a Ford and a Chevy. That was the extent of the options."

"We drove Chevys," offers their younger sister Marilyn.

"Fords," says Bucky, gently correcting her. "You girls and mom always wanted Chevys because they were fancier."

The memory prompts Bucky to flash a broad smile. A college professor in San Jose, California, he has returned for his annual visit. His given name is Alfred, but nobody has called him that since their mother died in 1989. Pushing six and a half feet tall, he still moves with the graceful ease that made him a celebrity on the basketball court as a teenager. His long silver ponytail lengthens the loose, lanky frame of a man whose favorite mode of transportation is his own two legs. His eyes are bright, translucent gray, while his smooth baritone voice seems to shape its words at the bottom of a well.

"Fords held up better on the roads, but Chevys were pretty. So, you had to decide whether you wanted to get to town on four wheels and a frame, or freeze to death out in the middle of nowhere in a nice-looking car."

"I thought we drove a Chrysler," says Phyllis.

Bucky scoffs with mock contempt. "Dad wouldn't have been caught dead in a Chrysler."

"Well, that's one thing he doesn't have to worry about anymore."

The road suddenly stops atop low-lying, windswept bluffs. Here, less than a mile from the lake, Old State Road Number Eight suddenly became a weed-choked trail. This final stretch, skirting the remnants of an old homestead, has not carried regular traffic in decades. The wreckage of abandoned dreams lies strewn about everywhere in a sea of whorled grass — a bullet-riddled wind-mill; a collapsed stock tank; an old Ford pickup, rusting to air; a homesteader's one-story cabin with a roof of sky. A few hundred yards downslope from the cabin, the van pulls over in the tall grass and stops. There, the road makes one final bend to the left, then slips beneath the green waves of Lake Sakakawea.

The same thing happens to Old Number Eight on Sakakawea's southern shore, five miles away across the whitecapped lake. These two segments of road, one from the north and one from the south, eventually meet on the main square in the village of Elbowoods. The town's tree-lined streets, the government buildings and boarding school, Simon's and Twilling's general stores and the country hospital, now sit at the center of the lake under two hundred feet of water. Elbowoods has been home to schools of walleyed perch and northern pike for almost fifty years. But to Phyllis and her siblings, who were born and raised at the bottom of the lake, it seems like yesterday. Around these parts, folks still refer to what happened here as simply, "The Flood." With thirteen hundred miles of shoreline, Lake Sakakawea material-izes on the horizon like an inland sea, a mini-ocean trapped in an arid waste-land. From certain vantage points on the lake's eastern shore, water touches the horizon in every direction.

When Congress gave its approval for the construction of Garrison Dam by enacting the Flood Control Act of 1944, their thinking was a straightfor-ward response to a century of catastrophic flooding on the Lower Missouri River. Major floods in the spring of 1943 had caused billions of dollars in damage and flooded thousands of farms in Nebraska and Iowa. The Missouri River portion of the resulting flood-control legislation would be called the Pick-Sloan Plan. This ambitious scheme was devised by marrying competing water development plans proposed by the Army Corps of Engineers and the Bureau of Reclamation. When the two proposals were folded together, the Pick-Sloan master plan called for the construction of 110 dams of varying sizes, all designed to tame the hydraulic tyrant known as the Big Muddy.

The key to the entire project, the jewel in the crown, would be the first and largest dam. Engineers had already selected a spot for this dam, a nar-rowing of the river valley that locals called the Mandan Bluffs. This site was located a few miles west of the small town of Garrison, and sixty miles up-stream from the state capitol at Bismarck. When Garrison Dam and its five smaller siblings were completed, their combined storage capacity would even-tually exceed 60 million acre-feet of snow melt and runoff from the Rocky

Mountains and High Plains. This was four times the annual runoff of the Colorado alone, or enough to form a column of water the size of a football field twelve thousand miles high.

The Bureau of Reclamation knew just what it would do with all that water. Less than a decade earlier, dryland farmers in the Upper Midwest had endured the most devastating drought in history. In less than five years, more than forty thousand family farms were abandoned. Instead of being transformed into a Garden of Eden by waves of immigrant homesteaders, the prairie had suddenly returned to grass, wind, and sky. For centuries, their native neighbors on the nearby bottomlands had survived the whimsical vicissitudes of the river by planting their gardens on the floodplains. There, like farmlands in the Nile Delta of Egypt, the soils were recharged with mineral nutrients by the river's annual flooding. During the dry months of summer, crops were naturally irrigated from below by the shallow water table. These farming methods had guaranteed the Village Indians good harvests even during drought years, but the dust bowl of the 1930s was so severe that even the Indian crops failed when they were planted at a distance from the river. During one three-year period in the "dirty 30s," meteorologists recorded less than ten inches of precipitation.

Farmers who had managed to survive the devastating dust-bowl decade had viewed the promise of irrigation in the Pick-Sloan Plan as the opening act for the Second Coming. Tens of thousands of families lured west by a succession of nineteenth-century homestead acts had been hostages to the whims of nature. Every year, millions of acre-feet of water flowed past the parched farms that straddled the Missouri. Annual rainfall west of the Hundredth meridian teetered back and forth over the break-even point of fifteen inches. An inch above that benchmark meant sustenance, a bumper crop, a pair of new school shoes for the kids, a down payment on a milch cow, real glass for the kitchen window, and a few dollars in the cookie jar. An inch below meant hungry children, months of wasted backbreaking effort behind a horse-drawn plow, the long silent stare that measured the interminable winters. Toil, sweat, determination, and sacrifice were not enough. The only long-term solution to the poverty and despair of life on the Great Plains was irrigation, and lots of it, the kind of irrigation that only the federal government could finance. Once the main-stem dams were built, Pick-Sloan promised to deliver irrigation to 4 million acres of bone-dry prairie. To survivors of the "dirty 30s," Pick-Sloan was a last-minute pardon for a condemned man.

After congratulating itself for expediting passage of a national flood-control program, Congress realized that Pick-Sloan was going to put the Mandan, Hidatsa, and Arikara tribes under a six-hundred-square-mile lake. Lawmakers in Washington immediately launched a regionwide search for replacement lands of equivalent value. But this was a task more easily imagined in a committee room on Capitol Hill than one that could be accomplished on the ground on the Northern Plains. A survey of the Upper Missouri Valley by field agents for the Army Corps of Engineers showed that such land did not exist, for love or money.

With doors to alternative solutions closing all around them, efforts to head off a disaster with these people appeared destined to fail. Heroic figures such as Martin Cross and Senator Joseph O'Mahoney emerged in Elbowoods and Washington, hoping to forestall the inevitable catastrophe. But by 1949, Congress' patience had worn thin under the constant chafing of downstream states, and its early altruism began circling the drain. Four years of sustained effort by tribal leaders and their allies in Washington succeeded in producing little more than futility and a mounting sense of desperation.

"This was all going on at the same time President Truman nominated a guy named Dillon Myer to be the new commissioner of Indian affairs," says Bucky, putting the era in context. "Myer and a senator from Utah, Arthur Watkins, decided the time had come for all of us Indians to get out and see the world. So Myer launched a program to round up all the Indians, put us on trains and buses, and scatter us in the big cities."

"It was the same thing he did to the Japanese at the end of the war," chimes in Phyllis. "Myer ran the internment camps, then they made him Indian commissioner. So there was The Flood, and now we had to deal with relocation."

"People we'd known our whole lives were put on trains in Minot and vanished," says Bucky. "Years later, in San Francisco, you'd read about some guy who jumped off the bridge the day before. 'Hey, I know that guy. I was in school with that guy in Elbowoods.'"

"Myer and Watkins called it the Termination Era," says Phyllis. "We owned too much land, too many resources, too many treaties. They thought things would be better for everybody if we just went away."

"Our dad challenged those guys face-to-face, in Washington," says Bucky. "They blew spit at each other in committee hearings. Dad and Harold Ickes, Roosevelt's secretary of the interior, and Felix Cohen, the human rights attorney, accused [Myer and Watkins] of genocide, which they denied, of course.

It got nasty. Time proved them right. What Indians learned from that experience is that truth comes out in the end, but it can kill you to be patient."

There was one more ironic twist to the story of "The Flood that stayed forever," a turnabout that none of the residents of Parshall and Elbowoods could have foreseen. As the floodwaters rose in Lake Sakakawea, many lifelong residents of Elbowoods chose to move to higher ground in Parshall. Most of them had done business in Parshall. Its streets, schools, and neighborhoods were familiar. The residents of Parshall had remained strangely quiet throughout the long fight to stop the dam. Now, hundreds of Indians began immigrating into the tidy little town of straight fences and perfect lawns built by Norwegian homesteaders. The racial divide between Indians and Norwegians, once scarcely noticeable, widened overnight to a chasm.

When the lake had finally filled, government surveyors were sent out by the U.S. Geological Survey office in Washington to reestablish the legal boundary lines of the reservation. With that accomplished, the citizens of Parshall were called to a town meeting by officials from Bismarck and Washington, who had come with news. It seemed that someone had made a mistake, way back when. The town of Parshall, explained the spokesman for the government, lay two miles inside the northern boundary of the land held in trust by the federal government for the Mandan, Hidatsa, and Arikara people. So it seemed, they told their stunned audience, the tidy homes, schools, and churches of Parshall had been in Indian Country all along.

☙

Phyllis and her siblings make the drive down to the lake a couple times a year. They take in the sights from the bluffs, visit family cemeteries, and reminisce with old friends over lunch in the town of Garrison, the dam's eponymous neighbor. When Phyllis's brothers and sisters visit from out of town on a nice spring day, an afternoon drive to the lake is a good excuse to put off errands in New Town or Bismarck. Michael is behind the wheel today, with Marilyn and Phyllis riding in the backseat. At sixty, Michael is a study in contrast with his sisters. He's tall, like Bucky, but was built with the thicker chest and broader shoulders of his father. At six foot four, boy number three inherited the arresting looks of his paternal grandfather, Chief Old Dog. Old Dog and his half brother, White Duck, were such striking-looking men that the famed turn-of-the-century photographer Edward S. Curtis made portraits of both of them when he visited Elbowoods in 1906. Old Dog would be astonished by his mirror image in his grandson.

His sister Marilyn, the middle child, was always the "lively one" when they were kids. Recently retired from a career with the Bureau of Indian Affairs, she is now the curator of the tribe's Four Bears Museum in New Town. Marilyn was the daughter Dorothy Cross relied on to entertain "the little ones" and to help them with their schoolwork. She was the valedictorian of her high school class and has a memory like flypaper, so Phyllis and Michael defer to her quick grasp of elusive details even though each of the Cross children has laid claim to particular fragments of his or her shared history.

Michael turns off-road onto an open bench of sage and cheatgrass. After bouncing across the trackless prairie for several minutes, he brings the van to a stop. He steps out, takes five steps, then rubs the toe of his tennis shoe over the burnished surface of a bronze surveyor's stake from the nineteenth century. This stake, placed here by federal surveyors more than a century ago, is not much larger than a silver dollar. It was stamped with the precise coordinates of latitude and longitude, down to the seconds of arc, and fixed with a U.S. Geological Survey code. This spot marks the northwest corner of Grandfather Old Dog's property.

"I will never know how you can remember things like this," Phyllis calls from the window. "You always drive right to it."

Michael's soft chuckle is his way of agreeing. "I couldn't tell you what I had for lunch yesterday, but I could find this blindfolded in a snowstorm."

The abandoned ranch house where their father died sits on a broad piece of level ground about a mile west of the bronze stake. Off and on as a teenager, Michael lived there with his dad. By then, in the stormy days that followed The Flood, Dorothy had seen enough of the ranching life. She moved to Parshall with the three youngest children, while Martin, a cattleman from his boot heels to the crown of his hat, built this place and tried to make another run at the cow business. The older boys followed him to the ranch and pitched in, but even in the best years, raising cattle "on top" was a great way to go broke. One generation later, there is little evidence of those efforts. The barn burned down years ago. Plank by plank, the shiplap siding has fallen into splintered piles skirting the foundation. The door to the room where Martin Cross died hangs partway open by a single cockeyed hinge. The wind-shredded fragments of a curtain flutter against the blue sky in a broken window. What is left of this place is in a race to fall down.

Martin Cross was buried at the Old Scout Cemetery, just up the road from his ranch. This tidy, well-kept cemetery, with straight rows of white crosses, is a place of honor for the Three Affiliated Tribes of Mandan, Hidatsa, and Arikara. He lies alongside the Arikara and Hidatsa scouts who worked for the U.S. Army during the American Indian Wars of the 1860s and 70s. Many of these tribal members were recruited to scout for the fateful Custer campaign in the spring of 1876. All but three of the Arikara and Crow who cautioned Custer against pressing his luck in the valley of the Little Bighorn returned to tell the story of that June afternoon. Those three were buried here. A few miles away is the Sacred Heart Cemetery, where Cross family ancestors were reinterred in the final hectic months before the floodgates closed at Garrison Dam. Thousands of graves had to be moved from cemeteries on the bottomlands to higher ground. As a result of that chaos, the remains of tribal ancestors now lie scattered in cemeteries across 400,000 acres of prairie. Marilyn pays her respects as often as she can. She brings flowers on holidays and cuts the grass around the family headstones.

Phyllis quietly drifts away and kneels in front of a headstone the next row over. Kissing her fingertips, she runs them over the lettering of her brother Forrest's name. This is the grave of Cross child number five. They called him Brother.

"I always wonder how Brother would have turned out," she says, turning back to the car. "He had the sweetest temperament in the family. Brother and Ray would have been a lot alike. I've never stopped missing him."

Marilyn takes her elbow. Together they walk back to the van in silence. The drive down Old State Road Number Eight is always a pilgrimage to the past, a sojourn to childhood, a distant time that seems more actual and immediate at these landmarks than it does in the vague abstractions of scrapbooks and photo albums. Lake Sakakawea is just a short jaunt down the road from Parshall, but the ride is not always a painless one. The familial pathology gets complicated the closer the Cross kids get to the lake. Bucky, for example, has returned to Fort Berthold on numerous occasions, but he has no use for the dam or the lake. Like the experience of many of the people who lived through The Flood, his memories of that era are still raw.

"A lot of our tribal people have never seen Garrison Dam," says Marilyn. "One day soon there won't be anyone left who remembers Elbowoods, or Nishu, Lucky Mound, or Beaver Creek. That day will mark the end of something for our people. It's best not to think about it."

Psychologists studying the long-term effects of extreme hardship on groups and communities have coined a new term to describe what they encountered: *transgenerational trauma*. A bit awkward at first glance, the term is nonetheless an apt description of the experience of the Mandan, Hidatsa, and

Arikara people over the past fifty years. Unless the pathology resulting from a traumatic event is quickly interrupted, long-term psychological damage can sweep through a community like a viral epidemic. Untreated, the effects of the trauma linger for generations, often long after the causal event is forgotten. The most immediate symptoms include a sudden increase in alcoholism and drug addiction, joblessness, child abuse, domestic violence, clinical depression, and suicides. Equally common are widespread diabetes and heart disease, disabling afflictions which usually accompany a crippling assortment of lesser maladies. Life expectancy plummets. Indian Country in general, and Fort Berthold in particular, have become frontline laboratories for the study of transgenerational trauma. As a registered nurse and a mental health specialist, Phyllis has spent a lifetime thinking about The Flood and its consequences. In her own family, for example, decades passed before her parents and siblings were willing to talk.

"I've come to the conclusion that our thinking failed us. Our thinking failed us because suddenly our landmarks, our social and physical landmarks, the framework for everything we were, was gone. Our identity derived from our villages. Those were destroyed. We were born into very dynamic and complex social networks that connected those identities across forty generations. Those went when the villages went. When everything was gone, there was no one waiting to help us put the world back in order. No jobs, no communities, no gardens, no homes. Gone."

As the Cross children grew older and their lives began to stabilize, each became more willing to compare notes. What jumped out was not the similarities of their experiences but the differences. "It turned out we were complete strangers in many ways," says Marilyn. "We went from being a deeply integrated family and community in July 1954 to being a society of totally isolated individuals who went into social free fall for the next fifty years. This happened to thousands of people simultaneously."

Of all the Cross children it was probably the youngest, Carol and Raymond, who were most vulnerable to the emotional fallout of The Flood. Young, defenseless, and as rootless as tumbleweeds, they were thrown headlong into the darkest and meanest days of the storm that descended on Parshall. Their new small-town home on the High Plains suddenly transformed itself from an idyllic farming village into a racial war zone.

"Craziness, dis-integration, and racial hatred were completely normal to Raymond and Carol," says Phyllis. "Little children, elders, were dying all around us. Meals were breaks between funerals. Raymond and Carol grew up thinking it was normal to see the mothers and fathers of their friends passed out drunk in the streets at twenty below. In that world, either you learn to step over the bodies and keep going, or you lie down beside them. Raymond will never talk about those years. He could walk through a burning house today and not know it was on fire. He has that ability to detach, to focus on a distant point, that came from walling himself off from the world in order to survive.

"The more we studied trauma, the more clearly we saw how it was being passed on to the next generation. How do you bury the past when your identity is trapped in its lasting effects? What do you call your life as a community, as a people, when despair is the only emotion you can trust?"

Michael angled the wheels of the van into a thick patch of buffalo grass, then got out and walked the last twenty feet to the edge of the bluffs. In the distance were the twin smokestacks of a coal-fired power plant at Stanton, and the irregular blemish on the far shore called Pick City, a community of two hundred residents who work at the dam and supporting service industries. Aside from that, and a few white clouds that merged with the horizon, there was little to see for fifty miles.

"This is the spot where Dad used to drop us off and make us walk home," said Michael, chuckling to break the silence.

"Right here?" exclaimed Marilyn, coming up beside him. "I always wondered where that was! Are you sure?"

"Right here." Michael scuffed the ground with his foot and looked out across the lake. "It'd take us the rest of the afternoon to walk home. We'd stop and eat apples in somebody's orchard. If it was hot we'd take a swim in somebody's pond. We'd make it home just in time for supper. If you did that today, they'd throw you in jail for child abuse."

"You know why he did it, don't you?" asked Phyllis. "He was a sly one, that Martin Cross."

"Sure." Michael grinned as if they were about to share a secret they had kept in the dark for sixty years. "He wanted to run home and get some nooky from Mom. He ditched us out here and raced home. 'Take your time, kids,' he'd say. 'Have fun.'"

Michael laughed, and after a moment of mild embarrassment, the sisters were laughing, too. "With ten kids there was never a minute of peace in that house," said Marilyn.

"Well," added Phyllis, "somewhere along the way they got enough to make ten of us. That's not exactly the same thing as living without."

Michael wandered off and followed the last fifty yards of Old Number Eight down to the edge of the lake. There, a set of wheel tracks trailed off into the water where small wavelets lapped against the shoreline. The light at water's edge had a spectral, burnished quality, but the wind had a bite to it, a cutting edge that hinted at winter. Killdeers wheeled and dove on gusting currents. Out in the middle, windrows of whitecaps raced across the lake.

"These are recent," he said, running his fingers along the hardened impression of a tire track. "The car that made these tracks was written up in the Garrison newspaper not too long ago. Seems that one night last summer, five or six fancy dancers at the powwow in New Town took off for a joy ride in an old Chevy Impala. They were drumming and singing and hauling ass down the road, having a great time, when they passed one of the county cops, down the road there, by the cemetery. He saw this carload of Indians dressed up in feathers and paint, so he pulls out behind them and turns on his lights. He told the paper that he clocked those kids at just over a hundred miles an hour when they hit the end of the pavement. Nothing was going to stop them. You can see how they skidded through this last turn before they hit the water. As for the cop, he slammed on his brakes just in time. The last thing he saw was the Impala's taillights going out of sight underwater. Cop said he could still hear the drumming and the sound of those boys singing as the lights disappeared, right out there."

Michael heaved a rock out over the lake. After a while there was a little splash.

"Cop said, 'Never see those boys again. They were going back to Elbowoods.'"

CHAPTER II

Savages and Infidels

❧

*"We saw that the white man did not take his religion any more seriously
than he did his laws, and that he kept both of them just behind him, like
helpers, to use when they might do him good. These were not our ways.
We kept the laws we made and lived our religion. We have never
understood the white man, who fools no one but himself."*

PLENTY COUPS, CROW

Like a fall chinook swimming home after years at sea, the white Subaru
station wagon navigates the early-morning traffic in Portland, Oregon, purposefully thrusting its nose into the oncoming current. Ever since
Raymond Cross was learning to swim in the back eddies of the Missouri
River, half a mile from his childhood home in Elbowoods, his instincts have
steered him into life's stronger currents. This is a law of nature he learned
early on from his father, Martin Cross. Slack water inevitably leads to a
blocked pathway and stagnation. The strongest current runs right alongside
it, and while its resistance poses another set of challenges, it always points to
the open channel — free-flowing water and possibilities.

For Raymond Cross, the early-morning drive through Portland's busy
downtown streets is a homecoming of sorts. He fought his first big legal battles in this city back in the late 1970s. He likes Portland and has always felt at
home here. This is a clean, well-lit city known for its progressive politics, urban-growth boundaries, and a diverse, open-minded citizenry.

Throughout his life, Raymond Cross has consciously made choices that
oriented his intellect and energies to the open channel, to the future. "The
older I get, the less use I seem to have for the past," he says, in a rare moment
of self-revelation. "The truth is, I never had much use for it to begin with."

When Cross was still in his twenties, federal courtrooms in Portland became his doorway to the future. Doorways alone, however, were not enough to ensure a young lawyer's passage into the rarefied world of federal statutes and Indian law. By fate and good fortune, generous judges were willing to hold the door open while the young Mandan attorney, fresh out of Yale Law School, polished his legal education in their courtrooms. Thanks to that mentoring, particularly by a federal district judge named Gus Solomon, Cross won his first major legal victories here.

But on a November morning in 2001, those victories seem like the outcome of battles that took place a lifetime ago. Much has changed in twenty-five years. Raymond was single then, and maybe thirty-five pounds lighter. Now he is married with two kids, and as a law professor at the University of Montana in Missoula, he himself is a mentor to a new generation of legal eagles. Much of the cityscape that passes by his window is in sync with his memory, but regardless of his physical surroundings, the intellectual carnival in Raymond Cross's mind, with so many interesting booths, spinning lights, and alluring rides, will always be his primary preoccupation. That is why he shaves no more carefully today than he did when he was twenty-nine, leaving errant tufts of whiskers on his chin and jowl. And he is still famous for arriving at airports with neither luggage nor tickets, details that somehow go missing with predictable regularity. These are the stories families tell, fables that are embellished around kitchen tables in order to keep their most extraordinary members human sized.

᛭

This trip to Portland is a mix of business and pleasure. Months ago, officials at the Bonneville Power Administration invited Cross to hold an Indian law clinic for its legal staff of seventy attorneys. The BPA, as the agency is better known in the Pacific Northwest, sells and distributes electrical power generated by hydroelectric dams in the Columbia River Basin. Dozens of BPA dams, large and small, are scattered across a diverse geologic region, a contiguous five-state area roughly the size of France. Beneath the agency's wide net are the homelands of dozens of federally recognized treaty tribes. With five state governments, hundreds of cities and municipalities, and dozens of tribal councils involved in the agency's decision-making process, the region has evolved into a legal crazy quilt of overlapping treaty provisions, state laws, federal statutes and environmental regulations, and competing jurisdictions. While the Columbia Basin accounts for a small percentage of the 600,000 miles of American rivers that have been bottled up behind the 75,000 dams on the National Inventory of Dams, the BPA network — with its Grand

Coulee, John Day, the Dalles, and Bonneville dams built like stair steps to the sea — is among the nation's largest.

This powerful and intricate hydroelectric system, tapping energy released in water flowing from hundreds of tributaries and mountain lakes, also happens to be the principal route of migration for more than a dozen native stocks of salmon and oceangoing steelhead trout. After completing a three-year round-trip to Japan and back, a sockeye salmon returns to its home waters at the Columbia's turbulent mouth, near Astoria, Oregon. From here, the twenty-five-pound adult will travel nine hundred miles up the river, climbing from sea level to seven thousand feet to spawn in high mountain lakes in Idaho's Sawtooth Range. At every turn in this journey, dams lengthen the odds against nature's intended outcome. Millions of dollars and decades later, marine biologists studying these fish have concluded that the damming of the Columbia and its tributaries has brought many native species, such as the sockeye, perilously close to extinction. Chinook salmon, a species which numbered as many as 50 million a century ago, dropped below 50,000 in the year 2000.

When the first large dams were built on the Columbia at midcentury, salmon appeared to hold their own. But as soon as the Army Corps of Engineers built five more dams in the 1960s and 70s on the Columbia's main tributary, the Snake River, fish counts plummeted. The Snake was also the main corridor to the largest salmon spawning ground in North America. That corridor was now blocked. Several Columbia Basin stocks, such as the Snake River coho salmon, were declared extinct by the 1980s. Tens of millions of salmon-recovery dollars later, in August of 1991, a lone sockeye salmon returned to Redfish Lake in the mountains of central Idaho. Over the growing protests of industry and agriculture, marine biologists at the National Marine Fisheries Service, the agency charged with monitoring fish populations in federally controlled waters, closed out the twentieth century by declaring a dozen native stocks in the Columbia River Basin as endangered species. All twelve, said the scientists, were on a trajectory leading to imminent extinction.

This rash of listings instantly became a point of no return in the growing crisis over what to do about dwindling fish counts. The moment these stocks were declared endangered, nineteenth-century treaties with Columbia River Indian tribes were back on the table. When the federal government negotiated these treaties in exchange for land concessions 150 years ago, forward-looking tribal leaders such as Chief Seattle insisted on provisions which guaranteed their descendants a right *en perpetua* to maintain a tribal fishing economy on their ancestral waters. When the salmon were declared endangered, by inference so were the treaties. The problem for the federal government and the BPA was now twofold. These fish were protected from man-made causes of extinction by the Endangered Species Act, a law with jaws of steel that was passed by Congress in 1973. Similarly, treaties with the Columbia River Basin tribes were protected by Article VI of the U.S. Constitution as "the supreme law of the land." This *supremacy clause,* relating specifically to treaties, was approved by the original thirteen states in 1789. To the dismay of state governments, industry, and agriculture, these two separate protections combined to erect a formidable legal bulwark around the fish and the tribes in the year 2000.

In this new predicament, the BPA was itself a fish out of water. The agency was suddenly obligated to mediate conflicts between the competing interests of a dozen separate entities, including states, tribes, city and county governments, and industry, transportation, and agriculture. Almost overnight, the agency went from being a distributor of watts, volts, and amperes to being the spider at the center of a web of bewildering legal complexities. When the National Marine Fisheries Service unveiled its long-awaited recovery plan for salmon in July 2000, the formal announcement was prefaced with a telling disclaimer. No model was known to exist, said NMFS officials, for reconciling the mind-boggling array of competing legal demands at play in the Columbia River Basin.

Setting the fish aside, the recovery plan's legal aspects represented a daunting, if not impossible, challenge for the BPA. Compounding its task, the agency found that few of its attorneys had any formal training in federal Indian law. In hopes of closing that gap, they asked Raymond Cross to come to Portland to help them begin sorting out the agency's responsibilities to the Columbia Basin's treaty tribes. Specialized legal concepts such as "domestic sovereign nations" have helped to make Indian law the most Byzantine branch of federal law, one that confounds even Supreme Court justices with its history of contradictory and nuanced precedents. In the past two centuries, the high court has heard more than fourteen hundred cases involving Native American sovereignty and jurisdiction.

Despite this high visibility, federal Indian law until recently was the exclusive domain of a small but brilliant group of white men; legal theorists such as Felix Cohen, author of the *Handbook of Federal Indian Law,* and Charles Kappler and Francis Paul Prucha, the leading twentieth-century authorities on the 370 active treaties that legally bind members of the national legislature, as the trustees, to the 2 million citizens of Indian Country.

Then, a hundred years to the day after U.S. Army general William Tecumseh Sherman sued Chief Red Cloud for peace at the treaty council of Fort
Laramie in November 1868, Richard Nixon was elected to the White House.
This event heralded a new era in Indian Country, particularly in the once rarefied arena of federal Indian law. Raymond Cross's generation was the first to
benefit, intellectually and materially, from radically progressive reforms introduced into federal Indian policy by the Nixon administration. Making good
on a promise to Native American leaders, Richard Nixon became the first sitting president to deliver a speech to Congress on the subject of federal Indian
policy and Native American rights. Calling the Termination Era of the Eisenhower years "a shameful disgrace," Nixon challenged Congress to turn a new
page in the "long and sorry history of Indian affairs" by reaffirming the sanctity of treaties and tribal sovereignty, and by taking measures to permanently
safeguard tribal self-determination in all domestic affairs.

Nixon then asked South Dakota senator James Abourezk, the son of
Lebanese immigrants who settled on the Pine Ridge Reservation fifty years
earlier, to assist his administration in writing the Indian Self-Determination
Act of 1975. This was landmark legislation, a comprehensive act that imagined an entirely new day in federal Indian policy. Its partners, the Indian Education and Health Care Improvement Acts passed by Congress in 1972 and
1976, opened the doors of the white man's educational system to thousands of
young Indians. In the 1960s, fewer than five hundred Indian students were
enrolled in schools of higher education. By September 2002, seventy thousand young Indians were taking college course work. Thousands more had already finished law school and joined the bar.

"Tribes began developing legal personalities for the very first time because
they realized that federal policies had been a disaster for well over a hundred
years," says Cross. "The time had come to change all that."

Coincidentally, this was also the era when fish counts on the Columbia
began to plummet. By then, virtually every tribe in the West had its own legal department and its own courts and judges. Today, many tribes staff their
own biological laboratories and natural-resource departments with native scientists. Every law school west of the Mississippi offers courses in contemporary Indian law, public lands, and environmental law. Simultaneously, lawyers
at agencies such as the BPA were awakening to a new set of twenty-first-
century realities. With increasing regularity, natural resource law and federal
environmental policies were crossing paths with federal Indian law. In the
modern world, BPA lawyers would now have to figure out how treaties signed
in 1855 might skew the agency's mandate from Congress in 2002 to provide

power on demand to public utilities in southern California and the Midwest. Dams on the Columbia were more than concrete structures with fish ladders and hydroelectric turbines. They had become the point of intersection between laws written by the founding fathers, century-old treaties, environmental legislation, and a confounding array of state and municipal laws. What was at stake with each turn of a turbine was the fate of tribal societies whose cultural survival was legally recognized to be inextricably linked to the survival of a fish. Somehow, the BPA had to find a way to balance existing commitments against the economic survival of those industrial and agricultural interests fueled by the Columbia's water, by the inexpensive transportation afforded by its lakes, and by the unlimited power generated at bargain rates by its dams.

Annually, the BPA spends half a billion dollars to protect native salmon stocks and habitat. But one day soon, that investment could well seem trivial. A compact signed in 1995 by the twelve basin tribes and the Canadian and American governments hung a sword of Damocles over Congress' head. If the federal government's salmon-recovery plan fails and the fish become extinct, the tribes are guaranteed a lump sum payout of 10 billion dollars from American taxpayers for the abrogation of their treaty rights. Every year since the compact was signed, fewer and fewer native salmon have returned to spawn in basin headwaters. Barring a dramatic and unforeseeable turnabout, the trajectory of the current "extinction model" projected by National Marine Fisheries biologists will touch the zero-line in 2017. Author David James Duncan has argued that Columbia River fish counts should be printed daily on the front page of the *Wall Street Journal*. Peering into their crystal ball in 2000, the BPA legal staff realized the time had come for a crash course in federal Indian law.

"I first heard Raymond speak a couple of years ago at a conference on natural resource policy," says Philip Key, the staff attorney who organized the workshop at the BPA headquarters in Portland. "In the first five minutes I knew we were in the presence of something very special. Here's a tall, powerful-looking Indian man addressing a roomful of egomaniacs on the subject of recent environmental case law. Before he was finished, people were holding their heads in their hands. This was our guy."

⋇

Raymond's wife, Kathleen Johnston Cross, and their two children, Helena and Cade, came along for a quick trip to the big city before the Missoula winter set in. Raymond and Kathy met at Harvard's John F. Kennedy School of Government back in 1988, when both were taking scholastic sabbaticals from work; Raymond, from his job as a tribal attorney, and Kathy, from her career as an administrator with philanthropic foundations. At ages forty and thirty-eight, respectively, neither had ever been married. It was love at first sight. Raymond and Kathy tied the knot in New York City the following year, then moved to San Luis Obispo, California, where Raymond took a position teaching law at the local college. Daughter Helena came along in 1991, and son Cade arrived the following year. It was about this time that a legendary pioneer in Indian law, Professor Marjorie Brown, decided to retire from her post at the University of Montana School of Law in Missoula. When Raymond was invited to fill her vacancy, he accepted without hesitation. He's held the position ever since.

Raymond had earned his undergraduate degree in political science at Stanford University in Palo Alto, California. For a while, he toyed with the idea that he might do graduate work abroad, preferably at the London School of Economics. But neither political science nor economics seemed to be avenues that would lead to a practical career path for a twenty-one-year-old Indian who felt rich when he had two nickels to rub together. So, in his senior year at Stanford, he applied to four law schools: Harvard, Yale, Notre Dame, and Stanford. He was admitted to all four on full scholarship. Raymond flipped a coin. By now he felt completely at home in the white world. He had thrived on the intellectual stimulation at Stanford, but that was the relaxed, laid-back milieu of the West Coast. At Yale, life in New Haven would be a galaxy removed from the familiar landmarks of Palo Alto, California, and Parshall, North Dakota. "Yale was a real cultural challenge for me, coming from Parshall, North Dakota, but you don't learn much real-life law there. What you learn at Yale is professional posture, your rank in the social order. The main thing I knew, coming out of Yale, was that I wasn't headed for Wall Street. I considered myself very lucky." California Indian Legal Services hired Raymond straight out of Yale Law School in 1973. The move back West felt like a homecoming after three years in New Haven.

The little Subaru swerves onto Southwest Broadway, then slowly cruises past the federal courthouse. Raymond cranes his neck for a better look at his old haunt. His face suddenly lights up. A bronze plaque mounted on the front of the building reads GUS J. SOLOMON FEDERAL COURTHOUSE. "Well I'll be damned. They named it after Gus. Isn't that great. It's a common misconception that you go to law school to learn the law," explains Raymond. "That's a lot of hooey. You go to law school to pass the bar. You learn law out here in the world, from judges who come to work in buildings like that one."

Cross is referring to Federal District Judge Gus Solomon, who presided over the first big case he took to trial when he went to work for NARF — the Native American Rights Fund, based in Boulder, Colorado — after his stint at California Indian Legal Services. The outcome of this case, now a textbook study in water law known simply as *Adair,* impacted dozens of state governments and hundreds of tribes with treaty-protected water rights. Like so many battles in the West, *Adair* turned into a cowboys-and-Indians shoot-out over stream flows and acre-feet of water. Judge Solomon's 1981 ruling in favor of the tribes was so reviled by white ranchers and farmers that they decided to battle it out all over again twenty years later. Farmers in the arid Klamath Basin of southern Oregon spent a lot of money trying to get Solomon reversed on technicalities. Their challenge proved feeble. None of the new claims struck a sympathetic chord with Federal District Judge Owen Panner. In February 2002, Panner issued a forceful reaffirmation of Gus Solomon's original ruling.

At stake in this contest were the treaty-protected water rights of the Klamath Indians, a tribe that was formally terminated by the U.S. Congress in the early 1950s. In a later act of contrition complete with formal apologies, Congress restored the Klamath people to their former status as a federally recognized treaty tribe. When the state of Oregon denied their rights to water in the Klamath Basin, the penniless tribe turned to the legal staff at the Native American Rights Fund. In court, the Klamath argued that their original treaty rights had not been forfeited by Congress' illegal termination. If the termination was itself illegal, argued Cross, then their first-in-line water rights — for all manner of uses, including fishing and irrigation — had remained intact throughout the ordeal.

The state of Oregon and the tribe's white neighbors vehemently disagreed. Farmers wanted unrestricted access to the basin's limited water resources to irrigate their crops. In his reaffirmation of Gus Solomon's earlier ruling, Judge Panner found that the Klamath's claim to enough water to maintain a healthy fishery was not only intact but also a right grounded "in time immemorial," predating all others. Once again a federal court declared that the Klamath's claim was superior to all competing demands, a decision with dozens of contemporary echoes from federal courtrooms across the arid West.

During his tenure with California Indian Legal Services in the mid-1970s, Raymond pined for a shot at a big case, one that could have far-reaching consequences in Indian Country. When he moved to Boulder, Colorado, to join the staff at NARF in 1975, that opportunity walked through his door on a blustery spring day in 1978. He won the assignment to argue *Adair.* As the new guy at NARF, the chance of that happening had been slim to none. High-profile cases like *Adair* were usually assigned to attorneys with more experience in the courtroom. But his luck was running. *Adair* presented itself at a time when the staff veterans were overextended with other cases.

When Raymond filed the Klamath tribe's claims in federal court, the suit set off alarm bells across the West. Predictably, a counterchallenge from the Oregon attorney general's office was instantaneous. It seemed the suit had no sooner been entered into the court's log than the volley of motion and countermotion turned feverish. Against the odds and into the current, Cross was soon on his way to Portland. The flurry of paperwork and fast-breaking developments made it obvious that there was no effective way to fight this battle from Boulder. By moving to Portland and camping out in Solomon's courthouse, Raymond could beat the state at its own game. It was in that courthouse, says Cross, that he got his real education in the law.

"This was not the kind of case you give to a twenty-nine-year-old kid," says Cross, smiling all these years later at his improbable good fortune. "On the other hand, none of us at NARF really saw where this thing was headed. We knew it was big, but we didn't know it was *that* big. For me this was like going from the neighborhood blacktop to the NBA in one big step."

※

Raymond's audience at the Bonneville Power Administration headquarters is scattered out among two dozen tables. They've given themselves plenty of room to stretch and fidget, with notebooks open, pens in hand. Windows run the length of the wall on both sides, overlooking a city park. He's relaxed at the podium, and guffaws with genuine laughter at a casual joke. For the next eight hours he will lead a roomful of mostly white Anglo-Saxon male and female attorneys on an intellectual scavenger hunt through a bewildering legal maze known as federal Indian law.

"I was really pleased on the way over here this morning to see that they named the new federal courthouse after Judge Solomon," he begins. This is a calculated opening, a way to set his audience at ease. Everyone in the room knows of Judge Solomon. Many of the agency's veteran attorneys argued cases in Solomon's courtroom. Moreover, all present know that Raymond Cross was the principal architect behind Judge Solomon's *Adair* ruling, a decision that tends to dominate the legal foreground in current disputes between states, municipal governments, and tribes throughout the Columbia River Basin.

"In hindsight, I'd have to say what I learned from Gus Solomon was part two of my legal education. You could say it was the practical side, the one that taught me how to work the important details of a case from beginning to end. But for all of Judge Solomon's wisdom and fine counsel, it wouldn't have done me much good without part one. Part one came from a man whose genius was certainly unique in the history of American jurisprudence, a man who understood better than any of our founding fathers that we are held together as a nation by our mutual willingness to embrace a system of laws, our foundational laws.

"I am here today to talk about Indian law, because Indian law is the oldest branch of our nation's foundational law. It surprises my law-school students to learn that Indian law predates the founding of the republic. But as every lawyer and legislator knows, creating law is one thing. Some say it's the easy part of this law business, and I tend to agree. Once the law is on the books, somebody has to make those abstractions work in the real world, right here on the Columbia River. How does that happen? Well, for that answer we have to go back and take a second look at our founding fathers.

"While they all made important contributions, particularly Mr. Madison and Mr. Hamilton, most were probably dispensable. But when it comes to Chief Justice John Marshall, I'm not so sure that's the case. As time goes by, it gets more and more difficult for me to imagine where we would be today without him. We've certainly never had a more visionary chief justice, or one with a greater legal intellect. He was like a world-class chess player, a man who could see eight, ten, twelve moves into the game. He knew that the young American republic was headed for trouble. There was no way around it. The fractures were there in our founding laws, and they would have to be addressed somewhere along the way. It came thirty years later, at Gettysburg and Appomattox. Marshall said, 'Okay, look, there's going to be trouble, big trouble. If we manage to survive as a nation, what can we do today to help reconcile those fractures in our law when that day comes?' Marshall was absolutely the right man at the right time. It's historically astonishing. To really get a handle on his contributions, what he was grappling with, let me take you back for a moment and show you the world as it looked through his eyes."

The federal Indian law that applied to dams and fish counts on the Columbia River in 2001, Cross told his audience, could be said to have its origins in the presidential election of 1800. President John Adams lost his bid for a second term to his chief political rival, Thomas Jefferson. The contest in 1800 was as fiercely divisive as the presidential election two centuries later in 2000, a contentious standoff that was still fresh in everyone's mind. In 1800, the young republic had grown to sixteen states and had a population of 5.5 million people. The government was still carrying $81 million in debts incurred during the War of Independence from King George III. The seat of government had moved a year earlier from Philadelphia to Washington. When Adams left the presidency in March 1801, his parting act of ill will toward the incoming president was to nominate Jefferson's arch nemesis, a federalist by the name of John Marshall, to be the new chief justice of the U.S. Supreme Court.

In Adams's view, the Marshall nomination was a well-aimed blow. Marshall's superior intellect and judicial independence would bedevil Jefferson throughout his presidency. A tall, dignified Virginian with an impeccable reputation for integrity, the self-possessed, soft-spoken jurist from Fauquier County commanded greater respect from friends and adversaries — as a gentleman, civil servant, and legal scholar — than any man in early America. In character and intellect, Marshall towered above the politicians of the day. He inspired awe in his peers and foes. The great lawyer and orator from New Hampshire, Senator Daniel Webster, would one day tell Supreme Court Associate Justice Joseph Storey, "I have never known a man of whose intellect I had a higher opinion than Judge Marshall's. His black eyes proclaimed the imperious powers of the mind that sat enthroned within, a gigantic genius that trampled all with disdain. No matter how gnarled the oak, John Marshall would, without effort, penetrate the knot."

Marshall's groundbreaking opinion for the majority in *Marbury v. Madison* established the principle of judicial review for the Supreme Court, a decision that secured the court's power to determine the constitutionality of laws passed by Congress. *Marbury* is only one of hundreds of decisions issued by the Marshall court over a thirty-four-year period that continues to define the boundaries and powers of the federal and state governments, and illuminate the civil rights and liberties of individuals. Marshall consistently frustrated Jefferson, the ardent states' rights activist, by subordinating state power to federal authority. As time went on, he increasingly demonstrated a quiet devotion to the rights of property and to the idea of steady governance by wise and good men. Marshall viewed public service by those same wise and good men as life's highest and most noble calling. Yet like his federalist allies Madison and Hamilton, Marshall could survey the world with the cold eye of a true pragmatist.

To the end of his life, John Marshall believed that the democratic ideal of government by the common man was a promise that could never be fulfilled. He quietly harbored profound doubts as to the average citizen's ability to legislate against his own self-interests, a quality of personal character that Marshall viewed essential for enlightened leadership in government. Time and experience would reinforce his views, convincing the chief justice that the ideal form of government was a limited democracy run by enlightened and benevolent despots.

Cross tells the BPA attorneys that as a legal theorist, Marshall had an impact on the eventual outcome of the salmon crisis in the Columbia River Basin that can be found in his formulation of the ground rules that today control the playing field of Indian tribes, states, and the federal government. Marshall's Indian law schemes began to take shape in the early 1820s, with a trio of cases involving the Cherokee nations. The court would hear these three cases — *Johnson v. McIntosh, Cherokee Nation v. Georgia,* and *Worcester v. Georgia* — over a ten-year period from 1822 to 1832.

The final contest, *Worcester,* pitted the property rights of the Cherokee nations against the state sovereignty of Georgia, a bitterly fought battle that laid at the feet of the court the problematic questions pertaining to Indian sovereignty and the nature of tribal government.

In his opinion for the majority in *Worcester v. Georgia,* Marshall predicted a long and stormy relationship between whites and native peoples: "The condition of the Indians in relation to the United States is perhaps unlike that of any other two people in existence." Over the next two centuries, the truth of that statement would be borne out time and again. Marshall's opinions in the trio of Cherokee cases have been since memorialized by Indian law scholars as the Marshall Trilogy. To the untrained eye, the Trilogy might appear to be a throwback to a forgotten era, yet the legal boundaries it drew into the framework of federalism still play out in federal courtrooms.

"In the Trilogy," explains Cross, "Marshall accomplished an intellectual feat that is still a source of condemnation or praise, depending on which side of the bed you wake up on." In these opinions, Marshall laid bare the contradictions that were built into federalism. In reconciling those contradictions, Marshall succeeded in making American law different from indigenous law anywhere else in the world. In post-Trilogy America, the power sharing between states and the federal government would be obligated to include Indian tribes. In ruling on these three cases, Marshall created a new legal distinction for tribes. For the purpose of securing them a place in the legal framework of federalism, he defined them as "domestic dependent sovereign nations." The glaring omission of the Indians by the founding fathers created a hairline fracture in the U.S. Constitution, one which forced the Marshall court to recognize tribes as having a legal status that located them somewhere between the federal government and the states. States, said Marshall, could not override Indian sovereignty. Only Congress had the power to circumscribe a tribe's sovereign authority, a plenary power that was balanced and tempered by Congress' paramount responsibility to the tribes as its all seeing, all knowing trustee.

"I was invited to Ottawa, Canada, recently, to a First Nations legal forum," says Cross. "Jurists in Canada, New Zealand, and Australia still can't get over what Marshall did, and how he did it. It was an extraordinary intellectual achievement.

"The first thing he did was break new legal ground by recognizing Indian tribes as the original governments on the North American continent. Now, let's think about this for a moment. The original governments. That's a pretty big deal in the 1820s, especially for a lot of white folks who were more or less going about their business pretending that the Indians didn't exist at all. Let's say you run a land syndicate in Philadelphia. When you woke up this morning, you figured you had clear sailing all the way to the Pacific Ocean. Nothing can stop you. Then along comes word from Washington telling you that John Marshall says, 'Nope, sorry, you've got it all wrong, boys. Those Indians out there are independent nations, and the only body that has the authority to make land deals with the tribes is the federal government. Sorry about that.'

"Well, suffice it to say that Mr. Marshall's popularity had its highs and its lows. He wasn't very popular with a lot of folks, especially with people like Thomas Jefferson, who found it a lot more convenient to argue that red men were just a bunch of savages wandering around in the forest." Marshall did not want to leave things to chance in future courts. He was using his combined opinions in the Trilogy to remind judges in the far-off future that treaties were "confirmatory doctrines which recognized the tribes to possess the rights of nationhood." In other words, Marshall took it to be self-evident that sovereignty existed as a precondition to treaties between self-governing entities, a condition that acted as a legal shield protecting all privileges, both reserved and implied, by the standard rights of nationhood as those were construed in the Law of Nations.

"To really appreciate this guy's intellectual and moral courage," says Cross, "it helps to look at his opinions in the context of his day. The Cherokee cases asked the Marshall court to answer a very loaded question: 'What kind of animals are these savages?' This was no trifling issue back then. Nor was it one that was easily resolved, ignored, or set aside. Somebody, sooner or later, was going to have to answer this question."

This question put the chief justice at the center of a predicament. He was surrounded by such men as Justice Baldwin and Justice Johnson, who argued that Indians were little more than a bunch of wandering hordes and barbaric savages devoid of any legal standing. Essentially, this was the same "natural law" justification used by crusaders seven centuries earlier to cast the Muslims out of the Holy Lands and seize Jerusalem. It was also the same rationalization used by Spanish conquistadors to destroy the Inca and Aztec civilizations. Marshall's fellow justices saw the Cherokee cases as an opportunity to project the same ecclesiastically derived law on the native people of North America. By ruling in favor of the state of Georgia in *Cherokee Nation v. Georgia,* the court, Baldwin argued, could simply reaffirm the claims of conquests made by the original "discoverers" and let the government be finished with its "Indian problems." To recognize the tribes as sovereign entities was to "do a grave injustice and disservice to the future of our American republic." From the perspective of the Euro-American immigrants, Baldwin anticipated the interests of extraction industries — such as mining and logging — and the arguments of states' rights groups and right-wing think tanks — such as the Heritage Foundation — that would be heard in federal courtrooms 180 years later.

Baldwin's solutions were too simplistic to dissuade Chief Justice Marshall. If adopted, his argument would eventually require a dismantling of the republic's foundational law. In practice, it could also mean rewriting the Constitution and disavowing the Law of Nations. Besides, by 1776 even the European governments of the original "discoverers" had evolved beyond discovery-era doctrines. Most had come around to formally recognizing native claims to property. As things stood, the American legal system was already deeply compromised by its own internal conflicts of interests with regard to land, Indians, and the rights of the discoverer. In many ways, it remained wedded to medieval law primarily because it promoted the interest of the emerging aristocracy. In 1776, John Adams commented that the lofty but attainable goals of the Revolution were being postponed by "that avarice of land, which has made upon this continent so many votaries to mammon that I sometimes dread the consequence." In his examination of Revolutionary War–era land syndicates in *The American Indian in Western Legal Thought,* legal scholar Robert Williams concludes, "Few legislative bodies in history have so mired themselves in corrupted self-interest parading as principle as did the Revolutionary-era American Continental Congress." Marshall responded to Baldwin's argument by first turning it upside down, then dropping it on its head.

"Marshall does something really ingenious and unique in the *Georgia* opinion," Cross tells his audience. "He says, 'Look, these Indian tribes are domestically dependent sovereign nations. But nothing in our own Constitution, or in the existing body of law governing European nations, gets me out of the woods. So what I'm going to do is borrow the existing concept of sovereignty, and I'm going to bifurcate it, I'm going to cut it in half. I'm going to apply the domestic rights and privileges of nationhood to the tribes. From here forward, they will retain all the domestic rights to self-regulation and governance that pertain to any sovereign nation. But what they give up in this deal is the rights of a foreign sovereign. We just can't let them go off and make their own treaties with foreign governments, and they can't establish their own rules for international commerce. That's where we draw the line. But within the borders of the United States, these are sovereign, domestically dependent nations.' Now, this was really big. This was a revolutionary idea, and he used the Trilogy to make it stick."

As an example of his last point, Cross cites Marshall's landmark 1823 case, *Johnson v. McIntosh,* as one whose outcome reverberates in federal courtrooms to this day. Marshall's opinion would tailor a claim made by European kings to the legal blueprint of the new American republic. The feudal rights of conquest over new lands and the savages who lived there had been seen as the exclusive domain of the crown. With a simple sleight of hand, Marshall substituted discovery-era monarchs with the republic of the United States. In Marshall's perfect world, the federal government's new role in Indian Country would be that of the enlightened and benevolent despot.

"We call this Marshall's Velvet Revolution," Cross tells the BPA attorneys. "The consequences of the Velvet Revolution are very much with us today. Marshall cleared the way for the federal government to take paramount title over Indian lands without having to resort to bloody battles. He knew the Indian nations would never surrender their land peacefully. Instead of hand-to-hand fighting, which the new republic would likely as not have lost, they accomplished the same thing through a protracted policy of attrition. But he did it by making the federal government a partner with the tribes. He named Congress as the trustee responsible for safeguarding their interests, resources — their lands. Properly managed, this would put their land beyond the reach of speculators and states. It was a brilliant solution, and it could have worked. But the temptation for Congress to reach into the treasure chest was too great. Asking white lawmakers to be responsible trustees, faithful partners to the tribes, was putting the wolves inside the henhouse."

⋇

No one living between the Mandan Villages on the Knife River and Washington, D.C., on the Potomac could foresee how Chief Justice Marshall's realignment of federalism was going to play out as the young country moved west. Like other pragmatists of his day, Marshall believed that given time, tribal structures would gradually break down. As that political entropy progressed, little by little Indian people would be absorbed into mainstream society. One day in the not-too-distant future, Marshall believed, the thorny questions posed by the trio of Cherokee cases would most likely be moot.

But in 1832, congressmen were restless, and citizens on the frontier were unwilling to put off westward expansion for several more generations. By establishing a new Indian Territory in Oklahoma, legislators believed they had crafted a clever stopgap measure that would buy some time for westward expansion until the inevitable assimilation of the Indian was complete. To achieve that goal as quickly as possible, Congress lent its full support to President Andrew Jackson's proposal for removing the last remnants of native tribes from the eastern forests. Jackson's removal policies became law with unanimous support from Congress.

Chief Justice Marshall was not swayed by Congress' enthusiasm for removal. His 1832 opinion in *Worcester* declared Jackson's removal policy as unconstitutional. When President Jackson was told of Marshall's ruling forbidding the removal, the president is said to have retorted, "If that is Mr. Marshall's decision, then let *him* enforce it!" Under pressure from impatient southern politicians, Jackson ordered the U.S. Army to proceed with the plan with all haste. In the following two years, tens of thousands of Indians would be forcibly removed from their treaty-protected homelands east of the Mississippi River and escorted at gunpoint to the new Indian Territory in Oklahoma. Along what the Indians called the "trail of tears," thousands would perish. The only advocate they had in Washington was the chief justice, and President Jackson knew full well that the power to enforce the laws of the land fell to him and to Congress.

For Marshall, President Jackson's dismissal of the federal protections guaranteed to the tribes in the *Cherokee Nation* decision underscored his theory that common men made common presidents and common legislators who were lacking in the character necessary to enforce laws that ran counter to their self-interests. In Marshall's view, Thomas Jefferson, the slave-owning champion of the common man, epitomized these contradictions. By enacting this policy and forcibly removing thousands of Indians from their ancestral homelands in eastern forests, President Jackson and Congress had formalized those contradictions as official policies of the state. Ignoring Marshall's opinion, gleeful lawmakers declared the eastern third of the continent open to white settlement and assured white citizens that the nation's "Indian problems" had been solved once and for all.

But Congress' assurances to the public were premature. The government's policy of removal left it unprepared to respond to events that were about to unfold out west. The national legislature had no strategy for dealing with the wild tribes of the plains and Rocky Mountains. Nevertheless, by the 1840s, Texas, the Oregon Country, and the Mexican territories of the Southwest were all incorporated into the rapidly expanding American empire. Also, the restless energy pent up in frontier settlements was a force beyond Congress' control. The American people, wrote William Gilpin in 1848, were "possessed of an untransected destiny . . . to subdue the continent, to rush over this vast field to the Pacific Ocean, and to establish a new order in human affairs."

Just how the American pioneers and homesteaders would manage those affairs, and how they would conduct themselves while fulfilling their destiny, was a Gordian knot that would vex Congress throughout the nineteenth century. In a nutshell, the problem was how to square Thomas Jefferson's dreams of empire with Marshall's Trilogy and the admonition of Attorney General William Wirt:

> So long as a tribe exists and remains in possession of its lands, its title and possession are sovereign and exclusive; and there exists no authority to enter upon their lands, for any purpose whatever, without their consent. . . . They do not hold under the states, nor under the

United States; their title is original, sovereign, and exclusive. We have no more right to enter upon their territory, without their consent, than we have to enter upon the territory of a foreign prince.

Clearly, fulfilling Jefferson's dream of empire to the Pacific Ocean could not be realized without balancing "the new order in the affairs of men" against the practical problem of making peace and coexisting with dozens of nomadic Indian tribes. It was one thing to round up the scattered remnants of tribes in the eastern forests and relocate the survivors to Oklahoma. The vast, unknown territories in the West presented a different dilemma. Extending Jackson's removal policies to the Sioux and Cheyenne, the Comanche, Arapaho, Navajo, and Apache, the Flathead, Nez Percé, and Mandan, and dozens of other sovereign nations, was not a solution that could be imposed on the unmapped West.

In fact, it seemed that lawmakers had no sooner set aside the new Indian Territory in Oklahoma than word reached Washington of a momentous achievement. An intrepid, one-handed Irishman by the name of Thomas Fitzpatrick had guided a young Presbyterian missionary couple, Marcus and Narcissa Whitman, to the Oregon Territory. There, the Whitmans intended to answer their calling by opening a mission among the Cayuse Indians of the Walla Walla Valley. Fitzpatrick set out with the missionaries in the spring of 1836. Five months later the trio arrived at their destination on the Columbia River. Though the Cayuse took a dim view of Marcus Whitman's liturgical fervor and scalped him, he and his wife went to their early reward little knowing how prescient was their intention "to aid the white settlement of this country." Fitzpatrick's wagon tracks across the Great Plains, connecting St. Joseph, Missouri, to the Columbia River, would soon be known as the Oregon Trail. When gold was discovered in California in 1848, Fitzpatrick's highway across the plains became the principal route for the largest sustained family migration in recorded human history.

For the next forty years, Conestoga wagons poured west by the thousands. The journey was so arduous that future trail bosses referred to the Oregon Trail as "the longest graveyard in the world." Until the railroads replaced the Conestoga in the 1880s, the steel-rimmed wagon wheels that carried settlers across the continent's broad back would wear ten-inch grooves into limestone bedrock in eastern Oregon. Fitzpatrick's trail bisected an unbroken grassland, a region of prairie and plains a thousand miles wide and fifteen hundred miles deep. Congress was slow to realize that the western tribes would not stand idly by as the endless flood of settlers destroyed a world that had sustained them for centuries.

⋇

As gold fever swept through communities along the eastern seaboard, the new Indian commissioner in Washington, William Medill, was growing increasingly alarmed by reports filtering back from his Indian superintendents on the frontier. The Oregon Trail now bisected the continent. The great herds of buffalo would no longer migrate from north to south across this man-made boundary. Soon faced with starvation, leaders of the tribes dependent on the buffalo's north-south migration were growing increasingly uneasy over the river of immigrants moving through their lands. Every summer, wagon trains of white settlers stretched from horizon to horizon. Many tribes in the north were now cut off from the only food supply that saw them through the long winters. Medill and his superintendents knew that dwindling resources would inevitably lead to bloody encounters between tribes and settlers. Something had to be done, and quickly.

A man of clear vision and steadfast loyalty to the native people, Medill sternly reminded lawmakers of their moral responsibilities to the continent's original inhabitants. At the very least, he told Congress, "Whatever may be the nature and extent of [the tribes'] original title to the lands, I think it would be sound policy to make them some annual compensation for the right of way through their country." The alternative, he warned them, would be written in settlers' blood.

"These were some of the legal and sociological conditions that set up what we now call the second great era of treaty making," Cross tells the attorneys. "The first era came earlier in the century, when the new government had to make a lot of quick deals with the eastern tribes to acquire land. Getting its hands on that land was the new government's only way to start paying off all the debts it ran up with the French in the war against mad King George."

The second era of treaty making would be different from the first era, both in kind and quantity. Many of the treaties between tribes and the federal government during this later period were treaties of peace, agreements in which no land was exchanged. Instead, annuities were offered and rights formally conferred on these widely dispersed Indian nations, in exchange for guarantees of peaceful coexistence.

"Uncle Sam simply wanted to make peace with these people and guarantee its citizens safe passage on the Oregon Trail. The treaties that apply today to the salmon tribes on the Columbia came from that second big wave of treaties. All Congress really wanted from the Indians was a guarantee of peace. In order to get that, they were pretty much willing to guarantee the Indians anything they wanted, such as perpetual access to their hunting grounds — such as guarantees that their salmon fishery would be protected in perpetuity."

The typical treaty from this era struck bargains between the American people and the tribal nations that would be in effect "for as long as the waters shall flow." Western tribes with little previous experience in dealing with the white men quickly learned that water in white communities seldom flowed for more than ten or fifteen years. The ink had no sooner dried on one treaty than a new president or a new Congress was dispatching more agents to Indian Country to bring back new treaties. In these second- and third-generation contracts, Congress was bargaining not for peace and safe passage for pioneers but for land, and more land. To achieve that end, the legislature ratified in less than fifty years more than three hundred treaties. Some tribes signed four and five agreements, each with overlapping conditions, a new exchange of values, and reconfigured boundaries to their homelands. Federal courts are now routinely asked to sort through the myriad of conflicting conditions to divine what tribal leaders understood at the time the treaty was made, and to rule on which "as long as the rivers shall flow" clause controls the conditions and boundaries being contested in the twenty-first century.

Great leaders such as Red Cloud, Black Kettle, Sitting Bull, and Plenty Coups were not fooled by the conflicting conditions offered by Indian agents in treaty negotiations. What the left hand took in friendship and peace, namely Indian land, the right hand of government gave away to settlers and homesteaders a few years later. "If you can find one man in Washington who speaks the truth," Sitting Bull told General Sherman at Fort Laramie, "I will gladly meet with him."

"What you are now dealing with here on the Columbia is a result of all that treaty history," says Cross. "It's obvious to us today that the federal government didn't do a very good job of thinking things through in the last phase of the treaty era. Congress' final treaty was made with the leaders of the Nez Percé nation in 1871. Today, that's one of the treaties that has your backs against the wall here at the BPA. The Nez Percé were guaranteed their fishing livelihood on the Columbia and Snake Rivers, in perpetuity.

"So, as you can see, it is no fault of the tribes that the BPA, the states, the agricultural interests, the aluminum industry, and the cities of Portland and

Seattle all find themselves in such a predicament over the salmon. As long as Congress secured its desired short-term goals in the nineteenth century, legislators tended to ignore the long-term consequences, not to mention their responsibilities as trustees. But that didn't matter to the Indian people in the short term. The Indian people were always willing to take the long view, to think far out into the future. They were thinking about today."

To illustrate that point from his own family history, Raymond Cross notes that hundreds of land-claims cases brought by tribes such as the Mandan, Hidatsa, and Arikara, all filed in the final decades of the twentieth century, have a common point of origin. As often as not, a modern tribe's complaints of malfeasance against the United States government reach back across 150 years to retrace the sacred lines drawn by hand on a sheet of parchment beside a meandering tributary of the Platte River. For three weeks in September 1851, at the peak of the second era of treaty making, the greatest peace council in the history of the American republic was convened by Superintendent of Indian Affairs David Mitchell, at Fort Laramie in the Nebraska Territory.

With visions of white women's scalps dangling before their eyes, lawmakers in Washington had finally acted on William Medill's dire warnings. In the winter of 1851, Congress appropriated $100,000 for "the expense of holding treaties with all the wild tribes of the prairie and for bringing delegates to the seat of government." Fortunately for David Mitchell, when word of Congress' formal action reached him in St. Louis, Thomas Fitzpatrick, the father of the Oregon Trail, happened to be in town on his annual business trip from the Wyoming Territory. Congress' approval came as great news to the new treaty commissioners, but it came with a challenge that was equally daunting. Nothing of this scale had ever before been attempted with nomadic tribes. With no time to waste, Mitchell and Fitzpatrick scattered runners across a million square miles of "territory unknown" with invitations to leaders of all the great western tribes. Promising gifts, Mitchell invited them to bring their men, women, and children so they could all gather in September for a great peace council at Fort Laramie.

The peace conference proposed by Congress would include dozens of tribes, many of which were mortal enemies. The council would also require the services of every interpreter Mitchell and Fitzpatrick could scour up from far-flung trading posts. Fitzpatrick calculated that once underway, the formal proceedings would be conducted in no fewer than twelve languages. Many of those whose talents the new treaty commissioners called upon — frontiersmen such as Jim Bridger and Robert Meldrum — were already legendary figures in the mountain West. At the top of their list were Alexander Culbertson, the veteran trader at Fort Union at the confluence of the Missouri and the Yellowstone, and the distinguished Belgian Jesuit priest Father Pierre-Jean DeSmet, who was currently teaching at the nearby St. Louis University.

DeSmet had recently returned to the city after spending fifteen years among the tribes of the Northwest. He was renowned among Indians and whites alike for his pacific demeanor and physical stamina. Mitchell sent a messenger specifically asking Culbertson to meet DeSmet at the Mandan Villages, eighteen hundred miles up the Missouri. Mitchell hoped that his emissaries could coax the Mandan, Hidatsa, and Arikara into making the rugged eight-hundred-mile overland trek to Fort Laramie. He would have no way of knowing if his gamble paid off until they all arrived at Fort Laramie three months later. The white men who traveled to this distant outpost would call it the Fort Laramie Peace Council of 1851. The Indians would call it the Miracle at Horse Creek.

CHAPTER III

Miracle at Horse Creek

"You speak by papers and record your words in books.
We speak from our hearts, and memory writes our words
on the hearts of our people."

GRIZZLY BEAR, MENOMINEE

Commissioner Mitchell's invitation to Father DeSmet and Alexander Culbertson came at propitious moments for both men. The Fort Union trader had already made plans to travel downriver for his annual rendezvous with the Mandan. The Belgian priest in turn had been actively lobbying his superiors at St. Louis University to release him back to his vocation as a sojourning "black robe" among the western tribes. After spending fifteen years wandering the West and living among the Indians, DeSmet chaffed against the yoke of cloistered priesthood. DeSmet's superiors relented and agreed to send his close friend, Father Christian Hoecken, to accompany him as far as Fort Berthold, the American Fur Company trading post at the Mandan's new village of Like-a-Fishhook, a day's journey upstream from the Knife River.

The priests' fellow passengers on the paddle wheeler *St. Ange* were mostly young French, German, and Swiss emigrants, wide-eyed adventurers who had hired themselves out to the American Fur Company to trap beaver in the Rocky Mountains. But this was the last voyage many of them would make. To the horror of all those trapped aboard the small ship, one of the deckhands soon fell ill with cholera. Less than two weeks into the voyage, the dreaded scourge swept through the ship like fire. Dozens of passengers and crew perished within days. Thousands of miles from friends and family, the dead were buried ashore whenever possible, or simply slipped over the gunwales into the Missouri. DeSmet's companion, Father Hoecken, tirelessly attended to the sick, then perished himself in DeSmet's arms. After hastily burying Father Hoecken on a small island near the mouth of the Little Sioux River, DeSmet and the *St. Ange* continued on their way upstream, fighting day and night against the Missouri's dangerous currents. The Belgian priest was by nature a hard-nosed pragmatist, yet he now wrote in his journal that his brush with death on the *St. Ange* had unhinged his nerve. He feared the advancing plague could only be a dark omen for the tribes of the Great Plains.

As the *St. Ange* was approaching the big bend of the Upper Missouri River, word of the cholera outbreak reached Commissioner Mitchell's wagon train as it lumbered across the plains toward Fort Laramie. For Mitchell, already burdened with doubts about his enterprise, this was discouraging news. His secretary, a young lawyer and future governor of Missouri named B. Gratz Brown, reported in the commission's official log that the new outbreak was sweeping across the Northern Plains like the smallpox epidemic of 1837. Mitchell pressed onward, knowing that this epidemic could upend any hopes for long-term peace with western tribes.

⋇

By 1851, the Mandan, Hidatsa, and Arikara had been dealing with white men for more than a century. Measured against the French, Spanish, and English, the Americans had the shortest history, and they were the least trustworthy. It seemed to leaders such as Cherry Necklace that the tribes had paid a high price for friendship with the Americans. Since the departure of Lewis and Clark in 1806, the ensuing parade of profiteering vagabonds, explorers, and fur traders had brought far more grief to the Mandan Villages than could be offset by promises of material wealth. Fourteen years before, in 1837, smallpox had cut a deadly path up the Missouri aboard an American Fur Company steamboat, the *St. Peters.*

Though the origin of the great smallpox epidemic of 1837 will forever be shrouded in mystery, the virus is believed to have traveled up the river from St. Louis, finally coming ashore at the Fort Clark landing on June 18, on a blanket wrapped around the shoulders of an Arikara woman. On July 14, the white trader at Fort Clark, a semiliterate alcoholic cur named Francis A. Chardon, recorded the first Mandan death in the trading post's log. After carefully listing various business transactions that took place throughout the day, Chardon ends his entry with a matter-of-fact postscript: "A young Mandan died today of the smallpox. Several others has caught it. The Indians all being out making dried meat has saved several of them."

By summer's end, the piles of rotting bodies in the villages had become so extensive and commonplace, and the wails of grief so constant, that Chardon himself became semideranged. After watching more than a thousand villagers perish in six weeks, Chardon wrote in his journal on the last day of August that a friend in the village had taken ill and killed himself. Rather than waste away in physical agony and grief, the young man's wife then "killed her two children, one a fine boy of eight, and the other six, and to complete the affair, she hung herself." Two weeks later, he entered a final note on the epidemic without a further word of explanation: "My youngest son died today. . . . What a bundle of rascals has been used up [by the epidemic]."

From the Mandan Villages at the Knife River, the plague cut a deadly path through the nearby communities of Hidatsa and Arikara. Fortunately for both, their hunters had scattered on the plains in pursuit of buffalo and were spared from the brunt of the epidemic. The Hidatsa lost only half of their people before the first winter snows. The strain of pox was so virulent that its victims often died within hours of showing the first symptoms. Bodies turned black and swelled to three times their normal size in the prairie sun. Before it had run its course, the epidemic of 1837 claimed half a million Indian lives.

This was the second devastating epidemic to visit the Village Indians in two generations. A previous outbreak, in 1781, reduced their population from fourteen thousand to fewer than three thousand in just four weeks. The survivors moved upstream and built two new villages near the mouth of the Knife River, close to their longtime allies, the Hidatsa. It was here that Lewis and Clark found them in October 1804. Two more generations would live at the Knife before the epidemic arrived on the *St. Peters* and reduced the Mandan tribe to fewer than two hundred people. The survivors abandoned the Knife River and commenced a migration upstream in search of a new village site. A few miles upstream, they found a high spit of land on the northeastern bank of the river. There, the Mandan and Hidatsa joined their tribes for the first time. Together they built a small village that they named Like-a-Fishhook.

When Father DeSmet disembarked at the new village, his spirits brightened when he learned that his longtime friend Alexander Culbertson had arrived from Fort Union several days ahead of him. The two men had not seen each other since DeSmet returned to St. Louis from Montana five years before. By the time DeSmet arrived, Culbertson had already extended Mitchell's invitation to the Mandan and Hidatsa leaders. The trip to Fort Laramie would cross hundreds of miles of hostile country. To Cherry Necklace the risks entailed in such a venture appeared to outweigh the potential rewards. Where the Mandan's bellicose neighbors, such as the Sioux and the Blackfeet, seemed to have flourished, the fortunes of the Village Indians had suffered greatly. The contrast was lost on no one, but the chiefs nevertheless agreed to postpone their decision until they met with the black robe.

"We get no help at all from our old friends, the *mah-shi*," the chiefs told the trader and the priest. "When the men go off hunting, the women cannot work in the cornfields without being raped and murdered by the Sioux. When we ask for the help of our friends, the white men, they grow scarce and are nowhere to be found."

As he listened to the litany of complaints from the elders, Father DeSmet waited for the right moment to present his arguments. The Great White Father asked for this treaty council, he told them, in hopes of putting an end to all the fighting among the Indians. Gifts were promised to all the tribes who attended the peace council at Fort Laramie. DeSmet assured them that future generations of Mandan, Hidatsa, and Arikara children would reap the benefits. He personally knew the commissioner, David Mitchell, and he could vouch for the honesty and character of this man. Mitchell wanted to protect the Village Indians by making peace with the Sioux.

Culbertson translated DeSmet's apology. If the conference was an opportunity to make lasting peace with the Yankton and Lakota Sioux, then Cherry Necklace agreed that their tribes must attend and proposed that they proceed with the selection of representatives. Raven Chief and Red Roan Cow would speak for the Mandan. The Hidatsa selected their young war chief, Four Bears, and the Arikara tapped their elder chief, Gray Prairie Eagle. With two wagons and a small herd of horses, DeSmet, Culbertson, and the small band of headmen and their families set off into the unknown on July 31, 1851.

※

As the widely dispersed tribes approached Fort Laramie and the rendezvous with David Mitchell, many saw the "Great Medicine Road" of the white man for the first time. After a journey of eight hundred miles across unmapped wilderness, DeSmet, Culbertson, and their small party of war chiefs met the Oregon Trail about fifty miles west of Fort Laramie. The vision that now filled the Indians' disbelieving eyes, wrote DeSmet, "was the broadest, longest, and most beautiful road in the whole world, a highway as smooth as a barn floor swept by the winds, and not a blade of grass can shoot on it on account of the continual passing."

The last wagon trains of the year had passed this way three months earlier. By September the trains that left St. Joseph, Missouri, in mid-March were approaching the Columbia River across the high desert of eastern Oregon. The Nebraska plains were now silent, but the evidence of their passing was strewn everywhere: cooking utensils, knives, axes, hammers and kettles, barrel staves and parts of wagons and wheels, rotting carcasses of oxen, discarded furniture and clothing, and hastily dug graves marked with simple crosses.

When they came upon this spectacle, Four Bears, Raven Chief, and Gray Prairie Eagle stared speechlessly in both directions. These were men accustomed to traveling hundreds of miles across the prairie on trails no wider than their shoulders. Surely, they told DeSmet and Culbertson, a road such as this was made by so many people that the exodus had left their homelands empty. To the contrary, DeSmet assured them, the whites that made this trail would not be missed from the great cities of the East. The silver-haired black robe was the most trusted *mah-shi* they had ever known, but Gray Prairie Eagle told the priest that the Indian's eyes did not lie. What he told them could not be so.

The men in Washington who called for peace and friendship with the "wild tribes" of the West could no more imagine the scale of the endeavor being undertaken by Mitchell and Fitzpatrick than Four Bears and Gray Prairie Eagle could imagine life in an eastern city. Despite Mitchell's promise to shower the tribes with gifts, when the government's five-mile-long wagon train left St. Louis on the final day of July, the anxious Mitchell had no way of knowing how his invitations had been received, nor whether any of the tribes would accept. Before he left, he wired Congress and told them that he and Fitzpatrick were hoping to meet with as many as five thousand Indians. As the wagon train approached Fort Laramie on September 3, he saw the answer to his question swarming in the distance. The small fort was surrounded by an encampment of twelve thousand Indians. Fifty thousand Indian ponies ranged loose on the plains. The Mandan, Hidatsa, Arikara, Assiniboin, Sioux and Cheyenne, Shoshone, and Arapaho and Gros Ventre had all come to smoke the pipe of peace with the Great White Fathers. Yet Mitchell had no sooner swung down off his horse than word reached him that problems were already brewing between enemy tribes. Buffalo, it seemed, were scarce, and there was not enough water for the herd of ponies. And as far as the eye could see there was not a blade of grass left on the prairie.

After reuniting with Fitzpatrick, Mitchell immediately called for a council of the chiefs. Runners carried Mitchell's invitation to all of the Indian camps. Soon, the chiefs were gathered inside the walls of the fort. After formal greetings were exchanged all around, the Brule Sioux leader, Terra Blue, appraised Mitchell of the chiefs' complaints and suggested that the entire camp move thirty miles to the east. There, where the Platte and Horse Creek met beneath a swale of cottonwood trees, the Brule chief said, there was plenty of fresh grass and running water for the horses. Also, it was far removed from the white man's Medicine Road. The hunters would have better success at finding buffalo in the country around Horse Creek.

Mitchell readily agreed and proposed to reconvene at the new venue. Feasts were held in all the camps that night, and when Mitchell woke the following morning, he stepped out of his tent and gazed in astonishment at the mute and grassless plain. Without a sound, twelve thousand Indians had packed up their lodges and disappeared over the hills toward the Platte.

∗

When the Indians and the treaty commissioners finally met on the banks of Horse Creek on September 8, before them was a blank map of the West, a map with no interior lines other than geographic features that gave the country its essential character. They could draw any lines on this map that they pleased. This was the very solution to the "Indian problem" promoted by Chief Justice John Marshall thirty years before, when he ruled that tribal claims to land were made through aboriginal title that predated the "discovery" of the Americas by Europeans. The million square miles of territory that Congress wanted to divide between the principal tribes of the West was four times greater than the combined area of the original thirteen states. But if Washington was serious about taking steps to avoid bloodshed in the coming years, Mitchell told Congress, it had no choice but to lie down in its own bed. They were asking the tribes to accept boundaries to their home territories and grant white immigrants safe passage on the Oregon Trail. For these concessions Congress was offering the tribes annuities and the formal recognition of their perpetual right to hunt, gather, and fish in their accustomed forests and waters. Anything short of this, Mitchell told Congress, would be rejected out of hand. From the Indians' perspective, the Great White Fathers in Washington were in no position to drive hard bargains.

No one better appreciated what was riding on the success of this council than its portly commissioner, David Mitchell, and his tall, one-handed partner, Thomas Fitzpatrick. Their master plan envisioned peace with tribes from the desert Southwest to the Canadian border. When Mitchell and Fitzpatrick arrived at Fort Laramie, news awaited them that the Apache and Comanche had elected not to make the long trek to the Platte. This setback was not entirely unexpected. More unsettling to both men was the unexplained absence of the Crow. Months ago in St. Louis, both had identified the Crow as holding the key to the success of the master plan. Occupying prime buffalo country between the Tongue and Yellowstone Rivers, the Crow were surrounded on every side by fierce enemies. Despite incessant encroachments on their homelands for thirty years, the Hidatsa's first cousins had easily repulsed the Sioux, Cheyenne, and Blackfeet. Living with ceaseless hostilities had transformed the nomadic Crow into the most fearsome warriors and finest horsemen on the Northern Plains, and their prized homeland was the central piece in the commissioners' million-square-mile puzzle. Even in their absence, the commissioners would have to establish boundaries for the tribe in order to have any hope of brokering peace with so many of the Crow's enemies.

꙳

At daybreak on the first morning, David Mitchell raised the American flag above the thatched canopy of the council circle. The arbor was a simple affair, a canopy of cottonwood branches that served the dual purpose of providing shade and avoiding diplomatic pitfalls. No position in the circle could be construed as favoring one leader more than another.

Shortly after nine o'clock, Mitchell touched the ash of his cigar to the fuse of a cannon to announce the opening ceremony. The council's secretary, B. Gratz Brown, opened his journal and quickly scribbled a note to himself: "I deeply regret that among our many fine American artists there is not one present." Instead, the young attorney climbed a low-lying hill above the council circle and described what he saw after "the cannon gave forth its thunder":

> The whole plains seemed to be covered with the moving masses of chiefs, warriors, men, women, and children. . . . Each nation approached with its own peculiar song or demonstration and such a combination of rude, wild, and fantastic manners and dances, never before was witnessed. It is not probable that an opportunity will again be presented of seeing so many tribes assembled together displaying all the peculiarities, features, dress, equipments, and horses.

They came out this morning not armed or painted for war, but decked out in all their best regalia, pomp, paint, and display for peace. The Chiefs and Braves were dressed with punctilious attention to imposing effect. . . . It must be confessed that the prairie dandy, after his manner, displays quite as much sense and taste as his city prototype. . . . The "belles" (there are Indian as well as civilized belles) were out in all they could raise of finery, and the way they flaunted, tittered, and talked and made efforts to show off to the best advantage before the bucks justly entitled them to the civilized appellation we have given them. . . . A novice in this wild country, surrounded by the excitement of transpiring scenes, has scarcely the time to put all he observes on paper.

As the pageant of Indians closed around the council circle, Mitchell announced that only the principal headmen of each nation would be seated beneath the peace arbor. Mitchell and Fitzpatrick greeted each chief by name as he stepped forward. Four Bears, Raven Chief, and Gray Prairie Eagle were the first to take their seats beneath the arbor. Though they were a small band compared to their neighbors, they had overcome the greatest hardships in getting there. Joining them as their translators were DeSmet and Culbertson. Once all the chiefs had been greeted by the commissioners, a coterie of dignitaries who had come at Mitchell's invitation to witness the proceedings formed an outer circle around the peace council.

As he surveyed the faces around the arbor, Father DeSmet realized that the only person there who actually looked out of place was Commissioner Mitchell himself. His short heavy body, the thick shoulders and ponderous brow, struck DeSmet as an undistinguished presence cast among this stately congress of chiefs. For the first time in American history, nearly all the chiefs of all the great western Indian nations were assembled in one place, surrounded by thousands of their tribesmen and women. "For quietness, decorum, and general good behavior," wrote B. Gratz Brown, "the Indians might be models for more civilized society. . . . Everything was as quiet as a church."

After welcoming all the "red children" to the council, Mitchell assured the chiefs that "the Great Father at Washington does not want your land, your horses, or your robes, nor anything you have. We come to confer with you, and to make a treaty with you for your own good. When the red man intends to tell the truth, and faithfully fulfills his promises, he takes an oath by smoking to the Great Spirit," said Mitchell. "The Great Spirit sees it all and knows it all, and for that reason, I do not wish any Indian to smoke with me that has any deceit or lies in his heart."

All watched in silence as Mitchell lit the bowl of tobacco in the ceremonial pipe. Momentarily, he disappeared in a cloud that rose from the pipe's three-foot-long stem. The redstone pipe, beautifully decorated with beaded ornaments, feathers, and various talismans intended to bring good fortune, was passed first to Terra Blue, who passed it to the Cheyenne, the Assiniboin, and the Shoshone, then to the Arikara, Hidatsa, and Mandan, and finally to the Arapaho. Several of the chiefs rose to their feet and presented the pipe to the four points of the compass, to the Great Spirit, "and down to the Bad." When the smoking had concluded, Mitchell stood to address them as the cadre of translators stepped up to sit with their assigned chiefs.

"I am glad we have all smoked together like brothers," he told them. "The ears of your Great Father are open, and he has been alarmed to hear that the white children have driven off the buffalo. The White Fathers desire to pay the tribes fairly for things being destroyed by his white children, but for these payments, they expect you to allow the white people to travel over the Great Medicine Road in peace."

Mitchell told them that times had changed. The days when they could roam freely across the continent were fast coming to an end. Congress had sent him to ask them to divide the country into tribal territories. Henceforth, each tribe would own its own territory, its own homeland. Washington desired to make peace with all of the Indian people, but each tribe needed to select its principal spokesman with whom Congress would transact all future business. If they agreed to these conditions, Mitchell told them, the Great Fathers in Washington promised to give each of the tribes $50,000 a year for fifty years.

"This is all I have to say to you today," said Mitchell. "Go back to your lodges, think about what you have heard. Talk about what I have proposed to you. Make peace and visit each other."

When Mitchell had finished, twelve thousand Indians rose to their feet. As the council circle broke up, the Brule patriarch, Terra Blue, stepped forward to shake hands with both commissioners, addressing Mitchell through his interpreter.

"I have heard you were coming, ever since the grass began to grow," the old warrior told him. "Now you are here. I have not two hearts. My ears have been open. It seems good to me, and I believe our Great Father is good, but I will go home and talk to my people. We will think on what you have told us."

As the Sioux chief finished and turned from the circle to rejoin his people, the chiefs from Like-a-Fishhook waited for their turn to shake Mitchell's hand. B. Gratz Brown recorded their remarks through their translator, Alexander Culbertson. "Your talk is good," Gray Prairie Eagle told Mitchell. "The ears of my people have not been on the ground. They have been open. We feel good in our hearts at what you have told us. The ground is not as it used to be. We come here from a long way off, from the Missouri River. We arrived hungry. We found no buffalo on our trail, but we found friends when we arrived here and they fed us. This makes our hearts glad. We live far away. We wish to satisfy the Great Father so he will send us more buffalo."

※

Mitchell's presentation had made for a long session, but more had been accomplished than either he or Fitzpatrick had dared to hope. The only nagging disappointment was the absence of the Crow.

For the next several days, chiefs and warriors of each nation met in lengthy council sessions. Shortly before noon on September 11, Mitchell's secretary, B. Gratz Brown, accompanied him on a ride out to the Sioux camp. They found the chiefs sequestered at the center of the village, their shoulders pressed close together in a council circle. Terra Blue's loosely formed confederacy was the most troublesome on the plains. Rather than being a cohesive tribe, the Sioux were instead a confederation of wide-ranging bands that were hopelessly tangled in a web of blood relationships, ceremonial rituals, vague boundaries, and mercurial political alliances. Reluctant to interrupt, Mitchell and Brown quietly left the village, mounted their horses, and rode back to their camp beside Horse Creek.

Early the next morning, Fitzpatrick raised the Stars and Stripes above the arbor. The cannon again boomed out across the plains. Mitchell, up before dawn, had wrestled with his doubts through a sleepless night. Yet when the cannon roared, nothing moved on the plains. The surrounding country lay still and utterly silent. Commissioner Mitchell's darkest fears raced through his mind. This must be their answer, he told Fitzpatrick. They must be going home.

The commissioners gazed across the Platte at the silent encampments. Before the two men could panic, a voice yelled the news from the Shoshone camp. *"The Crow are coming . . ."*

Both men sprang to their horses, charging across the Platte at a gallop toward a nearby hilltop to meet the approaching tribe. What they saw as they crested the hill, wrote Brown, abruptly brought them to a halt. Arriving from a journey of eight hundred miles

> The Crow were all mounted and their horses, though jaded and reduced by the long trip, were beautiful animals. The Crow Indian rides better than any other, and he sits his horse with ease and elegance. This is much the finest delegation of Indians we have yet seen, as they came down the plain in a solid column, singing their national melody. . . . They were dressed with more taste, especially the headdresses of the chiefs, than any of the other tribes, and though they rode down into the midst of their enemies the whole plain seemed now alive with a moving mass of redskins, and amidst it all, riding through the middle, they were not the least disturbed or alarmed.

The commissioners turned and rode back to the council grounds as the Crow came riding triumphantly over the hill and down through the scattered Indian villages toward the government camp. Thousands of Indians followed them on foot from the surrounding encampments. As the two Crow headmen dismounted, Mitchell gave a brief speech of welcome and offered the tribe the campground nearest his own. As the women moved off to set up their camp, the warriors hobbled their horses and took their places outside the arbor. The two chiefs chose seats at the east end of the circle beside the Arapaho named Cat Nose.

One by one, the chiefs now rose to report the results of their deliberations. Terra Blue was the first to speak. The Sioux leader quickly confirmed what Mitchell already suspected.

"We want a chief for each of our bands," the Brule chief demanded. "The White Father does not understand. We are many bands. If you make two chiefs for each band, it will be better for you whites. It is not possible to make one chief to speak for all of us."

Several other Sioux now rose to echo Terra Blue's message. Big Yankton reminded Mitchell that the western tribes could go where they wanted, as they pleased. No one could tell them where to live. "We have moved around in this country with the freedom of the wind, and we still like it this way."

When the Sioux had finished, a heavy silence hung under the arbor. Cat Nose, the distinguished chief of the Arapaho, finally rose to his feet to address the commissioners.

"I thank the Great Spirit for putting us on this earth," he began. "It is a good earth. We Arapaho hope there will be no more fighting on it. I hope that the water will fall from the sky and make the grass grow and bring plenty of buffalo. I come to tell you that we have heard your words, and we think there is much good in what you say. We will go home from here satisfied if we do not have to watch our horses at night, or be afraid for the safety of women and children. We have to live on these streams and in the hills. I would be glad if the whites would pick out a place for themselves and not come into our country anymore. We have chosen our chief as you requested. Whatever he does we will support him in it, and we expect the whites to support him also. That is all I have to say."

Mitchell thanked Cat Nose, and for the benefit of the Crow, he repeated the proposals that the tribes had heard two days before. When they gathered under the arbor the following morning, the Crow chief informed Mitchell that they had spent the entire night in council deliberating the proposals from Washington. The Crow were ready to speak with one voice. A man named Big Robber now rose to face the commissioners. He was a prepossessing figure of size and physical power, and like many of his Hidatsa cousins, Big Robber was fully a head taller than either commissioner.

"Father," he began, "we live a great way off, and we have but little to do with the whites, but we are willing to be at peace with them. We believe it would be for the good of all to be at peace and have no more war. We listen to our old men. They told us to come and see you and to listen to what you had to tell us. Father, what I promise I will perform, and my people will sustain me. For our part, we will keep the peace. I have been asked to speak as the voice of my people. The sun, moon, and earth are all witnesses of the truth, and all that I have promised here will be fulfilled."

Acceptance of territorial boundaries by the Crow immediately shifted the political debate taking place in the Sioux's Tribal Council. Because the Crow's homeland was the most productive buffalo ground north of the white man's Medicine Road, the Crow declaration now put Terra Blue and his subchiefs under pressure to join in the peace. Big Robber's surprising speech underscored Mitchell and Fitzpatrick's belief that the success of the treaty conference would ride on the shoulders of the Crow. The Sioux were now obliged to deal with Congress in good faith. They could not afford to have both the whites and the Crow as their enemies. After Big Robber's speech, their only alternative to peace was to go home empty-handed and prepare for war with the whites and all of their neighbors.

Mitchell now announced that henceforth, deliberations in the council circle would take a different form. The new scheme would commence the following morning. He instructed the chiefs to bring five or six of their principal men to the arbor. Each group would meet together with individual interpreters and the commissioners. The interpreters, men such as Culbertson and Jim Bridger, had lived with the tribes for years. These men knew the rivers and mountains of their homelands as well as anyone in the tribes.

"Tomorrow begins the most important task before us," Mitchell told them through the interpreters. "We will begin to draw the boundaries around your home territories. When you agree to this peace, that land will be yours, for as long as the waters flow. Now, go make great feasts."

⋇

There is no man living so extensively and correctly informed as to the geography of the headwaters of the Mississippi, the Yellowstone, and the Columbia Rivers, and their tributaries and lakes, and the mountains from whence they rise, or through which they pass, and how they interlock and pass each other, than Father DeSmet," wrote David Mitchell in his personal journal. And as for the foulmouthed, unwashed rogue named Jim Bridger, "He has traversed the mountains from East and West, and seems to have an intuitive knowledge of the topography of the country, the courses of the streams, the direction of the mountains, and is never lost, we are told, wherever he may be." Without the well-versed services of these two men of opposite callings and personal character, the peace council at Horse Creek, Mitchell admitted to himself, would have amounted to a fool's errand.

No sooner had the smoking ceremony concluded the morning following Big Robber's speech than Terra Blue rose to voice a protest. Speaking for the other Sioux chiefs, he told Mitchell that the Sioux bands were very concerned about disputes that would arise over boundaries between themselves, the Cheyenne, and the Arapaho. This new complaint was an attempt to regain lost bargaining power by asserting dominion over a larger territory than they had any right to claim. The Platte River was a natural line of demarcation between the Sioux and the Arapaho. Terra Blue was claiming territory on both sides of the Platte, in addition to the Brule's right to hunt as far south as the Republican Fork of the Kansas River. The Oglala's chief, Black Hawk, then rose to voice similar concerns. With a growing sense of foreboding, Mitchell and Fitzpatrick listened patiently as the Sioux's objections were quickly echoed by the Snake and Cheyenne.

The Sioux's tactic, aimed at disrupting Congress' proposal for tribal boundaries, quickly took hold among the other tribes. Before he understood what had happened, Mitchell found himself hamstrung between a myriad of claims and counterclaims. Although each tribe occupied a homeland that was recognized by all the others, territorial boundaries were completely foreign to their thinking. Mitchell called for a recess and withdrew to his camp. After devising a new strategy over lunch with Fitzpatrick, Mitchell reconvened the council of chiefs.

Now taking the offensive, Mitchell preempted any further protests by re-framing the government's purpose for demarcating tribal territories. This time, the commissioner presented the plan in terms the Indians could easily translate and explain to their people. Fixing boundaries to tribal territories, he assured them, was simply a formal recognition by the Great White Fathers of the Indian world as it already existed. Formal boundaries would in no way limit the tribes' right to travel or hunt in the country of another nation. As long as they remained at peace with each other and the white settlers, they would be free to travel and hunt as always.

Mitchell's distinction seemed to allay the Indians' greatest fears. His caveat gave the chiefs an escape from the trap set for them by the Sioux. The commissioners were now free to advance Congress' condition for established territories without requiring the tribes to give up their widely scattered hunt-ing grounds. In this, Mitchell had overstepped his instructions from Wash-ington, but in light of John Marshall's Trilogy, the tribes' rights to hunt, gather, and fish as they were accustomed was a moot point. The government was in no position to strip the tribes of rights that were already legally pro-tected. In Mitchell's view, he and Fitzpatrick had agreed to a demand that succeeded in securing the peace without costing the government a single bar-gaining chip. Without this condition, Mitchell knew there would be no peace. Lawmakers in Congress wanted one thing: to avoid bloodshed on the Oregon Trail. This simple concession, so easily and reasonably granted, would still be confounding federal courts in the twenty-first century.

For the next two weeks, the business of establishing territories for the principal tribes of the West continued. Negotiations filled the days, while dancing and feasting went on till dawn. By the middle of the second week, Brown wrote, the commissioners and interpreters were delirious from lack of sleep. Mitchell, the chiefs, and their interpreters were creating a blueprint for governance that translated the abstractions of John Marshall's Trilogy into a real-world model for federalism that formally vested the American Indian tribes with constitutionally guaranteed powers of self-government. Day after day, the leaders of each tribe worked with Mitchell, DeSmet, Culbertson, and Bridger toward consensus with the chiefs of other Indian nations on identifying the basic geographic features that outlined their home territories. For the Mandan, Hidatsa, and Arikara, Raven Chief, Four Bears, and Gray Prairie Eagle agreed to band together for the purpose of establishing a common homeland for their three peoples.

As the process of drawing boundaries proceeded, Father DeSmet and Jim Bridger quickly discovered that in the world of realpolitick, it was one thing to get each tribal group to claim its territorial boundaries; once those boundaries were established, it was an undertaking of a different kind to square the results of these individual agreements on one large map. Midway through the second week, Bridger, DeSmet, Culbertson, and Fitzpatrick met after dinner one evening and struck upon a new plan. Rather than each of them working with individual tribes, Fitzpatrick suggested, the four of them should meet with each tribal delegation. One by one, starting at the North with the Blackfeet, they could work their way south across the Great Plains to the Arkansas River.

As the mapmakers called the roll of the tribes, each group of chiefs gathered around a large sheet of parchment. Bunched together in the shade, the unlikely band of adventurers, priests, traders, Indian chiefs, and loners, such as Jim Bridger and Robert Meldrum, knelt shoulder to shoulder in the dust. Line by line, geographic features slowly shaped a map of the new American West. When the map was finished at the end of the second day, the lines drawn on the sheet of parchment by DeSmet and Bridger had legally defined a dozen new tribal territories. At the formal signing ceremony officiated by Mitchell and Fitzpatrick three days later, Four Bears, Gray Prairie Eagle, Raven Chief, Terra Blue, Big Robber, Cat Nose, and all the lesser chiefs made Xs beside their names on the final document that between them divided up 640 million acres, or a million square miles, of North American landscape. The territory described by the treaty covered ten future states in the Great Plains and far West, and included the sites of modern cities such as Denver and Kansas City; Billings and Cheyenne; Bismarck and Fort Collins, Colorado; Salt Lake City; Sioux Falls, South Dakota; Omaha, Nebraska; and Des Moines, Iowa.

The text of the final agreement was brief and simply stated. The Indians agreed to allow white settlers to pass unharmed through their country. It also granted Washington the privilege of building military posts along the trail to protect Indians and whites alike. The tribes promised to keep peace with white settlers and among each other. For these concessions and privileges, the commissioners guaranteed each tribe an annual payment of $50,000 for fifty years. The government also promised to honor the new boundaries of their tribal territories as defined by the treaty: white settlers would be prohibited from settling in those territories for "as long as the rivers shall flow."

Alexander Culbertson described the ancestral territory claimed by the Mandan, Hidatsa, and Arikara tribes: Since they were now living as one tribal people on the Upper Missouri, the Mandan, Hidatsa, and Arikara were granted a common homeland in the following manner: commencing at the mouth of the Heart River, thence up the Missouri River to the mouth of the Yellowstone, thence up the Yellowstone to the mouth of the Powder River, thence from the Powder River to the headwaters of the Little Missouri, and along the range of the Black Hills to the headwaters of the Heart River, then following that watercourse back to the place of the beginning.

For the three tribes of Village Indians, this was a formal recognition of what had been an informal arrangement since the fifteenth century. The new boundaries enclosed 12 million acres containing many of the tribe's sacred sites and traditional hunting grounds. A century later, the area set aside for the Mandan, Hidatsa, and Arikara would fall in parts of eastern Montana, northeastern Wyoming, and western North Dakota.

After the official treaty signing concluded on September 17, 1851, Mitchell, Fitzpatrick, and several of the older chiefs made speeches to the young warriors. Terra Blue and Cat Nose entreated them to be wide awake, attentive to their promises. Long after we are gone, you will be bound by this peace, Terra Blue told them. You must keep the peace with whites, and not molest them in passing through the country. Equally important, you must keep peace with each other.

The celebrations that marked the end of the peace council at Horse Creek went on through the night and well into morning. Mitchell's long-awaited wagon train arrived later that morning bearing the goods and gifts he had promised to the tribes months before. After presenting the principal chiefs with new military uniforms and gilt swords, Mitchell and Fitzpatrick distributed the twenty-seven wagonloads of gifts. Each band patiently waited to receive its share. In minutes, it seemed, the wagons were empty.

Twelve thousand Indians had spent the last three weeks camped at the confluence of Horse Creek and the Platte River. "Glad or satisfied, but always so quiet," wrote Brown, they now loaded up their lodges, their families, and slipped away over the horizon. The small party of Mandan, Hidatsa, and Arikara parted from their fellow traveler Father DeSmet, who returned to St. Louis with Commissioner Mitchell. Four Bears, Raven Chief, and Gray Prairie Eagle would journey overland with the Crow as far as the Yellowstone. They had little hope of reaching Like-a-Fishhook ahead of the first snows. The other tribes would turn south from Horse Creek. Many buffalo, they had heard, had roamed into the country of the South Platte. The Sioux, Arapaho, and Cheyenne were particularly anxious to have one last hunt before winter drove them back to their camps.

⚜

Thomas Fitzpatrick, the man who had blazed the Oregon Trail thirteen years earlier, watched the closing moments of the monthlong drama with "a feeling of quiet elation." He believed that the peace council had established a benchmark for Indian and white relations on the plains. This honorable, unassuming Irishman had played a leading role in two of the most pivotal events in the history of the American West. Less than two years later, it would fall to Fitzpatrick to shoulder the humiliating duty of revisiting each of the tribes and informing them that Congress had altered the agreement they had made at Horse Creek. In the intervening months, Congress decided that its original offer was too generous. Washington now wanted to reduce the promised annuities to $25,000 a year, and cut the terms of the payout from fifty years to ten. When Fitzpatrick tracked down Terra Blue in the Wyoming Territory, the Sioux chief spoke for many when he asked, "Where is our incentive to comply with these conditions when the White Fathers change every agreement to suit their own needs?"

Tribal leaders expressed bitter resignation over the revised provisions. Nevertheless, all but the Crow would eventually agree to the proposed amendments. By the time Congress finally acted on the treaty late in 1853, Mitchell and Fitzpatrick knew there was little hope that the original terms of peace with the Sioux would last out the decade. Every spring, new Indian agents made their way to the Oregon Territory with instructions to broker new treaties of friendship with tribes in the Northwest. Nearly every day, reports filtered back to Washington from agents on the frontier telling of Sioux atrocities against white emigrants and neighboring tribes. Despite DeSmet's solemn pledge to Cherry Necklace, the council at Horse Creek would not lead to an era of peace and tranquility for the Village Indians. Immediately following the peace council, Sioux hostility seemed to abate for a brief period.

By the end of the decade, however, the frequency and lethal consequence of their battles with the Mandan, Hidatsa, and Arikara would increase dramatically.

While Fitzpatrick was circulating the revised treaty among disgruntled tribal leaders, Congress passed the Kansas-Nebraska Act of 1854 and opened the eastern bank of the Missouri River to settlement by whites, immediately prompting a land rush into territory owned by the Sioux, Arapaho, and Pawnee. With the Civil War brewing in the east, fewer federal troops were being dispatched to the western frontier to keep the peace. Though the new amendments did not change the territorial boundaries of any of the tribes, a rising tide of settlers was encroaching on Indian lands. Each passing year recorded an increase in hostilities between Indians and whites. Neither side showed any willingness to back away from the bloodshed.

As the cycle of violence deepened, leaders of the great western tribes began to realize that the Great White Fathers in Washington had little, if any, control over their people. Time and again, white citizens demonstrated brazen contempt for the laws and treaty obligations of their government. When the ice broke on the Upper Missouri in the spring of 1860, more than a hundred steamboats left St. Louis with passengers bound for the High Plains and the gold-bearing hills of the Dakota Territory. The average trip from St. Louis to Sioux City, Iowa, took nine days and required the wood of fifty mature oak trees to fire a paddle wheeler's boilers. The once-dense woodlands along hundreds of miles of river bottoms vanished like the buffalo.

Ten years after Horse Creek, the material condition of the village tribes was "pitiable," writes Roy W. Meyer, a leading historian of the Mandan, Hidatsa, and Arikara people. With their number of able-bodied warriors greatly diminished by disease and war, they were increasingly more cautious in their dealings with the pugnacious Sioux. Cholera and deteriorating conditions with their nomadic neighbors finally drove the Arikara inside the protective walls of Like-a-Fishhook. From 1862 onward, the three tribes would engage the external world as a single political and economic unit. Though diminished from 25,000 to fewer than 1,000, the three tribes were still intact and culturally solvent. Each had retained its own language and its own religious traditions, clans, and secret societies. Despite the decades of adversity they had weathered since the smallpox epidemic at the Knife River, the tribes, according to reports from agents and traders during the 1860s, had a continuing sense of dignity and cohesive tribal identity. Often outnumbered ten to one, they seldom lost a face-to-face battle with the Sioux, yet increasingly their isolation forced them to live like prisoners inside the walls of their own village. The Sioux, by contrast, were chronically hostile to whites and other tribes but still managed to obtain horses, firearms, annuity goods, and treaty concessions from both government agents and private traders.

The Sioux reached the zenith of their military power in the 1860s just as the three tribes reached their low, a perfect reversal of the balance of power of a hundred years before. Driven west by the rapid encroachment of settlers from the east, the Sioux pushed across the plains at a furious pace. The Mandan, Hidatsa, and Arikara lay directly in their path. The three tribes' long history of friendship with the whites did little to promote peaceful relations with their rivals. Washington's lax attention to its treaty commitments, combined with the widespread corruption of federal Indian agents at frontier outposts, made the government's presence more of a liability than an asset.

Combined with the sudden disappearance of the buffalo on the plains, these mounting adversities seemed to assail the three tribes from all quarters. By the late 1860s, living conditions at Like-a-Fishhook were dire and rapidly worsening. In the winter of 1871, Captain Walter Clifford, the new officer in charge of the cavalry post at the nearby Fort Berthold, saw no choice but to send the tribes' youngest and strongest hunters into the Yellowstone country of the Crow. Otherwise, fifteen hundred Indians at Like-a-Fishhook faced the prospect of imminent starvation. Clifford gambled that the hunters would find game in the Yellowstone River country and be able to feed themselves through the winter. Using up the reserves of his own meager supplies, Clifford managed to keep the remaining five hundred women, children, and elders alive through the winter. For weeks on end, they huddled around bonfires inside the walls of the fort and survived from day to day on rations of soup.

This was a humiliating ordeal. Thankfully Clifford's gamble paid off. The hunters found elk and deer on the Yellowstone, enough to sustain them through the bitter cold winter. It was during this forced march into the country of the Crow that a Hidatsa matriarch named Yellow Corn gave birth to a girl in a tepee on the banks of the Yellowstone, a week's march upstream from the trading post at Fort Union. At a naming ceremony ten days after her birth, the baby girl was called Many Dances. She was a healthy, robust little girl who would one day marry a legendary warrior named Old Dog, a man twenty years her senior, and they would have five children. The couple's fourth child, a boy named Martin Old Dog Cross, would marry a Norwegian girl and make Many Dances a grandmother — ten times over.

That same year, 1871, the young Hidatsa warrior named Old Dog killed two Sioux warriors in hand-to-hand battle a stone's throw from the palisades of Like-a-Fishhook. At the age of twenty-one, the grandson of Cherry Necklace had already earned a reputation for fearlessness in combat. If he survived the exploits of early manhood, Old Dog would one day be a chief. After killing the two Sioux interlopers, he added to his glory by chasing a young Hunkpapa warrior named Sitting Bull completely out of their country.

⚜

The surrender of Crazy Horse and Sitting Bull in the years that followed the Battle of the Little Bighorn in 1876 brought a long-awaited cessation of hostilities between the Sioux and the Village Indians. The Sioux's two-hundred-year history of conflict with the Arikara would cost them dearly in the end. For many years they had held the upper hand. In the spring of 1876, the Arikara were the first to sign on as scouts for the 7th Cavalry's last great campaign against the plains tribes. Though Sitting Bull and Crazy Horse would vanquish their nemesis George Armstrong Custer, the cooler heads of General Terry and General Miles would prevail in the end. The Arikara would lead them to their ultimate military victory over the Sioux and Cheyenne.

As the American Indian Wars were approaching a denouement on the Northern Plains, the new commissioner of Indian affairs, Amasa Walker, would declare to Congress in 1872: "What shall be done about the Indian as an obstacle to the progress of settlement and industry? . . . They must yield or perish, as they are altogether barbarous and incompatible with civilization."

Walker's rhetorical flourishes would make a profound impression on the administration of President Benjamin Harrison. Though the president himself would not embrace Walker's extermination proposals, the policies enacted by Congress with Harrison's full approval would achieve the same results. In 1887, with the passage of a law known as the Dawes Act, Congress not only turned its back on the "supremacy clause" in Article VI of the U.S. Constitution, which stated that federal treaties would be the "supreme law of the land," but also upended the promise George Washington made to the tribes in the Northwest Ordinance of 1787, vowing never to take their land without their expressed permission. The Dawes Act, also known as the Allotment Era, abrogated dozens of treaties and opened treaty-protected Indian lands to white settlement. The long-anticipated agrarian expansion onto the Great Plains could now move forward, blessed with the high hopes and expectations of the Harrison administration. Railroads, with a twofold interest, were given a free hand to promote the scheme. They were anxious to sell to settlers the land they had been awarded for building the roads in order to create future markets. With Crazy Horse dead, Red Cloud imprisoned on a reservation, and Sitting Bull riding as a featured attraction in Buffalo Bill's Wild West Show, a new page had turned in the unfolding story of America. At the Chicago Exposition of 1893, historian Frederick Jackson Turner declared that Americans had fulfilled their "manifest destiny" by reaching the Pacific Ocean. "The American frontier," he announced, "is closed."

On the Upper Missouri, women from Like-a-Fishhook could return to their fields without warrior chaperones. Encouraged by new government policies promoting private ownership of land, twenty families left the village by 1882 to farm their own "allotments." By late 1885, the remaining families in the village were told that if they did not begin farming their allotments, their government assistance would cease. Within two years, Like-a-Fishhook was a ghost town.

In 1885, the new agent at Fort Berthold reported to his superiors in Washington that thus far, he had succeeded in preventing the Indians from organizing "dancings and other heathen rituals that celebrated their savage past." Slowly but surely, Congress was told, the wild children of the plains would be transformed into respectable gentleman farmers. As evidence of their progress toward this goal, he noted that the last resident of Like-a-Fishhook, a withered little old man named Red Roan Cow, a veteran of the Fort Laramie Peace Council of 1851, lived alone in his earth lodge in the company of bleached buffalo skulls and cold medicine pipes. In contrast to this last holdout at Like-a-Fishhook, the Hidatsa tribe's newest leader, Chief Old Dog, had moved upstream to his allotment on a wooded plain near a north turning bend in the river. Others were certain to follow.

By the spring of 1894, the agent's predictions had proven accurate. Government surveyors began laying out the streets of a new agency town, about a mile south of Chief Old Dog's log cabin and earth lodge. And since it would rise in a small forest of live oaks, wild plums, and maple trees at a deep bend in the river, they would call this town Elbowoods.

CHAPTER IV

Great White Fathers

☙

*"The European is to other races of men what man in general
is to animate nature. When he cannot bend them to his use or
make them serve his self-interests, he destroys them and makes them
vanish little by little before him."*

ALEXIS DE TOCQUEVILLE

A few miles downstream from the mouth of the Heart River in central
North Dakota, a bronze plaque marks the spot on the west bank of
the Missouri River where the Lewis and Clark expedition met up with its
first grizzly bear. What followed, rather hastily, was a one-sided tête-à-tête
between the toothsome critter and the captains' feeble-eyed subordinate,
Pierre Cruzat. Firing wildly at the animal from close range, the Frenchman
threw down his single-shot flintlock and ran for his life. Lewis named this
animal "white bear" for the silver coloring in the adult grizzly's fur. "I saw
several fresh tracks," he wrote in his journal on October 20, 1804, "three
times as large as a man's track." These ferocious, short-tempered monarchs
of the plains would continue to bedevil the expedition for the next two
years.

Wildlife biologists estimate that fifty thousand grizzly bears roamed the
Great Plains at the turn of the nineteenth century. For millennia, Homo sapi-
ens and Ursus horribilis thrived side by side at the top of the food chain in the
lush ecosystem of the Missouri River floodplain. This semi-isolated reserve
provided both man and beast with a rich diet of protein, vegetables, and wild
fruits and berries. "They flourished because they didn't have to eat each other
to survive," explains natural historian Ken Rogers. "For the alpha species,
these river bottoms were the modern equivalent of a strip of fast-food take-
out windows."

In a mere lightning strike of geologic time, the silver-tipped bear with the humped shoulders and large footprint has vanished altogether from the plains. The westward migration of European immigrants put the animal's natural habitat inside a fence and under the plow. The last grizzly bear walked off the plains at about the same time the Sioux warrior Crazy Horse surrendered at Fort Robinson in 1877. When the "wild tribes of the West" had been subdued by starvation and the cavalry had herded them onto reservations, the great white bear lumbered off to islands of seclusion in the "shining mountains" of the Rockies. There, in ever dwindling numbers, the grizzly has remained.

The plaque commemorating the encounter between the bear and Monsieur Cruzat is mounted beside the Missouri's last stretch of free-flowing water between the Montana border and the state of Iowa. Rogers says that this seventy miles of river, between the Garrison Dam and the Oahe Reservoir, is the only segment of the Big Muddy that Lewis and Clark would recognize for hundreds of miles in either direction. One-part historian and one-part ethnographer, Rogers is an avid canoeist who has several times retraced the explorers' water route on the Upper Missouri.

"These guys were the last in a long line of explorers to come into this country. What made them different from all the others was the underlying nature of their mission. Everybody else wanted to secure a trading monopoly with the Mandan. Lewis and Clark wanted that and a lot more." Where the French, English, and Spanish saw piles of beaver pelts they could sell at a premium in Europe, the young Americans saw a wide-open empire. "They were the first to stand on the banks of this river and see not just a river but a national resource," says Rogers. "That assessment has pretty much dictated the story of the Missouri, and the people who live beside it, ever since."

After measuring the bear's enormous paw print and noting its size in his field journal, Lewis climbed a steep embankment to reconnoiter the abandoned Mandan village of On-a-Slant. Lewis described the village's defenses as formidable and estimated the area inside the walls to be six to eight acres in size. The earth lodges were intact. He found cache pits of dried corn and squash, and cairns of weather-bleached human skulls. Through his Arikara guide, Lewis learned that when the Mandan abandoned On-a-Slant, the village had been occupied for three centuries. The golden age of Mandan prosperity had ended right where they were standing, less than twenty years before.

"When that first wave of smallpox hit in 1781," says Rogers, "the Mandan died by the thousands. For all they knew, this was a curse from God. Whatever the cause, the tribal leaders knew that they had arrived at a defining crossroads. They had to make a decision. They had to choose between pulling up stakes and moving on by themselves, as they had for hundreds of years, or opening up their culture and merging with other societies."

Surrounded by heaps of bodies that grew higher by the day, the Mandan leaders decided that the tribe's survival now called for a break with seven centuries of tradition. When the epidemic's survivors migrated upstream to the Knife in 1781, they began to share their customs, ceremonies, language, and lodges with the Hidatsa and Arikara. This commingling, says Rogers, gave the Mandan the wherewithal to survive the second wave of smallpox in 1837 and the catastrophic flood of 1949.

"In many respects, Garrison Dam is the great-grandchild of the Corps of Discovery. It would finally turn this mad elephant of a river into a resource. But for the tribes, Garrison Dam was as devastating as the 1837 smallpox epidemic. This series of disasters, starting back in 1781 at On-a-Slant, created the great future leaders in the tribes: the Cross family, the Baker family, the Walkers and Lone Fights."

Rogers argues that the twentieth-century composition of these clans, and the great leaders they produced, resulted from the daring decision made by the leaders at On-a-Slant in 1781 to open up the Mandan society. Had the Mandan, Hidatsa, and Arikara leaders decided to remain isolated from one another, the three tribes could not have emerged intact from the disastrous wars and plagues of the nineteenth century.

※

What lay between the placid river flowing past the Mandan Villages at the Knife River in 1804 and Lewis and Clark's vision for the Missouri was 150 years, and billions of federal dollars, that would be required to transform a national menace into a national resource. Jefferson's fact finders had no way of knowing that they were camped beside the most unpredictable river in North America, a concourse that might be idyllic one moment and deadly the next. As Missouri River Valley farmers would learn in the 1800s, their neighbor was the most promiscuous waterway on the High Plains. It seldom slept in the same bed and was forever jumping its banks and crossing state lines, and changing its course from one week to the next without knowing where it was headed. The river went dry when farmers were desperate for water, and brought torrents when they were saturated. In 1863, the editor of the *Sioux*

City Register newspaper wrote: "Of all the variable things in creation, the most uncertain are the actions of juries, the state of a woman's mind, and the condition of the Missouri River."

So when the first of three large floods inundated Omaha, Nebraska, in the spring of 1943, nothing about the deluge seemed out of the ordinary. In the first week of April that year, a sudden thaw on the Northern Plains coincided with a low-pressure system that was racing north from the Gulf of Mexico. Rapidly melting snow and ice along the Rocky Mountain front had already pushed the upper segment of the river over its banks, saturating hundreds of miles of floodplains. Then came the downpour. In Omaha, the river crested three feet above flood stage at two o'clock in the morning on April 12. Sullen skies wrung themselves out for days on end, dumping torrents of warm rain on waterlogged farmlands. With nothing to hold back the deluge, and no place to store the excess water, the river quickly filled to capacity and spilled over its banks. For residents of east Omaha and Kansas City, the coincidence of thaw and downpour was devastating. The only way to reach the airport from downtown Omaha that week was by canoe or powerboat.

But in the spring of 1943, the nation's attention was focused elsewhere. Allied armed forces were fully engaged in the war in Europe and the Pacific. The first reports of the flooding on the Missouri were buried in the second and third sections of the *New York Times*. General Patton's Fourth Army had just routed Rommel's elite Afrika Korps at El Guetar in north Africa, and American bombers were pounding Japanese rail installations in Burma. In late May, when the second flood carried away entire communities in Iowa and Nebraska, the story was bumped up to the inside pages of the *New York Times'* front section.

When the third flood crested on the thirteenth of June, millions of acres of rich farmland were inundated. Midwestern states lay beneath the largest lake on the continent. Hundreds of homes were carried off in the night by the river's rampaging currents. Drowned horses and cows came to rest in treetops in city parks. Claims for property damage climbed into the hundreds of millions of dollars. Day after day, the stiff-legged carcasses of farm animals floated past waterfronts at St. Louis and New Orleans. From Sioux City, Iowa, to the Gulf of Mexico, the foul stench of rotting flesh hung over the nation's heartland. When the third flood finally pushed the river onto the front page of the *New York Times,* Congress and the White House declared war on the Missouri.

While researching her now classic study of the Missouri, *Down by the*

River, Constance Elizabeth Hunt discovered that prior to the floods of 1943, the Army Corps of Engineers had spent three decades building an extensive network of dikes and levees along the lower stretch of the river. When the first surge of water pushed down from the north in April 1943, the Corps' artificial riverbanks prevented rising waters from dissipating into low-lying marshes and wetlands. Floodplains adjacent to the Corps' new levees had been pumped dry and planted with crops. The riprap banks had successfully protected at least one generation of farmers from the river's menacing temper. But when the downpour of Gulf rain collided with the heavy spring runoff, the resulting bulge of water had nowhere to go but over the levees. Prior to the building of those levees, the floodplains and wetlands along hundreds of miles of river bottoms would have absorbed the heavy runoff. Hunt's study led her to a disquieting conclusion: the devastating floods of 1943 were man-made.

⋇

Fed by runoff from the Rocky Mountains, the Missouri weaves itself together from the icy yarn of mountain streams near Three Forks, Montana. Once it collects the Ruby, the Madison, and the Jefferson, the river meanders another five hundred miles before joining up with the Yellowstone at the North Dakota border. There, the reinvigorated river suddenly doubles its size, becoming from head to tail the second longest river on the continent, and the seventh largest in volume. Yet even these figures can be misleading. Flash floods on any of the river's many tributaries could cause it to leap out of its bed at a moment's notice. The river's unpredictable upstream behavior often had lethal consequences in downstream farm states. The annual outflow of the Little Missouri could range from a mere trickle of four thousand acre-feet per year at Alzada, Montana, to a roaring million acre-feet at its mouth, four miles upstream from the small community of Elbowoods. The mercurial nature of these larger tributaries continually reinforced the Missouri's demonic reputation.

When Congress created the Army Corps of Engineers in 1824, the military's civil engineers were assigned the mission of regulating navigation on the nation's inland waters. The agency's first commission on the Missouri came in the spring of 1838. Engineers sent two boats up the river to remove snags that were continually impeding and befouling the burgeoning flotilla of commercial steamboats. With mounting reluctance and at ever-increasing expense, the Army engineers maintained navigation channels on the Missouri until railroads spanned the continent in the 1880s. Unable to compete with the railroads in speed, price, or tonnage, the steamboat vanished from the Upper Missouri. When the Army engineers ended a half century of duty on the Missouri, they reported back to Congress that if left to its own, the river could be expected to return to its "former state of uselessness" in short order. The agency cheerfully conceded defeat and redeployed its engineers to more worthwhile rivers.

At the same time the Army Corps of Engineers were waving a white flag on the Missouri, the Bureau of Reclamation was being created by Congress to build civilian water projects and irrigation systems for farmers and communities in the arid West. Federally funded water projects on the High Plains had been the dream of dryland farmers for decades. Ever since white men had stepped out of the woods and sunk plows into the short-grass prairie, western rivers had taunted them with their limitless but inaccessible resources. None of the West's great rivers was more contemptuous of man's hubris in controlling nature than the river known as the Big Muddy.

The river, it seemed, was a living thing with a capricious will and a mercurial temper. The Missouri appeared determined to defy human schemes to shackle its energy, or make greater use of its flowing resource. In the 1920s, politicians from Upper Missouri states approached the Bureau of Reclamation hoping to sweet-talk the agency into building a regionwide irrigation system for dryland farmers. But the civilian engineers were as reluctant to get involved on the Upper Missouri as their counterparts in the military. The bureau's early experience with irrigation projects on the Colorado plateau had taught them a harsh lesson in the economics of cold-terrain farming. Schemes to bring water to the arid plateaus quickly turned into losing propositions for taxpayers. Congress intended the bureau to act as a low-interest banker to fund economically viable water projects, not as a pawnbroker for destitute farmers. Projects that looked economically viable on paper commonly turned into bottomless sinkholes for the Department of the Treasury. Against its better judgment, the agency yielded to pressure in Washington and built nine moderately sized irrigation projects on the Upper Missouri. The system was scheduled to be paid off in the 1960s. When the due date came and went, the bureau estimated that the farmers still owed the American taxpayers $55 million. The bureau projected that at the rate the debt was being paid off, the irrigation systems they built in the 1920s would be free and clear in the year 2140. If this was the outcome of a modest irrigation system costing less than $100 million, what, asked the bureau's bookkeepers, would the schedule of payments look like following an investment of billions?

Despite the bureau's humble efforts on the Upper Missouri, most dryland farmers on the Great Plains in the 1920s had made peace with the idea that moisture sufficient to grow their crops would have to fall from the sky. The historian Samuel Eliot Morison argued that "the conquest of the Great Plains, land that had for so long posed a formidable barrier to settlement, had been America's most notable achievement" in the first decades of the twentieth century. In 1890, the United States had seventy-seven acres of land under cultivation for each of its citizens. Many of those acres had been virgin prairie just a few years before. By World War I, that figure dropped to four acres per citizen. Advances in agricultural methods had revolutionized the small family farm. Moreover, moderate climate and consistently high rainfall during the 1910s and 1920s produced bumper crops and heady optimism among High Plains farmers. In the two decades prior to the disastrous dust bowl years of the 1930s, agriculture on the plains looked like the new American gold rush.

In the first years of the century, Norwegians, Swedes, and Swiss and German immigrants turned millions of acres of virgin prairie and High Plains topsoil under the plow. For an all too brief period in the early 20s, everybody farming land beside the Missouri River was getting rich. Postwar demands for wheat soared. In 1920, the population of North Dakota was the highest it would be for the next eighty years. Through intensive resource development and the good luck of steady rain, the American homesteader fell into the comfortable habit of expecting miracles. By 1930, farmers on the northern Great Plains supplied the entire country with butter, beef, leather, wheat, and numerous other valuable commodities. The visionary logic of the Homestead Acts had paid off, relieving pressure on eastern cities and putting the continent's valuable resources to the most beneficial use of a growing American society.

But to anyone who knew the region, and to any farmer accustomed to glancing overhead at the inscrutable dome of sky, the idea that man could somehow "conquer" the elements that governed life on the Great Plains was a dangerous conceit. Any farmer familiar with the natural history of the Great Plains knew that the bumper-crop years of the 1910s and 20s would sooner or later come to an end.

After mapping the West's great river systems in the late 1800s, John Wesley Powell of the U.S. Geological Survey recommended to Congress that the federal government should promote settlement in the West by river systems rather than by geographically organizing the continent according to arbitrary boundaries drawn across empty deserts by railroad magnates in eastern cities. He also warned Washington that the boosterism of western congressmen was a pied piper's tune that would soon lead them, and hordes of emigrants, down the path to disaster. Sustainable agriculture on the Northern Plains was simply not possible, warned Powell, without a massive investment of federal dollars in public waterworks and irrigation projects. If scarcity of moisture was not intimidating enough in the continent's heartland, the growing season between killer frosts across northern tier states was often less than 130 days. In other words, life for homesteaders on the Great Plains would be a devil's gambit. If one demon did not get them, Powell told Congress, another surely would.

In the two decades following Powell's report, homesteaders arrived in Minot and Fargo by the tens of thousands on trains, foot, horseback, and wagons. In the 1870s, there were fewer than 2,500 immigrant farmers in North Dakota. By the late 1920s, railroad land sales and Homestead Acts had increased that number to 690,000. Basinwide, more than 70 million acres of virgin sod — an area the size of France, Germany, and Spain combined — had been sectioned off by government surveyors and turned under the homesteader's plow. The alluvial topsoils left behind 16 millennia before by receding glaciers were uniformly high in fertility across the entire region. As long as the annual rainfall stayed above the magical fifteen inches, the soil produced bumper crops. But when the drought years returned in the 1930s, Bureau of Reclamation hydrologists told Congress that homesteaders had in less than three years gone from celebrating good fortune to learning a cruel lesson of nature. It was a lesson, they told Congress, that they had better learn as well. Beyond the Hundredth meridian, climatic realities of the Great Plains transformed Thomas Jefferson's vision of a nation of gentlemen farmers, on 160-acre homesteads, from a pretty mythology into a vast graveyard now forming between the rock of the western mountains and a dry place called Fargo.

In hopes of heading off a complete disaster, Congress spent a billion and a half Depression-era dollars to bring relief to farmers in the Northern Plains states. Despite this infusion of cash, commodities, and good intentions, it soon became apparent that no amount of money could stem the exodus. In less than five years, first-generation homesteaders abandoned 300,000 family farms. In the *Atlantic Monthly,* E. V. Smalley wrote that "an alarming amount of insanity occurs in the new prairie states among farmers and their wives. In proportion to their numbers, the Scandinavians furnish the largest contingent to the asylums." At forty below zero, the harsh conditions of life on the Great Plains played out in the maddening silence of 10,000 homestead kitchens. Engineers and hydrologists in both federal water agencies knew that halfhearted stopgap measures by long-winded congressmen were not going to restore the people in those kitchens to sanity. The only way to subdue this land, if that was possible, would be through a massive, federally sponsored program of public works. It took the dust-bowl disaster to chasten the western congressmen who had scoffed at John Wesley Powell fifty years earlier. Now, no one in Washington dared guess what such an enterprise would cost. Coming off the "dirty 30s," farmers agreed that the only sensible alternative to a federally funded water project was to give it all back to nature.

The Bureau of Reclamation's negative attitude toward the Missouri served as a reminder to their cross-town rivals, the Army Corps of Engineers, of their own half century of frustration on the river. In the first three decades of the twentieth century, the Corps continued to build and maintain dikes and levees on the lower portion of the river, but when it came to the Upper Missouri, above the border at Sioux City, Iowa, they busied themselves elsewhere. Then, after nature asserted her dominion with a series of nationwide floods in 1927, Congress turned again to the Army engineers and asked the agency to prepare a formal hydrological study of the Missouri, from its headwaters in Montana to its confluence with the Mississippi above St. Louis.

Time and again since the turn of the century, proposals for bringing the Missouri under man's control had been rejected out of hand as too expensive. But if anyone could get the pig of a publicly funded basinwide water project through the snake of the national treasury, it was the National Farmers Union. In the prosperous years following World War I, the national union of small farmers had grown into a powerful political force in Washington. This group of independent, single family farmers was broadly allied with the larger industrially based labor movements. The National Farmers Union fused rural populism with urban socialism across America's vast rural center. Seeing its moment of opportunity in the aftermath of the 1927 floods, the union stepped forward to flex its muscle with Congress, hoping that one more big push would bring a huge infusion of federal water-project dollars to the Missouri Basin.

For its part, the Army Corps of Engineers viewed Congress' request for a basinwide study of the Missouri as an opportunity to shut the door forever on the senseless hydrologic adventures being promoted by farmers and politicians. On February 5, 1934, the agency submitted a 1,245 page report to Congress that specifically assessed the river's potential for hydroelectric production, navigation, irrigation, recreation, and flood control. The Corps' study, five years in preparation, was the first comprehensive analysis ever made on the

Missouri. Presented by the chief of engineers, Major General Lytle Brown, the study informed Congress that in the opinion of the Army engineers, expenditure of federal funds for flood control on the Missouri would be an egregious waste of taxpayer money and goodwill. General Brown conceded that hydroelectric facilities could become feasible on the Missouri under more favorable economic conditions. However, he declared, this provisional concession should not be taken as an endorsement for building the dam on the Mandan Bluffs at Garrison, North Dakota, that is often proposed by politicians and farmers. This site, in the view of field engineers, was "entirely impracticable." The underlying geology lacked the stability necessary to support a high dam, and any dam of that size would be constructed with the Achilles' heel of rapid siltation. In order to achieve some control over downstream flooding and navigation, the Corps recommended that Congress consider building a massive earthen dam above the Yellowstone at Fort Peck, Montana. Other than that, Brown told Congress, his agency could not recommend any water projects that would alter the river above Sioux City, Iowa. When Brown concluded, the subject of the Missouri was tabled.

The following year, however, one of the Missouri's notorious tributaries struck again. A ferocious storm materialized without warning on the Republican River in the summer of 1935. Those who saw the deluge described it as a river falling from the sky. The resulting flash flood killed 105 Nebraska residents in minutes. The maelstrom on the Republican quickly prompted Congress to pass the first nationwide legislation to address the problem of untamed rivers in the West. The Flood Control Act of 1936, which passed without opposition, was followed three years later with the more powerful Reclamation Project Act of 1939, a bill that authorized civilian engineers at the Bureau of Reclamation to once again prepare for Congress a comprehensive study of potential multiple-use developments on the Missouri River. Specifically, Congress wanted to know how much it would cost to acquire the property necessary to develop irrigation, municipal, and industrial water systems. Despite the clear and well-grounded recommendations of the Army engineers' report of the year before — the 1,245 page document that was now gathering dust at the Library of Congress — the new law also directed bureau engineers to work with the Army engineers on flood control above Sioux City, Iowa, and enhancement of downriver navigation.

This time around, Congress anticipated the rash of legal tangles that would inevitably grow out of any new engineering adventures on the Missouri. Land acquisitions would have to be accomplished through a combination of condemnation and "eminent domain." The Missouri had proven that it was a 2,600-mile-long enigma. One way or another, Washington was determined to bring the mad elephant to heel.

⋇

As Patton's Fourth Army was chasing General Rommel's battered Afrika Corps across North Africa in April 1943, on the home front, Errol Flynn and Ann Sheridan were starring in *Edge of Darkness* at Radio City Music Hall. A deep wave cut at the Saks Fifth Avenue beauty parlor cost $1.50, and as the Midwest was drying out from its first flood of the season, farther west an Army Air Corps enlistee named Martin Cross was making his way home by bus to Elbowoods, North Dakota, after spending a year at a training base in Utah. To their great surprise, airman Martin Cross' superiors had discovered that their enlistee from North Dakota had a wife and seven children, and his eighth child, son Milton, was on the way. Martin was immediately issued a hardship discharge and put on the next bus home.

"We've never been quite sure who got to him first, Mom or the Army," says Phyllis, retelling the story.

"I'm not sure which would have been worse," chimes in her brother Martin Jr., a tall, thick-bodied man better known to friends and family as Crusoe. Two years younger than Phyllis, Crusoe is visiting Parshall from his home in Saskatoon, Canada, where he recently retired from a career in social work. His broad friendly face, snow-white beard, and baritone voice fill up the room with genuine levity.

"I am," answers Phyllis without hesitation. "Mom. Why do you think so many men were anxious to go off to war?"

"To get a break from the women and kids," answers Crusoe. "That was the first time they were apart in fourteen years."

Martin and Dorothy had met in 1928. Both were twenty-two years old. Martin had recently left the Indian boarding school at Wahpeton, South Dakota, where he discovered that he had talents for language and composition, for playing the saxophone, and for riding broncs. When he left school he worked close to home and spent all of his free time with friends, following the rodeo circuit from town to town. When Dorothy graduated from the one-room schoolhouse in Van Hook, she wasted no time getting herself enrolled in the nursing program at St. Alexius Hospital in Bismarck. While Martin was off being a footloose rodeo cowboy, the daughter of his oldest sister, Maggie Grinnell, was severely burned in a house fire. The little girl was rushed to the hospital in Bismarck in the back of a wagon. While there, the little girl was cared for and brought back to health by a young nursing student from Van Hook named Dorothy Bartel.

This adventurous, high-spirited Norwegian girl became fast friends with Martin's sister Maggie. When the daughter made a speedy recovery from her burns and returned home to Elbowoods, her nurse followed. Rather than returning to Van Hook to spend holidays and long weekends with her parents, Dorothy started getting off the bus at Garrison and hitching a ride to Elbowoods on the mail truck. There, she soon became a regular houseguest at the Grinnell family home.

"She was a pretty Norwegian girl, the only daughter of first-generation homesteaders, and he was the dashing rodeo cowboy, the son of a tribal chief," says her daughter, Marilyn. "With our dad, life for this high-spirited girl from dreary Van Hook was suddenly very exciting."

Throughout her teenage years, Dorothy had secretly planned her escape from the Lutheran austerity of her parents' home. Once she had left the nurse's training program in Bismarck, Dorothy ignored her parents' continuous appeals to return to Van Hook. For a time, she moved in with Maggie Grinnell and helped her new friend care for her growing family, but the Bartels of Van Hook were nothing if not persistent. They drove down to Elbowoods on several occasions, parked in front of the Grinnell house, and sat outside honking the horn. Convinced their only child had fallen under an evil spell, the Bartels were determined to rescue their daughter and bring her back to her right mind. But each time they came to Elbowoods, their headstrong daughter sent them slinking back to Van Hook with an empty luggage rack. "Life in those small farming towns was pretty tough," says Marilyn. "I spent summers with my grandparents. They weren't the most fun-loving people you'd ever want to meet. There was no way Mom was going back."

Martin and Dorothy eloped and were married in September 1928 by a judge at the county courthouse in Washburn, North Dakota. The couple had a "pretty high time" of it through their first years of marriage. Dressed in white Stetsons and raccoon coats, they traveled all over the country in Martin's roadster, going from rodeo to rodeo and taking in the dances along the way. Through the first spring and summer of their marriage, they were buoyed by the invulnerability and carefree optimism of youth. The landscape the young couple called home was neither Indian nor white. Farm country was prosperous, rodeos were numerous, and all roads in the country seemed

to lead back to the secure refuge of family, friends, and the familiar surroundings of Elbowoods.

When Martin and Dorothy returned to Elbowoods after their first summer on the rodeo circuit, the couple moved into the farmhouse that Old Dog
had built shortly before he died. While Martin took over the responsibilities
of running a small ranch and providing for his sisters, Dorothy planted a garden, cooked the meals, tended to the livestock, and soon discovered that their
first child was on the way.

From the very beginning of the marriage it seemed that good fortune was
smiling on the young couple. Wealth being produced by industrious Norwegian and German farmers was filtering into reservation communities like
Elbowoods and Nishu, Lucky Mound and Independence. Many of the Mandan, Hidatsa, and Arikara Indians could rely on steady income by leasing
their bottomland allotments to white farmers. Most of this rich, untilled
ground was irrigated from below by the shallow water table lying inches beneath the valley floor. For their own subsistence, the Indians continued to
cultivate extensive gardens.

In addition to bountiful crops and material well-being, in 1930 the tribe
celebrated a long-awaited verdict in a lawsuit they had brought against the
U.S. Congress in the Court of Federal Claims. Attorneys for the tribe had
filed the suit years earlier, seeking restitution from the government for land
that was taken by executive order in 1870 and 1880, reducing the original 12-
million-acre territory by half. Their claims charged the federal government
with unilateral abrogation of the Fort Laramie Peace Council of 1851. The ten-
year wait for a decision from the Court of Federal Claims proved fortuitous.
Just as banks were failing from coast to coast and the country was plunging
toward the Great Depression, this victory brought an unexpected windfall to
the Three Affiliated Tribes. After adjustments for expenses, the court awarded
$1,000 to every member of the tribe, an enormous sum of money to a society
of people still conducting most of their economic activity on barter. With the
money, hundreds of new homes were built, older ones were updated, and new
equipment and livestock were purchased for farms and ranches. The Court of
Federal Claims settlement cushioned the tribes from the harshest days of the
Depression. The sudden windfall of cash also brought many of the Indians
into contact with the white world for the very first time. As late as the 1930s,
fewer than half the tribal membership spoke a word of English.

More than fifty years after black men were officially recognized as citizens,
and four years after women were given the right to vote, in 1924 Congress

officially recognized Indians as American citizens. Four years later, the Institute for Government Research released the first-ever investigation into living conditions in Indian Country. The famous Merriam Report, the Pentagon Papers case of its day, confirmed the darkest allegations of the critics of federal Indian policy: the Dawes Act of 1887 had been an unqualified disaster for the American Indian tribes. Contrary to claims made by its most ardent promoters, the Allotment Era of the Dawes Act had neither set Indians free nor succeeded in assimilating a single native into white society. Instead, the Merriam Report found, the Dawes Act had officially sanctioned the theft of hundreds of millions of acres of treaty-protected Indian land. At the same time, it had given government agents a free license to take thousands of Indian children from their parents' homes and send them off to boarding schools for assimilation into white society. This policy, concluded the report, had only succeeded in transforming America's original citizens into fragmented enclaves of demoralized beggars.

The public's outrage over the Merriam Report's findings was directly responsible for the uncontested passage of the Indian Reorganization Act (IRA) of 1934. The IRA was a sweeping new policy, one fiercely championed by President Franklin Roosevelt, his secretary of the interior, Harold Ickes, and the new commissioner of Indian affairs, John Collier. The IRA asked Congress to reverse a century of paternalistic efforts by the federal government and churches to assimilate the natives into mainstream society. It instructed Congress to replace these policies with John Marshall's concept of tribal self-government. Congress, in no mood to buck the Merriam Report or the new president, quietly ushered in a new era of federal Indian policy with the nearly unanimous passage of the IRA.

The Mandan, Hidatsa, and Arikara were among the first tribes in the nation to embrace this radical new proposal. On June 29, 1936, in the Great Depression's darkest days, the three tribes leaped into the modern political era by formally adopting a tribal constitution under the IRA's new guidelines. Tribal support for this decision, from the most progressive members like Martin Cross to the most traditional — those still living in such small isolated villages as Independence and Nishu — was nearly universal. The following year, when Secretary of the Interior Harold Ickes approved the tribes' corporate charter, the Tribal Council of the Three Affiliated Tribes came into being as the official lawmaking body and government on the Fort Berthold Reservation, which had been formally established fifty years earlier during the Dawes era.

One of the council's first acts was to engage the federal government in a cooperative cattle-raising program, a program that thrived and grew each year through the end of World War II. Despite the economic hardships sustained by farmers and ranchers on the surrounding plateau, the default rate on federal loans to Indian ranchers on Fort Berthold was the lowest in the nation. On the Northern Plains, it was common knowledge that the three tribes were weathering the 30s better than their white neighbors. Many homesteaders from nearby towns survived the worst years of the Great Depression by finding paying work on Indian ranches and farms on the reservation.

At the onset of World War II, a Bureau of Indian Affairs survey of the Mandan, Hidatsa, and Arikara tribes found that the population in the tribes' nine small communities had doubled from 960 forty years earlier to 1,854, a number not seen in more than a century. Materially and economically, the BIA survey found that life on Fort Berthold was an economic step up from the poverty in surrounding white communities. Apart from four cases of tuberculosis, health problems among the Indians were virtually nonexistent. Cases of smallpox, typhoid fever, and diphtheria had been reported in Parshall, Garrison, and nearby Halliday, but none of these maladies had migrated onto the reservation. In 1943, the four-person medical staff at the hospital in Elbowoods assisted in sixty-two births, performed twenty-six minor surgeries, and inoculated a thousand tribal members against typhoid when spring flooding contaminated wells along the river. One person had been diagnosed with cancer, while diabetes and kidney ailments were virtually unknown. In the previous five years, heart disease was listed as the cause of death in fewer than 2 percent of the cases.

In the months following the Japanese attack on Pearl Harbor, 250 adults, mostly men, left the reservation to join the armed forces. To enlist, many had to walk or hitch a ride with a farmer to the nearest bus station in Garrison. From there, enlistees rode a bus to the induction center in Fargo, 250 miles away. In order to ease his own transition into a world of white men, Martin, the week before he left in the spring of 1942, officially changed the family name in Tribal Court from the Hidatsa surname of Old Dog to the more Anglo-Saxon sounding Cross. "Back then, a lot of Indians were anglicizing their names," says Martin's son Bucky. "Young men like our father believed that Indians were going to have to close the gap between the Indian and white culture in order to survive. Adopting a new name was one way of closing that gap. It's a real insight into their thinking, because that would never happen today."

For many enlistees from the three tribes, fighting a war on foreign soil was the first adventure beyond their reservation boundaries. Some, like Martin, had attended government boarding schools when they were teenagers, but most went to Fargo — leaving behind a world where they spoke their native language, harvested crops by hand, cut hay with horse-drawn mowers, and canned the food that would see them through the winter.

"When the men went off to war, the women really had their hands full," says Phyllis. "Mom had five school-age kids, a toddler on each hip, and she was pregnant with Milton, who was developmentally disabled from birth. She had all the hay fields to deal with, all the animals, horses, cows, pigs, goats, and chickens, the gardens, all the harvesting, canning, and cooking. It wasn't too long before she was telling my dad in letters, 'Hey, buster, your warrior days are over. Get your butt back here where you can help me with these kids and this ranch.'"

"That was the toughest year of our childhoods," remembers Crusoe, who clearly recalls the hardships the war brought to Elbowoods. Many of his father's responsibilities in the fields, with livestock and harvests, fell to the two oldest boys, Crusoe and Bucky. "Imagine, no money to speak of, growing your own food, Mom making your school clothes out of flour sacks, shooting coyotes by moonlight to keep them out of the chicken coop, hauling ice from the river and coal for the woodstove at thirty below. If you didn't have food, you didn't eat. It was that simple. Things got pretty lean. I was very angry that Christmas because there weren't any presents. Mom made us mittens out of some old coats she got from a church clothes barrel. Going to bed hungry when it's thirty below zero after you've hauled coal on a sled all afternoon isn't something you ever forget."

By the time Martin Cross hopped off the mail truck in Elbowoods in April 1943, the season's first floodwaters were receding in downstream Nebraska. But the river was just taking a breather before unleashing the real show, which it was saving for late May. Two weeks before, the *Sanish Sentinel*, a small-town newspaper published in a nearby community, reported a story that was long on rumor but sketchy on details. A team of engineers, it seemed, had quietly slipped into the town of Garrison and was conducting surveys of some kind down along the river and by the Mandan Bluffs.

"One of the things we all loved about growing up in Elbowoods was having our own horses," says Phyllis. "We rode from the time we could walk. I used to ride in the hills outside of town, and that's when I first saw the red surveyor's flags. That was way before anybody heard anything about the engineers. I had no idea what they were. Then the paper came out with the story about the engineers being down at Garrison. Those flags were the elevation lines for the lake."

It was not until a month later, in May, that the story about the engineering survey officially became public knowledge. Beneath a headline reading, A DAM QUESTION, the *Sanish Sentinel* made the vague observation that "there was big news in the air," but ruefully admitted that "we cannot get at it." When pressed for answers, a spokesman for the Army Corps of Engineers told reporters from the newspaper in Bismarck that they were gathering data to be "correlated with an aerial survey for a topographical map." By then, however, another local paper, the *Stanley Sun,* published confirmed reports that civil engineers were surveying the Upper Missouri for possible dam sites. "Hopefully," wrote the editor, "the dam will be located where it will do the most good to the most people." In the mind of at least one editor on the Upper Missouri River, a major dam was already a foregone conclusion.

Then, the second flood of the season inundated much of Iowa and Nebraska and was soon followed by a third. Congress immediately directed the Committee on Rivers and Harbors to convene an emergency hearing on the Missouri floods. Despite millions of dollars spent conducting surveys, a viable, cost-effective solution for managing the Missouri Basin had thus far eluded Congress and the federal water agencies. To veterans on Capitol Hill, the call for emergency hearings in April of 1943 sounded like the boy crying wolf. President Roosevelt had heard all the high-toned rhetoric and explanations for the Missouri's irascible behavior. Now he wanted to hear how Congress and the water agencies proposed to put an end to that behavior, once and for all. The president directed his secretary of the interior, Harold Ickes, and General Wheeler to have their respective agencies, the Bureau of Reclamation and the Army Corps of Engineers, draw up basinwide proposals that would bring this devastating cycle of flooding on the Missouri to a halt. Before the floodwaters had receded, each agency was hard at work formulating its plan.

✺

The Congress that passed the Reclamation Project Act of 1939 was boxed in on the Missouri by a legal paradox whose pedigree had its origins in royal courts. Somehow, a legal riddle that originated in Elizabethan England had survived the turmoil of the eighteenth and nineteenth centuries, only to become the "takings" mechanism of choice for American legislators in the twentieth. The father of the U.S. Constitution, James Madison, had predicted as much. On the eve of the Constitutional Convention in the summer of 1787, the thirty-six-year-old political theorist told his protégé, Alexander Hamilton, that any work they left unfinished in Philadelphia would come back to haunt future generations. In some cases, however, it was already too late to set it right.

In the summer of 1787, Madison and his chief ally in Philadelphia, Benjamin Franklin, knew that where the law of the land ended — somewhere out on the western frontier — self-interest would inevitably work to unhinge the authority of the new government. After all, colonial leaders were students of their own behavior. For more than a generation they had promoted their own self-interest in defiance of King George III. Now that they were in charge, the young republic's leaders were determined to discourage that same self-interested anarchy in their own citizenry. With the full support of President Washington, the First Congress moved to foreclose on the temptations of frontier anarchy by passing the Indian Trade and Intercourse Act in 1790. This law was a broadside assault on narrow interests of individual states, most notably Virginia, which persisted in claiming that its original Jacobean charter granted it a swath of land that stretched from the Atlantic seaboard to the western ocean. Those Virginia patricians are delusional, said members of the First Congress, realizing that claims like Virginia's left it no alternative but to act. The federal government was determined to protect its exclusive right to engage in commerce with Indian tribes and to control all the future exchange of Indian lands. Without specifically saying so, that meant every acre west of the Appalachians.

The irony underlying the Indian Trade and Intercourse Act was the fact that it owed its legal efficacy to King George III himself. The king had imposed a very similar set of restrictions on colonial land syndicates a generation earlier. Compounding the irony, the most prominent of these syndicates was run by Benjamin Franklin and George Washington. At the time, Franklin's group was seeking to obtain title to all the lands in the Ohio Valley. But King George III's Royal Proclamation of 1763, issued to warrant the English victory over the French in the Thirty Years' War, denied colonists the right to acquire land from western tribes. All commercial enterprises with the tribes, said the crown, were the exclusive prerogative of the king.

The question King George III had addressed in the Royal Proclamation of 1763 was whether the "savage infidels" had natural law rights to legal ownership of the lands they occupied when they were "discovered" by European explorers. George III's proclamation answered the natural law question in the affirmative. Indians indeed held aboriginal title to their land. George III's proclamation reasserted the crown's exclusive privilege for dealing with the tribes, as one nation to another, one king to another king. Once and forever, the crown's proclamation dashed the land syndicates' dreams for privately owned empires against the rock of the mad king's reasoning.

Franklin sailed to England to argue that since the Indians' natural law rights perfected their aboriginal title to land, it followed that the tribes also possessed an undeniable right to sell it to whomever they pleased. George III summarily rejected the syndicates' argument. Behind the curtains in the royal court, London merchants had forced the king's hand by arguing that colonial land syndicates would put settlements in the West beyond the control of London bankers and merchants. Losing those markets would slowly bleed the king's treasury of its vitality. The king's caveat emptor enraged the colonial aristocrats, who viewed Indian lands as their personal path to riches. London merchants had won the day, but the colonials now had their justification for a break with the crown.

But no sooner had the colonists won the War of Independence than their legal theories about natural law and Indian title made an abrupt about-face. With the passage of the Non-Intercourse Act of 1790, land speculators on the frontier were told that they would now have to answer to the new Congress, whose members declared their earlier "natural law" arguments to be null and void. The Great White Fathers unilaterally dissolved all claims to Indian lands by individuals, land syndicates, and states. Benjamin Franklin and George Washington were among the chief proponents of this reversal.

The Indian Trade and Intercourse Act was a poignant reminder that dreams of empire may be born in idealism, but the details of conquest are underwritten by the coin of the realm. During the nation's centennial celebration of the Constitution, the Dawes Act would reverse the government's policy by opening Indian Country to private ownership under the pretext of bringing the "savages" out of the cold and into the warm house of civilization and Christian fellowship. Before the end of the century, the Dawes Act turned the ownership of Indian lands into a confused puzzle of private deeds and treaty-protected trusts. Nearly 150 years after Congress passed the Non-Intercourse Act, the legislators who passed the Reclamation Project Act of 1939 found themselves face-to-face with questions they were unprepared to answer. In the federal government's solemn trust relationship with the tribes, who exactly held title to treaty-protected Indian lands on the Upper Missouri

River? And if Congress, the trustee, decides to take that land away under eminent domain in violation of its solemn "supreme law of the land" treaty pledges to the tribes, how does the government legally square that with its constitutional obligations to the Indians? Assuming the knot could be cut, who would then decide what that land was worth?

*

When the floods of 1943 inundated Iowa and Nebraska, the insoluble legal paradox posed by a "taking" of treaty-protected land was of no concern to the Army Corps of Engineers' Colonel Lewis Pick, or Bureau of Reclamation engineer Glenn Sloan. Sloan, a middle-of-the-deck bureaucrat in the bureau's Billings, Montana, office, would prove his mettle as a politician and a diplomat in coming years. A young maverick with a history of being in hot water with his superiors, Sloan liked to think big and work alone. Ever since it was requisitioned by Congress in 1939, Sloan had been diligently working on a water-management plan for the Upper Missouri Basin. His sweeping proposal featured a strategically designed network of ninety reservoirs and irrigation systems. The galaxy of collection basins would efficiently distribute the Missouri's resources and deliver irrigation to tens of thousands of small family farms across a half million square miles of arid plains. The plan was designed to manage the river by controlling the flow of its largest tributaries. By creating an interconnected network of upstream catch basins, Secretary Ickes told Roosevelt, Sloan's "two-for-one approach" allowed for extensive upstream irrigation projects at the same time as it provided flood control along the lower river. Sloan's reservoirs could store tens of millions of acre-feet of water, more than enough to prevent all three floods in 1943.

Sloan had been working on his plan for more than three years when the river jumped its banks on April 12, 1943. A few hundred miles south of Billings, Colonel Lewis Pick, the director of the regional office of the Army Corps of Engineers, was poling a rowboat through the downtown streets of Omaha. To his subordinates, Pick's anger over the deluge seemed to rise with the floodwaters. The short-fused, no-nonsense colonel was animated by an indomitable self-confidence in his own abilities, a polar opposite to his self-effacing counterpart in Billings. But like Sloan, his professional standing among his superiors was chronically unstable. Pick had recently emerged from a session in the woodshed with his boss, General Wheeler. At the beginning of the war, Pick so badly botched the construction of an Army Air Corps training facility that planes could not land on his roller-coaster runways without crashing. When the entire base had to be abandoned, the Air Corps' General Robbins told Wheeler that his star engineer had the distinction for building the most dangerous runways in the history of aviation. A chastened Pick was reassigned to the Corps' office in Omaha, where it was thought that he could do little damage while pondering his transgressions.

Despite the embarrassing contretemps, Pick remained a hot-tempered autocrat who took challenges from nature as personal affronts. As floodwaters rose in the streets outside his offices, Pick jumped up on a desk and bellowed at his subordinates: "I want to control the Missouri!" On May 13, when Congress ordered the Army Corps of Engineers to produce a new survey for the purpose of controlling its floods, Colonel Pick commanded his subordinates to shelve all other projects. The Missouri would get their full attention until they had produced a workable master plan for taming the river. In contrast to the plan being designed by Sloan, a basinwide network of reservoirs and small dams addressing the region's perennial need for irrigation and drought relief, the Corps proposed to build a flood-control system that also promised to enhance downstream navigation for barge traffic between New Orleans and Sioux City, Iowa. But there was a catch. Either plan would force the American taxpayer to borrow from generations that were not yet born.

General Wheeler rushed his subordinate's master plan, a scant ten pages in length, into the waiting hands of Congress. The Pick Plan, as it would soon be known, called for the construction of 2,500 miles of new protective levees along the lower river. He also proposed a constellation of fourteen tributary reservoirs that would supplement the holding capacity of his plan's cornerstone: a massive new multipurpose flood-control dam at the Mandan Bluffs near Garrison, North Dakota. That crown jewel would be surrounded by four smaller dams, like stair steps descending from the high plateau at the base of the Rockies to the Iowa border. Harnessed together, these "rolled-earth" structures would put the forces of the imperious Missouri into the hands of man, once and for all.

With the help of the devastating floods of 1943, Colonel Pick succeeded in upending the Corps' long-held "hands-off" policy regarding water projects on the Central Plains, transforming a century of wariness into an agencywide obsession with the Missouri that infected everyone from General Wheeler on down. For more than four decades, funding public works on the Missouri had been deemed fiscal lunacy. The construction of Hoover Dam had been an enormous undertaking, one that lifted the nation's spirits out of the darkest depths of the Great Depression. To tackle the Missouri with five Hoover

Dams, and dozens of lesser reservoirs, would require a domestic public-relations campaign unlike any Congress had ever envisioned outside of war. But as the months went by, rather than question the overall efficacy of either plan, legislators acted as if the only unanswered question was which of the two would get the final nod of approval. Would it be Pick's plan, with its emphasis on navigation and flood control, or Sloan's plan, focusing on irrigation and a basinwide network of containment reservoirs?

The Corps infuriated high-level bureaucrats at the Department of the Interior by quietly rushing the sketchy Pick Plan into the hands of anxious congressmen on the Committee on Rivers and Harbors. Nevertheless, the rough proposal sailed through an enthusiastic, one-day review without a single alteration. The Pick Plan was on its way to a full vote by the House when President Roosevelt intervened. The President had serious problems with the plan. For one, he was furious when he learned that Pick had already met with the Missouri River States Commission to promote the plan behind the administration's back. Newspaper editors in the Missouri Valley were hailing the plan as a *fait accompli* before the president even saw the first draft. Echoing a now familiar charge, Roosevelt accused the Corps of attempting to make national policy without consulting either Congress or the administration.

Roosevelt's secretary of the interior, Harold Ickes, was fearless in his official rebuke of the Pick Plan: "The Corps' reputation for arrogance . . . is legendary, and every effort that has been made to induce the Corps to listen to recommendations made by the ablest civil engineers in the country has been resisted with an obduracy that is beyond belief." Furthermore, the Pick Plan was sketchy and vague, said Roosevelt. It appeared to leave many questions deliberately unanswered, or intentionally vague. Flowage estimates and distribution of power and irrigation water were all missing. The upstream governors would spike it on sight, said Roosevelt, because it ignored their demands for irrigation. Finally, he instructed Congress to delay its decision until the Bureau of Reclamation plan was completed, which should be at any time.

Secretary Ickes ordered the Sloan project rushed to completion. Ickes nurtured a quiet hatred for the Corps and was not reluctant to use his clout with Congress, and his influence with the president, to keep from being upstaged by a brash colonel. Thus a basinwide survey of reservoir sites was conducted by bureau engineers with such haste that $30 million irrigation projects were referred to as "windshield reconnaissance" because they were mapped out on the dashboards of cars speeding to the next valley. Bureau of Reclamation engineers spewed out project proposals in a blizzard of paper. Despite mounting pressures from Congress and Secretary Ickes, the 211 page Sloan Plan took months more to finish.

Behind the scenes, Colonel Pick used this interval to promote his own plan on the banquet circuit, drumming up support for navigation and flood control. Without saying so, Pick's public-relations campaign, aided and abetted by politicians from the lower Missouri states, made it clear that Pick was claiming sole jurisdiction on the Missouri. At the invitation of North Dakota governor John Moses, the colonel traveled to Bismarck in August 1943 and addressed a gathering of business leaders from the upper river states. Pick had good reason for wanting to head off incursions on his turf by civilian upstarts like Glenn Sloan. Sloan, in turn, told Congress that the bureau's plan could accomplish the same goals as the Pick Plan with three fewer dams. The instinctive distrust Pick and Sloan developed for each other during these months would grow into open contempt, nurtured along by leaders in both agencies.

Secretary Ickes explained to Roosevelt and Congress that the Sloan Plan, featuring the widespread use of smaller reservoirs and containment ponds, would easily impound enough water to prevent downstream flooding. A single 2 million acre-foot reservoir "could have easily regulated" all three floods in Iowa and Nebraska in the spring of 1943. Yet the Corps was proposing to impound 60 million acre-feet, ten times what was needed for effective flood control in a hundred-year flood. A key selling point to the Sloan Plan was its provision for bringing long-promised drought relief to small family farms on the Great Plains. Annually, turbines at the reservoirs would generate $17 million in power receipts; the plan would increase regional land values by an estimated $600 million dollars; and at current price levels the additional irrigation would increase crop values by $130 million each year. Population would grow, basinwide, by 630,000 people over the next thirty years, stabilizing the region's cities and towns. All of this, in addition to the downstream flood protection, could be accomplished with a savings of hundreds of millions of dollars simply "by eliminating the Army's proposed Garrison Reservoir."

In the previous two decades, Congress had spent billions of dollars to coerce meager to nonexistent harvests of low-value crops from marginal soil in the desert of the central Colorado plateau. Now, the passage of either plan would require billions more in spending in order to flood hundreds of thousands of acres of the most fertile farmland in North America, land that year after year did not require a single additional drop of water to produce bumper crops.

Before the plans arrived in Congress for the formal debate, each side sought to reinforce its own base of support. Upstream politicians favored the Sloan Plan. Lower river states stood as a solid block behind the Army Corps of Engineers. Debates erupted with such rancorous enmity between the two sides that the challenge for Congress was twofold: settle on a scheme, and find a way to make the financing for this enormous undertaking plausible to the nation.

Pick believed he had divined a method of plucking the thorn from his rose. If anyone bothered to take a close look at the Corps' plan, the bulk of the "land takings" would be borne by the twenty-three Indian nations on the Missouri. All twenty-three nations, from the Northern Cheyenne and Crow to the Standing Rock and Yankton Sioux, were signatories to the Fort Laramie Peace Council of 1851. There is no evidence to suggest that treaty rights factored into Pick's strategy, but in the unlikely event that Pick was aware of the government's obligations under the Treaty of Horse Creek, he ignored them in the interest of selecting dam sites that would avoid flooding white communities such as Williston and Bismarck. Of the eight hundred square miles of rich bottomland that would disappear above Yankton, South Dakota, less than 10 percent was owned by white farmers. Only a few small towns, such as Van Hook and Sanish, would be affected by the floodwaters. The bulk of the land to be "taken," approximately six hundred square miles, was owned by tribes. And right in the middle, at the center of the two-hundred-mile-long lake that would form behind the dam near Garrison, North Dakota, sat the Mandan, Hidatsa, and Arikara nations.

Spun about by the turmoil of all this legislative logrolling, everybody engaged in the Pick-Sloan debate in Washington overlooked an important aspect of protocol. Neither Pick nor Sloan, nor General Wheeler, Secretary Ickes, Governor Moses, or President Roosevelt ever bothered to consult with the Mandan, Hidatsa, and Arikara people about either plan. Details about both schemes were drifting back to Elbowoods in disjointed bits of information and rumor. As late as the fall of 1943 nothing official had yet been announced by either Congress or the White House. The editor of the *Sanish Sentinel* counseled everyone to be patient and to hope for the best. The Tribal Council nonetheless gathered the bits and pieces of rumor floating around the valley and put them together. On November 15, 1943, the Tribal Council passed a resolution condemning any plan proposing a dam at the

Mandan Bluffs. The following day the tribe sent copies of the resolution to members of Congress, the White House, and to Indian commissioner William Brophy:

A dam below the Fort Berthold Reservation is being contemplated for future action by the Congress of the United States in cooperation with the state of North Dakota, which action, if realized, will destroy by permanent flood all the bottomland of the said reservation, causing untold material and economic damage to the Three Affiliated Tribes . . . and deprive approximately 250 boys from our reservation who are now serving in the armed forces from land rightfully theirs as the lands of these Indians were inherent property from time immemorial and in no sense [were] given to them by any human power arriving from somewhere else.

When the telegrams arrived on desks in Washington, Congress' attention was focused instead on the competing plans. For months, a blizzard of acrimonious letters demanded alterations, suggested recommendations, and promised challenges to both plans from members of Congress, regional governors, senators, and the White House. In congressional hearings, Colonel Pick attempted to portray the Missouri River as a great, unused highway that could easily pump economic vitality back into the nation's midsection. To approve the other plan, he said, would be a waste of the taxpayer's money. To politicians from upriver states, Pick's testimony was a shameless attempt to cover up the fact that American taxpayers were being asked to spend half a billion dollars for downstream navigation channels that would never see more than a few hundred barges a year. The lower states knew that upriver politicians could block the Pick Plan in its entirety unless farmers were given an equal shake in the final package.

In order to remedy this oversight, an amendment was tacked on to the bill by two senators from Colorado and Wyoming. Their caveat stipulated that in any future contest over the river's resources, the irrigation requirements of upstream farmers would trump downstream navigation. Water flowing out of western mountains could not be used for navigation unless the latter in no way conflicted "with any beneficial consumptive use . . . in states lying wholly or partly west of the ninety-eighth meridian."

Pick allies in Congress did not have the muscle to turn back what came to be known as the O'Mahoney-Millikin Amendment. Yet while western senators from the upriver states had played their cards wisely, the final strategy of the lower states would win out in the end. Despite the clearly worded conditions of the amendment, lower-river politicians have systematically ignored it ever since. The strategy adopted by the lower-river states in 1944 has kept barges floating between St. Louis and Sioux City, without interruption, for more than fifty years.

The day arrived, as Secretary Ickes had long predicted, when President Roosevelt had to play King Solomon. Congress was hopelessly deadlocked between the Pick and Sloan plans. In the fall of 1944, it fell to the president to choose between them. In the end, he threw his hands in the air and ordered the agencies to hammer out a compromise that would stop the flooding in the lower states, supply cheap hydroelectric power to the region's growing cities, and offer drought relief to dryland farmers in the upper states. Roosevelt told General Wheeler and Secretary Ickes that he wanted to see the compromise built into the Flood Control Act of 1944, which Congress was already in the process of writing.

Glenn Sloan flew to Omaha to hammer out a compromise with the Army Corps of Engineers on October 15, 1944. Colonel Pick, having since been sent to Burma to finish the Ledo Road, could not attend. Each agency arrived at the meeting determined to fight for every line item in its own plan. Neither side was willing to give up an inch of the river, or a dam, or a mile of levees, or an acre of irrigation. By late afternoon on the same day, the plans were quietly "reconciled" and sent back to Congress. Not counting the project at Garrison, they embraced more than $18 million worth of projects that one or the other had previously deemed worthless. No attempt was made to consolidate or justify costs. Project dimensions and the duplication of services were kept intact. Of the 113 major projects proposed by the combined plans, 110 survived the meeting in Omaha. The Pick-Sloan "compromise" sent to Congress was the very result critics of both agencies had predicted. When Congress passed the Flood Control Act of 1944 on December 22, Farmers Union president James Patton called the final package "a shameless, loveless shotgun wedding."

※

Two weeks after the bureau and the Corps met in Omaha, a new chairman was elected for the Tribal Council of the Three Affiliated Tribes in Elbowoods. Following in his father's footsteps, thirty-eight-year-old Martin Cross was sworn into office as the new chairman of the Mandan, Hidatsa, and Arikara nations. News of the Pick and Sloan Plans had by now been disseminated throughout the region. Several members of the Tribal Council had met with the North Dakota Reclamation Association in Minot, the largest town upstream from Elbowoods. It was clear now that all nine of the Mandan, Hidatsa, and Arikara communities — Elbowoods, Nishu, Charging Eagle, Lucky Mound, Shell Creek, Red Butte, Independence, Beaver Creek, and Square Butte — and all their farms and ranches along the bottomlands, 152,000 acres in all, would be inundated by the flood. Wasting no time, Martin Cross scheduled a meeting with North Dakota's new governor, Fred Aandahl, hoping to derail the dam before the plans could gain any more momentum. Aandahl told the new tribal chairman that he was foursquare behind the construction of Garrison Dam. In a follow-up letter, Governor Aandahl told Chairman Cross that until the tribes were ready to accept the damming of the river as inevitable, the two sides had nothing further to discuss.

Since the governor's office sat at the high end of a one-way road to inundation, Cross and the Tribal Council decided to go over the governor's head by appealing to Roosevelt himself through the commissioner of Indian affairs, William Brophy. Cross telegraphed a letter to Brophy inviting him to meet with the Tribal Council in Elbowoods. "We Indians on the Fort Berthold Reservation oppose the construction of the Garrison Dam one hundred percent," read the telegram. "Can you come and attend a conference with us?"

Though he had never visited Elbowoods, Brophy was well acquainted with the Mandan, Hidatsa, and Arikara. A few months earlier he was present when Martin Cross was elected vice president of the new national organization of tribes, the National Congress of American Indians. Brophy declined the invitation with regrets, however, citing scheduling conflicts. President Roosevelt had died and was no sooner buried than Brophy found himself in a full-scale political battle to preserve his own agency. With the president gone, a new contest over the Indian bureau was rapidly coming to a boil in Congress. Hearings were opened to investigate the possibility of removing all federal protections from the tribes, tribal trust lands, and resources held in trust such as timber, gold, uranium, and silver. This coincided with a scheme being advanced by western congressmen to dismantle the Bureau of Indian Affairs altogether.

Brophy dashed off a letter to Senator O'Mahoney, the chairman of the Senate Select Committee on Indian Affairs, alerting him to the predicament of the Mandan, Hidatsa, and Arikara tribes. In a parallel note to Chairman Cross, Brophy included a copy of his letter to Senator O'Mahoney and counseled the new tribal chairman that his best strategy for opposing the dam would be to work through friendly forces in O'Mahoney's committee. The letter from Brophy was a sobering disappointment to the new tribal chairman.

The Pick-Sloan juggernaut was beginning to look unstoppable. The Army engineers had built their entire plan for the Missouri on the shoulders of Garrison Dam. By hook and crook, Pick had persuaded Congress to ignore the scientific recommendations of his own agency, convincing lawmakers instead that Garrison Dam was the key to flood control on the entire river. Before a single shot had been fired in defense of the Mandan, Hidatsa, and Arikara treaty rights, the commissioner of Indian affairs was waving a white flag above the ramparts. The agency responsible for safeguarding the federal government's obligations to Indian tribes seemed to have surrendered without a fight. As he looked out his office window in the Department of the Interior to the bright white dome of the Capitol building, Brophy knew that nothing in Washington, D.C., was easier to swallow, or harder to kill, than a bad idea.

CHAPTER V

Hell and High Water

※

"The uttermost good faith shall always be observed toward the Indians.
Their lands and property shall never be taken from them without their
consent: and in their property, rights, and liberty they shall never
be invaded or disturbed. . . ."

NORTHWEST ORDINANCE OF 1787
U.S. CONGRESS

A week before the U.S. Senate Select Committee on Indian Affairs met
with Martin Cross, the tribal chairman of the Three Affiliated Tribes,
to hear the Indians' views on the Garrison Dam and the Pick-Sloan Plan, a
brief obituary appeared in the *Sanish Sentinel* newspaper. Forrest Cross, the
seven-year-old son of Martin and Dorothy Cross, died early in the morning
hours of October 2 at the agency hospital in Elbowoods. The boy's death
was blamed on a ruptured appendix.

"It was the first day of October," recalls Phyllis, "and for reasons that none
of us can remember, school let out early that day. I was walking down the hall
when somebody came running up from the playground and told me Forrest
was hurt. A boy named Saunders Bearstail had kicked him in the stomach."

Phyllis found her little brother out in front of the school, where kids from
Beaver Creek and Lucky Mound were boarding buses for the ride home. Forrest was crouched over and crying on the front steps. Saunders Bearstail had
kicked him in the stomach in a playground scuffle, he told her, and it hurt
right here, just below his ribs. His little sister, Uppy, wiped the tears off his
cheeks as Phyllis lifted his shirt and checked for bruises. Nothing visible presented itself or gave her cause for alarm, so after reassuring him that the walk
home would make him feel better, Phyllis and Uppy held his hands and the
three Cross children started off down the dirt road for home.

Phyllis remembers that it was a crisp autumn afternoon, with the smell of burning leaves in the air, and the nostalgic honking of migrating geese ringing from the October sky. She and Uppy tried to take Forrest's mind off his stomach, but their little brother's misery only seemed to worsen with every step. When their house finally came into view, Phyllis's heart sank. The green pickup truck was gone. Her mother and father had gone off shopping to Parshall, or to Halliday, and there was no way of knowing when they would return home.

"I hated it when they left like that," says Phyllis. "I had to run the house and feed everybody and make sure all the chores were done and get the little ones to bed. When Mom and Dad left like that, their world landed in my lap."

By the time they reached home, Forrest had become inconsolable. As dusk turned to night his shrill cries of pain filled the rooms of the small house. Phyllis despaired at his bedside as Crusoe stood watch at the front window, hoping against hope that the next set of headlights on the road from Parshall would materialize into a green truck. But as evening became night, not a single car approached on Old Number Eight. By the time Martin and Dorothy finally returned home, sometime around midnight, Forrest had slipped into delirium. They gathered him up in a blanket and rushed out the door. Phyllis lay in her bed and listened to the truck race off down the road to Elbowoods. The kids all remember the weight of the silence that closed around their parents' sudden departure, the sound of the truck going away, and waking suddenly hours later, sometime before dawn, when their father roused them out of bed and called them together in the front room.

"Dad asked all of us to kneel in a circle," says Marilyn. "Then he told us, 'Brother's really sick and we all need to pray extra hard because Brother needs our prayers right now.'"

Kneeling shoulder to shoulder around the coffee table, the Cross children sent their prayers into the silent darkness. Pretty soon Martin stood up and covered his face with his hands. Without a word, he turned and walked out the front door and down the steps. The door of the pickup clanged shut and the engine roared to life as the headlights swung against the house and the truck sped off down the road to Elbowoods.

"I was standing at the window the next morning when Mom and Dad pulled up in front of the house," says Bucky. "They sat there in the cab of the truck for a long time. They weren't talking."

Finally, Martin and Dorothy stepped down out of the truck and walked across the yard and up the plank steps to the front door. Before entering,

Martin held Dorothy's shoulders. She put her forehead against his chest and wept into her hands. Bucky stood in the window and stared blankly at the pale gray dawn that lit the bare limbs of the trees.

"He died of blood poisoning. There was nothing the doctor could do," says Phyllis.

"Mom walled it off in her heart somehow, but Dad had to wall it off in his head," says Crusoe. "A long time later, Mom told me that just before he died, Brother was hallucinating that water was rising all around him. He was delirious, but he kept telling her that he couldn't get away from the water. He was drowning. Mom told me that she held on to his little hands and felt him slip away."

"After they brought him home in the little casket, Dad and I went up to Pem Hall's house," says Bucky. "Pem met us at the door. Dad asked him if he would help with the funeral for his little boy who had died in the middle of the night. I just stood there staring at my shoes when Dad fell apart. This great big man started sobbing. I'd never seen a grown man break down and cry like that."

"Of all of us, I think Forrest had the sweetest spirit," says Crusoe. "You can see it in his face, in the old pictures. He and Raymond were a lot alike. I don't think any of us have ever held it against the Bearstail boy. I never believed the incident on the playground had anything to do with Forrest dying. But it probably kept us from seeing what was really going on with him. Would it have made a difference? I don't know. Would we have gotten him to the hospital earlier? We'll never know."

"Before the funeral, they put Forrest's casket in our bedroom," says Bucky. "I'm so glad they did that because I've always had that memory. He was a beautiful little boy. He looked like he was sleeping. I combed his hair."

Probably no one in the immediate family was more traumatized by Forrest's death than his shadow and little sister, the six-year-old Uppy. Ever since they were old enough to crawl, Uppy and Forrest were inseparable. With Forrest suddenly gone, her siblings remember Uppy sitting in the front room of the house and staring out the window for hours on end, as she rocked back and forth in a private world of grief. For more than a year after Forrest's death, Uppy did not utter a word, or make a sound.

"When Mom died in 1989, we found an unmarked envelope among her things," recalls Marilyn. "Inside was all of Brother's schoolwork, his little pictures, his projects from second grade, his homework, crayons, the stuff somebody collected out of his desk at school. Fifty years, she carried that envelope."

"A day or two after the funeral," says Crusoe, "I woke up early and went into the kitchen looking for breakfast. Mom was in there by herself. I must have surprised her. I could tell she'd been crying. She turned away from me and wiped her cheek. I said, 'Morning, Mom. Where's Dad?'"

"Your father?" said Dorothy, slightly surprised by the question. "Didn't he tell you? He's gone to Washington to fight the dam."

Late one afternoon in the autumn of 1945, Donald Goodbird hopped off the back of the Garrison mail truck at the agency post office in Elbowoods. Shouldering his duffel bag, Goodbird set off down the dirt road toward Martin Cross's house, where he had left his horse for safekeeping three years before. After a home-cooked meal in Dorothy's kitchen, he saddled his horse and rode off up the river toward his home in Independence, retracing the tracks he made when he went off to war.

"That's the way a lot of our guys came home," says Crusoe, recalling that all but 6 of the 250 Mandan, Hidatsa, and Arikara enlisted men and women returned home safely at the end of World War II. "They came walking in over the hills, or down Old State Road Number Eight, with a duffel on their shoulder and pocketfuls of cash. No parades, no fanfare, but they were our heroes. For the first time in our history, most of our people were fluent in English, and a lot of us had had our first experience with the outside world."

The Mandan, Hidatsa, and Arikara nations that Martin Cross was leading into the postwar era were no longer the reclusive, ethnocentric remnants of the once-great tribes championed by his father, Chief Old Dog. Forty years before Martin left for Washington, Old Dog made news in papers across the region when he rejected Congress' offer of citizenship. The chief had lived a long life, long enough to watch many of the Great White Fathers' promises vanish on prairie winds. In Old Dog's view, they had already lost too many of their rights, rights they had foolishly believed to be given freely to all people by the Great Spirit, not doled out like beads and trinkets by the Great White Fathers in Washington. Old Dog's own notions of "inalienable rights" had governed tribal culture for countless generations. By the turn of the twentieth century, Congress was telling Indian leaders that henceforth, Congress would be the final arbiter of just which privileges would enhance the overall well-being of the Great White Fathers' "red children."

To enforce its will, Congress passed the Religious Crimes Code in 1887 as an adjunct to the Dawes Act during President Harrison's administration. This

law, written by Methodist missionaries, banned all Indian religious ceremonies in an effort to drive Indian spiritual leaders out of business. Despite
the freedom of religion protections in the First Amendment, lawmakers gave
Indian agents the power to suppress and jail any native holy men caught prac-
ticing rituals such as the Mandan Okeepa ceremony, the original Sun Dance
practiced widely by plains tribes. Despite James Madison's establishment
clause in the Constitution, which was designed to act as a legal firewall between civil law (and liberties) and the encroachments of organized religion,
Washington put the management of Indian Country into the hands of Christian missionaries. With the blessings of Congress, Methodist and Congrega-
tional missionaries initiated the practice of sending Indian children to boarding
schools in hopes of "killing the Indian to save the man." The first missionary
to live among the Mandan, Hidatsa, and Arikara, a Congregationalist named
Reverend Charles Hall, arrived at Fort Berthold in May of 1876 on a steamboat from St. Louis that was piled high with provisions for Colonel George
Custer and the 7th Cavalry.

Not long after Reverend Hall and his bride disembarked at Like-a-
Fishhook Village, the straight-laced patrician summarily denied a request by
Chief Old Dog to hold a traditional dance in celebration of the harvest. A few
years later, in 1894, Old Dog apparently remembered the religion of the man
who denied him the right to dance. Rather than attend church at the Con-
gregational mission, he took the sacrament of baptism in the Sacred Heart
Catholic mission. Yet, to Reverend Hall's own amazement, the fifty years he
spent among the three tribes transformed him into one of Indian Country's
most distinguished and vocal advocates in Washington, D.C. "The people of
these tribes turned the tables on me," wrote Hall. "I came to convert them,
and have myself been converted." Becoming fluent in all three tribal languages, he set about preserving their vocabularies and grammar in writing. At
the end of his career, the Congregationalist missionary from the Bronx was
widely regarded as one of white America's most fierce defenders of native
rights.

By 1945, Hall's half century of activism was bearing latent fruit on the Upper Missouri River bottomlands. The Mandan, Hidatsa, and Arikara communities were growing rapidly and bustling with vitality. A census conducted
that year by the Bureau of Indian Affairs found that the tribes had grown to
2,034 enrolled members, almost doubling their population since the turn of
the century. The census also found that 80 percent of the tribal members attended weekly church services, and every child on the reservation went home

each evening to a two-parent family. Divorce among the Indians was virtually unknown. Cohabitation outside of marriage would quickly turn into a formal invitation from the Tribal Court to make a trip to the altar, or enlist in the Army. "Living in sin" was prohibited by tribal laws. By the end of the war, less than 3 percent of the reservation population received federal assistance. Most of the federal money distributed by the superintendent in Elbowoods went to elderly, or handicapped, tribal members. All five hundred of the tribes' school-age children, who a generation earlier would have been shipped to distant boarding schools, were enrolled at one of the nine agency day schools, or living at the boarding school in Elbowoods. Even with half of the tribes' adult men in the armed forces, the BIA survey found that women such as Dorothy Cross and Maggie Grinnell had managed to increase the reservation's agricultural production during each year of the war.

Despite the tribes' achievements, new wealth created by the economic boom in postwar America would bypass Indian Country. The average income on the Fort Berthold reservation in 1945 was $250 per year. The $2 million the tribe received from the 1930s land claims settlement had all been spent. As long as the tribes remained in relative isolation from the white world, $250 was sufficient to see most families through the year in Elbowoods. But with so many soldiers returning from distant countries, their heads filled with new ideas and their pockets bulging with cash, and with the threat of the dam inching its way toward reality with each passing week, Martin Cross, the thirty-nine-year-old leader of the Three Affiliated Tribes, knew that the isolation that once protected the people of Old Dog's era from the outside world had suddenly become their grandchildren's greatest liability. Like tribal leaders in 1781, like his great-grandfather Cherry Necklace in 1851, Martin Cross knew that the Mandan, Hidatsa, and Arikara nations had once again arrived at a fork in the road. Just as before, tribal leaders were being asked to divine the path that would lead to survival.

The Soo Line passenger train that left daily from the Northern Pacific station in Minot, North Dakota, took three days to reach Washington, D.C. On that October day in 1945, the four Indians that stepped up onto the train from the station's brick herringbone siding were heading into a foreign country. This was their first trip to the nation's capital as official representatives of the tribes. In the weeks prior to the journey, the Tribal Council had to decide on a strategy for stopping the dam before construction began. Yet the tribe had very little money with which to wage such a campaign, certainly not enough to buy train tickets to Washington, D.C., and foot the bill for big city hotels and meals. In order to make ends meet, fund-raising dances were held in all the communities. Marilyn Hudson remembers their neighbor, Lillie Wolf, going from door-to-door collecting dimes and quarters in a Bull Durham sack to help the council buy train tickets.

"Not one of those guys had a stitch of clothes they could wear to a hearing in Congress," remembers Crusoe. "Dad and I drove all over the country, from church to church, digging through mission barrels for suits, hats, shoes, and socks, whatever they could find to make them look halfway presentable."

The four tribal delegates from Elbowoods were met at Union Station in Washington by the Department of the Interior's acting solicitor, Felix Cohen. Cohen, a forty-year-old bespectacled Jewish lawyer from New York, held a doctorate in philosophy from Columbia University and was regarded in legal circles as one of Washington's brightest stars. In recent years, the dauntless Cohen had made his mark as a fearless and formidable defender of Indian rights. In fact, he had just completed his legal opus, the *Handbook of Federal Indian Law,* an encyclopedic project undertaken at the urging of his boss, Harold Ickes, the secretary of the interior under Roosevelt. Anxious to help the contingent from Elbowoods, Cohen found rooms for Cross and his fellow councilmen at the New Ebbits Hotel, at Tenth and H Streets in northwest Washington. For Martin, the following day's hearings in the Senate would be the first of dozens of appearances he would make before committees in Congress over the next several years. Before the end of the decade, people back home would start calling their councilmen "suitcase Indians," a reference to their frequent trips to Capitol Hill. But none of the later meetings would carry as much weight, or as much anticipation, as the one that now awaited them.

"Dad loved the responsibility of being the tribal chairman," says Bucky. "As the son of Old Dog, it was a role he'd inherited, even though he got into it by choice. He shoved his canoe into the river on a beautiful, calm morning. The next thing he knew, the current had him and the river was boiling all around him. From then on, the only thing he could do was ride it out or fall in and drown."

"He was trapped between two eras, and he knew it," says Marilyn. "He had one foot in the past, one in the future. He loved to play the saxophone. After dinner on summer evenings, he'd sit out on the back porch and light a cigarette and play Hoagy Carmichael's 'Stardust.' An hour later, he'd be singing us lullabies in Hidatsa. At times, it must have been very lonely being Martin Cross. I never saw him show his fear."

"Once he got on that train there was no way back," says Bucky. "A lot of people were stuck in the past and couldn't face the fact that The Flood was coming. It was like the Ghost Dance, when people thought their Ghost Dance shirts would stop the white man's bullets. All the dead were wearing those shirts at Wounded Knee. "

※

The historic meeting between Martin Cross and members of the Senate Select Committee on Indian Affairs was called to order promptly at ten-thirty a.m. on the morning of October 9, 1945. Cross was accompanied into the Capitol by Tribal Council members Jefferson Smith, Martin Fox, and Earl Bateman. The hearing was held in room 424 of the Senate Office Building, with Senator Joseph O'Mahoney presiding. O'Mahoney was a powerful Democrat and veteran Capitol Hill power broker with a reputation as a ruthless deal maker. For its part, Congress tended to regard this meeting as a formality. Officially, it was listed as an investigation into a claim made by the Three Affiliated Tribes that "Garrison Dam, the construction of which is embodied in the engineering plan for the development of the Missouri River . . . will, if constructed, take or inundate 221,000 acres of Indian lands in violation of the treaty between the United States and the Indians." As the hearing was brought to order, Senator O'Mahoney explained that Congress' joint resolution, SJ Res. 79, was the "vehicle under which the committee can today hear a protest . . . by a delegation of Indians representing the Three Affiliated Tribes of North Dakota." In addition to the committee members and tribal councillors, also present were Walter Woehlke, the number-two man at the Bureau of Indian Affairs, and the Department of the Interior's leading solicitor, Felix Cohen.

For Martin Cross and the tribal representatives, this hearing was the most important face-to-face encounter with white people since the Treaty of Horse Creek. Yet for many members of the 79th Congress, the hearing of Indian claims was a charade. Congress agreed to endure the ritual in order to claim a richer prize once the complaints were aired and the colorful parade of tribes through the corridors of Congress had finally concluded. The real petard of SJ Res. 79 was concealed in the resolution's fine print: "To investigate the administration of Indian affairs." This, in fact, was the sharp end of the wedge that many lawmakers hoped would eventually lead to the dismantling of the Bureau of Indian Affairs altogether.

In Cross's mind, the resolution itself was a wedge that held open the door to the possibility of a full hearing in Congress over the violation of the solemn agreements the tribes made at Horse Creek. When Senator O'Mahoney's committee had invited the Three Affiliated Tribes to come to Washington to testify, Chairman Cross immediately sent a telegram to Commissioner Brophy requesting him to make a formal appeal to Congress in support of the tribes' protest of Garrison Dam. Brophy responded to Cross's second appeal with a more upbeat telegram. This time, the commissioner promised his full and vigorous support in defense of the tribes' protest. On the eve of their departure for Washington, the council interpreted this as an encouraging sign. Unfortunately, while Brophy was being distracted by congressional assaults on his agency, the Trojan horse of SJ Res. 79 had already slipped through the gate.

When Martin Cross stepped into room 424 of the Senate Office Building, he was immediately buttonholed by Brophy's assistant, Walter Woehlke. Was the memorandum to Congress written? Cross asked Woehlke. Yes, said Woehlke, it was written, but complications had arisen regarding SJ Res. 79, complications that prevented the commissioner from signing his own memorandum. The memo was written and ready to deliver, but attorneys on the Water Resources Committee at the Department of the Interior warned Brophy that if he followed through with his memo, he could expect another round of attacks on the BIA from hostile western senators.

In other words, Congress' tacit threats had succeeded in silencing the Indian commissioner. The Indians would get their day in Washington, but as an advocate for the tribes, Brophy and the Indian bureau had been cleverly preempted by their foes on Capitol Hill. As Martin Cross stepped forward to take his seat at the witness table, the tribal chairman realized, for the second time in as many months, that the bureau was again throwing in the towel. The agency's powerful enemies in Congress had quietly disabled the bureau behind closed doors. As he raised his right hand to take the oath of honesty, Chairman Cross had no choice but to take a deep breath and accept the fact that the Mandan, Hidatsa, and Arikara nations were on their own.

※

Senator O'Mahoney rapped the gavel, then opened the hearings with a brief statement outlining the purpose of the meeting. He introduced the six committee members who were present and their guest, Lieutenant Colonel Goodall of the Omaha office of the Army Corps of Engineers. O'Mahoney then welcomed the representatives of the Three Affiliated Tribes, and noted for the official record the attendance of Acting Solicitor Felix Cohen and Assistant Indian Commissioner Walter Woehlke. "A delegation of Indians has come from the Fort Berthold Reservation to present the point of view of the Indians with respect to the construction of Garrison Dam," he explained to the committee members. "Mr. Chairman, would you please take a seat at the table?"

Martin Cross moved to the center table. Once seated, he squared his broad shoulders to the dais of white men in dark suits. Even seated in a chair, his physical presence dominated the room. After Senator O'Mahoney entered the text of SJ Res. 79, and the previous Tribal Council resolution protesting the dam, into the record, Cross delivered a brief statement summarizing the events that led to this meeting. Then, following through on the agreed-upon strategy, he closed his opening statement by broaching the thorny issue of treaty rights.

"Mr. Chairman, senators," began Chairman Cross, "the Corps of Engineers seems to think that the Indian land in the flooded area can be acquired by eminent domain, if necessary. We question the legality of this process on the grounds that the treaty law between the United States government and the Indians is binding, and not subject to eminent domain. Since I have no legal talent, I must rely on other authority to interpret this legal point. I want to come out openly against the construction of the Garrison Dam, not only from the legal standpoint but from destructiveness and the setback of our Indian people. I believe that this group of men, composing this honorable body, are adamant foes of abuse and, being such, that they will not permit the Army engineers to carry out their program, their plan."

"Mr. Cross," said Senator O'Mahoney, "I understand you to say that if the Garrison Dam were constructed, a large amount of that land would be flooded. Is that right?"

"That is right, about two hundred twenty-one thousand acres."

"What is the character of that land?"

"It's the best land we have, along the river, the best irrigable land, and most of our homes are situated along this valley."

"You say the homes of the Indians are now built upon the land that would be flooded?"

"That's right."

"How many homes are there?"

"Of our five hundred thirty-one homes, four hundred thirty-six would be in the flooded area."

The committee chairman scribbled a note to himself, then glanced over at

Felix Cohen before returning to Chairman Cross. "What you are saying, then, is that three-fourths of the homes of the Affiliated Tribes would be flooded."

"That is right."

"And you would have to move off and take up your homes somewhere else?"

"That's right."

"Do these Indians raise agricultural crops?"

"We raise spring wheat, oats, corn, potatoes, and a little alfalfa. We have a thriving tribal cattle cooperative."

"And how much of your land do you use for grazing?"

"Well, I would say out of the six hundred thousand acres, about half of it is used for grazing."

"So, one half of your land is grazing land, the other half is agricultural. And of the agricultural land, two-thirds would be taken if the dam were built," stated the senator, clarifying his own mental picture of Fort Berthold. "Would the Indians be willing to exchange that land for other land, if other land were available?"

"No, sir."

"I see. What is the value of this land, per acre? Have you any idea?"

"I'm not permitted to say that," said Cross. "In my personal opinion, I would say around one hundred fifty dollars per acre."

"You say you were not permitted. By whom?"

"We are not here on the question of selling our land. We want to keep it," said Cross.

A murmur swept through the room. Martin Cross's voice was steely and controlled. Now, his eyes moved from senator to senator. The committee chairman adjusted his glasses on the bridge of his nose as he pondered the approaching impasse.

"You mean . . . the Indians did not want to disclose the value of their land?"

"That's right."

Senator Langer of North Dakota suddenly jumped in. "It is not for sale at all?"

"That's right," said Cross firmly. "Senator, with all due respect, I am not here to sell land. I am here to keep the land."

Senator O'Mahoney looked up and down the dais. "Are there any other questions?"

"How long have your ancestors been living there?" asked Senator Langer.

"From time immemorial we have been living there."

As these facts were sinking in, Senator O'Mahoney asked for an explanation of the Army engineers' rationale for building Garrison Dam. The committee's counsel reported that the dam's primary purpose was to form "a reservoir for a flood menace." It also came to light that thus far, Congress had only appropriated $2.5 million for work on the dam, against a total appropriation of $7.6 million. Once these figures had been reviewed by the committee members, the chairman gave Martin Cross a second breath of life.

"Of course, nothing can be done to dispossess these Indians without a formal taking of this land," said Senator O'Mahoney, tipping his hand.

"It raises pretty much of a legal question," interjected Senator E. H. Moore of Oklahoma.

"Well, considering the general disregard of Indian rights, which has characterized our dealings with Indians, I think it's a very important question," said O'Mahoney. "What do you stand to gain from this dam, Mr. Cross?"

"We will gain nothing from this dam but our own destruction," said Cross.

"It would not enhance the value of the balance of your land?" asked Senator Moore.

"No, sir, it would not."

"I want to say," began Senator Langer, "as a member of this committee, that I know these lands. Everything Mr. Cross has said is absolutely true. This dam would take by far the best land and leave the tops of the hills, which will not begin to compare with the soil in the valley."

"That is right," said Martin Cross, clearly appreciative of the sympathetic support from his own senator.

The committee then heard brief statements from Jefferson Smith and Councilman Earl Bateman, who told the committee that the Tribal Council's recent resolutions in opposition to the dam "contain some records relative to the treaties of 1851 between the Government of the United States and the three tribes — the Arikara, Gros Ventre [Hidatsa], and Mandan." Furthermore, said Bateman, the land near the Killdeer Mountains that the Army engineers had proposed to exchange for the land that would be lost to flooding was completely unacceptable. Chairman Cross agreed, telling the committee that the land where the Corps proposed to relocate the tribes was "fit for rattlesnakes and horned toads," but not for humans.

Senator O'Mahoney then asked Assistant Commissioner Woehlke to present the position being taken by the BIA. Cross braced himself for bureaucratic double-talk, but to his surprise, despite the phantom memo, Woehlke made a strong defense of the tribes and successfully thwarted open hostility from several members of the committee. It had long been the agency's position, began Woehlke, that the Sloan Plan was the only responsible answer to the chronic water-management problems on the Missouri River. Conversely, in the opinion of both the BIA and the Bureau of Reclamation, the Pick Plan should never have seen the light of day. Weathering a torrent of hostile questions, Woehlke offered an explanation of the agency's reasoning. First, there was not nearly enough money allocated by Congress for the Garrison project to compensate the Indians for their potential loss of land. Second, as Secretary Ickes explained to Congress and President Roosevelt in his report earlier that summer, just ten years earlier engineers in both water agencies had concluded that Garrison was an unnecessary extravagance. Building the dam would devastate the lives of the people who had lived in that valley for a thousand years. Woehlke concluded his remarks by saying that the BIA was in complete agreement with the secretary of the interior. Garrison Dam was a boondoggle from top to bottom, one that needed to be killed before the Corps had a chance to turn its first shovelful of dirt. If and when that happened, warned Woehlke, it would be too late to stop.

Woehlke's assault on the Pick Plan came as a complete surprise to the tribal delegates. Chairman Cross was heartened by the force of his arguments. Senators on the committee were now clearly baffled by some of the unresolved legal problems. The chairman then called on Solicitor Cohen for clarification. Cohen knew his audience. As the country's leading authority on federal Indian law, Cohen staked out the perimeters of the legal battlefield that lay before them, taking pains to underscore the delicate nature of what was being asked of the tribes, and their trustee, the government.

"These Indians were at their present location one hundred forty years ago, when Lewis and Clark went through that country," explained Cohen. "They have never been removed from their original homelands. On the specific question of eminent domain, the fact is, whatever moral obligations we may have to respect the homes of the Indians, Congress has the authority to condemn allotted lands. It also has the authority, under extreme circumstances, to abrogate treaties, whether they were made with foreign nations or Indian nations."

However, said Cohen, that was not an end point for the purpose of clarifying the law in this situation. Rather, it should be viewed by the committee as a starting point, which is why the treaty business gets so sticky. Cohen explained that Congress made a very bad and fateful decision when it turned its back on Marshall in the 1880s and opened Indian lands to private ownership. The Dawes Act effectively divided the ownership of land between private land and trust lands. Now, the two kinds of titles were hopelessly intermingled. In creating two kinds of status, the government laid a trap which it could not avoid springing on itself. Congress, explained Cohen, cannot condemn lands it holds in trust for the Indians as a trustee. Yet faced with this dilemma, every time the government wants to build a road or a dam or an irrigation project across Indian land, lawmakers have to decide which of their own laws they want to break. "As far as I have been able to determine," concluded Cohen, "Congress never has authorized condemnation of tribal lands, as distinguished from allotted lands." In other words, condemnation of trust lands was not legally possible.

"And this is tribal land?" asked Senator Moore.

"Some is tribal, some is allotted."

"And the rights of the Fort Berthold Indians to ownership and control of their land was recognized by this treaty?"

Cohen held up the frontispiece map in the 1945 edition of the *Handbook of Federal Indian Law,* showing the lands set aside for the Three Affiliated Tribes by the Fort Laramie Peace Council. "As a result of a series of cessions, they now have a small remnant of the land which was once theirs."

"Did Congress recognize specific boundaries, or did the Government of the United States recognize specific boundaries in this treaty?"

"Both. An executive order on April 12, 1870, defined the boundaries very specifically."

Senator Moore and others seemed thoroughly confused by the distinction between allotted lands and trust lands. Cohen conceded that allotted lands could be condemned by Congress without any further action. Conversely, trust lands were held in common ownership by tribal members, with the federal government as the tribes' trustee. Fort Berthold was a checkerboard of allotted and trust lands. Setting aside the moral considerations, the legal problem that now confounded the committee was how could they go about flooding one type of land without flooding the other? The chairman thanked Cohen, who promised a written memorandum on the question of condemnation of trust lands, and then returned to Martin Cross.

"Mr. Cross, let me say to you and your delegation that this committee will pursue this matter further as soon as we have received the memorandum from the Department of the Interior regarding the legal phases of the treaty. It is my opinion at the moment that you can tell your Indian fellows that these lands cannot be taken away from you without the passage of a special act of Congress authorizing the condemnation."

"Which is the problem," said Senator Moore. "We can't very well inundate allotted lands without inundating trust lands." And, by inference, Congress was legally barred from inundating trust lands by their obligations as trustee to the tribes.

"That is so," said Senator O'Mahoney. "At this time the committee will stand adjourned."

*

Felix Cohen was at work on a report to the committee before the delegates from Fort Berthold had arrived back in Elbowoods. Cohen's memorandum was distributed without delay to members of Senator O'Mahoney's committee. The tightly worded analysis attempted to fully explicate the narrow range of issues the committee had been dancing around during the hearing. In a famous turn-of-the-century case known simply as *Lone Wolf,* the U.S. Supreme Court had ruled that Congress indeed had the plenary power over the tribes and could legally abrogate the Fort Laramie Peace Council. But there was a fly in the ointment, cautioned Cohen. Congress indeed possessed the plenary power to abrogate ratified conditions agreed to at the Fort Laramie Peace Council. However, he cautioned, it could only do so by simultaneously violating its legally binding responsibilities to the tribes as trustee for the tribal commons. In other words, the federal "trust doctrine" clarified by Justice John Marshall a century before acted as a preemptive check on Congress' broad authority.

As for the sanctity of treaties, Cohen reiterated the position of former attorney general William Wirt, who had told Congress a century earlier that "so long as a tribe exists and remains in possession of its lands, its title and possession are sovereign and exclusive, and there exists no authority to enter upon their lands without their consent."

The Wirt Principle, Cohen explained, constituted a guarantee to the tribes from the federal government against any future taking of Indian land, for whatever purposes. Wirt had intentionally set a high bar in order to discourage state governments and opportunistic lawmakers by making it clear that tribal land "has always been sacred and can never be disturbed but by their consent." As a coda to his own remarks, Cohen added that Attorney General Wirt's axiom was also articulated in the text of the Fort Laramie Peace Council. "[The tribes] do not hold under the States," concluded Wirt, "nor under the United States; their title is original, sovereign, and exclusive." It was Cohen's opinion that Wirt's exegesis on tribal sovereignty of "domestic dependent nations" was an exquisite articulation of what might better be called the Marshall Doctrine.

This was the sort of problem that untethered the Corps' chief administrators from their legal moorings. The Army's engineers were in the business of taming rivers, not interpreting the law. Consequently, it came as no surprise to Felix Cohen in the late summer of 1945 when he learned that the Corps had begun construction on Garrison Dam without receiving the first word of approval from Congress. The Corps viewed final approval as a formality. Yet after a careful review of Mr. Cohen's memorandum, O'Mahoney's committee voted to attach a rider to a deficiency appropriations bill then moving through Congress. This last-minute addendum, rubber-stamped by Congress on December 28, 1945, stipulated that no money could be spent on the construction of Garrison Dam until the tribes had been given suitable and sufficient land in exchange for the land they would lose to the flood. The Corps, however, took that to mean that they could go ahead and build the supporting infrastructure, such as new towns for all the workers and rail spurs to bring in material. Congress was simply delaying the actual excavation of dirt.

Back home, Chairman Cross told local newspapers that the trip to Washington, D.C., had been a great success. On hearing their objections to the building of Garrison Dam at the Mandan Bluffs, Congress had promised that nothing would go forward until the legal issues raised by the tribe were resolved to the Tribal Council's satisfaction. Upon the council's return, the first official act was to remain on the offensive by hiring their own point man in Washington, D.C. — attorney Ralph Hoyt Case, whom they had met on their trip. Case's job would be to safeguard the tribes' interests in Congress and to coordinate the council's campaign with other advocates for tribal rights at the Department of the Interior and the Bureau of Indian Affairs. With this first crucial meeting behind them, a collective sigh seemed to quietly rise from the council. A future that had looked so dark just weeks before seemed to have brightened considerably.

As winter closed in and once again shut the tribes off from the outside world, the council struck upon the idea of offering the government a way out of its own trap. In February, they hired an engineering firm to investigate alternate sites for the dam. Working with the council and attorney Case, a civilian engineer named Daniel C. Walser soon arrived at a conclusion identical to the one reflected in Glenn Sloan's basinwide master plan. Walser's written opinion to the tribe also echoed that of Secretary Ickes: the Garrison Dam was an unnecessary extravagance. Fort Peck, combined with the other four large-scale dams proposed by the Corps, would provide more than enough storage for downstream flood control, upstream irrigation, and barge navigation to Sioux City.

Building an enormous dam hundreds of miles from a road, railhead, or town made little sense. With just such a point of intersection in mind, Walser proposed that the Corps consider an alternative to the Garrison site another forty miles upstream from Elbowoods. The site above the town of Sanish featured several significant improvements over the Garrison site: It would only flood the upper portion of the reservation, leaving all nine communities intact; it would generate power more cheaply; and the government would save 1 million dollars in construction costs. In late May 1946, the Tribal Council, certain they had been dealt an ace in the hole, approved a resolution offering the upstream dam site as a gift to the American people, with no strings attached.

As soon as he was notified of the plans for the alternate site, Case launched a campaign to turn the tide on the Upper Missouri through personal appeals to congressmen friendly to the tribes. Case and the council hoped that a handful of lawmakers such as Senator Joseph O'Mahoney could be persuaded to create a groundswell and stop the Pick Plan before it gained momentum.

Having recently returned from an assignment in Burma, Colonel Pick rallied his allies and promptly shot down the Walser alternative before Case could win a single supporter for the alternative site. Already incensed by the legislative delays, Pick dismissed the Walser proposal with a summary judgment. "It would not be a project that we could justify or that I would recommend," said Pick, effectively consigning the Walser alternative to legislative purgatory.

The tribes' friends in Congress were not yet willing to concede defeat. When Congress passed the War Department Civil Appropriations Act for 1947 in early May of 1946, Congress stipulated that the secretary of the interior would have to certify any "lieu lands" as being "comparable in quality and sufficient in area" to make the tribe whole for the land they were losing. Only after this exchange, which "shall be consummated before January 1, 1947," could the actual construction of the dam then proceed. The interim secretary of the interior, Oscar Chapman, sent a letter to Case assuring him and the Tribal Council that the tribes would have to sign off on any lieu-lands offer before the dam could be built.

A resolute Pick decided to press his advantage by arranging a meeting with the Indians themselves. Along with representatives from the BIA's office in Aberdeen, South Dakota, and Lieutenant Colonel Delbert Freeman — the chief engineer assigned to manage the Garrison project — Pick and North Dakota governor Fred Aandahl rolled into Elbowoods in a caravan of shiny black government cars on May 27, 1946. Before the caravan turned down Old State Road Number Eight, no agreement had been reached between the Indians and their guests as to the purpose of the get-together. The press arrived to report on the meeting with its own set of assumptions. The *New York Times* titled its May 26 story on the meeting, TRIBES ON THE WARPATH. Locally, the *Sanish Sentinel* explained that the meeting with Pick and the governor was being convened "for the purpose of blocking the construction of the Garrison Dam, if possible."

Indians streamed from all the distant villages into the Elbowoods High School auditorium. Horses, wagons, buckboards, and old cars and pickups converged on Elbowoods and lined every street of town. "I'd never seen so many people in Elbowoods," says Crusoe. "I was standing at the back door when Pick got up to speak. You could hear a pin drop."

Tribal chairman Cross brought the meeting to order and opened the floor to new business by welcoming the guests to Elbowoods. When Pick rose to speak, the packed auditorium awaited the colonel's comments with stony civility.

"Several conferences have been held with you people, during which the plan for the construction of this dam has been discussed," began Pick. "During these conferences it was recognized that you were particularly desirous of preventing the construction of the dam at the Garrison site rather than obtaining compensation for the lands to be inundated. Under the law passed by Congress in 1944, the Army engineers are charged with building the Garrison Dam. We are meeting here today to work out ways and means of building the dam. When it is built, it will create a large lake. Before that lake can be completed, a large number of people living in this valley must be moved out to new locations. We are here as friends. We are here asking that you cooperate with the Army engineers and your official Indian affairs office in carrying out the law as now written. Mr. Cross, I would like to have this statement distributed in English and then interpreted."

Colonel Pick's raspy, high-pitched voice sounded like a ball-peen hammer banging on a metal washtub. No one stirred. Hundreds of blank, enigmatic faces peered back at the expressionless queue of bald-headed white men arrayed in chairs behind the table at the head of the room. Pick's opening remarks had just confirmed the Indians' darkest suspicions. This is what they had come to hear with their own ears, and see with their own eyes. As Pick's final words dissolved into a restive silence, James Driver, an elder from the community of Shell Creek, rose from his chair in the middle of the audience.

"I hear that you have come here to ask us to give up our lands," began the old man, who was one of the last living tribal members to be born at Like-a-Fishhook Village. "I am an old-time Indian. I have little knowledge of the English language. You will understand me when I tell you that there are some things that are dear to me, above all others. For instance, the land I am standing on is dear to me. From time immemorial, we have resided on this land. The land beneath our feet is the dearest thing in the world to us, and I am here to tell you that we are going to stay here. We refuse to be flooded. As members of the white race, you have come from across the pond as newcomers to this land. In the years that have come and gone, the time when our chief Four Bears was alive, he made treaties with your government that promised this land would be ours forever. Forever! What confuses the Indian is how he and the white man can have such a different interpretation of that word. We are here today to remind you that we were on this land long before the first white man came, and we are going to remain here forever. I have seen a good many white people with bald heads, and when a person is in that shape, he is usually the most gifted liar in the country. His promises are taken with a smile, but they are not worth the paper they are written on."

James Driver quietly returned to his seat. The audience stirred in the silence that followed his speech, but no one at the head table dared to respond. Finally, Chester Smith, another elder, rose to his feet and spoke briefly, reminding the white guests that America had just finished a war to preserve freedom, and many Indians from Fort Berthold had fought for those same freedoms.

Daniel Wolf, of Elbowoods, then followed with remarks that addressed Colonel Pick directly.

"I heard your saying that you would do your best to give us the best land in exchange for our lands. I must tell you that I doubt your word. You have fooled us before. Why do I know this? Because there is no land that compares to what we have here. I am here to tell you that if we are forced to move somewhere else, to leave this land, the Indian people who called this place home before the white man came across the water will pass away with loneliness and sadness."

The Indians' initial comments indicated that neither Pick's flashy arrival nor his starched uniform and phalanx of aides had succeeded in nudging this crowd any closer to accepting the Corps' plan for the Upper Missouri. Later, reflecting on the encounter in Elbowoods, the Indians told Arthur Morgan, author of *Dams and Other Disasters* and director of President Roosevelt's Tennessee Valley Authority, that they believed Colonel Pick had specifically chosen words calculated to provoke the crowd's anger. As each speaker finished, the meeting's well-mannered decorum seemed to lose a little more of its fragile civility. The upwelling emotions were about to spill into a flood of anger. Thomas Spotted Wolf now rose, wearing a full headdress, a bolo tie, and a beaded vest.

"Gentlemen, I won't say that I am glad to see you, neither will I shake your hands," began Spotted Wolf. His speech then boiled over into a furious attack of words that were delivered no more than an arm's length from Colonel Pick's nose. When Spotted Wolf had finished, the colonel decided he had heard all he wanted to hear from the Indians. As attorney Case presented his appeal for the upper dam, Pick stood up without apology to Chairman Cross and stormed out the door, followed by the governor and his aides.

This was Pick's first and last meeting with the many Indian tribes who owned land that would be inundated by his management plan for the Missouri. As for the stated purpose of promoting a free exchange of ideas between the Indians and the men at the head table, Thomas Spotted Wolf had gotten the last word. The lessons of the aborted meeting were not lost on Pick or the governor. As the official caravan made its way back to high ground, they both knew that they were engaged in a battle with a foe who would not be intimidated or bullied at the negotiating table. Pick, however, turned the incident to his advantage by reporting back to his friends in Congress that the event went just as he predicted. He and the governor had gone to Elbowoods with the intention of building a bridge of friendship with the Indians. Their best efforts were rewarded by insults from a belligerent and uncooperative tribe of backward natives who had no interest in the welfare of their fellow citizens on the Missouri.

As the Corps geared up its public relations campaign among farmers, promising that the new dam would "bring immeasurable wealth to North Dakota . . . which can hardly be visualized in advance of its creation," the War Department reported to President Truman's new secretary of the interior,

Julius Krug, that the search for "lieu lands" was proving to be a snipe hunt. There were no lieu lands to be found. For a brief period in the autumn of 1946, they believed they had located a possible exchange of bottomlands near the town of Washburn, currently being farmed by whites. When word of this leaked out, once sympathetic whites suddenly became the tribes' fiercest enemies. News of the proposed land swap was met with a "stunned silence" that quickly gave way to a storm of protests in town meetings and local papers. Yet even this land did not meet the "comparable and sufficient" standard required by Congress. Affirming the argument the Indians had made all along, and with regrets, the Washburn exchange was spiked.

As Congress' deadline for an exchange of land rapidly approached, the search for lieu lands suddenly turned frantic. By now, lawmakers were losing patience with this expensive and fruitless search for replacement lands. Some members of the Tribal Council were under the impression that if no "comparable and sufficient" lands could be found, then talk of Garrison Dam would end. More than 6 million dollars had already been spent by the Corps in preliminary engineering work. They had laid a new rail spur to the site and built the town of Riverdale from scratch to house future workers. If anyone thought the government was going to walk away from all that work and money "for a handful of Indians," wrote the editor of the *Hazen Star* newspaper, "they were crazy."

The War Department finally admitted that "comparable and sufficient" lands did not exist. At last the charade was called off. In the closing months of 1946, administrators at the Corps and bureau began openly discussing a cash settlement for the tribes. Clearly, anxiety was also mounting on Capitol Hill. Lawmakers wanted to see bulldozers moving dirt. With the "drop-dead" day fast approaching, members of the powerful Appropriations Committee in the House began echoing the War Department's call for a cash settlement. The fact that no money had been allocated for a "taking" in the original appropriation for the dam could be easily remedied. As for the legal problems surrounding the status of trust lands, well, that could be finessed somehow. Neither hell nor high water was going to stop the Corps. The agency now appeared to have a monopoly on both.

Without risking the liability of actually spelling out its dirty little legal problem, Congress had made its decision. Lawmakers would simply lift their eyes above the troubling distinction between trust lands and allotted lands, and pretend the former was the latter in order to wiggle out of its overarching treaty obligations as a trustee to the tribes. Rather than sending in the cavalry,

Congress had learned that it could exert its will in Indian Country simply by passing new statutes. Incidents such as Wounded Knee and the Sand Creek Massacre had put up a foul odor that lingered over federal Indian policy for decades. A hundred years from now, who would know the difference, or remember the cause and effect of a simple statute? As he watched the drama unfold from the sidelines as an observer, engineer, author, and the former director for the Tennessee Valley Authority, Arthur Morgan wrote in his journal that nothing the Corps did could surprise him. In a letter to the former secretary of the interior Harold Ickes, Morgan argued that nothing could be worse for the country than a "willful and expensive Corps" that made up its own rules in defiance of Congress and in contempt of public welfare. Out on the Missouri, continued Morgan, they were witnessing the destruction of an "ideal human community, the Three Affiliated Tribes, a group of people who have lived in a community of goodwill and economic independence" for countless centuries.

The January 1, 1947, deadline came and went with no agreement on lieu lands. Attorney Case wrote a letter to Cross to inform him that the Department of the Interior was being flooded with letters supporting the tribes, but there was little chance these sentiments would have an effect on policy. Both the BIA and the Department of the Interior were resigned to the fact that the dam was going to be built. The Corps interpreted Congress' frustration with the lieu-lands deadline as a green light to ignore the ban on construction. When the Tribal Council complained that Army engineers had resumed work on a new rail spur near Sanish, the protest was ignored in Washington. What had taken a day to cobble together in Omaha would take forever and a day to build and pay for.

A fourth tribal delegation traveled to Washington and testified against a cash settlement on July 17, 1947. A newly elected tribal councilman, Mark Mahto, threw down a gauntlet in a hearing with the House Appropriations Committee.

"The quickest and most merciful way to exterminate the three tribes is by mass execution, like they did to the Jews in Germany. We find it strange that the treaty made between you and the aggressor nations of Japan and Germany are more sacred than the treaty you made with the three tribes. Everything will be lost if Garrison is built. We will lose our homes, our communities, our economy, our resources. We took in the Lewis and Clark expedition in the winter of 1804. We took those men in and watched them like hawks to keep them from freezing and starving to death. If you are determined to remove us from our land, you might as well take a gun and put a bullet through us. The principles that we fought for in this last war, right beside you, was for the very homes, lands, and resources that you are trying to take from us today."

The campaign to pay off the tribes with a lump sum cash settlement arrived at a moment of truth in the early weeks of 1947. Jefferson Smith and Mark Mahto had no sooner boarded the Empire Builder for the trip back to Elbowoods than Congress huddled with officials from the War Department and quietly hammered out Public Law 296. Before the ink was dry, P.L. 296 was passed by the full House, without a word of protest. With this law, Congress now formally proposed to sidestep its earlier obligations by compensating the tribes with a lump sum payment of $5,105,625. According to the text of P.L. 296, this figure would represent full payment for the "acquisition of the lands and rights therein within the taking line of Garrison Reservoir . . . including all improvements, severance damages, and reestablishment and relocation costs." The Corps, in other words, could now move forward with work on the dam itself without having to anticipate any further irritating delays.

When their train pulled out of Union Station, councilmen Smith and Mahto were convinced that this latest round of testimony had cinched the deal. Congress, they were certain, would now move decisively to stop the Pick juggernaut in its tracks. Unbeknownst to them, Smith and Mahto had fallen for the oldest trick in the book by believing their own press. As the councilmen's train rumbled down the tracks, Congress, instead of cinching the deal to stop Pick-Sloan, was quietly approving the lump-sum buyout. Word of Congress' betrayal would beat them home. When they arrived back in Elbowoods and heard the news, Mahto and Smith sat through an emergency meeting of the council in stunned silence. After Chairman Cross distributed copies of Congress' latest bait-and-switch offer, not a word was uttered. The entire council pored over the new law with disbelieving eyes.

Between the lines, Congress had cut a deal with itself. Lawmakers were not going to get lured into a trap that tangled them up in the finer points of the law. The 5-million-dollar compensation package was intended to cover all bases. Not only would it have to compensate them for their land, but it would also have to cover the relocation and reconstruction expenses for more than four hundred families, in addition to rebuilding schools, hospitals, and roads. Congress had chosen to ignore the valuations provided by private appraisers, who had already estimated the value of the bare land at 21 million dollars. The $150 an acre figure Martin Cross had cited three years earlier to O'Mahoney's committee as the value of an acre of bottomland had now been reduced by

Congress to less than $15. And be forewarned, said the bill's fine print, this is the best offer you are going to get. And one last thing, said Congress. The tribes had five months to consider the offer. Congress wanted an answer no later than June 1, 1948. If the tribes failed to accept the offer, the money would revert back to the federal treasury, and the council could then take its chances in the court.

The take-it-or-leave-it subtext conveyed by this offer was deeply unsettling to the Tribal Council members. Privately, Martin Cross knew the tribes had run out of options. The future that looked so promising after his first trip to Washington in October 1945 had been systematically eroded by political forces that proved greater than the tribes or their allies. The Bureau of Indian Affairs had become a liability. Now, under a vicious attack by western congressmen such as Senator Arthur Watkins of Utah, Congress appeared more determined than ever to abolish the agency altogether. With the lieu-lands provisions now null and void, the tribal councilmen searched one another's eyes. Each of them knew that from this day forward, the people of the Mandan, Hidatsa, and Arikara nations were in a losing race against the white man's clock.

⚘

Phyllis Old Dog Cross turned seventeen in January 1947, the same year Congress gave the Army Corps of Engineers the final go-ahead to build Garrison Dam. It would be her last winter in Elbowoods. When the search for lieu lands failed, the early optimism her father expressed about stopping the dam suddenly began to diminish, before finally fading out altogether. The twelve-hundred-square-foot Cross house was now home to ten people. Her father's mood was gloomy, day in and day out. Determined to go to nursing school that fall, Phyllis worked every day that summer chopping fence posts in the woods by the river, earning a dime per post. This was the first "folding money" she had ever called her own, and she never worked that hard again. But she knew she came from a long line of strong-willed, tough-minded women. If she had to work twenty hours a day through the summer in order to go away to school, then that was what she would do.

"The dam had gradually taken over our dad's life," says Phyllis. "Mom was getting more and more withdrawn. By the time I left home, her only social activity was the school. Their common ground had gotten smaller and smaller."

Martin Cross must have sensed that his marriage was adrift. When he came up for reelection early in 1948, he made an unexpected decision not to seek another term on the Tribal Council. Martin stuck to that decision despite the pressure that was brought to bear by the elders. The four years he spent fighting the dam, since early 1944, had been an education in the ways of the white man's world.

"Mom and Dad were two very complex people, trying to mesh their lives as best they could," says Marilyn. "By nineteen forty-seven or forty-eight, there were too many forces out there working against them. Dad loved to play the saxophone, and Mom played the accordion and the banjo. After Forrest died, they never played together again."

"It doesn't take long for politics to turn you into something your family doesn't much like anymore," reflects Michael. "Dad got progressively harder to get along with. He could be a bear at home with us kids, but he was so effective in public as a politician. He was caught between the past and the future, and between dual personalities, and between responsibilities to his family and his responsibilities, as Old Dog's son, to the tribe. I think his life just got more and more impossible."

All things that rise tend to converge. When the search for lieu lands collapsed and her father left the Tribal Council, Phyllis, like her mother before her, enrolled in the nursing program at St. Alexius Hospital in Bismarck. Unlike her mother, Phyllis was determined to finish the program and not return to Elbowoods. When the day finally came to leave home, her mother and father gave her a ride as far as Garrison. From there she caught the bus to Bismarck.

"I knew I had to get out, but I also felt like I was deserting my little brothers and sisters. When they left me at Garrison, they looked back through the window with their beautiful little innocent faces, waving their little hands. I thought my heart would break."

Phyllis got on the bus wearing a new pair of mail-order shoes that she had purchased from a Sears catalog for $2.50. She wore a new calico dress sewn by her mother, and the suitcase she checked through to Bismarck contained all her worldly belongings. "I took a seat toward the rear of the bus and looked out the window. When the bus pulled onto the street and turned away from Elbowoods, it hit me all at once. I couldn't believe it. There I was, alone in the world for the very first time in my whole life, heading off into the unknown."

Phyllis settled quickly and easily into her new life at the hospital. The dormitory itself seemed luxurious compared to the world she had left behind. Water came out of faucets, she could take a warm bath every night, and there was central heat and electric lights in every room. Her first paycheck for a month's work came to $191, a sum that made her rich beyond her wildest imaginings. She sent money home to her mother every month, completed the three-year nursing program in just two, and still graduated at the top of her class. The nuns at the hospital were very strict, but Phyllis thrived in the regular routine of hospital life. Soon she made new friends in Bismarck, started going to picture shows, and volunteered to work extra shifts at the hospital on the weekends. As the months went by, the world of her childhood drifted farther and farther away.

"The trip home was just a hundred miles, but it would take all day," remembers Phyllis. "When I went back at Christmas, in 1947, I couldn't believe it. So much had changed, or the way I was seeing it had changed. That trip home was very hard for me. Then Mom told me she was pregnant again. I thought, when is this ever going to end? I couldn't wait to get back to Bismarck."

⚶

The nine communities of the Three Affiliated Tribes voted on the compensation package in May 1948. Congress' offer was accepted by 625 of the 960 eligible voters. There were notable holdouts, such as Lillie Wolf, who years before had gone door-to-door collecting dimes and nickels to pay for train tickets to Washington. She spoke for many when she told the tribes' new chairman, George Gillette, "I will not accept any money from the sale of the tribal land and timber. I refuse to sell my share."

The tribe was face-to-face with a "prisoner's dilemma." Gillette felt he had little choice but to argue in favor of accepting the offer. At the very least, he could argue that the contract guaranteed the tribes' grazing rights, and hunting and fishing rights, in the taking area. It also protected the tribe's subsurface mineral rights and promised that if the $5 million proved insufficient for "relocation" costs, Congress would cover the overruns. The official signing ceremony was held in Secretary Julius Krug's office in Washington, D.C., on May 20, 1948. As Krug fixed his signature to the contract, flashbulbs popped at the moment emotion overwhelmed Chairman Gillette. He buried his face in his hands and wept. The picture ran on the front page of newspapers across the country.

"As everyone knows," Gillette told the press following the ceremony, "our treaty of 1851, and our tribal constitution, are being torn into shreds by this contract. My heart is very heavy. What will become of our people?"

Not everyone in Congress was celebrating the government's dismissal of its "supreme law of the land" obligations to the Mandan, Hidatsa, and Arikara people. Yet many of the tribes' early supporters were no longer in office. A postwar sea change had seen Republicans take control of both houses of Congress for the first time in more than twenty years. For Pick, who had since been promoted to general, this was reason to celebrate. Republican control of Congress was a guarantee that what had been done on the Upper Missouri would not be undone. Besides, a new cadre of anti-Indian legislators, led by the hard-charging senator from Utah, Arthur Watkins, was in control of important committees. With Watkins watching the Indians' every move from his position as the new chairman of the Select Committee on Indian Affairs, it was generally conceded on Capitol Hill that nothing short of an act of God could stop the Garrison Dam from being built.

Yet the tribes were not yet completely friendless in Washington. Men such as Senator Langer, O'Mahoney, and North Dakota's idealistic champion of Indian rights in the House of Representatives, William Lemke, were determined that the $5 million settlement offered by Congress should not be the final word on the abrogation of the treaty made at Horse Creek. As the contract was being drawn up for the signing ceremony in the spring of 1949, Langer introduced a bill that upped the ante by demanding that the tribes be given $1 million in compensation for their flooded land and $30 million in damages for their forced removal. Removal, in context of the bill, was a sanitary euphemism for the abrogation of constitutionally protected treaty rights.

Langer's bill sailed into heavy seas from the outset. Though the first draft was rejected out of hand, Langer and Lemke managed to attach a $9.5 million rider to the "takings act" as additional compensation. In committee hearings, Ralph Case produced experts who told Congress that the tribes' claims in a court case could easily exceed $25 million. The logrolling now began in earnest. In January of 1949, Lemke's bill called for a compensation package totaling $14.6 million and officially became House Joint Resolution 33. This proposal was immediately referred back to Senator Watkins's Indian committee in the Senate. There, without explanation, Watkins reduced the House figure to $4 million. After months of haggling back and forth through the summer and fall of 1949, Congress arrived at a compromise package of $12.5 million.

The committee haggling over compensation was a bitter defeat for Lemke. The rookie congressman was powerless to curb the mean-spirited atmosphere that now prevailed on the Senate's Indian committee. Nevertheless, Lemke told the House that a great crime was being committed against the Indians. Garrison Dam was probably a mistake to begin with, he said, but the "taking" of treaty-protected lands only compounded the crime. "We are again violating a treaty solemnly entered into with these tribes, a treaty in which we promised never to disturb them again. Unfortunately, the Indians have no choice. There is no honor in this settlement."

Watkins's strong-arm tactics had sent the tribes a clear but subliminal message: take the money. Another round of negotiations in Watkins's committee would likely cut the figure even further. Martin Cross advised the Tribal Council to throw the entire package back in the laps of Congress and take their chances in the courts. On a hastily arranged trip to Washington in 1948 as an at-large representative for the tribes, Cross told a joint committee hearing that the new "taking" act would most likely be ruled unconstitutional. Yet when Congress' compensation offer was put to a vote, the tribe approved the latest offer by a thin majority. Members themselves were more deeply divided than ever, a political split that did not bode well for the coming months and years. In the end, Martin Cross set his personal opinions aside and pressed Congress to abide by the will of his people. The official "taking" act, Public Law 437, was signed into law by President Truman on October 29, 1949.

Lemke's arm-twisting managed to secure a monetary settlement that was more than twice the original figure. On the other hand, Watkins had succeeded in cutting what they were legally due by half. Now, as far as Congress was concerned, P.L. 437 swept aside any unresolved claims the tribes might have regarding violations of their agreement at Horse Creek. The question that remained was, by the time they were removed from the valley, lock, stock, and barrel; and new homes were built; and thousands of graves were moved to high ground from bottomland cemeteries; and new schools and roads were built, how much of the money would be left in the treasury to assist individuals faced with rebuilding their lives, and communities, from the ground up?

Human suffering aside, the money had come with hidden costs which slipped through Congress with no discussion. In the compromise that came out of Watkins's committee, the best parts had gone missing. The tribes' fishing and hunting rights, the promise of discounted power, and the guarantee of irrigation and of perpetual grazing and mineral rights in the taking area were quietly stripped from the bill. The most sinister wrinkle of all was tucked into the final section by Watkins himself. He emerged from a private lunch with his friend General Pick and tacked a clause onto the end of Section 12 that prevented the Indians from ever using the settlement money to bring claims against the government.

This issue was close to Watkins's heart. For years, Secretary Ickes and the Roosevelt administration had denied the mineral industry access to the treasure chest of resources in Indian Country. Now, with the Republicans in charge, Indian Country uranium, gold, copper, oil, zinc, silver, timber, and water fell within their reach. For years, Watkins and Mormon politicians had tried to force the Ute tribe of southern Utah to sell its treaty lands to the state and mining companies. In recent years, lawyers for the tribes had turned the tables on Watkins and his business associates. Federal courts awarded the Ute huge cash settlements for violations of their treaty rights by Mormon settlers and unscrupulous politicians. Watkins and his allies could now get to the agenda they had been forced to postpone when Roosevelt and his commissioner of Indian affairs, John Collier, put Indian Country off-limits to the extraction industries with the Indian Reorganization Act of 1934.

As the final version of the takings act was being drafted in his committee, Watkins's colleague in the House, Representative Reva Beck, formally instigated the "Termination Era," a slate of bills that would clog committee dockets over the next five years with the intention of disbanding tribes and the Bureau of Indian Affairs, and transferring federal control over the tribes to the states. Watkins argued that by stripping the Three Affiliated Tribes of their mineral rights, grazing rights, and hunting and fishing rights, he was simply looking to the future. What sense did it make for Congress to guarantee the tribes' cheap electricity and irrigation, or protect their aboriginal hunting and fishing rights, when they were already in the crosshairs for termination?

The predicament that the Three Affiliated Tribes found themselves in was a sign to Senator Watkins that tables had turned in Indian Country. The takings act had been a dress rehearsal for the coming termination battles. Recent judicial history in his own home state had reinforced Watkins's dim view of federal courts: federal judges could not be trusted. Given its plenary power over Indian Country, Watkins reasoned, Congress alone could determine a just and fair settlement for the Three Affiliated Tribes. While Watkins was busy laying the groundwork for termination, Secretary of the Interior Julius Krug sent a brief missive to Watkins suggesting that a clean sweep of the issues with the Mandan, Hidatsa, and Arikara nations would go a long way toward reducing the likelihood of a protracted showdown in a court of claims at some future time.

Krug's cautionary warning prompted Watkins to tell members of his committee to ignore any proposals out of the House that recognized the Indians' right to just compensation, and to formulate a settlement that reasserted

Congress' plenary authority over the tribes. The trick would be to deny the tribes access to the courts. With luck, Congress could forestall judicial review in a final settlement conference. Although they could not legally deny the tribes access to federal courts, Watkins knew he could effect a similar outcome by cutting off their access to funds for legal representation. When the Select Committee on Indian Affairs completed work on the compromise, Congressman Lemke read the draft in astonished silence. What he had in his hands bore no resemblance to the bill passed by the House.

At the same time his committee was clipping the horns of the House bill, Watkins was publicly promising the Three Affiliated Tribes a fair shake in the Senate. Martin Cross alerted Case to be on the lookout for any shenanigans in the Senate, then sat back to wait and see. The chairman's wait was not a long one. Denying the tribes the right to use settlement money to hire legal counsel was like hanging a padlock on their casket. Not only had they lost their *usufructuary* rights to hunt, fish, and gather food, but Watkins also eliminated all language from the House version of the takings act that referred to the "abrogation of treaties." The bill was so radically altered from its original form that the Senate was obliged to give it a new name before sending it back to the House. Now it was simply called, "A joint resolution to vest title to certain lands and to provide compensation therefor."

Historian Roy Meyer argues that the $3 million earmarked by the Lemke bill for "consolidation of lands" could have transformed the tribes' fractionated holdings into economically viable and contiguous units. Instead, Watkins eliminated this line item from the final draft and dug in his heels when the two houses met in conference. As a result of this fierce intransigence, Representative Lemke and his allies failed to get the Land Readjustment Fund reinstated. Members of the House who had worked diligently to write a fair and equitable takings bill were appalled by the bill that emerged from Watkins's committee. Lemke immediately demanded a new conference. Watkins stonewalled. After the Senate agreed to a final compensation figure of $12.5 million, the House waved a white flag and capitulated.

Congress' abdication of its trust responsibilities to the Three Affiliated Tribes, the failure that Felix Cohen had warned them about four years earlier, was the legislative outcome that Chief Justice John Marshall had most feared. The Indians held aboriginal title to the land. As such, they enjoyed rights that were guaranteed to them by treaty, the Northwest Ordinance, and the U.S. Constitution. With the takings act of 1949, Congress inadvertently became a latter-day agent for Pope Innocent III. Lawmakers could follow their "taking" back to *Quod super his* to find the origin of its preemptive legal justification for forcing the "infidel" to relinquish title to his aboriginal homeland. Yet just as Felix Cohen had warned, Congress could only do so by sawing through a load-bearing beam that supported the American house of democracy.

᠕

In the years immediately following the war, the Elbowoods Warriors always won a berth in the North Dakota state basketball championships. The year after the takings act passed in Congress, the team was snowed in by a late-season storm. There was no chance of getting to Minot by road. Instead, their resourceful superintendent, Rex Quinn, came up with a plan. He and the men of Elbowoods plowed the streets of town to make a landing strip. On a snowy March day in 1951, the U.S. Air Force landed on the main street of Elbowoods with a DC-3 and picked up the team and their coaches. They landed sixty miles away, in Minot, a half hour before tip-off. The Warriors won.

The following autumn, the Elbowoods Warriors had the best record in the state in football. Going into the final game of the season, against the boys from the high school in the new town of Riverdale, the Warriors were undefeated. So were their opponents, the Knights, who had been soundly beaten by the Indians in their two previous contests. These were the sons of the engineers brought in by the Army Corps of Engineers to build Garrison Dam. They knew about the tall and lanky Cross kid named Bucky. He had great hands as a receiver, and a fair turn of speed, and if he got loose on the sidelines it usually meant six points. But the young man they were laying for that week was already a high school football legend in North Dakota. Arnie Charging, a young Arikara fullback, had already been offered six scholarships to play college ball, including a full-ride offer from Notre Dame. No one in the history of North Dakota football had scored as many touchdowns, or piled up as many rushing yards, as Arnie Charging. Against the Underwood Comets the previous Friday, Charging rushed for four touchdowns, kicked two extra points, passed for another two touchdowns, and gained 194 yards on the ground. And that was an off night.

The matchup against Riverdale was the final game of the season. This time, the Warriors would be playing on Riverdale's home field. Like most games played late in the season, it was a nasty, bitter cold day. These were perfect conditions for an Indian fullback from Elbowoods.

"The only thing we've ever been able to figure is somebody got to those refs before the game," says Charging. "On the first play of the game, I ran a sweep around the right end and went seventy-eight yards for a touchdown."

The referees called the touchdown back. A line judge said Charging had stepped out of bounds when he turned up the field. On the very next play, Charging took a handoff from the quarterback and flicked the ball to Bucky Cross, who ran the length of the field for another touchdown.

"They called that one back, too, on a clipping penalty," says Charging. Soon, the weather deteriorated along with the game. An Arctic storm was howling across the plains. By the start of the second half, the frigid winds had kicked up a ground blizzard that made it impossible to see the far side of the field. When the final whistle blew, the Riverdale Knights had won the game, fourteen to three. According to the story in the *Minot Daily News,* by all rights the Elbowoods Warriors probably should have won the game handily. But the referees, who had all been brought up from Bismarck, called back all six of their touchdowns.

"We lost that game before we ever set foot on the bus," says Charging. "It's the kind of thing that stays with you for a long, long time."

※

Martin and Dorothy Cross's biggest surprise of the postwar years would be the birth of their tenth and final child. The little boy, born at the hospital in Elbowoods on August 24, 1948, was named White Duck. As dictated by custom, a relative from the father's family organized a traditional Hidatsa naming ceremony two weeks after the child was born. A generation earlier, another White Duck, Alice's uncle and Chief Old Dog's brother, became a celebrated warrior in tribal legends that immortalized his bravery and exploits in battles against the Sioux. When White Duck's namesake was baptized at the Sacred Heart Mission, Father Reinhart, the same priest that had buried his brother Forrest three years earlier, asked the parents, "And how will this child be known?" Martin and Dorothy Cross answered, "His name will be Raymond."

CHAPTER VI

Leaving Elbowoods

🌿

"I wish all to know that I do not propose to sell any part of my country.
I am particularly fond of the little groves of oak trees. I love to look
at them because they endure the winter storms and summer heat
and, not unlike ourselves, seem to flourish by them."

TATANKA YOTANKA, HUNKPAPA
(SITTING BULL)

I n late May of 1951, Louise Holding Eagle had just celebrated her twenty-first birthday with her husband and their two young children. The couple had eloped and gotten married as soon as they graduated from the high school in Elbowoods in 1948. Early the following summer, the couple moved into a small farmhouse on the outskirts of town. There they raised a few cows in the pasture and put in a crop of oats and durum wheat. The winter of 1951 had been exceptionally long. By May, Louise's pantry shelves were bare. Indians had always called late spring "the starving time." On a warm and sunny afternoon a few days after her birthday, Louise left her two children with her husband and drove to the grocery store in Beulah, thirty miles away. After shopping for sugar, flour, beans, and potatoes, she stopped for a bite of dinner at the home of some old school friends, then turned for home in the twilight.

"Nobody had a phone back then, so I couldn't call my husband and let him know I'd be a little late," remembers Louise. "He was an easygoing man, and I knew he wouldn't mind."

The long summer evening suddenly darkened when the road home dropped into the valley. When Louise reached the turn to her house on Old State Road Number Eight, she thought she must have been disoriented by the gathering darkness. Inadvertently, she had turned down a long driveway that ended abruptly in an empty field.

"It took me a minute before I realized I was in the right place. I was home, all right. Everything was right where it was supposed to be. Except my house."

The house, the barn, and the chicken coop were gone. The Corps had come in that afternoon with a crew and a flatbed truck and driven off with the house and two outbuildings. The only thing they left behind was the old foundation. Louise Holding Eagle spent the next two hours chasing her house across the prairie.

"It was just like that for a lot of folks," says Louise, a bright-eyed, cheerful woman who now entertains her grandchildren at her small home in Parshall. "For years and years we heard stories like that," she says, chuckling with a tinge of sadness. "I know one lady who had to chase her house on horseback."

The challenge for tribal leaders was to penetrate the hardened silence of their members when it came to moving to higher ground. Nearly all of the Indians still considered the high ground foreign country. The Tribal Council finally realized that as long as the Bureau of Indian Affairs' offices remained in Elbowoods, nobody wanted to make the first move. But the Corps had an answer for that problem. In the summer of 1951, two years before the scheduled evacuation of government personnel, they began moving homes out of Elbowoods and surrounding environs. Arnie Charging was having dinner with his new bride one evening when they heard a racket outside their house. The couple continued eating and thought little of it until they felt the room lifting beneath them. "They never told us a thing or gave us a word of notice," says Charging. "I ran outside to find out what the heck was going on. There was a bunch of white guys out there with jacks and sledgehammers. 'Oh, sorry, we didn't know you were home. We're moving your house, Mister. Where do you want us to put it?'"

If there was reluctance in Elbowoods to accept the inevitability of relocation, by the summer of 1951 the dam was fait accompli in Washington and Bismarck. Sixty miles upstream from the state capital, a permanent cloud of dust now hung over the eastern horizon, day after day, like smoke rising from a wind-driven prairie fire. Charles Pickering, the editor of the *Sanish Sentinel*, got in his black '46 Buick and took a drive down the valley to see for himself. "Earth-movers are at work excavating the powerhouse and a test diversion tunnel on the west side of the river," he told readers. "Visible from the dam site are the water tower, the powerhouse, and dwellings of the government-built town of Riverdale. White people in the valley are about to get a taste of what the Indian has been experiencing for the past hundred years." In other words, whites and Indians alike who lived in the flood area could protest the dam until they turned blue in the face, but they had better be doing it while they were packing their bags.

☿

In Washington, a storm of a different kind had suddenly blown up over the implementation of the Pick-Sloan Plan. Torrential rains in the spring of 1951 once again brought a "hundred-year flood" to Nebraska and Iowa. Seeing a golden opportunity in the Missouri's rising waters, the newly promoted General Pick had his picture taken on a stack of sandbags outside of Omaha and blamed this new wave of devastation on Congress' "needless foot-dragging" in funding the main stem flood-control dams. Pick's widely published accusations made legislators look like dunces. This time, the general had overplayed his hand. A newspaper editor in Kansas City wrote that Pick's "stampede tactics . . . made General MacArthur look like a small-time operator." Furious congressmen demanded a review of the general's conduct. Anxious to cooperate with the goose that laid the golden egg, the Corps' top brass publicly censured the general.

Pick's censure was immediately underscored in a long-awaited report on public works released by a high-profile commission headed by former president Herbert Hoover. Produced at the request of the Truman administration, the Hoover Commission study could not have been released at a more inopportune moment for the Corps and the bureau. Himself an engineer, Hoover appointed former Wyoming governor Leslie Miller to write the report on natural resources. After studying federal water projects for two years, Miller launched a broadside attack against both federal water agencies in the *Saturday Evening Post.* The bureau and the Corps were so violently jealous of each other, wrote Miller, that their "senseless competition" was leading America to the poorhouse. Both were guilty of "cockeyed" cost overruns in the billions of dollars, and the Pick-Sloan Plan, which was shaping up to be the most extravagant public works project in the nation's history, was "a conscienceless bit of political compromising. The Engineers will use navigation and flood control as a guise for a hydroelectric project, while the Reclamationists use irrigation as their alibi for hydroelectric development. . . . Do you want to pay a fifty-two-billion-dollar water bill?" asked the governor. "You may have to if someone doesn't stop the money-spending contest between the Army engineers and the Reclamation Bureau."

Although the Hoover report got the most attention in the national press,

Governor Miller's diatribes were not the Corps' biggest worry. Word had filtered through the legislative grapevine that the takings law passed by the previous Congress had serious problems. Somebody in committee had jumped the gun. The tribes' new attorney, James E. Curry, was asking thorny questions about the act's underlying legalities, and even the government's own attorneys at the Department of the Interior admitted that Congress had gone too far. The bill Congress wrote to resolve the Indian issues, once and for all, had created a raft of new ones.

An undeterred Senator Watkins reassured the Corps that any problems with the bill would be ironed out forthwith. Construction on the dam should proceed at full throttle. The massive excavation work was ahead of schedule. The Corps had started moving the homes of tribal members to higher ground, and a relocation team had set up shop in Elbowoods. Also, a crew from the Department of the Interior was on the scene and had started building new roads.

As a feat of engineering, Garrison Dam was an ambitious, impressive undertaking. Site selection for any dam was a tricky "science" at best. For a "rolled earth" structure such as Garrison, in which various kinds of soils would be built up in thick layers to form the main body of the dam, the stability of subsurface geology was a critical factor in site selection. At full capacity, the dam would have to be strong enough to hold back 24.5 million acre-feet of water, enough to form a lake hundreds of feet deep and hundreds of miles long. To engineers poring over the blueprints, the cross sections of the dam were breathtaking. What they were about to build here would be unlike any structure ever constructed by man and machine.

At a cost of $600 million, Garrison Dam was Lewis Pick's monument to American know-how. The crest of the completed dam would be four miles across, spanning the entire breadth of the Missouri River Valley. Half a mile wide at its base, the entire monolithic structure would sit on an impermeable, ten-foot-thick clay blanket that covered the lake bed for almost a mile upstream. From its base to its crown, the dam would be formed by layers of "rolled earth" that would measure 210 feet high. Set down in New York City, Garrison Dam would swallow twenty-story buildings on a continuous run from Washington Square to Central Park. Heavy equipment operators moved a million cubic yards of dirt every week for two years to stay on schedule. Nearly all of the 65 million cubic yards of earth and rock that were poured into the dam's massive breastworks were excavated from nearby bluffs and upstream bottomlands. The huge scars made by the steam shovels, bulldozers, and earth-movers would eventually be hidden beneath the lake's placid surface. Byron Sneva, the grandson of a Norwegian emigrant who settled in Fergus Falls, Minnesota, in 1879, had just graduated with a degree in civil engineering when the call came from the personnel office of the general contractor, Peter Kiewit Sons of Grand Island, Nebraska, to report for work at the dam. Now retired from a lifelong career as a civil engineer, he still marvels at the engineering challenges that were posed by the Garrison project.

"For a bunch of young engineers who were full of piss and vinegar, Garrison was a great experience," he says. "Most of us would never be involved in anything like it again. When I remember that site in my mind's eye, I'm awed by it."

Sneva spent two years at Garrison, but he did not see the finished dam until he revisited the site in the mid-1960s. A two-lane road ran along the crest of the dam. Sneva recalls his astonishment at his first sight of the lake as he drove across the dam.

"When I looked out over that stretch of water, all I could think about was the bitter cold days I spent four hundred feet beneath the surface of that lake at the outlet channel. What was in front of me was this enormous lake, but what I saw in my mind's eye was this huge expanse of dirt, with hundreds of huge pieces of earth-moving equipment. It was really strange."

Sneva worked on the west side of the dam, where he set the elevations for the diversion channels, huge culvertlike structures that would allow the dam's operators to control the release of water once the lake had filled. Similar channels, called the intake towers, were built on the upstream side of the dam. These were 20-foot-wide tunnels that would direct the river's flow through turbines to produce electricity. Both the intake tunnels and the diversion channels, or spillways, had to be built into the 210-foot-high pile of dirt.

"We used a massive dragline to carve out those channels. Those buckets scooped up three average-size dump-truck loads with every pass." When finished, the diversion channel spillway would be two thousand feet wide and hundreds of feet deep. The dump wagons hauling earth out of the cut through the bluffs never stopped moving. "It took a crew of five hundred men just to keep that equipment running. They made two bucks an hour, and from Monday morning till Saturday afternoon, there was always a line at the employment office in Riverdale."

Sneva's responsibility was to direct the excavations in the spillway cut and to calculate the volumes of earth that needed to be moved. Once he staked out the shape of the channels and the elevations for the cut, the big scoop shovels and bulldozers went to work. "Those dozer drivers were crazy. They'd bring those huge blades right up to the edge of the bluff, lower the blade, start the cut, and ride that avalanche all the way to the bottom, straight down, hundreds of feet, with their legs braced on the dashboard. The things they could do with those bulldozers, you had to see with your own eyes."

For men like Byron Sneva, work on Garrison seemed more like a race against time than a race against the river. In winter, high winds, blizzards, and subzero temperatures directed the pace of the work. Instead of bringing relief, summer brought its own catalog of miseries. By mid-June the humidity in the bottom of the cut approached 100 percent. Temperatures routinely soared past one hundred, and black clouds of mosquitos and gnats made life miserable. The only relief from the extremes came in autumn. Late September and October brought crisp nights, warm days, and brilliant blue skies. It was then that Sneva and his pals first headed for the floodplains along the river bottoms to hunt grouse and deer.

"Those river bottomlands were a different world. There was so much game in the fields and woodlands of the bottom that we never bought meat at the grocery store." It was on one of those October hunts, in the wooded bottomlands between the dam and the mouth of the Knife River, that Sneva first saw the Indian farms and villages. In his two years at the dam, he does not remember anyone ever discussing how The Flood might change the Indians' world.

"You didn't have to spend more than one winter there to know that nobody could survive that country on top. When I saw the lake for the first time, I was stunned. We destroyed hundreds of square miles of beautiful river bottomland. What a terrible thing. We gave them no choice."

⚜

The clouds of red dust streaking the sky above the town of Garrison in the autumn of 1951 put farmers in a state of giddy excitement. The dam taking shape beneath those streamers was an answer to their prayers, a long-awaited reward for hard work and sacrifice. Their bone-breaking, mind-numbing trials on the Upper Great Plains were about to come to an end. White-knuckled men behind plows had outlasted the demons of the natural world. God and Governor Aandahl had intervened. Surely, if not next year then the following, Pick-Sloan irrigation would turn their prairie into a garden of plenty.

For Martin Cross, the red sky above the sandstone bluffs east of Elbowoods spoke of something quite different. In a letter to Robert Yellowtail, the tribal chairman of the Crow tribe in eastern Montana, Martin predicted that what was being done to the Three Affiliated Tribes was only the beginning for tribes on the Missouri and elsewhere — a prediction that would prove prescient.

Martin Cross's intended hiatus from council work was short-lived. Judging from the stack of letters in his desk drawer, the stubs of train tickets, and the nonstop parade of tribal members through the Cross family living room, Martin was spending as much time on tribal business as he had when he was chairman. The intensifying crisis between Elbowoods and Washington suddenly mushroomed from a small taking on the Upper Missouri to a full-scale assault on treaty rights of the Yankton, Brule, Standing Rock, and Cheyenne River Sioux, and the Arapaho, Shoshone, Chippewa, Blackfeet, Crow, Cree, and Assiniboin. As Pick-Sloan's consequences for Indian Country became clear, tribes across the nation began following every turn of events on the Upper Missouri. The escalating conflict was transforming Martin Cross from a small-time Indian rancher into a national leader for Indian people.

Martin's friend and mentor, Robert Yellowtail, had been beating the drum for strong leadership in Indian Country since the release of the 1928 Merriam Report. A self-taught lawyer who passed the bar without the benefit of a formal education, the elder Yellowtail took Cross under his wing. As new elections approached for the Three Affiliated Tribes, he wrote Martin a personal letter in April 1953 from his home in Lodge Grass, Montana, and appealed to Cross's sense of duty: "Native Indian leadership is what the Indians need right now . . . when their political, constitutional, and treaty rights are being assaulted by white men. Get that, Martin, as your people look to you for intelligent and effective leadership."

Though he was off the council between 1947 and 1950, Martin made numerous trips to Washington for the tribe. These sojourns took him away for weeks at a time, leaving the care of the home and ranch to Dorothy and the older children. Increasingly, his work for the council competed with his responsibilities at home, a daunting conflict that left his loyalties hamstrung by quandary. In the end, the more visible and urgent needs of the tribes won out. Willy-nilly, the small-time rancher from Elbowoods had become one of the most recognized and respected Native leaders in the United States. At home, he was the most trusted leader the three tribes had known since they were led by his father. On any given evening, elders and clan leaders would start knocking on the Cross's front door right about dinnertime. Without fail, guests were offered a meal and a seat at the table, and it was not uncommon for them to linger in the front room into the wee hours of the morning, discussing politics and the dam. Then, first light often arrived accompanied by the sound of typewriter keys banging away in the living room at Martin's makeshift desk, which he set in front of the window beside the old cherry-wood radio. Cross wrote thousands of letters on that typewriter. A stickler for accuracy and standards of professionalism, he seldom let an official letter leave his desk with a typographical error or a misspelled word. In her final years of high school, his daughter Marilyn helped him proof hundreds of letters.

"I think he knew nothing would ever be simple again," reflects Marilyn. "By 1951, he was fighting to salvage a piece of his pride, and to live up to his father's name."

Martin won his early political victories by arguing that Indians could only succeed in the modern world by closing the economic gap that separated them from white men. His experience with Congress had revised his views. Now, in a letter distributed to all the tribes on the Missouri, he called for formation of a Missouri Valley Indian Defense Committee to "try and control the whims and fancies of the starry-eyed politicians . . . who think they are Davy Crocketts or Indian fighters who still think the Indian's rights are an impediment to the progress of the nation and should be wiped out." Better than anyone in Indian Country, Cross knew that their fight was not simply an isolated showdown over a single dam. The outcome of this battle would most likely have an adverse and lasting impact on tribes living beside every major river system in the western United States.

When Martin Cross returned to the council following the tribal elections in 1950, he was more convinced than ever that the takings act was unconstitutional. Their only way out now was to turn to the courts. The fundamental problems with P.L. 437 grew out of the very nexus of concerns that were first articulated by Felix Cohen in Senator O'Mahoney's committee six years before. While various drafts of the act bounced around in committees, Cohen's caveats were consistently ignored by a Republican-controlled Congress that was determined to abolish the Bureau of Indian Affairs. The deteriorating situation at the BIA left the Three Affiliated Tribes dangerously exposed to the whims of senators such as Arthur Watkins and his close ally from New Mexico, the tall, silver-haired, smooth-talking power broker Clinton Anderson. Underscoring those threats were the widely reported remarks of President Truman's new commissioner of Indian affairs, Dillon Myer, who told the *New York Times* that his primary objectives were to "end the federal trust relationship with the tribes" and to work himself out of a job.

Lawmakers like Watkins and Anderson could hardly contain their glee. They now had an ideological cohort at the Bureau of Indian Affairs, and they intended to help him accomplish his goals as swiftly as possible. With a little cooperation from fellow lawmakers, the decommissioning of tribal governments could begin within the next two years. Every field office of the BIA was instructed to draw up plans for turning its agency over to state governments. Robert Yellowtail and Martin Cross wrote an open letter to tribal leaders charging that white politicians viewed "Indians with their tax-free land holdings as a thorn in the flesh of the states." This long-festering resentment had been aggravated by white politicians who allowed that the general public was "to forget that the United States practically stole everything, including the lands of the Indians from coast to coast."

Without mentioning the new commissioner by name, Felix Cohen and former secretary of the interior Harold Ickes joined forces to publicly lament what they called "the banality of evil" on Capitol Hill. Cohen told the *Washington Post* that Dillon Myer's appointment to the BIA gave Congress and the agency license "to disregard past promises, and to repeat past mistakes, without awareness of either." Soon, citizens of Indian Country would lose their greatest advocate in modern times.

Just months after Harold Ickes passed away from old age in 1952, Felix Cohen succumbed to lung cancer at the age of forty-six. In his brief life, he had done more to protect the sanctity and civil rights of tribal cultures than any other jurist since John Marshall. In the foreword to the first edition of his compendium on federal Indian law, Cohen summarized the focal point of his philosophy with great brevity: "The American Indian is the miner's canary of our society." His old friend John Collier, the former commissioner of Indian affairs under Franklin Roosevelt, spoke for Indian Country when he eulogized Cohen's passing: "Felix's death has shattered me as no death since my mother's and father's. . . . The agony is on account of all the Indians, but it is more. Felix was my highest experience of the power of thought united with disinterested power of action."

As things went from bad to worse in Washington, the council's festering doubts about their attorney, Ralph Case, came to the fore. Some suspected that Case had been co-opted early on by the Pick-Sloan people. He never seemed to grasp the tribes' attachment to their homelands. In Case's mind everything had a price tag, including their land. Shortly after Martin Cross returned to the council in 1950, the tribes canceled their contract. The only hope for the future was to find someone now who could think like an Indian. Felix Cohen had once urged Cross to contact Cohen's good friend and law school contemporary, James Curry. Curry had helped Cohen and former BIA director John Collier to establish their tribal governments under the Indian Reorganization Act of 1934. The tall, bespectacled Indian law expert had emerged in recent years as a fearless and formidable advocate for Indian rights. Working with numerous western tribes, Curry had become as familiar with the arcane ins and outs of federal Indian law as any private solicitor in America. Cross now moved quickly to retain Curry's services. But unbeknownst to either man, Curry was a man with a price on his head. He was already in the crosshairs of the new commissioner at the Bureau of Indian Affairs, Dillon Myer.

※

Dillon Myer's new strategy for isolating the tribes and minimizing the effects of "hired guns" such as Cohen and Curry was to take control of the tribes' source of funds. In 1951 Myer began notifying tribes that money for private counsel would no longer be made available. Felix Cohen had incensed the new commissioner by offering his services pro bono to the Blackfeet in Montana. In an interview with the *New York Times* in November 1951, Myer explained that taxpayers' dollars were being wasted on private attorneys when government attorneys could better perform the task. To Myer's great dismay, the public's outcry was so shrill following the publication of these stories that President Truman's new secretary of the interior, Oscar Chapman, responded to Myer's remarks by calling for public hearings.

Chapman's predecessor, Harold Ickes, had once reminded him that the top post at Interior came with both a legal and moral obligation to prevent people such as Dillon Myer and Arthur Watkins "from stomping on Indians." While obligations to Indian Country were viewed as an annoyance by Washington bureaucrats, no love was lost between Chapman and Myer. When Chapman scheduled hearings over Myer's protests, the commissioner's detractors, including Senator O'Mahoney and Ickes, pressured President Truman to sack Myer before he could cause any more embarrassment. Ickes regretted not ending the commissioner's career himself, when Myer was his subordinate at the Department of the Interior. For Ickes, Myer's career with the Japanese internment camps, and now with the Indians, represented the darkest side of American racism. In an interview with the *New York Times,* Ickes described Myer as a "blundering and dictatorial tin-Hitler."

Myer shrugged off his critics and pressed forward with his objectives. Senators Watkins and Anderson rallied to his defense with the president, but they were powerless to stop Chapman's hearings, which opened on January 4, 1952,

Karl Bodmer's famous 1834 etching of Mih-Tutta-Hang-Kusch,
a Mandan Village near Fort Clark on the Upper Missouri River.
(Courtesy of the Three Tribes Museum)

Chief Old Dog, second from left, with members of the Fox society,
circa 1890s. *(Courtesy of the Cross family)*

Martin as a boy, with his sisters (LEFT TO RIGHT) Virginia, Alice, and Lucy. *(Courtesy of the Cross family)*

LEFT: Chief Old Dog, photographed by Edward Curtis in the autumn of 1909. *(Courtesy of the Three Tribes Museum)* RIGHT: Elbowoods rodeo dandies, circa 1925. *(Courtesy of the Three Tribes Museum)*

A snapshot from the home front during the difficult war years.
LEFT TO RIGHT: (BACK) Alfred (Bucky), Phyllis holding Michael, Marilyn,
and Martin Jr. (Crusoe); (FRONT) Dorothy (Uppy) and Forrest.
(Courtesy of the Cross family)

ABOVE: The only known photograph
of Martin and Dorothy, taken
shortly after they were married.
(Courtesy of the Cross family)

RIGHT: As a young rodeo cowboy,
Martin Cross was both a roper
and a bronc rider.
(Courtesy of the Cross family)

Thomas Spotted Wolf challenges General Lewis Pick at the 1946 hearing in Elbowoods. *(Courtesy of the Three Tribes Museum)*

Garrison Dam's massive powerful tunnels under construction.
(ND Archives, Bismarck)

As flashbulbs pop to record the formal signing of the takings act
of 1949, tribal chairman George Gillette chokes back his emotions as
Secretary of the Interior Julius Krug signs the bill that would flood
the ancestral home of the Mandan, Hidatsa, and Arikara people.
(AP/Worldwide Photos)

A rare gathering of the Cross kids on the front porch of their childhood home. LEFT TO RIGHT: Phyllis, Martin Jr. (Crusoe), Dorothy (mother, behind), Marilyn, Dorothy (Uppy), Michael, Milton, Carol, and Raymond. *(Courtesy of the Cross family)*

As tribal chairman of the Three Affiliated Tribes and the first vice president of the National Congress of American Indians, Martin Cross became one of the first Indian leaders of the modern era to use the law and the U.S. Constitution to fight his tribe's battles in the U.S. Congress. *(J. W. Schmidt)*

The Cross brothers. LEFT TO RIGHT: Martin Jr. (Crusoe), Alfred (Bucky), Raymond, and Michael at a gathering in Parshall after cousin Richard's funeral. *(Courtesy of the Cross family)*

The massive gates at the spillway of the Garrison Dam hold back more than 20 million acre-feet of water, nearly twice the annual flow of the Colorado River. *(Paul VanDevelder)*

North Dakota Supreme Court chief justice Ralph Erickstad, the man who found himself trapped between Chief Justice John Marshall's "federal trust doctrine" and the U.S. Congress' "unlawful exercise of its plenary power." *(Paul VanDevelder)*

The Cross children, forty years after The Flood.
LEFT TO RIGHT: (BACK) Phyllis, Marilyn, Dorothy (Uppy), and Carol;
(FRONT) Michael, Alfred (Bucky), Raymond, and Martin Jr. (Crusoe).
(Courtesy of the Cross family)

to heavy media coverage. The *New York Times'* opening story carried the headline: INDIAN WAR WHOOP MARKS HEARINGS. The *whoop,* it turned out, was made by Popovi Da, the former governor of the San Ildefonso Pueblo tribe. Popovi Da, an engineer who worked on the atomic bomb at Los Alamos, put a question to the panel that no one seemed ready to answer. "If the government trusted me with its most sensitive wartime secrets, why would it now not trust me to hire a lawyer of my own choosing?"

Thomas Main, a tribal chief of the Gros Ventre tribe from Fort Belknap in central Montana, followed Da with an assault on Myer's policies. "We Indians in Montana thought we were making real progress towards freedom until a couple of years ago. Then something happened . . . and during the last couple of years that attitude of paternalism, treating us like prisoners in a concentration camp, has become the attitude of the Indian bureau."

Myer rose from his seat and stormed out of the hearing, refusing to return. The hearings went on without him for several more days, but despite a tidal wave of negative press, the commissioner weathered the storm by falling in behind an impregnable wall of western congressmen who fully supported his policies. When Chapman's hearings ended, Myer redoubled his efforts against what he called the "wily Indians and their champertous attorneys" and issued a blanket policy that prohibited the tribes from hiring their own attorneys. In a note to Watkins, Myer justified his policy on the grounds that he was simply performing his "statutory duty." As far as Watkins was concerned, Chapman could hold hearings until hell froze over. Myer's new policy was the final word.

Ideologically, Watkins and Myer were as close as Siamese twins. A third-generation corn farmer, Myer was born in Licking County, Ohio, in 1891. His paternal grandfather turned virgin sod when Licking County "abounded in snakes, wolves, and Indians." Methodism and self-reliance, honesty and thrift were the core values that forged the young Myer and his views of the world. As a grown man, Myer never doubted that he knew what was best for the Japanese, and later, for the Indians. Consequently, every victory by Curry or Cohen was seen by Myer and his allies as a challenge to the government of the righteous. The commissioner had no intention of allowing attorneys in his bureau to argue tribal claims in federal courts.

Ignoring Myer's new policy, the Three Affiliated Tribes' new counsel made one reading of P.L. 437 and demanded new hearings on Capitol Hill. In a twist on the legal paradox first illuminated by Felix Cohen's memorandum to Senator O'Mahoney's committee six years earlier, Curry realized that the "settlement" in the takings bill was a fiction masquerading as law. The government had neither paid the tribes for their trust lands nor compensated them for violation of their treaty rights. Instead of resolving its constitutional dilemma, Congress' P.L. 437 had put the solution to both of these paradoxes out of reach. The trust lands had been taken in violation of constitutional guarantees, and private lands had been taken without "making the citizens whole," or paying them fair market value for their land, as required by the Fifth Amendment.

At Curry's urging, the Tribal Council filed a new claim with the Indian Claims Commission in May 1954, seeking compensation for the illegal executive orders of presidents Grant and Harrison, which reduced the tribes' land holdings by 6 million acres in the 1880s. The orders were made on behalf of homesteaders and railroads. Regardless of the rationale, the U.S. Supreme Court had since ruled that presidents were prohibited from changing a treaty without the approval of Congress. The picture in Curry's mind was beginning to clear: P.L. 437 was simply a new violation to be added to a long list of actionable grievances. Unless this cycle could be broken, the pattern would go on repeating itself until there was nothing left in Indian Country.

As the eviction of the Mandan, Hidatsa, and Arikara people from the bottomlands began accelerating in 1952, the eastern press started picking up the story. Reporters such as Ruth Mulvey Harmer of *The Atlantic Monthly* were beginning to ask embarrassing questions by linking various committee chairmen in Congress to policy decisions being issued by Dillon Myer. She also pointed out that the timing of Myer's nationwide "removal policy" happened to coincide with the eviction of the Mandan, Hidatsa, and Arikara people from their ancestral homelands. The Department of the Interior's own inhouse sociologist, Gordon Macgregor, reported to Congress that the people and the land on the Upper Missouri River "form an inseparable unit. These Indians were never assigned this land, or forced to reside on it as prisoners of war. This was the land of their ancestors, where they farmed and hunted long before the coming of the white man."

Sympathetic accounts of the plight of the Three Affiliated Tribes suddenly began appearing under bold headlines in newspapers around the country, including the *New York Times*, the *Minneapolis Star Tribune*, and the *Chicago Tribune*. In her fearless attack on Myer and Congress, Harmer concluded that while "termination" and "removal" were both immoral and unconstitutional, they paled in comparison to what was happening on the Upper Missouri, where actions by the federal government had resulted in "one of the most extraordinary forced migrations in history." Echoing Curry's opinion, Harmer and others asserted that Congress' passage of the takings act in 1949 had shredded the tribes' constitutional guarantees.

John Marshall had tried to keep the Indians' aboriginal title intact by incorporating Indian lands under the umbrella of federal trust doctrine. In practice, the trust doctrine created what legal experts called "high spots," or pressure points, that had the unintended consequence of eroding stable and consistent policies between the tribes and their federal trustees. Commonly, these high spots were felt in conflicts that triangulated the competing interests of the federal government, their Indian wards, and the states.

Marshall's difficulties arose from the fact that the federal government recognized tribes as independent nations. Legally, this made it possible for the tribes to bargain away their land. Marshall recognized that conflicts would inevitably arise between the moral conscience of the courts and the political expediency of lawmakers. In the end, Marshall crafted his solution out of federalism itself by putting the federal government and the tribes in a legally binding partnership. This still left Congress and the courts with the practical problem of guaranteeing the tribes that American society would expand across the North American continent in an orderly fashion. Inevitably, as disorderly expansion became the norm, the conflict of interest embedded in federalism gradually eclipsed the rights of the tribes. For a time in the late-nineteenth and early-twentieth centuries, Congress was able to finesse the inconvenient obligations of its partnership with the tribes. But once later courts made Marshall's legal alignments more visible through controversial decisions that consistently favored the tribes and reminded the federal government of its binding obligations, state governments quickly learned to regard the Indians with jealous hostility and to view the tribes' partner, the federal government, as a heavy-handed interloper.

Marshall had hoped that the Trilogy would encourage the best of human nature to prevail until the Indians were assimilated into white society. Yet by 1952, assimilation of the two cultures was no closer to a reality than it was a century before. The Three Affiliated Tribes' new attorney, James Curry, regarded P.L. 437 as proof that Marshall's dim view of the common man had been well informed. The takings act of 1949 was a poignant reminder of Cherokee philosopher John Ross's disarming insight: "The perpetrator of a wrong never forgives his victims."

In a letter to Chairman Cross in February 1952, Curry argued that P.L. 437 needed to be scrapped and rewritten from the beginning. With the construction of the dam proceeding at a furious pace, both men knew the odds of that happening were next to zero. With the help of Senator O'Mahoney, Curry instead demanded that Congress address the biggest problems in the act with new amendments. Senator O'Mahoney agreed and guided two new bills through the Senate which sought to restore rights and privileges that had mysteriously disappeared in Senator Watkins's committee. Hearings on O'Mahoney's amendments were scheduled for the first week of April 1952. Commissioner Myer would be present, and Senator Clinton Anderson would preside. Anderson was a fierce champion of banking, mining, and timber interests, and regarded the Indians as a legal nuisance and a blight of barnacles on the ship of state. As the new chairman of the powerful Interior and Insular Affairs Committee, the senator from New Mexico made it his personal mission to convert Indian Country's "communal holdings into individual ownership by siphoning off tribespeople into the mainstream."

While Senator Anderson was taking center stage, in the wings Watkins and Myer were carefully coordinating their respective policies to converge on Indian Country simultaneously. All the fuss over Pick-Sloan, the Hoover Commission report, and the takings act would vanish like so much political vapor as soon as termination kicked into high gear. Congressman Beck's original termination bill had been spiked in committee in 1949, but by 1952, Beck's offspring had looped back under a different name and with renewed vigor. Republicans now controlled congressional committees, and the protermination forces were taking no chances with freshman legislators. Beck's newly resurrected bill was now sponsored by Watkins himself. Known as Public Law 280, this far-reaching law would formally open the door to the larger, carefully choreographed termination movement by initiating the transfer of jurisdiction over Indian Country from the federal government to the states. This time the bill would be attended by anxious midwives on Capitol Hill, in the Bureau of Indian Affairs, and in the Department of the Interior. In a confidential letter from the assistant secretary of the interior, Orme Lewis, Senator Watkins was assured that Interior wanted to get out of the Indian business once and for all. "Federal responsibility for administering the affairs of individual Indian tribes should be terminated as rapidly as the circumstances of each tribe will permit."

Dillon Myer, meanwhile, had identified the first sixty tribes that would disappear in the initial wave of termination. The Three Affiliated Tribes were at the top of the list, along with the Menominee of Wisconsin and the Klamath tribe of southern Oregon. Leaders such as Martin Cross and Robert

Yellowtail would learn of this at the same time as department bureaucrats. Someone inside the agency leaked a secret letter sent by Myer to all of his area directors. This epistle, dated August 5, 1952, outlined the government's new strategy for bringing about the termination of federal trust. A clandestine carbon copy of the letter was slipped through the mail slot at 1345 Connecticut Avenue N.W. in Washington, D.C., where it landed on the desk of N. B. Johnson, the new president of the National Congress of American Indians.

Johnson immediately alerted the NCAI membership to the government's plan. Myer and Watkins had concocted a multipronged strategy that was designed to immediately implement the fifteen new termination bills moving through Congress. Myer was seeking to "dispose of tribal lands, tribal funds, tribal water rights, irrigation systems, or other tribal property at his own discretion, without tribal consent." The commissioner had quietly petitioned Congress for the blanket authority to terminate trusteeship of land, to remove tax-exempt status from Indian Country, and to veto any tribal expenditure of funds. Most egregious of all in Johnson's view was Myer's request that Congress exempt the BIA "from review or correction in any court in all the foregoing activities." In other words, the commissioner was asking his friends in Congress to put his agency above the law.

None of the news in Johnson's bulletin caught Martin Cross by surprise. Yet as Myer's motives became better known to an unsuspecting public, Cross saw an opportunity for a counteroffensive and sent a carefully worded declaration to newspapers around the country by Western Union telegraph: "The Government of the United States first dealt with our tribal governments as sovereign equals," he reminded white audiences. "We have never asked anything except that this protection be continued and these benefits be provided as agreed, in good faith. . . . These proposals, if adopted, will tend to destroy our tribal governments. From our point of view, if these laws are passed, they will be a new monument to the white man's persistent efforts to force native people of this continent to vanish or become like himself."

At the end of World War II, Myer "reintroduced" more than 100,000 Japanese internees into mainstream society by loading them onto buses and dropping them off in urban centers. Ethnic slums blossomed overnight in a dozen western cities. Nevertheless, Myer's plan was hailed in Washington as a great success. Now, the commissioner proposed to do the same thing with Indians. This new policy, called "relocation," was officially unveiled at the end of 1951. Its objective, explained Myer, was "to liberate the Indian into mainstream society." With relocation successfully launched to coincide with Congress' termination legislation, the long-awaited end to the nation's ongoing Indian problem now seemed within reach.

At the same time Myer was launching his relocation campaign, he submitted a new bill to Congress — "A Bill to Authorize the Indian Bureau to Make Arrests Without Warrant for Violation of Indian Bureau Regulations" — that would empower the agency director to act as judge and jury over Indians suspected of committing crimes. If the bill was approved, the director would also wield the authority to deny Indians independent access to legal representation. For example, if Martin Cross got into a fight with a fellow tribe member over damages incurred by an errant cow, this new law would give Dillon Myer the right to decide the chairman's fate. The stealthlike fashion in which this bill was introduced when the McCarthy hearings were distracting the national media suggests that Myer and his partners in Congress were advancing their agenda with great confidence. Yet Myer's newest initiative was so bold that even the white media lifted its eyebrows. "Could it be that those who propose such legislation still think of Indians as savages without rights?" asked the *Great Falls Tribune.* This was echoed in the *Houston Post* with, "The Indian bureau is asking for gestapo power. . . . This is one bill Congress would do well to file and forget pronto."

Meanwhile, as these new initiatives were being debated in the press, a diplomat at the United Nations in New York City named Raphael Lemkin joined the root of the Greek word *genos,* or race, to the Latin suffix *cide,* to kill, and coined the word *genocide.* Still in shock over the horrific atrocities committed in World War II, the United Nations General Assembly convened the first international conference on genocide in 1950, a decision which ultimately led to the passage of a formal resolution that recognized genocide as a "crime against humanity." *Genocide,* said the congress of nations, was the act of denying people the right of existence, in whole or in part, by undermining the foundations underlying their national or ethnic identity, with the aim of destroying that group. Virtually every member nation of the UN endorsed the sweeping new addition to the formal body of international law.

As details about termination began leaking onto the pages of eastern newspapers, former Indian commissioner Collier openly charged Commissioner Myer and members of Congress with committing acts of genocide against the Indian people of North America. Termination, said Collier, was nothing more than a sanitized euphemism for genocide. Under Collier's own watch, the BIA sought to end the "forced atomization, cultural prescription, and administrative absolutism" over the tribes that had characterized a century of abuse. The Roosevelt administration had reshaped federal Indian policy to recognize the importance of tribal culture, native languages, customs, and religious ceremonies. Collier asked, "How could so much have changed in ten short years?"

Given the feverish loyalty mania of the early 1950s, an atmosphere in which every liberal was viewed as a quasi communist, Myer easily deflected Collier's accusation as left-wing hysteria. In his own defense, he pointed to the fact that the United States had abstained from joining the United Nations' resolution on genocide. As these charges and countercharges passed one another in the nation's newspapers, Martin Cross and Councilman Ben Youngbird boarded the train in Minot for another three-day trip to Washington.

ᴗᴇ

Before the gavel opened the hearings in April 1952 on a new slate of amendments to P.L. 437, Senator Anderson knew what to expect from the Three Affiliated Tribes' attorney. Curry and Anderson had locked horns on previous occasions. In the days leading up to the hearings, Curry told the press that he was after big game, both literally and figuratively. He wanted the historic rights of the Three Affiliated Tribes to "hunt, gather, and fish," and their mineral rights, restored immediately. Also, in Curry's opinion, the $12.5 million Congress approved for the tribes was an insult. This sum did not begin to address the Fifth Amendment issues swamping this case. If lawmakers missed this opportunity to correct their errors, they would only be inviting a constitutional crisis. Clocks were ticking. Construction was moving swiftly, the power tunnels were being cut for the hydroelectric turbines, yet not one Indian holding a title to land had seen the first dime of compensation. Curry was not shy when it came to laying his cards on the table. Congress' Fifth Amendment obligations to landowners were not negotiable. As things stood, P.L. 437 was a criminal breach of the tribes' constitutional guarantees, not to mention their treaty rights. Either Congress would clean up the mess or the tribes would take their case to the courts.

The first questions put to Curry made it clear that many of the committee members were confounded by the array of issues before them. Senator Morris wanted to know how, and why, the guarantees had been stripped in the first place.

"Frankly, sir, we'd like to have an answer to that ourselves, but we're not holding our breaths," said Curry, glancing at Senator Anderson.

"You're telling us that the original bill that came to this committee provided for restoration of mineral rights?"

"Yes, sir. If you have any doubts about that, I urge you to discuss it with Congressman Lemke."

"And we provided for harbor rights on the lake?"

"Exactly," agreed Curry.

"And fishing rights?"

"Yes, fishing and hunting rights were intact. We are asking for nothing that your committee did not give us in the original bill, which stated, if I might . . ."

"Please."

"To paraphrase, the contract that the Corps made with the Indians permitted them to continue making use of the waters behind the dam. Congress cannot meet its obligation to make these Indians whole unless these rights and guarantees are restored."

Sensing a reversal in sympathies in favor of the tribes, Anderson jumped in with bristling indignation.

"This was all resolved in the last Congress to the satisfaction of the Indians!"

"Not the Indians I represent," shot Curry.

"Mr. Curry, I remember distinctly, Senator Kerr came back from conference and declared it was all settled. In fact, his very words were, 'Well, that should take care of the Indians once and for all.' Does anybody else remember that?"

"That's what he said," agreed Senator Langer.

"So, I don't understand why we're back here."

"I thought we'd made that clear, Senator. The Indians never agreed that they would give up these rights. When they objected, they were told by Senator O'Mahoney, in writing, that they could reclaim them after the bill was passed. That's what we're doing."

"Did he really say that?" asked Senator Ecton.

"Yes, he did, Senator," said Chairman Cross. "We have it in writing. If I may, Senator . . ."

"Please, Mr. Cross, go right ahead."

"Aside from restoring our mineral rights, and providing irrigation and electricity, which was promised to us when we negotiated this contract way back when . . . for some reason, the final draft of the bill forbids us to use our money to hire attorneys or agents to represent us. It seems to me that the Indian should be as entitled to legal counsel of his own choice as a white man . . ."

Dillon Myer immediately rose in defense of Indian bureau policy. His brow furrowed, but his gray-green eyes were unblinking behind the steel-rimmed spectacles. "We do not believe it is essential, or in the tribes' best interest, to use this money for attorneys, since there are other moneys available for paying attorney's fees. We're simply trying to do our duty by protecting the interests of the tribe. We do not agree with your reading of this, Mr. Curry."

"The act, as it is written, forbids the Indians to use these funds to hire attorneys to represent them. Surely you don't intend to leave that in there."

"I don't think that it would be wise to revisit this," offered Myer. "We're quite happy with it the way it is."

Myer was playing his cards from strength to weakness. He knew he had enough friends in Congress to make his policy stick. Following the hearing, as the Three Affiliated Tribes' petition languished in committee, Myer sent a telegram to Chairman Cross ordering him to make a final payment to James Curry for services already rendered. Once made, Cross was ordered to formally sever the tribes' relationship with Curry. Reading and rereading the telegram, Cross and the council concluded that the commissioner left them no choice. Curry agreed to let the tribe out of its contract, provided the council could pay him the balance owed. He assured Cross that he would always be available pro bono if the tribe needed help in Washington.

Despite Cross's reputation as a visionary leader of his people, every time he went to Washington, his troubles back home grew increasingly dire. By the time Martin Cross's oldest son, Crusoe, turned eighteen, the young man knew in his bones what no one in the family was willing to say out loud at the evening dinner table. Martin Cross was wearing out the railroad tracks to Washington, D.C., but the only thing he ever brought home was more bad news, more disappointments, more frequent and long-lasting bouts with alcohol. As he watched his father's decline, Crusoe began to suspect that Dorothy and Martin's marriage had entered its final act. By the time he graduated from high school in 1951, all that remained to play out now, in the final days of Elbowoods, were the ugly details of their own personal endgame.

"It didn't help their marriage that Dad was in Washington almost every spare minute," remembers Marilyn. "By then, things had gotten to the point where I think Mom and the older boys felt it was a relief when he was gone."

The sooner their mother got out of Elbowoods, the better off she would be. For ten years she had worked eighteen hours a day, keeping hearth and home intact. Without the simple conveniences of running water, electricity, a phone, or refrigeration, she was feeding and clothing nine children, her husband and his friends, and a small army of in-laws. From Crusoe's vantage point, Dorothy's tireless sacrifices had only earned her endless fights with her husband and ever-deepening isolation from the Indians in her midst.

"In the last years we were in Elbowoods, from 1950 until 1953, nobody talked in that house," says Bucky. "We were prisoners of our own thoughts. That was the way people dealt with their *angst* back then."

"My Dad and I were mortal enemies throughout my high school years," says Crusoe. "I just wanted to escape."

Two weeks after he graduated from high school, Crusoe got his chance. On a beautiful June morning, his friend Russell Gillette pulled up behind the house and yelled out his car window. "Hey, Crusoe, I'm off to join the Air Force. You want to come?"

After his father wrote him a check for twenty dollars, he gave his mother a kiss good-bye and walked out the kitchen door. "That was the last time I saw Elbowoods. We drove out State Road Number Eight, hung a right at Garrison, and drove nonstop to Fargo. I had the clothes on my back. That was it. The recruiters bought us a meal and put us on the bus to Lackland Air Force Base for basic training. The next time I walked into that house, four years later, it was in Parshall. It sure was strange. Same door, different town. I'd come home, but I was completely lost.

"Elbowoods was a beautiful little village," says Crusoe. "All the people in the outlying communities came into town once a month. They gathered on the big main square, beneath the monument to the chiefs who went to the Treaty of Horse Creek. The women would sit on the porch of the agency with their shawls pulled around their shoulders and talk for hours. The men would sit in circles on the ground and smoke and talk and tell stories, and they had a different, tobacco smell that was very strong in young nostrils. You knew everybody in the world by their first name, what clan they belonged to, who their ancestors were, which societies they belonged to, who had the medicine bundles. My grandfather was a Water Buster and a member of the Fox society. Our grandmother's family had been in the Prairie Chicken clan, long before Cherry Necklace took Sakakawea as his sister. It's difficult for outsiders to understand the complexity of these relationships, how they formed us. The clans, all the religious rites and ceremonies and rituals of passage, developed over many centuries. You learned these things as a kid, the way you learned language, how to track a fox, or plant a hill of beans. There was nothing easy about that life. It was tough, but we laughed and we sang and we never stopped dancing. When people say 'Elbowoods,' they're not remembering the actual place as much as a state of being and spiritual peace. When you mention Elbowoods to the old people, they turn their heads away. They go off by themselves and weep."

Many elders told the Tribal Council that no force on earth could make them abandon their homes. Some vowed they would rather drown than be exiled to the world "on top." As dignitaries converged on North Dakota for the official dedication of the dam on June 11, 1953, the owner of the dry-goods store in Elbowoods, Hal Simon, was found dead in his home behind the store. Leaving a young wife and a six-year-old daughter behind, Simon had taken his own life, said his note, because he could not face losing the world they had built in Elbowoods. The mute testimony of their bitter despair would not be recorded in committee meetings on Capitol Hill but would continue to appear on the obituary pages of small-town local newspapers for years to come.

By the late summer of 1954, the Missouri River was rising rapidly. Day by day, the floodplains and gooseberry woods around Elbowoods disappeared beneath the Missouri's turbid waters. Many residents began to realize that they had waited too long to make their preparations for the move. Every Sunday morning for the past year, Reverend Case and Father Reinhart led their congregations in Elbowoods in singing "Plant Your Feet on Higher Ground," yet when The Flood finally came, the evacuation came off as a mad scramble. Many homes were left intact, still sitting on their foundations. In the final dash to high ground, someone realized that all the school's athletic trophies had been left behind in the trophy case at the high school. Armed with flashlights, a group of former basketball players assembled a small flotilla of rowboats, returned to Elbowoods on a moonlit night, and rowed down the school's main corridor to the trophy case. The Elbowoods Warriors trophies were the last things to be rescued from the green depths of Lake Sakakawea. As the boatmen swung their sterns toward the drowning village, clouds scuttled across the face of the moon in a rising wind. The boats raced for shore, battling to stay one stroke ahead of the gathering storm. Familiar voices greeted them at lake's edge. Flashlights crisscrossed in the leafless treetops and swirling flurries of snow. For the first time in nine hundred years, the winter moon would not rise on Mandan Villages in the gooseberry woods of the Missouri River Valley.

"When it's fifty below in February, the sheet of ice on the river can get to be a couple of feet thick," says Crusoe. "People think it fractures and breaks apart in the spring, piece by piece, but that's not what happens. As snow starts melting upstream, the flow of water beneath the ice builds up pressure. In a sudden thaw, that pressure builds so quickly that the entire ice sheet explodes. You can hear it miles away, like a sonic boom, disintegrating into ten zillion pieces. That's exactly what happened to us when The Flood came to El-bowoods."

※

Unwilling to entrust her own future to whims of chance, Dorothy Cross filed for divorce from Martin, then arranged for a crew of Army engineers to move Old Dog's house to one of several lots the tribe had purchased in Par-shall. The divorce went through in early 1954, but establishing a new resi-dence "on top" soon proved to be more difficult than ending her twenty-six-year marriage. Along with hundreds of other exiles from Elbowoods, Dorothy ar-rived in Parshall with two suitcases full of her belongings, a young child un-der each arm, and her son Milton, a mentally retarded teenager. The two oldest kids had enlisted in the Air Force. Uppy was finishing high school with a family in Garrison, and Marilyn was off to college in Minot. Bucky was do-ing odd jobs for the Corps, and Michael was floating back and forth between Martin's ranch and school in Parshall.

"When we first got to Parshall, we lived in some abandoned shacks that were moved to town at the last minute," says Raymond. "They weren't much more than chicken coops, really. For awhile there, we moved from shack to shack. The seminomadic life can get pretty chaotic. Mom didn't have the repertoire of skills to deal with everything that was happening. My earliest memories are of being completely alone in one of those shacks."

Eventually, Old Dog's house arrived in Parshall and was settled on its new foundation on East Second Street. The back door, which once looked out across sixty miles of bottomland and empty prairie to the lights of Minot, was now two blocks from the Grand movie theater, the bowling alley, and the American Legion Hall on Main Street. Plumbing and electricity were in-stalled, so for the first time in her adult life, Dorothy Cross would have an in-door bathroom, hot and cold running water in the kitchen, and electric lights. Her semi-estranged husband, however, was unwilling to give up life on the range for the relative luxury of town. Martin built a new ranch on Old Dog's allotment, twenty miles south of Parshall. He excavated a half basement from the hard scrabble, drilled a well, poured a concrete foundation, and turned the solid-frame structure of the Tribal Council offices he'd moved from government square in Elbowoods into his new ranch house. After living in Elbowoods all his life, his nearest neighbor at the ranch would be two miles away.

Martin Cross had probably been the first to realize that the battle to stop the dam was lost. A decade of fighting the power brokers on their own turf, in Washington, had hardened Chief Old Dog's son into a political realist. Now, as he sat between President Eisenhower and General Lewis Pick on the reviewing stand at the dedication ceremony for Garrison Dam, he knew that a larger war, to save the Three Affiliated Tribes from oblivion, had begun in earnest.

CHAPTER VII

Hitting Bottom On Top

"I have met a white man. He was fair to behold, very pleasant, very genial personality. He appealed to me as a high-type man. . . . I tell you, my people, the white man is your friend. Protect him, furnish him food, furnish him shelter, because he is our friend."

BLACK CAT, MANDAN

As the village of Elbowoods disappeared beneath the whitecaps on Lake Sakakawea in September 1954, legislation designed to terminate federal wardship over American Indian tribes was quietly moving through a dozen committees in Congress. Thus far, no one in Washington had raised a single objection to this menacing raft of laws. Since the deaths of Felix Cohen and Harold Ickes, and the exile of former Indian commissioner John Collier, it seemed that the tribes' few remaining allies in Washington had been thoroughly demoralized, or neutralized, or effectively run out of town. It was a new day in Washington, one the protermination forces were determined to translate quickly into a new day for Indian Country. The point of their spear was Public Law 280, the federal statute originally sponsored by Senator Arthur Watkins that initiated the transfer of jurisdiction over Indian tribes from the federal government to the states. While this law appeared innocuous enough to the general public, its "real-world" effect would be to summarily sweep aside all binding contracts between Congress and the Indians, and to declare null and void all constitutionally protected agreements, such as the Treaty of Horse Creek.

By 1954 state legislatures in New Mexico, Arizona, and Montana were using P.L. 280 to begin assuming jurisdiction over the tribes within their borders.

North Dakota's legislature was the latest to approve the measure, but many of the state's legislators were fish out of water when it came to the more exotic legislation being handed down by Washington. More familiar with farm futures and agricultural price supports than federal Indian law, North Dakota's lawmakers were uncertain as to how this new law was going to affect the state's relationship with the nine sovereign Indian nations residing within its borders. Just how these new civil and criminal jurisdiction laws were going to interact with federal law, not to mention state statutes, was anybody's guess. Since there was no road map out of this thicket, North Dakota's governor, C. Norman Brunsdale, decided that the new director for the Legislative Research Committee should be an adventuresome sort, a lawyer who was simultaneously fearless and creative. For the right person, this would be an exciting opportunity to camp out on the leading edge of untested legislative reforms.

When the governor put out the word, the name Emerson C. Murry turned up on two lists as the top choice. The first endorsement came from the dean of the University of North Dakota law school; the second, from the sitting chief justice of the North Dakota Supreme Court. Both described Murry as an energetic and highly competent young professional. While his résumé might have suggested that Murry was a little green for a post with such high visibility and political sway, both men assured Brunsdale that the young attorney from Rugby would be an excellent appointment. He was not your average thirty-year-old wheat farmer with a law degree. Murry had enlisted in the Army on December 6, 1941. As a paratrooper with the 17th Airborne, 82nd Infantry, he had seen combat across Europe, from Belgium and Luxembourg to the Ardennes and the Rhine. In the years right after the war, he had not only graduated at the top of his law school class but also clerked for the state supreme court. Governor Brunsdale looked no further.

"I considered myself the luckiest guy in the world," says Murry, a retired major general in the U.S. Army. "I'd survived the war, gotten through college and law school, and now the governor offered me the best job on earth."

When the legislature was in session, eighty-hour workweeks were routine. Once the flood of legislation started, it never seemed to stop. Double shifts and weekends would not be enough to keep up with the workload. Aside from Washington, it seemed that every legislator in the state was writing bills. Murry's primary responsibility was to read these new laws, absorb the content, and report back to the legislature on the merits of all proposed legislation. In his first month on the job, Murry began to recognize the "huge gaps" in his legal education. His first order of business was to get a working knowledge of federal Indian law, but that was a daunting task. When Public Law 280 dropped onto Murry's desk, he immediately recognized an opportunity to immerse himself in the unknown.

"It doesn't take long with Indian law before you realize you're breathing a different kind of air," reflects Murry. And while the work of a state legislature can intersect with federal Indian law on a dozen different planes, just how those intersections will play out in municipal, county, township, and statewide statutes is by nature an unknown. Complicating matters further, when Congress passed P.L. 280 and began transferring federal jurisdiction over the tribes to the states, not a single state legislator in North or South Dakota, Montana, Wyoming and Colorado, Arizona, or New Mexico was trained in federal Indian law.

Murry immediately realized that once it was enacted at the state level, the scope of P.L. 280 would be sweeping. Civil and criminal jurisdiction would dilate to include the management of Indian lands and natural resources, forests and rangeland, the implementation of irrigation and municipal water systems, the building of roads, and most important of all, the right to conduct land sales. Until now, all of these areas of the law were completely foreign to the states. To help him investigate what P.L. 280 might mean for both the Indians and the state of North Dakota, Murry hired a young Hidatsa lawyer named Hans Walker, whom he had met in law school. Walker had impressed Murry with his quiet manner and subtle but powerful talent for the law. Together, they began deconstructing P.L. 280 like the engine of a car, so they could examine its many pieces. For Murry and Walker, the report on P.L. 280 required total immersion in state land codes and federal Indian law. In the end, Murry and Walker recommended that the state legislature leave the adoption of this law up to the tribes. "In our view, this was the only way we could square the federal government's trust obligations to the tribes with the transfer of jurisdiction to the states."

While Emerson Murry and Hans Walker were busy writing their report on P.L. 280, Congress was busy in Washington, D.C., churning out another dozen pieces of termination legislation. The most prominent new initiatives were House Resolutions 89 and 108. The former stated that the objective of termination was to bring an end to "all Federal supervision and control over Indians." Committees reporting back to the full House urged Congress to expedite any legislation that promised to bring about the "full assimilation of the Indians into the nation's social and economic life" because existing policy was out of step with mainstream America. "Immigrants do not become citizens as tribal groups," reasoned Congress, "and neither should Indians."

Despite its treaty obligations, Congress had never bothered to explain its objectives to the citizens of Indian Country. The oft-quoted purpose of "making Indians whole" by "setting them free" was simply a legal cover for stripping them of their treaty protections. To the surprise of no one, the first round of termination hearings was scheduled between Senator Watkins's committee and the "Tribes of Utah," soon to be followed by the Three Affiliated Tribes. Both groups were deemed ready for "complete termination of wardship status." Chairman Cross responded to this news with a furious letter to North Dakota's congressional delegation telling them that the Mandan, Hidatsa, and Arikara people, having recently lost their homes and communities to the Army Corps of Engineers, were in complete disarray. In Cross's opinion, his people had never been less prepared, or less willing, "to take such a drastic cure."

Martin Cross was a man under siege. He was newly divorced, and his tribes were scattering to the four winds. Now the Bureau of Indian Affairs wanted to dissolve their tribal government by putting tribal members on buses and trains with one-way tickets to distant cities. Despite his personal misfortunes, he wanted Washington to know that he was prepared to stand and fight. "We are opposed to the withdrawal by the government of any help that they give us," Cross told Congress. "We only oppose their interference in the management of our own property and money."

Yet even as members of his tribe were battling to survive their first bitter winter "on top," Cross knew that he could not let down his guard. The fictions now being advanced by the BIA seemed extraordinary even to Cross: "The tribes are now enjoying the highest level of resources in their history," said a new BIA report in 1955, noting that tribal members believed "their present plight is up to us to do something about." The report concluded that since the construction of Garrison Dam coerced members of the Three Affiliated Tribes to make major readjustments to their lives, the forced march to higher ground was "an excellent opportunity [for the tribes] to break with the past. We can see no particular gain for the Indian people by delaying the institution of a planned withdrawal of all special government services. The shock of such a program will have immediate repercussions, but the negative effect of such reaction can be considerably reduced if the problem is properly presented in positive terms. It is our belief that the time is ripe for early consideration [for termination] at the Washington level."

Chairman Cross went on the offensive, arguing publicly that the BIA was becoming more reckless by the day. As it had done so often in the past, the agency chose to ignore known facts when the facts did not serve their objectives. As it had so often throughout its history, the very agency responsible for safeguarding the Indians' interests had become the tribes' principal adversary. Eisenhower's Indian commissioner, Glenn Emmons, hailed a new protermination report produced by his own agency as "an opportunity waiting to be seized." In February 1955, Emmons sent his personal representative, Homer Jenkins, to New Town to meet with the Tribal Council. In so many words, Jenkins conveyed Emmons's opinion that the time had come for the Three Affiliated Tribes "to get out on their own" and begin the move toward termination without delay. Jenkins urged the leaders to close the tribal rolls, demand a lump-sum payment from Congress for all money still due them from the 1949 taking, and agree to terminate their tribal government.

Cross and the council listened politely to the commissioner's emissary. Once Jenkins had said his piece, the council sent him on his way without tipping its hand. At the first opportunity, Cross loaded the entire tribal government onto the train in Minot and headed for a showdown with the secretary of the interior in Washington, D.C.

"Mr. Cross," began assistant BIA commissioner Warren Spaulding, "we understand that you desired to meet with some of the bureau people for certain discussions. You undoubtedly have something to say, so would you care to lead off?"

"I am packing some resolutions in my briefcase, and I'm wondering if I should bother presenting them to the Indian office at all."

"How does everybody else feel about this?" asked Spaulding.

Tribal councilman William Dean was the first to respond. "I have come after money, the money Congress owes us for taking our land, but I don't want to be turned loose by termination. Whenever we try to cooperate with the Indian bureau, we don't get to first base. All we do is spend lots of time and money going back and forth. It never gets us anywhere."

"In other words, you want the money owed you, but you also desire to retain the trust status of the land."

Mr. Cross interrupted. "The money belongs to us. Yet the way we're treated, we have to come here and beg for it. If you're using this as a way of bribing us to accept termination, then turn us loose. If we are incompetent, put it in writing. But you won't do that. I know what I'm talking about, Mr. Spaulding." Cross knew that if the agency declared the tribes incapable of managing their affairs, the bureau would be obligated to take the Three Affiliated Tribes off the list for termination. This, Cross knew, was something the bureau would not do. Therefore, if the three tribes were competent in the eyes of the bureau, what, then, demanded Cross, was the holdup with the money?

"Well, you know all of these things must be reviewed."

"No, sir, it must be decided today!" said Cross. "The secretary has the authority to authorize per capita payment, but he does not have the authority to force us into termination. Only Congress can do that. There is no sense in continuing this conference if you are not going to make a decision today."

"We thought we were here to talk about programming and planning."

"Look, our people are in a very bad way," said Councilman Sam Mathews.

"We recognize that," said Spaulding. "And the last thing you want now is to have the members that have left the reservation come back, since all you have left is hilltops. The valley is all gone, isn't that correct?"

"That is right, gone."

"You need to make arrangements to start moving more people out. We know what your problem is. You've been elected to get the money for the tribal members, but we have the responsibility to enforce policies that are going to lead to long-term benefits . . ."

"It's the older people who are asking for their money," said Mathews. "They have no other way of living, no way to grow food, no cattle business, no way of securing loans."

"I still believe that any group of people capable of handling twelve and a half million dollars is competent to handle themselves without supervision of the bureau," said Spaulding. "This whole thing is a question of whether or not you want to talk about it [termination], or whether you have closed your minds."

Chairman Cross had heard enough from Spaulding to know where he was headed. As far as Cross was concerned, Spaulding could get there alone. The Mandan and Hidatsa leader had spent too many days in the past ten years sitting around polished walnut tables just like this one not to recognize a setup when he saw one. He was no longer thrown off by his surroundings, or intimidated by the endless parade of expensive suits. At this juncture in the discussion the official transcript reports, simply: "Mr. Cross left the meeting."

Cross and Spaulding were both gambling. Both had hoped to come away from this meeting with a trophy. The government still owed the Mandan, Hidatsa, and Arikara people approximately $4.42 million. After taking their land, Congress had used the compensation money as leverage to extract more concessions from the tribes on completely unrelated matters. Now, Spaulding was hoping to extract guarantees from Cross that if the money was released by the agency, the tribe would agree to initiate the process of termination. Spaulding was coy. He knew that Cross had been reelected tribal chairman on a platform promising to force the government to release the remaining funds in per capita payments. The deputy commissioner's strategy was to pin the chairman's back to the wall by locking in linkage between termination and per capita payments, two completely unrelated issues. Cross knew that these so-called win-win arrangements somehow always turned into one-sided affairs that favored the white man and hurt the Indian.

This time, Spaulding misjudged the chairman's inner resolve. Although Cross was committed to bringing home the remaining money, he was not about to be blackmailed by the bureau. After Cross stormed out, Spaulding continued to press his initiative for linkage with the other tribal councilmen. These were well-meaning men who, to an individual, were naive about the deputy commissioner's ulterior motives. Intimidated by their surroundings and anxious to smooth the waters, they were quickly seduced into placing both feet squarely in Spaulding's trap. Before the meeting was over, they all agreed to negotiate over the remaining money.

Spaulding's victory would prove to be short-lived. Even as the Three Affiliated Tribes were disintegrating around him, Martin Cross kept his head in the contest and ultimately prevailed by refusing to allow the BIA or Congress to link the dispersal of funds to termination. Unbeknownst to most of his fellow councilmen, Cross had initiated a counteroffensive through North Dakota's congressional caucus and the National Congress of American Indians. In March 1956, President Eisenhower signed off on the tribal chairman's demand for a final per capita dispersal of the remaining funds. They had lost the bitter, decadelong battle over Garrison Dam, but Martin Cross had won the war to stave off termination.

"To defend the Indians in their rights," wrote his friend Robert Yellowtail, "inevitably means a lot of grief for whomever takes on the job."

⋇

The regionwide battle over termination unexpectedly flip-flopped when a report on Public Law 280 was released in 1956 by two young attorneys in North Dakota. The report written by Emerson Murry and Hans Walker recommended that lawmakers take a new approach to this radical law. "Hans and I recommended that they allow the tribes to decide whether they wanted to relinquish jurisdiction, and to their everlasting credit, and after much debate and drum pounding on the Capitol steps, that's what they did. Of course, the North Dakota tribes all elected to retain their own civil and criminal jurisdiction."

As a caveat to their general recommendations, Murry and Walker urged the tribes to surrender their civil jurisdiction over disputes with white businesses. That would allow state courts to reconcile any future disputes in civil cases. "We felt this was the only way we would ever see any kind of white investment on the reservations," says Murry. He and Walker reasoned that the non-Indian community would always be reluctant to invest in Indian Country without certain guarantees to legal remedies for malfeasance. "Unfortunately, the tribes didn't adopt that provision, and I think it hurt them in the long run. But it didn't take a brain surgeon to see that this was headed for the courts. It was only a matter of time."

Murry's prediction for P.L. 280 revealed his insights into the conflicts embedded in federalism. Eventually, something would have to give at the highest levels of government, and those conflicts would have to be resolved by the nation's highest court. Just as he and Walker predicted, the final years of the Eisenhower administration saw a reversal of fortunes for the protermination forces in Washington. As momentum and opinion began to swing in the other direction, protermination lawmakers made one last attempt to rally support. Eisenhower's assistant attorney general, Perry Morton, called a news conference to announce that "recent court decisions relating to old Indian land claims could now cost the federal government billions of dollars."

Newspapers across the country jumped on the story. The *Indianapolis Star* wrote, "A government attorney reported yesterday that the Indians are on the warpath again. This time, they want more wampum. The tribes are demanding that Washington pay a fair and honorable price for vast areas that were won by early settlers through firearms, fast-talk, and firewater. Indian memories, it seems, are long, and according to these same attorneys, it appears that the Indians are given unique rights and privileges not enjoyed by any other citizens."

This time, the old tactics had little effect. Through the National Congress of American Indians, once widely dispersed tribes had begun to rally around the clear voices of Robert Yellowtail and Martin Cross. The painful experiences of the previous decade were plainly reflected in the Declaration of Indian Purpose that was drafted by the NCAI at their Chicago conference in 1961:

When our lands are taken for a declared public purpose, scattering our people and threatening our continued existence, it grieves us to be told that a money payment is the equivalent of all the things we surrender. Our forefathers could be generous when all the continent was theirs. They could cast away whole empires for a handful of trinkets for their children. But in our day, each remaining acre is a promise that we will still be here tomorrow. Were we paid a thousand times the market value of our lost holdings, still the payment would not suffice. Money never mothered the Indian people, as the land has mothered them, nor have any people become more closely attached to the land, religiously and traditionally.

As termination policy began to lose steam in the final days of the Eisenhower administration, P.L. 280 and House Resolution 108 suddenly came under ferocious attacks from both the political left and right. In a speech delivered from the well of the Senate on March 9, 1959, Arizona senator Barry Goldwater took aim at termination and challenged Congress to cast off all previous resolutions made in support of terminating the federal trusteeship over Indian lands and resources. Goldwater was followed to the floor by Montana's Lee Metcalf, who lambasted termination as a national disgrace: "There is no satisfaction in our record of dealing with the American Indian, from the beginning to the present. Ultimately, Indians must be given the management of their own affairs."

Though encouraging, the chorus rising in defense of Indian tribes was not enough to banish the ghosts of termination from the halls of Congress. Wary tribes would continue to see termination lurking behind every legislative act directed at Indian Country. Their well-founded suspicions were based on the experience of half a dozen tribes, such as the Menominee and the Klamath, who had been coerced into dissolution against their will. Hard-fought battles in Washington would eventually restore terminated tribes to full tribal status in the 1960s. Although senators such as Watkins and Anderson were now long gone, the damage done to "terminated" tribes could not be undone. The Klamath, for example, were forced to sell half a million acres of virgin timberlands to private timber companies that, in turn, began harvesting those resources almost immediately. Entire forests in southern Oregon were reduced to a landscape of stumps.

As soon as President John F. Kennedy had taken the oath of office in January 1961, he declared that living conditions of the American Indian were a disgraceful blight on the conscience of the nation. The desperate condition of America's "first citizens," said Kennedy, was the direct result of federal Indian policy of the previous two administrations. The new president's commissioner of Indian affairs let it be known to western congressmen that a new day had dawned at the Bureau of Indian Affairs. "WASPs [white Anglo-Saxon Protestants] assume that the value system of the Anglo-Saxon is universal, and that the individual ownership of property is the only natural way for people to live," declared Commissioner Philleo Nash. Congress was told that the government's Indian agency was open for business, and the new man in the White House was determined to reverse recent trends and expand the agency's services.

For the Three Affiliated Tribes, the change of heart in Washington was probably too little, too late. The damage of the previous two decades could not be undone. By the time John F. Kennedy was elected in 1960, the former tribal chairman was living alone on his new ranch outside of Raub. His children had all been "relocated" to cities on the West Coast. Crusoe returned home for six-month intervals to help run the ranch, but ranching "on top" was a shortcut to financial ruin. Life for Martin had been reduced to a day-to-day struggle to keep the tribal cattle business solvent and intact. After winning the battle against termination, he had taken a much-needed leave of absence from tribal politics. From the first weeks of 1944 until December 1956, he had worked day and night at the business of the tribe. Most of that work was done without pay. Now, following a four-year respite from the burdens of leadership, Cross decided to return to the council when John F. Kennedy was elected to the White House in 1960. Emerging from long seclusion, Martin seemed reenergized by his return to politics. To Crusoe, the vigor his father had shown throughout his years as chairman had returned with a vengeance. For his distant children, his letters were once again filled with optimism and his signature enthusiasm for life. In a letter written to Marilyn in February 1963 during a trip to Washington, her father reflected on the bittersweet experience of returning to the city he had once known so well.

"I have been to Washington to see the Great White Father and other lesser white fathers to boot," he began, explaining that the "lessers" included the new secretary of the interior, Stewart Udall, and Kennedy's commissioner of Indian affairs, Philleo Nash. "I did not enjoy the visit there, as I found many new faces in the BIA . . . but anyway, I got to see and talk with President Kennedy."

By the time he met John F. Kennedy in the spring of 1963, a decade had passed since the evacuation of Elbowoods and his divorce from Dorothy. With the lake now filled all the way to the Montana border, and new dams being built downstream that would soon flood Sioux lands, the Bureau of Indian Affairs decided it would be a good idea to update previous profiles of the Three Affiliated Tribes. Specifically, they wanted to know how the Mandan, Hidatsa, and Arikara were meeting the challenges of building a new life "on top."

The winter the new study was conducted, 1964, was ferociously cold. Cattle and other range livestock perished on the High Plains by the thousands. Frigid temperatures imprisoned tribal members in desolate outposts, without food or fuel, for months on end. In a tersely worded summation, the BIA investigators reported: "Their poverty, coupled with the isolation of many in the remoter parts of the reservation, has created a situation in which actual starvation for many of these people is a real possibility." The dire conditions at Fort Berthold made assimilation into mainstream society more remote a possibility than it had been twenty years earlier. The tribal cattle program was in shambles. The herd of cattle the tribe had carefully built up over the past three decades had been sold off to buy food and propane. Their subsistence economy had been shattered by their eviction from the bottomlands. The tribes' material and social needs, once met with agricultural abundance and tight-knit communities, had crumbled. Tribal members were scattered far and wide across a desolate geographical area. The few jobs available in service or farm-labor sectors paid subpoverty wages. Opportunities for economic growth were nonexistent. The authors concluded that the forced relocation of the Mandan, Hidatsa, and Arikara people had effectively wiped out a century of progress.

On top, the Three Affiliated Tribes were finding it impossible to grow their own food or to feed themselves. Wild game, once so plentiful on the bottoms, had vanished. Even if the Indians could turn the soil and plant small gardens, either their wells were bad or there was not enough water to keep the crops alive. Materially and culturally, the Mandan, Hidatsa, and Arikara people were reexperiencing their ancestors' darkest days at Like-a-Fishhook in the early 1870s. Despite his native optimism, when he glanced ahead, Martin Cross saw no relief in sight.

As bitter weather gripped the Great Plains, Martin Cross was again back in Washington on Tribal Council business. Now they were meeting with officials from the Department of the Interior on the land-claim suit filed by James Curry ten years before. "Since I have time on my hands," he wrote his family in California, "I thought I would put them to good use and write you a few lines. This probably doesn't mean anything to you, but I have been on the water wagon for forty days now. Doctor Wilson tried to send me to the Jamestown alcoholic center for treatment, but I couldn't see it. I have no feeling in my toes, they seem numb, and I guess my blood circulation is punk. I have a letter from Mickey [Mike] with some disturbing news about Crusoe's behavior bouting [sic] with Jim Beam again. I was not too surprised to learn of it and suggested to Mickey to locate some AA clubs, take him in hand, and get him back on his feet. I have to get going now. We meet with our claims attorney this afternoon. I am very happy to be here again, and enjoy the business of meeting with authoritative groups again. . . . My health is not too bad. My feet are bothering me, but my appetite is good. My nerves can be relaxed without any sleeping pills or intoxicants. Try and write sometime soon. I like to know how you kids are doing."

※

For Crusoe, the thought of "coming home" to Parshall from the Air Force was a deeply incongruous one. Throughout his childhood in Elbowoods, Parshall was the "white town on top" where Martin bought their trucks and Dorothy occasionally went shopping. When Crusoe drove back to North Dakota in 1955 with his discharge papers in his duffel bag, the world he left behind on that summer morning four years before no longer existed. His mother and father had split up. Many people of his tribe were living on isolated farms scattered across half a million acres of High Plains. The streets and familiar landmarks of Elbowoods were at the bottom of a lake. Marilyn was in teachers' college in Minot. Uppy was finishing high school in Garrison, and Bucky had gone into self-imposed exile by joining the Army. After spending a year and a half in Parshall as shiftless nomads, Dorothy and her two youngest children, Raymond and Carol, were living in Old Dog's house at its new location on East Second Street. Coincidentally, Phyllis and Crusoe both came home from the Air Force at about the same time. The two oldest Cross children moved back into the house that Old Dog built and quickly slipped into what Phyllis calls "a state of functional shock."

"We couldn't believe what we were seeing," says Phyllis, recalling the early days in Parshall. "The dam money was gone, and the bars on Main Street were filled with Indians. People we'd known all our lives were passed out in the streets in the middle of winter. It seemed like every ten minutes we were going to a funeral. Sixteen-year-old girls went out on dates on Saturday night and came home two years later with a baby on each hip. In Elbowoods, if you got caught drinking, you went to jail. Babies out of wedlock were unheard-of. Overnight, these things had become commonplace."

When Phyllis left the Air Force she planned to get married and settle down on the reservation. A short stint of employment at the new medical clinic in New Town soon cured her of that notion. "It was big-city trauma-room medicine, out on the prairie. I wasn't cut out for that kind of nursing. I felt so disassociated from my past, my family, from everything I had ever known, I'd be driving home from work and not know where I was. I had to get out of there for my own survival, but that meant abandoning Raymond and Carol. They were so little. Their lives were crazy."

But people do not ask your consent at that age, says Raymond. "It's what you're given, what you have to deal with." The day he turned six years old, on August 24, 1955, his eight-year-old sister, Carol, had the responsibility for taking him to school. "She dumped me off at the front door," remembers Raymond. "I sat on the steps and started crying. Finally, some teacher came out and grabbed me by the scruff of the neck and hauled me into the building. That was my first day of school."

When Crusoe pulled up to his mother's house in Parshall on a sunny June morning in 1955, he had a roll of mustering-out pay in his pocket, a car with four good tires that was "bought and paid for," and a strong back that he planned to put to work doing odd jobs until something better came along. To his surprise, this remote, idyllic little community of Scandinavian Lutherans had been transformed by The Flood into an Indian village. Between time spent in Parshall, and his on-again, off-again life at Martin's ranch at Raub, the next five years for Crusoe evaporated into "a drunken haze between the dead end at the ranch and the dead end of town."

"Life was so drastically different from what it had been in Elbowoods that none of us could begin to make heads or tails of what was happening," says Crusoe, remembering a childhood friend named Billy Lockwood and his wife, Annie. The couple had gotten married right after high school. When Crusoe came home from the service, Billy and Annie lived directly across the street from Dorothy Cross, on East Second Street in Parshall.

"Billy and Annie had two little kids. I can still see those bright happy eyes, their beautiful little faces. The shack they lived in was maybe ten feet by fourteen feet. It had a dirt floor, no ceiling. They'd bundle the two babies in blankets and stuff them into a mattress up over the ceiling joists. We'd all sit in there in our coats in the middle of the winter, six or seven of us, each with a bottle of wine, and drink. When it got really cold, Billy would reach up and break off part of a joist, or one of the rafters, and stuff it into the wood stove for heat. We thought that was normal. Everybody we knew lived like that. We buried those babies."

Comatose drunks, self-inflicted gunshot wounds, wet brain, and the all-too-famous jalopy crashes and funerals became the currency of exchange of life "on top." Entire families lived in cars and in grain sheds on the outskirts of Parshall. White people's anger over the sudden transformation of their clean, well-lit community boiled over onto the streets, and in churches and school classrooms, in undisguised hatred. Nothing in the Indians' past experience prepared them for the racism that engulfed them. Among their many white neighbors in Elbowoods, racism had been nonexistent. But when hundreds of Indians landed in Parshall after The Flood, animosities once held in check beneath polite exteriors now colored every glance, every word and gesture at the grocery store and gas station. "Indian kids were dying of hunger and exposure all over the place," remembers Crusoe. "You can walk through the cemeteries today and see all the little graves from those years. There's dozens and dozens of them."

"What worried me most was little Ray and Carol," says Phyllis. "Mom had gotten chummy with the Seventh-Day Adventists, and Dad was drinking more than ever. He would come to Parshall and beg her to take him back. There were these horrible scenes. Mom would let him sleep it off in the basement, but she wouldn't take him back. Then he'd disappear again for weeks."

By the end of the 1950s, white people in neighboring communities were faring little better than the Indians. The familiar mosaic of long winters, hot, dry summers, and depressed crop prices was painfully reminiscent of the "dirty 30s." Strangely enough, ever since the Corps seduced white farmers into supporting the construction of Garrison Dam by promising them a million acres of irrigated croplands, the fortunes of farmers had soured at the very moment they expected improvements. Farmers had regarded the government's promise of irrigation to be as good as gold, better than cash in the bank. Banks, after all, could fail, but the Bureau of Reclamation would still be there to haul the water after the creeks rose and hell froze over.

But a new generation of farmers was learning that problems tend to merge in damaged habitats. From horizon to horizon, those one-hundred-sixty-acre Jeffersonian units of family and God, hard work and prosperity, were turning into a graveyard as big as the sky. Where dreams failed by the thousands, windmills clattered and clicked and pumped sand beneath an inscrutable blue dome. The wind and silence carried a message: free-market capitalism was no match for the fierce natural forces that had ruled the Northern Plains for ten thousand years. The cruel irony of the Pick-Sloan Plan was inescapable to those who dared to look. Without the support of farmers, the

Army Corps of Engineers could not have secured congressional approval for its extravagant scheme. Without ironclad guarantees to the region's dryland farmers that irrigation would be the crown jewel in the Flood Control Act of 1944, Garrison Dam would never have been built. Yet fifteen years after Congress promised farmers that their needs would come first, the first drop of irrigation water had yet to fall on the Northern Plains.

By 1960, the irrigation projects approved by Congress in 1944 were still nothing more than promises on paper. Farmers were running out of patience. No one could deny that they had done their part to make Pick-Sloan a reality; now they were calling in their debts. To make matters worse, as the farmers watched their crops wither from thirst, the Corps continued to build huge dams on the Missouri with missionary-like zeal. After the keystone project at Garrison was completed in 1954, the Corps turned next to the Oahe Dam, which was soon followed by the Fort Randall Dam and the Gavins Point Dam, near the South Dakota border. At the end of the decade, Pick dams had impounded nearly 50 million acre-feet of water, yet upstream farmers were still waiting to see the first mile of irrigation pipes. Quiet grumbling soon swelled to public anger.

Lawmakers realized that if irrigation was ever going to become a reality on the Upper Missouri River, they needed to create an independent administration to manage the Sloan Plan. As long as the two plans were connected, the Corps would get the lion's share of the funding. Though the two plans were created by the same law, in actual practice they had been anything but equal. To correct that imbalance, Congress created the Garrison Diversion Unit of the Missouri River Basin Project to mollify frustrated farmers. Anxious to show its good faith, Congress then sent a delegation to Devil's Lake, North Dakota, in the spring of 1960 to hear the long-suffering farmers' complaints. Unfortunately, Congressman Otto Krueger told them, they had picked a bad time to voice their demands. The Sloan Plan had recently come under attack by the United States Chamber of Commerce, which had declared war on "the entire federal reclamation program." An apologetic Krueger counseled farmers to bide their time until civility and common sense could be restored in Washington.

Farmers were beginning to suspect that irrigation had been nothing more than a cruel ploy all along. They had been duped into playing obedient pawns in the battle between two federal agencies fighting for control of the Missouri River. After the first dams were built and flooding ceased in downstream states, no one in Washington seemed much inclined to spend billions more dollars on irrigation projects. After yet more hearings in 1963, the editorial board of the *St. Louis Post-Dispatch* pulled the mask off the Pick-Sloan Plan: "This would be a good time for the governors and senators and representatives of the Missouri Valley states to decide whether they want to be held liable for the consequences of the most gigantic boondoggle in American history."

⚜

Dorothy Cross had no sooner moved out of Elbowoods than she realized that Parshall was no place for a single mother to be raising two young children. As the months went by, and she moved Raymond and Carol from one shack to another, she watched the once idyllic little town of Parshall falling apart all around her. Quietly but deliberately, Dorothy Cross began plotting her escape. When her daughter Marilyn and son-in-law Kent moved to California in 1959, she purchased bus tickets for herself and the two children, Raymond and Carol, and headed west for the summer. Eventually, by the time Raymond and Carol were in high school, they stayed in California year round. After Uppy and Bucky graduated from Haskell Indian Nations University in the early 1960s, they joined the rest of the family in the Bay Area.

For a half dozen years now, the BIA office at Fort Berthold had been actively "relocating" tribal members off the reservation as quickly as they could secure vouchers from Washington, D.C. The trail between Fort Berthold and the Bay Area was a well-worn groove. Crusoe was twice exiled from Parshall on Dillon Myer's relocation program — once to Chicago and later to San Francisco. By the early 1960s, the entire Cross family, and half of the tribal membership, had been relocated to Seattle and Los Angeles, Chicago, Denver, and the urban centers of northern California.

"There were a lot of tragedies in those years that will never get into the history books," says Bucky, who joined his brothers and sisters in the Bay Area in the 1960s, after he was discharged from the Army. Over the years he got to know hundreds of "relocation" drifters from places such as Pine Ridge, Lame Deer, and Shiprock. "Who knows how many thousands of Indians were dumped off in the cities? Years later you heard about the suicides in a bar on the North Beach from somebody who knew somebody, or headlines in the newspapers. NAMELESS INDIAN JUMPS OFF THE GOLDEN GATE BRIDGE, or NO-NAME JOE LEAPS FROM WINDOW. No known origin. No known survivors. No name, or, for that matter, no country."

For Crusoe and Bucky, every nameless Indian they read about in the newspaper was a kid they grew up with, a kid they swam with and rode horses with in the hills above Elbowoods. Thousands of "relocated" young Indians disappeared into America's urban ghettos and were never heard from again. Crusoe was determined to avoid that fate. Each time he returned to Parshall from Chicago or San Francisco, there were fewer lights burning in the windows of the house on East Second Street that Old Dog built. Eventually, one autumn night in 1960, he found the house completely dark, and himself completely alone. Instead of chasing down his old acquaintances at bars in town, he decided to keep on driving out Old State Road Number Eight and headed straight to the ranch.

"Dad really needed me. I knew it, even though he could never come right out and tell me. Before I left we couldn't spend five minutes in the same room without getting into a fight. Now we spent months out there on that ranch, just the two of us. Elbowoods was gone, the family was scattered all over the place, and he was out of politics. He must have asked himself a thousand times, 'How did this happen?' "

When winter's deep freeze caught them out on the ranch and held them captive in that tiny house for weeks at a time, he and his father became intimate strangers in their long silences. Despite all the trials Martin had endured in the past twenty years, Crusoe never heard his father complain or bemoan the defeats and burdens the fates had handed him.

"Of course, there was the drinking, too. There was a lot of that in the later years. And for awhile there, I couldn't seem to stay out of jail," says Crusoe. "Dad would come into town and bail me out. We'd go back out to the ranch and work our butts off to make it work and redeem our souls, so to speak, but it was hopeless. In our condition, the ranch and redemption were bigger than either one of us. In his successes, and there were many, Dad was humble. In his failures, he was stoic, like his father. In his self-destruction, he was profoundly human."

When Crusoe drove away from the ranch in 1960, he knew that Martin would now be alone to face the remaining years of his life. "By then the drinking was slow suicide. I couldn't watch it anymore without being a part of it, so I had to get out of there to save my own skin. There was no future for any of us there. He blamed himself for that, but it wasn't his fault."

Crusoe returned to San Francisco with a "relocation" voucher in his pocket. This time he was determined to stick it out and make a new life in the Bay Area. With his mother, brothers, and sisters close by, life seemed to offer real possibilities for the first time since he left the Air Force. With encouragement from his siblings and Dorothy, Crusoe picked up some college credits while holding down a job. Then one spring morning in the first week of April 1964, he awoke with a powerful sense that he needed to get back to Parshall on the next bus or train. He left that morning without telling anyone in the family. When the bus pulled into Parshall two days later, Crusoe knew right where to start looking for his father. With his suitcase in hand, he strode up the street toward the V.F.W. Club and swung open the front door. Martin was the first person he saw, hunched over a drink at the near end of the bar. After a boisterous reunion and a brace of boilermakers to celebrate Crusoe's homecoming, Martin bought two bottles of wine and the pair headed for the ranch. As the blood red sky drained to purple on the western horizon, Martin and Crusoe dragged two chairs off the front porch and drank their wine under the gathering stars. When the bottles were empty, the bleary-eyed pair helped each other up the steps and into the house, and passed out on their beds.

The following morning, father and son both awoke with "jangling nerves and atrocious hangovers," and neither stirred throughout the morning. Finally, Crusoe got dressed and walked down to his aunt Alice's house and brought back a plate of ham and bread, but Martin was too sick to eat. His father fell back against the pillows and did not move for the rest of the day.

Bright and early on Tuesday morning, Martin surprised them both by bounding out of bed at dawn. Crusoe listened to the meadowlarks and song sparrows through his open window, where chicory and wild mustard were in full bloom. Martin's spirits seemed miraculously restored by the crisp morning. He even whistled while he took a bath, and sang some of the old Hidatsa songs. When he had gotten dressed he said, "Wha'd'ya say we go into Raub, get some beer?"

A little "hair of the dog" might be just the thing, thought Crusoe. His nerves felt like a million rusty fishhooks. He hopped out of bed and jumped into his clothes, but when they stepped off the front porch, Martin took two faltering strides, then turned back toward the house. Maybe he should lie down for a few more minutes, he told Crusoe. It was still pretty early yet, and his feet seemed to be acting up again. Crusoe followed him to his bedroom and covered him with a blanket, then looked around in the kitchen for something to eat.

"I was telling him stories about everybody in California — Mom, Raymond and Carol, the bigger kids, about Bucky's new job, how Raymond was doing so well in school. That pleased him. School was the number-one thing with Dad. He never missed a PTA meeting the whole time we were growing up. After a few minutes he asked me to come in and lay down beside him, so I did. Then he asked me something about Mom and made a big yawn. He let out a sigh, real deep, and his hand dropped onto my leg, and then he didn't move. 'No,' I said, 'you can't do this to me. Not like this.'"

Crusoe lay still on the bed and stared at the plaster ceiling. His father's dead hand lay across his leg. He began mumbling things to himself, anything, any whispered noise to hold the silence at bay a few moments longer, until he could think of what to do next. Finally, he sat up on the bed and swung his feet down and walked to the sink in the kitchen, then drew some water into a porcelain basin from the hand pump at the window. Closing his eyes, he lowered his face to the basin and splashed his forehead and neck with the ice cold well water, then dried off with a hand towel. He stood at the sink a while longer and looked out the window at the new morning. Killdeer swooped and wheeled against the blue sky, and the bright sun squinted his eyes and felt warm on his cheeks. After a little while he closed his eyes and bowed his head and said a prayer. Then he turned from the window and walked back to the bedroom and stopped in the doorway. Finally, when he looked over at his father, the silence rushed in all at once, and Crusoe folded his arms over his head and sank to the floor.

Brother Martin died today," begins the April 7, 1964, entry in Martin's sister Alice's diary. Saying nothing more about their loss, the entry rambles on about the weather and the arrival of the coroner. The county coroner told Crusoe that the moment Martin yawned and sighed in the seconds before he died, a vein in his chest opened up like a broken zipper. "There's not a thing you could have done," he assured him. "He never knew what happened."

Along toward evening, a hearse arrived from the funeral home in Parshall. Martin's sisters, Alice and Lucy, drove to the BIA agency offices in New Town to inform the agency superintendent, and the Tribal Council, of Martin's death. Crusoe stayed behind at the ranch and started organizing his father's papers. In a small saucer on the windowsill, there was a quarter, a dime, and a nickel. Martin's bank account was empty. He had sold his last head of cattle in the fall. There was the house, the barn, the horizon, and blue sky.

What seemed the strangest of all at the moment, says Crusoe, was that Martin's favorite double-breasted suit had mysteriously disappeared. "I tore that house apart looking for that suit." He was buried three days later in a tattered brown suit in a place of honor at the Old Scout Cemetery. Dorothy and all the kids drove straight through from California and arrived the night before the funeral. The morning of the ceremony broke warm and clear over the prairie. As the mourners walked back to their cars from the graveside service, sixteen-year-old Raymond told Crusoe that maybe it was his turn now. Maybe that was how it should be.

As soon as the reception was over, Dorothy, Marilyn, Bucky, and the children reassembled the small caravan of cars and headed back for California. When Crusoe drove back to the ranch later that evening, it seemed like the silence of the prairie had reclaimed the ground. Making one last pass through the house, he found his father's double-breasted suit hanging on a hook on the back of a closet door. He threw the suit into the cab of the pickup truck and drove back to Parshall, where he had promised to spend a few days helping a friend with a construction project before returning to California.

"When I got back home from work one day, I knew right off that I'd had a visitor. The back door was standing wide open," remembers Crusoe.

In broad daylight, a burglar had broken into the Cross family home on East Second Street. The thief had helped himself to a pan of potatoes on the stove, a photo album that Crusoe had brought back from the ranch, and Martin Cross's suit coat, which Crusoe had left draped over the back of a chair in the living room. On a visit to Parshall two years later, Crusoe walked into a bar in New Town and saw an old school friend from Elbowoods, Eugene Spotted Wolf, sitting alone at the bar. Spotted Wolf was wearing Martin Cross's double-breasted suit coat.

"The coat was really trashed, but I didn't say a word. Neither would Dad. He would have laughed to himself and bought Eugene a drink. When they finished, he would have taken him outside and kicked his ass."

CHAPTER VIII

Return of the Natives

⚜

"The heavens and earth are my heart. The rising sun is my mouth.
My lips dare not lie to you. My friend, I ask the same from you.
Do not deceive us. Be strong and preserve your word inviolate.
I am old, but I shall never die. I shall always live in my children,
and my children's children."

NEW CORN, POTAWATOMI

More so than any of his big brothers and sisters, Raymond Cross is a product of Garrison Dam. His early years in Elbowoods and Parshall were shaped by the cultural entropy that engulfed both his family and the three tribes. In a few short years, the Mandan, Hidatsa, and Arikara people went from being the only self-sufficient tribal enclave in the United States to being one that was almost wholly dependent on outside help for day-to-day survival.

If poverty is the midwife of dreamers, Raymond was destined for a life of ideas and imagination from the time he was a young boy. Even in Elbowoods, from his birth until he moved with his mother and sister to Parshall at the age of five, he shaped his far-ranging imaginings by the amber light of a kerosene lantern. He remembers clearly that his first hero was the German rocket scientist Wernher von Braun. To the young Indian boy in Parshall, North Dakota, it seemed that he and the legendary rocket man shared a common dream. Both wanted to break the bounds of gravity.

"Life wasn't very good in those years," says Raymond. "It didn't hold out many possibilities. Mom and my sister Carol and I were no different than anyone else in Parshall. We survived on welfare. By the time I was nine or ten, things were pretty crazy for a lot of people. Even in our own family, we're still sorting it all out."

For a few years after The Flood, the Cross family managed to cling to its former identity, but by the time Raymond was getting out of elementary school, both his family and the tribes were in complete disarray. Brothers and sisters were scattered across the country. Every day brought news of another death in the tribe, or another tribal member who had "relocated" to Chicago or Los Angeles, never to be heard from again. "The whole time I was growing up in Parshall, I heard the stories about how wonderful our world was before the dam. Our communities were close and integrated. Farming and ranching were profitable. People were happy. It was hard to imagine."

By 1960, Milton was living at an institution for the mentally handicapped at Grafton, North Dakota, Michael had enlisted in the Army, and Dorothy and her two youngest children were spending their summers in California. Each time they went west, the return to Parshall grew a little more difficult. When Raymond became a teenager, Marilyn invited Raymond to move in with her family and attend school at Santa Clara. There, for the first time in his life, he began thinking about the future. For the tall, quiet Indian boy from North Dakota, public high school in Santa Clara, California, was a formative and exciting experience. It was there, with coaxing from teachers and guidance counselors who recognized his unusual gifts, that he finally began emerging from a private world shaped by chronic trauma. It was also there that he first began thinking about the law as a possible vocation. By the time Raymond was in high school, Wernher von Braun had been replaced in his pantheon of heroes by his father, Martin Cross.

"We all tend to bad-mouth our parents when we're kids. I'm sure I did my share of that. When I was little, Dad was pretty messed up. He was coping with his impotence as a man, as a leader, and his own sense of personal disintegration. Occasionally, he'd try to establish a connection with me. He'd make promises to take me to the movies. I'd wait for him to come pick me up, but he never came. Eventually, that kind of disappointment makes you a little withdrawn, a little more, and less, resourceful at the same time.

"When I was a sophomore in high school in California, I began to understand just how extraordinary my dad had been in the fight over Garrison Dam. He overcame the limitations of his education by the sheer force of will. He accepted the mantle of tribal leadership and sacrificed years of his life to that fight without looking for anything in return. When he lost, he continued to fight to hold the tribe together. He was the last of the old and the first of the new. As the last of the old, he accepted the loneliness and isolation that came with leadership. As the first of the new, I think he was far ahead of the average citizen in Indian Country. He was among the first to recognize that our survival would depend on stepping out of the isolation of our past.

"If you look at Plato's response to the Sophists, he says, I can show you that the only way to have a just man is to create a just society. This is an important exercise in myth making for any society, and I think it points to the nut of where American society has so often broken down. We build capable individuals like Frederick Douglass, Cesar Chavez, and Martin Cross, but then we deny them the resources to build a just society. The essence of native culture forces you to ask different kinds of questions about how a just society might look. What, for example, are the essential ingredients that make up a tribal society that already has its legal, economic, and cultural base of identity imbedded in its mountains and rivers and prairie? The physical world is the wellspring of a tribe's cultural identity. That has to be protected; at the same time the consciousness of the people has to transcend its isolation in order to survive. I think Martin Cross was one of the first leaders in Indian Country to fully understand the nuances of that challenge."

Against the great weight of the past, against the will of the national legislature and federal water agencies, against determined foes in the Bureau of Indian Affairs, Martin Cross, till his final days, fought to lead his people onto a road that would ensure the survival of tribal culture for unborn generations of Mandan, Hidatsa, and Arikara people. "To that end, which I believe was a noble one, you have to say he succeeded. Along toward my junior year in high school, I decided I needed to start thinking about carrying on with what he had started."

For all of the emotional and psychological challenges of Raymond's early life, being the youngest of ten children in the Cross family also brought advantages. Raymond was born at a time that eventually put him in law school in an era when Indian Country suddenly found itself undergoing dramatic and radical change, the very transformation that had been championed by his father. While Raymond was finishing his studies at Stanford in the late 1960s, the American Indian Movement, known as AIM, sprang to life almost overnight at the height of the civil rights era, a tumultuous age of cross-cultural political activism that saw blacks', Chicanos', and women's rights movements all merging with the growing protests against the Vietnam War in southeast Asia.

"What AIM helped people see for the first time was that our native cultures had been strip-mined by the Euro-American, Judeo-Christian civilization," says Raymond. "This was a big deal. An awful lot of Indians had been baptized Christians. But by then, the storm of protests and causes made it clear to us that we were dealing with a desperate society trapped inside a crumbling mythology. For four hundred years people had been living with the illusion that they could claw their way back to Eden on this continent. Now, their mythology was crumbling all around them. Blacks, Indians, Chicanos — we all had to start finding our own solutions because the white people were out of answers."

Yet an event that would have an even greater and longer-lasting impact on Indian Country than AIM occurred a century to the day after General William Tecumseh Sherman sued the Sioux chief Red Cloud for peace at Fort Laramie. Richard Nixon was elected as the thirty-seventh president of the United States.

On July 8, 1970, two months before Raymond Cross entered Yale Law School, Nixon presented Congress with a bold new vision for Indian Country. Calling for a governmentwide initiative to embrace the principle of Native American self-determination, Nixon's message was heralded by Indian leaders as a long-overdue break from the failed policies of the past. Nixon told Congress that its legislative history in Indian Country had created inexcusable horrors. "The American Indians have been oppressed and brutalized, deprived of their ancestral lands, and denied the opportunity to control their own destiny." Yet despite these travails, "The story of the Indian is a record of endurance or survival, of adaptation and creativity in the face of overwhelming obstacles. The time has come to break decisively with the past" because the "extreme policy of forced termination had more often produced excessive paternalism." In Nixon's view, one or the other of these "evils" had held the Indian down for 150 years. Indian tribes, he declared, "can become independent of federal control without being cut off from federal concern and federal support." This was in fact the very same argument that Martin Cross had used to challenge Senator Arthur Watkins and Dillon Myer twenty years before.

Nixon's speech was a powerful reaffirmation of John Marshall's original vision of "domestic sovereign nations" and precisely mirrored the demands that men such as Martin Cross and Robert Yellowtail had been urging on Congress for decades. All who heard and read the speech realized that the president had taken bold steps onto unmapped ground. Legal historian Alvin Josephy wrote that Nixon's address was the "strongest assertion ever made by an American president against the twin evils of paternalism and termination."

Perhaps it was his Quaker childhood, or a powerful empathy for the underdog, that nurtured Richard Nixon's vision for Indian Country. More likely still, it had its origin in his high school football coach, a Cherokee Indian whom he later credited with teaching him everything he needed to know to become President of the United States. Whatever it was, the alchemy of the ingredients that formed Richard Nixon combined to formally end the Termination Era on a July afternoon in 1970.

"By the mid-1970s," says Cross, "tribes were developing their own legal departments, their own strategies for engaging federal and state governments. You could say that was one of the unintended consequences of Public Law 280. Tribes realized that they were more vulnerable than ever to state governments, but they also had more power, so they started using that power to protect themselves. This was very different from the way things had been when my father was in tribal government, and it happened right about the time I was getting out of law school. Tribal councils were taking a hard look at their ancient wardship arrangement with the federal government, and they knew it wasn't working. Indian law was the hottest thing going."

Before he was driven from office by the Watergate scandal, Nixon persuaded Congress into passing the Indian Self-Determination Act of 1975. This legislation was proposed over the loud objections of western governors and state legislatures. It passed nevertheless, along with the Indian Education Act of 1972 and the Indian Health Improvement Act of 1976. Together, these laws made it possible for thousands of young Indian students to go to mainstream colleges and universities. By the time Raymond Cross graduated from Yale Law School and went to work for the Native American Rights Fund in 1977, a social revolution was sweeping across Indian Country. Dozens of tribes were finally stepping forward with long-dormant land claims and violations of treaty rights.

For young Indians such as Raymond Cross and Alyce Spotted Bear, the new tribal chairwoman of the Three Affiliated Tribes, the "century-of-longtime-sleeping" was officially over. As the 1970s drew to a close, the first wave of college-educated Indians was returning to its home reservations. Rather than disappearing into America's urban centers and suburbs, these coyote warriors were determined to protect their homelands and tribal cultures from further exploitation. In hogans and tar-paper shacks, from the hardwood forests of Wisconsin to the kivas of the Southwest, these spiritual descendants of Crazy Horse and Four Bears intended to map a new course. Few of them fully appreciated the obstacles ahead as well as Raymond Cross. After his dramatic victory in the *Adair* case in Portland, Oregon, he fulfilled a promise he had made years earlier to help the Yaqui people of Arizona to win federal recognition as a tribe. The *Adair* case had served as his legal education in the federal court system. The arduous campaign to win recognition for the Yaqui was his apprenticeship in the legislative system. Now, with these two victories behind him, the tall, well-spoken thirty-three-year-old Mandan attorney decided that he was ready to return to Fort Berthold and pick up where his father had left off.

⚜

Despite Richard Nixon's good intentions for Indian Country, people such as Emerson Murry and his colleague Chief Justice Gerald VandeWalle of the North Dakota Supreme Court point out that most western states were already paying the price for termination. Public Law 280 had caused irreparable damage to relations between tribal and state governments. Nixon's words were reassuring to tribal leaders, but most had learned to treat state legislatures like a nest of baby rattlesnakes. Fragments of Public Law 280 were still on the books. Once a federal law is grafted onto state statutes, the onerous effects of the law continue to infect local ordinances. Public Law 280 had swept through state legal systems like a self-replicating virus, quickly embedding itself in dozens of statutes controlling everything from license plates and water rights to contract law.

Chief Justice VandeWalle has spent a lot of time contending with the consequences of termination legislation. As president for the nation's Conference of Chief Justices, he was in a unique position to learn from the termination cases of numerous other high courts. "I was too young to be an active member in the original two-eighty debate," says VandeWalle, "but I remember the day Murry's report went to the legislature. Nobody would ever forget it, I'm sure. There was a lot of drumming and dancing in the hallways."

The very memory of those debates animates the judge's thick eyebrows, lifting his voice a full octave as he reconstructs the sequence of events. From the very beginning with P.L. 280, says Chief Justice VandeWalle, "residual jurisdiction" issues tended to pit a state's interest against a tribe's interest, effectively immobilizing the federal government between them.

"That's why it got so messy, so fast," says VandeWalle. "Residual jurisdiction is a situation where the state doesn't have full jurisdiction, but it has some. For example, who is supposed to oversee what goes on in criminal cases being tried in a Native American tribal court? Well, nobody had an answer for that one. Eventually, this is the kind of conflict that's going to find you, one way or another, and pin you down until it gets an answer. In North Dakota, it was the *Wold Engineering* case."

In the late 1970s, the Tribal Council for the Three Affiliated Tribes had hired a civil engineering firm, *Wold Engineering,* to build several pumping stations for municipal water supply. These stations would lift water out of the Missouri River and deliver it to the water treatment plant in New Town, four miles away. The specifications called for pumps that would work in a wide range of temperatures and guarantee a steady flow of fresh water when winter temperatures dipped to fifty below. The pumping stations were built according to specifications, but as soon as the weather turned cold, the pumps began to seize up. The tribes sued the engineering firm for breach of contract and nondelivery of services. The case was filed in state court. The state court said it had no jurisdiction to hear the case between a private party and a sovereign nation. An appeal by the tribes soon placed the "residual jurisdiction" question before the North Dakota Supreme Court in Bismarck. There, the seven justices ruled that the only way they could try the case was if the tribes relinquished their sovereign immunity. This was the very argument that was made against Public Law 280 by Martin Cross thirty years earlier, when he and Robert Yellowtail led the charge against termination in Congress.

"Our backs were to the wall," says VandeWalle, "but so were theirs. We were all looking for the king's X, you know, the bright line of escape, a final word, but we kept ending up back in the same trap, going around and around."

Lawsuits and hurricanes are often spawned by small local disturbances, tempests in out-of-the-way teacups. "The cases that end up in our court, or in the U.S. Supreme Court, generally begin as routine disputes over the ordinary application of governmental authority." Then, says VandeWalle, before the legal system finds a way to resolve the issues and send them on their way, a minuscule percentage of these tiny tempests pick up energy from new, often unexpected sources and end up asking enormously significant questions. As an example, he cites a case known as *Venatie* that recently arose in Alaska between a small tribe and a subcontractor over an invoice for twelve hundred dollars. By the time the case ended up in the U.S. Supreme Court, the twelve-hundred-dollar invoice had mushroomed into a battle over the ownership of millions of square miles of Alaskan wilderness.

"When *Wold Engineering* came in the door," says VandeWalle, "I remember thinking, 'Oh brother, here comes the train wreck.' This was going to be a watershed case, a referendum on Public Law 280, no doubt about it. So we told the tribe that we had no jurisdiction to resolve this thing. The only way we could hear this case was if the tribe waived its sovereign immunity. Short of that, we couldn't give them relief. It was beyond our reach, but it left them with no choice. They had to take it to the U.S. Supreme Court."

Their attorney would be Raymond Cross.

In 1982, when Raymond began making arrangements to return home to North Dakota from Portland, Oregon, across the country a professor of history at Cornell University in Ithaca, New York, was being tormented by dreams. Alyce Spotted Bear had been feeling "an unrelenting gravitational pull from the world of my origin." At the end of the school year, she and her husband packed up their children and their household belongings and moved "back home." After being gone for twenty years, she arrived back at Fort Berthold without any suspicions about the challenges life was about to lay at her feet.

"I was more naive about reservation life at thirty-six than I was at sixteen," says Alyce. "I came of school age just as the old world was falling apart during The Flood, so when I was only five years old I was sent off to a mission school in South Dakota. I came home in the summers, but nothing was ever the same again. When I left Cornell, I was stepping back into a world that had become foreign to me, even though I knew everybody by their first name. I figured I'd take it easy, settle in slowly."

The easiest way to settle in slowly was to move back to her home community of Twin Buttes. There, she could get her kids in school and help her siblings take care of their aging mother while she reacquainted herself with the reservation. But it soon became apparent that the journey from Ithaca to Twin Buttes was a longer one than Alyce had imagined. Nothing she saw looked familiar. Her memories, she finally realized, had been formed at her grandfather Spotted Bear's house, on the bottoms, in a world that was gone. To her dismay, instead of finding a proud and vibrant people, she found her tribe all but resigned to an uncertain fate.

Despite Alyce's resolve to settle in slowly, her instincts and character were soon leading her into the storm that had engulfed her tribe. By 1982, evidence of cultural collapse was visible everywhere: tribal schools were failing to meet minimum standards, the tribal coffers were empty, and the once vigorous tribal government was in a state of chronic disorganization and administrative disarray. A few months after she returned home, an ad hoc committee was formed to draft Alyce Spotted Bear into a candidacy for tribal chairmanship. In the fall of 1982, she was elected as the first tribal chairwoman for the Mandan, Hidatsa, and Arikara nations in what amounted to a landslide.

Alyce's first act as the chairwoman-elect was to convene a council of elders to seek their advice. The words she heard were laden with foreboding. Morale in tribal government had reached a new low. Nobody trusted the elected lead-ers. The tribal membership had grown to 5,500, but those statistics masked the darkness of high noon. Tribal members could no longer visualize a future for their children. The unemployment rate at Fort Berthold had risen to 85 percent. Four out of five school-age children were malnourished. Infant mor-tality rates were quadruple the national average. Life expectancy for men had dropped below fifty years. Moreover, soaring rates of alcoholism and drug ad-diction among the tribes' youth had created a social climate of hopelessness. If the tribes were to survive, the elders told Alyce, the time had come to make a radical break from the status quo.

There was a blush of serendipity to this new job that was not lost on Spot-ted Bear. Like Martin Cross, Alyce's father, Lorenzo Spotted Bear, was born in the first decade of the twentieth century. Like Dorothy Cross, Alyce's mother made her own soap, spun honey from wild beehives, and sewed her children's school clothes from bleached flour sacks. Athletically talented and intellectually endowed, Martin and Lorenzo became lifelong friends from their first face-to-face encounter as schoolboys. Both would marry the daugh-ters of Norwegian homesteaders, almost unheard-of at the time. As grown men they continued to enjoy each other's company, particularly when they were out howling at the moon, sharing a pint of bootlegged whiskey. In the end, both of their lives ended in circumstances that neither man would have imagined for the other: Lorenzo, from a fatal encounter with a policeman's bullet in a riddle of particulars that remain mysterious fifty years later, and Martin, from a tormented, diseased heart in a solitary ranch house in Raub, population: 11.

Like most Mandan families living at the Knife River, by the turn of the twentieth century the Spotted Bears had intermixed with Hidatsa clans, a tribal mingling that strengthened surviving clans and invariably brought with it blood relationships with the Crow, the Hidatsa's first cousins. On her mother, Olive's, side of the family, Alyce's grandparents met on the steerage deck of a steamship in the mid-Atlantic, emigrating from Norway. After find-ing the Minnesota countryside teeming with their countrymen, the young couple got married and pressed on to the West until they reached the High Plains grasslands astride the Upper Missouri River. In 1910, Alyce's grandfa-ther Ingwald made one last move by covered wagon, settling finally on a 160 acre homestead near the village of Raub, a stone's throw from Elbowoods. While Lorenzo and Martin were growing up in Elbowoods, Dorothy Bartel and Olive Shollas were growing up on the edge of Indian Country in towns that were forty miles apart. Between them, they raised twenty children without the benefit of electricity, plumbing, or modern conveniences. Both were disowned by their parents for marrying Indians, and both would bury their husbands in middle age. While each woman would live well into her eighties, neither would marry again.

"Growing up, the fact that our mothers were Norwegian had no bearing on our identity as Indians," says Alyce. "We've always been Indians. We grew up in the Indian culture. If our mothers ever gave it a second thought, they never let on."

⚜

After Alyce met with the elders, her instincts told her to put out the biggest fires first, then move on to the smaller ones. From where she sat, all the fires looked big, but nothing could be more important to their future than "getting food into the tummies of hungry children," says Spotted Bear, and getting them back into school classrooms. Once she had accomplished that by securing new sources of federal assistance, Alyce turned her attention to the tribes' desperate financial problems. Just hours after being sworn in as chairwoman, she discovered that the tribes' books were "a horrendous, scandalous mess." In fact, the tribes were legally bankrupt.

The accounts were in such disarray that before she could go to the Bureau of Indian Affairs to ask for emergency assistance, the council had to hire a team of accountants to bring some order to the chaos. Unless something was done to get the books in order very quickly, the auditors were legally obligated to put the tribes into federal receivership.

While accountants were frantically sorting through the chaos, she told the council that her next priority was to get the tribes' legal house in order. Unlike her fellow council members, Alyce knew that Raymond Cross was coming off a big victory in the *Adair* case. A loss would have been a legal setback for hundreds of tribes. When Raymond prevailed, the victory was hailed as one of the most important Indian water-law cases in decades. When he arrived back in North Dakota in 1982, he was thirty-four years old, single, highly trained, and fresh from an important victory.

"Hiring Ray was your classic no-brainer," says Alyce. "He must have heard a voice, just like I did. One day he walked in and offered his services. He could have gotten a job at the best law firms in the country, but he came home at the very time we needed him most. The council hired him by a six-to-five vote. The vote on the council wasn't a reflection on Ray at all. The tribes had been down for so long, they just didn't see how we could afford it. I couldn't see how we could *not* afford it. I told them, 'You'll walk him out over my dead body!' Then I went into his office. He was packing up his things. 'Don't go. Please, please, please stay!' We never spoke of it again. It's probably the smartest thing I ever did."

Under Alyce's diligent, sure-handed leadership, the Three Affiliated Tribes gradually altered course away from the abyss. In the tribes' darkest hours, providence, countless hours of unpaid work, and inspired leadership enabled the tribes to avert bankruptcy and dissolution as a tribal government. After bankruptcy was avoided, the next step toward solvency was a review of the tribes' unpaid bills. By forgoing fringe benefits for all employees, the tribes gradually cleared the books of bad debt over the next four years. By the mid-1980s, the Three Affiliated Tribes were back on sound financial footing for the first time since Martin Cross stepped down in 1956. Progress was slow and painful, but there were also causes for celebration. In 1983, Raymond Cross argued the tribes' case against Public Law 280 in *Wold Engineering* before the U.S. Supreme Court. A few months later, they got news that the tribe had won a split decision. The victory was Pyrrhic, however, because it was headed back to the high court and would have to be argued once again. Chief Justice VandeWalle remembers the case being remanded back to the North Dakota Supreme Court.

"The Supremes asked us to take another look, and this time Ralph Erickstad wrote our opinion," says Chief Justice VandeWalle.

VandeWalle's esteemed mentor, Chief Justice Ralph Erickstad, was a lifelong friend of the Indian tribes of North Dakota. Erickstad had not made his first ruling with the intention of thwarting the tribes, or denying them access to remedies in state courts. He simply could not see where the court had the authority to trump the tribe's sovereign immunity. "After another review, we again said we didn't see where we had jurisdiction in this matter. We sent it back up. We were asking them for a bright line. That's exactly what they were asking for from us."

In 1984, a month after the U.S. Supreme Court announced its first "non-decision decision" in the *Wold Engineering* case, Alyce was getting ready to leave for Washington one evening when her eye caught a small headline buried in the back pages of the *Bismarck Tribune* newspaper. As tribal leader, Alyce made it her daily habit to scan the legal notices of local newspapers in search of sales of property that fell inside reservation boundaries. That evening, instead of acreage for sale, she found an announcement released by the North

Dakota State Water Commission telling the public that the following day a new round of hearings would begin at the state capitol building in Bismarck on Pick-Sloan irrigation. The story was nothing more than a two-paragraph rewrite of a news release faxed to all the regional media by Senator Mark Andrews's office in Washington. Senator Andrews, the force behind the new hearings, was anxious to promote the Bismarck hearings in hopes of getting Pick-Sloan irrigation projects back on track in Congress.

The state had offered to help the new Garrison Commission to get the ball rolling. The hearings the following day would assist the commission in determining "the costs and benefits incurred, and opportunities foregone" by groups directly affected by the construction of the Garrison Dam. Congress was intentionally vesting this new commission with enough authority to break through the logjam that had held up the construction of Lone Tree Reservoir for nearly a decade. To achieve that end as quickly as possible, the state agreed to screen testimony and compile an official slate of witnesses for the commission being assembled in Washington, D.C., by the secretary of the interior, William Clark.

"I remember coming right out of my chair when I saw that story," says Alyce. "My first thought was, 'Why didn't anybody tell us about this? Where do we figure into this?' Then, my second thought was, 'Wow, if they're going to compensate anybody, it had better be us.'"

She circled the item in the paper, wrote out a quick missive to Raymond, then stuffed it in his mailbox on her way out of town early the next morning. The hearing was scheduled for ten a.m., 120 miles away. "Raymond," she scribbled in her perfunctory note, "I know you've got a full plate, but could you please attend this meeting? I'd do it, but I'm headed for Washington. Besides, you'll have a better feel for the legalities involved than I would. I have a hunch this thing could be very important for us. If they'll let you speak, make sure that they understand the tribes should be the first in line for any further compensation. Good luck." She sped toward the airport in Bismarck through the early morning darkness with her fingers crossed. She had no way of knowing if Raymond would find her note.

⚉

By the early 1980s, the ghost of the long-dormant Sloan Plan irrigation projects came back to haunt Congress like a guilty conscience. Veteran lawmakers had to admire the resilience of an idea that refused to die gracefully. But to dryland farmers on the Upper Missouri River, a promise was a promise.

Twenty years after Representative Krueger advised them to bide their time until common sense returned to Washington, and almost forty years after the Pick-Sloan Plan was passed into law, farmers were back at their drums. As the decades rolled by, Pick-Sloan's original price tag of $1.9 billion had risen 1,000 percent to $20 billion, yet upstream farmers, birds, wildlife, and crops continued to wither and perish from chronic thirst. High Plains farmers had yet to see the first drop of Pick-Sloan irrigation water.

When the "red scare" of Representative Krueger's day abated in the 1970s, pressure from western states brought long-delayed public works projects back to the table. North Dakota's congressional delegation, led by Senators Mark Andrews and Quentin Burdick, made certain that Garrison Diversion Unit irrigation was at the front of the line. Their arguments were unassailable. For thirty years, downstream farmers had been cashing in on benefits from Pick-Sloan, such as the lucrative farming of floodplains and subsidized barge transportation for their crops. Upstream, the Department of Commerce estimated that North Dakota's economy took a $100,000,000 hit every year from the income lost to vanished farmlands. The nation's debt to upstream farmers was long overdue.

Congress agreed. In the mid-1970s, lawmakers gave the bureau the green light to proceed with the construction of the McClusky Canal, the main trunk of the distribution system in the regionwide irrigation plan devised by Glenn Sloan. "The Ditch," as the canal that was deep enough to float a coastal freighter was called, would be a 120 mile long irrigation artery running east and west across the central portion of the state. The bureau hailed McClusky to skeptical farmers as their long-awaited reward.

Work had no sooner commenced on McClusky than the project was beset by problems, first small, then large. To allay the fears of environmentalists, bureau engineers announced that the new Lone Tree Reservoir, at the eastern end of the canal, would add 55,000 acres of waterfowl habitat to the central flyway. The strict new requirements mandated by NEPA, the National Environmental Policy Act, and the Endangered Species Act, compelled bureau engineers to make the protection of wildlife habitat a controlling feature of their master plan. But an investigation by the North Dakota Farmers Union showed that the bureau's numbers added up to a shell game. Lone Tree Reservoir would create 55,000 acres of new wetlands, as advertised, while destroying 65,000 acres of waterfowl habitat that already existed. The net loss of 10,000 acres came at a time when waterfowl habitat on the Upper Missouri was disappearing at an alarming rate. Furthermore, the right-of-way for the

McClusky Canal would destroy half as much productive farmland as the completed project would irrigate. Cooperating with the Corps and the bureau, the Farmers Union report concluded, was "the kind of working alliance the lamb is able to arrange with the lion."

If everything went according to plan, with no cost overruns or complications, each of the 250,000 irrigated acres would cost the American taxpayer $900, ten times the value of the bare ground. How could all of this make dollars and sense, asked the editors of the *Union Farmer*, when the total value of the state's tillable farmland was only $1.5 billion? "The reason people killed this idea when it first came up eighty years ago is simple," they concluded. "It was as crazy then as it is now."

But nobody in Washington was shedding tears for a handful of North Dakota farmers whose strongest economic trump card was silos full of surplus wheat. On the other hand, the loss of waterfowl habitat was a bird of a different feather. When the bureau began construction on The Ditch in 1976, the National Audubon Society immediately filed suit against the bureau in federal court. Their request for an injunction against the Garrison Diversion Unit for threatening to destroy federally protected waterfowl habitat was approved without delay. North Dakota farmers had waged a losing battle against the elements for a hundred years. Now, to end all ironies, the bulldozers bringing them relief had been stopped in their tracks by ducks and geese.

The fate of the canal would remain in limbo for another nine years. But like their constituents, Senators Andrews and Burdick were nothing if not persistent. In 1984 they brought the original Sloan Plan's irrigation projects back to Congress. Both senators had made numerous appeals for a congressional commission to break the impasse over the Audubon suit. Pick-Sloan had now dogged Congress for almost forty years. Something had to be done. At the moment Raymond Cross and Alyce Spotted Bear were arguing *Wold Engineering* and getting the tribes' books in order, Congress relented and appropriated half a million dollars to assemble the Garrison Diversion Unit Commission. Secretary of the Interior William Clark was directed to assemble a blue-ribbon panel of eleven investigators. Their charter specifically instructed the investigating team to resolve all outstanding legal issues impeding "the entitlement of the state of North Dakota to a federally funded water-development program as compensation for North Dakota's contributions to the Pick-Sloan Missouri Basin program."

In other words, said Congress, break the infernal deadlock with Audubon, get the bulldozers running again, and make this headache go away.

⅏

Like his father, Raymond was a habitual early riser. Reservation police often saw him driving to work at three-thirty in the morning. He found Alyce's note, bright and early, and ate breakfast in his car as he turned around and headed down Old State Road Number Eight to Bismarck.

Unbeknownst to either of them, tribal councilwoman Tillie Walker, the sister of attorney Hans Walker, had also seen the small story in the newspaper while she was in Bismarck on other business. To the surprise of both, Raymond and Tillie ran into each other at the hearing. Try as he might, the state water commissioners denied Cross the right to speak. As soon as he told them he was representing the tribes, he was dismissed. The commission being formed in Washington would not be entertaining any legal issues related to the tribes, they told him. If the tribes had unresolved grievances over the dam, the commissioners urged him to bring the matter to the proper authorities at the Department of the Interior, in Washington. Based on the instructions sent to them by Congress, the state water commissioners had no basis for putting the tribes on agenda for the upcoming hearings in Fargo.

As soon as Tillie Walker arrived back in New Town that evening, she put the water commission hearings at the top of the agenda for the next day's Tribal Council meeting. Alyce flew back from Washington early the next morning and raced home in order to make the weekly meeting. Tillie raised the issue as soon as Alyce called for new business. After the snubbing in Bismarck the day before, Raymond remembers that he went into the council meeting with mixed feelings. In fact, based on what he had learned in Bismarck, bringing old complaints to this new commission looked like a big waste of time.

"After going through *Adair,* I had a pretty good idea of the obstacles we would have to overcome to reopen the compensation issues. Besides, Congress was pretty clear. These were hearings with white farmers over irrigation, not with Indians over the dam. From a practical point of view, this was a real stretch."

The Cross and Walker clans had been neighbors for going on nine hundred years, so members of each family were known to be blunt with one another. After hearing Raymond's reservations, Tillie, a close friend of Raymond's older sister Phyllis, shrugged them off. Over the next two months, Walker held her ground with passion and persuasion at council meetings. Her friend and ally, fellow councilwoman Marie Wells, was in Tillie's camp. Wells had her own dark memories of The Flood, and she believed they should demand a hearing with the commission.

"Marie and Tillie were tight," says Alyce. "Once they'd made up their minds, you couldn't get a knife blade between them."

Perhaps this Garrison Diversion Unit Commission was a long shot, just like Raymond argued, and maybe the legal hurdles were insurmountable. But even if the opening was no bigger than the eye of a needle, argued Walker, what did the council have to lose?

"Let us never forget the people in these three tribes whose lives were destroyed by Garrison Dam," said Walker. "We all know people who are still living with the horror of dislocation and disintegration in their families and communities. I say the dead have a right to be heard. I believe we have a moral obligation to make certain that no opportunity is missed to set this right. Raymond is probably right. We probably won't get to first base. But we'll never know if we don't try."

The council voted unanimously to submit the Three Affiliated Tribes' outstanding grievances related to the dam to the Garrison Diversion Unit Commission when the hearings began in Fargo. Raymond, Tillie Walker, and Marie Wells would travel to the hearings. If he could find a way to get legal standing before the commission, Raymond agreed to present the tribes' case.

But before they made the drive to Fargo for one roll of the dice, Raymond wanted the Tribal Council members to understand that their chances for success were slim to none. The North Dakota State Water Commission had refused to recognize the tribes at the hearings in Bismarck. As far as Congress was concerned, the tribes had already been compensated for their loss thirty years earlier, so they could not be regarded as "a stakeholder group whose opportunities were forgone." In the eyes of Congress and the state of North Dakota, the compensation claim now being raised by the tribes' attorney these many years later was a nonstarter. Everyone on the council said he or she understood that the odds were a million to one, against.

What Raymond did not tell the council was that he may have found the eye of the needle, but he was loath to raise their hopes. By denying the tribes standing to air their grievances before the Garrison Diversion Unit Commission, the state had inadvertently exposed the only argument it could call on to bar the tribes from the hearings. Now all Raymond had to do was find another opening to the commission in Fargo, preferably one that the state had already deemed to meet the requirements for a legitimate claim.

Raymond remembers that when the answer came to him, no one was more surprised than he was. It had been right under their noses all along, lurking in one of the last places he would have looked. Now, the big question was whether the Garrison Diversion Unit Commission would give him standing at the hearings long enough to make his case. Would they let him speak? That was the imponderable question that remained to be answered in October 1984, when Martin Cross's youngest son turned east onto Interstate Ninety at Bismarck and headed for Fargo. The first snow flurries of the season swirled across the pavement on phantom zephyrs. The odds against him were still impossibly long, but Tillie Walker was right. After so much anguish and grief, it was worth the 250 mile drive to look into their eyes and ask, one last time, to be heard.

CHAPTER IX

The Last Train to Yuma

☙

"When the last red man shall have perished from the earth and his mem-
ory among white men shall have become a myth, these shores shall swarm
with the invisible dead of my tribe. Your children's children will not be
alone. Let the white man be just and deal kindly with my
people, for the dead are not altogether powerless."

CHIEF SEEALTH, DUWAMISH

It was an early October evening in Fargo, North Dakota, in 1984. Ronald
Reagan's campaign for a second term in the White House appeared to be
as unstoppable as the arctic winter that had swept down out of the north
and buried the Upper Midwest under the first blizzard of the year. Blowing
snow drifted against the concrete abutments that lined the highway off-
ramps at Fargo. Stoplights flashing over intersections of empty city streets
swung wildly in the frigid wind. Schools closed regionwide, and long-haul
truckers downshifted into towns such as Beach and Jamestown. There was
refuge here, in warm truck stops with bright lights and like-minded cast-
aways who had already gathered around endless pots of coffee, little piles of
loose change, and dog-eared decks of cards.

For weeks, the Garrison Diversion Unit Commission's arrival in Fargo
had been preceded by an expectant buzz in the regional press. With three former U.S. senators and three former governors among its eleven members, this
was the most distinguished group of outsiders to visit the state since the dedication of Garrison Dam, exactly thirty years before. In fact, while Congress'
requirements for appointment to the GDUC had seemed modest enough on
paper, suitable candidates had to be recruited from the top echelons of public service. Where, asked a stymied Secretary Clark, was he supposed to find
men and women with experience in municipal and industrial water systems

who were also well versed in western water law? And of those, how many would volunteer to serve pro bono for a period of months? The commission's charter was as complex as its goals would be elusive. In order to keep the investigation on track, the cost-conscious Clark wanted a chairman with a track record for delivering reports on schedule and under budget. In August, former Louisiana governor David Treen agreed to serve as the commission's chairman.

Unlike many of his colorful predecessors in the Cajun state, Treen was well known in government circles as a straight-shooting administrator. He combined a congenial manner with a low threshold for nonsense, and there was a charming mint-julep quality to his voice that put people at ease. The governor confessed to being a little fuzzy on western water law, but no one on the commission was better versed in Robert's rules. Clark asked him to have the commission's report to Congress no later than the last day of the year. At their first get-acquainted gathering in Washington in early September, all eleven commissioners and their twenty-member support staff seemed anxious to get started. They had less than four months to come up with realistic solutions to a problem that had befuddled Congress for three decades.

The GDUC hearings, which opened in Fargo in early October, were the first of several the commission would host in venues across the state. Despite the early snowstorm that blanketed the Great Plains, farmers from every corner of the wind-blasted prairie made the drive to Fargo. After battling the federal water agencies for forty years, they wanted to see these yahoos from Washington with their very own eyes.

The crowds had no sooner gathered in the lobby of the Old Fargo Theater in downtown Fargo than Chairman Treen's education in western water law commenced in earnest. Unlike the straightforward rules of supply and demand that governed the oil and gas trade in his native Louisiana, nothing about water in the West, whether it was a mountain stream or a raindrop, could be reduced to simple economics. By 1984 farmers owned a million and a half square miles of the American landscape. As a lobbying colossus, they had learned that they could make water flow uphill toward money. The titans of agriculture had sought to tie up every drop of water that would fall on, flow over, or be pumped out of the continent's arid heartland for the next hundred years. To further complicate that picture, Glenn Sloan's original plan for a regionwide system of water distribution had evolved into a confounding web of environmental and political protocols. Among the first up to testify, North Dakota's governor William Guy reminded the commission that the state's water subsidy to downstream barge transportation had been expressly forbidden by the O'Mahoney-Millikin Amendment to the Flood Control Act of 1944. Yet this lawless practice had been going on, unchecked, for thirty years. The Corps, said Guy, was the biggest group of thieves that Washington had ever turned loose on honest, hardworking citizens. Then, the National Wildlife Federation and National Audubon Society promised to bring further lawsuits if the central flyway wetlands were not protected. And finally, even the farmers seemed to have developed second thoughts. Some were simply fed up with the bureau and the Corps. Others aligned themselves with environmental groups such as the Sierra Club and threatened to go to court to preserve the last short-grass prairie in North America from being destroyed by Pick-Sloan reservoirs and irrigation whirligigs.

As the commissioners filed out of the theater at the end of a long day of testimony, Ike Livermore, who had served for eight years as California's secretary of natural resources under former governor Reagan, wondered privately if anyone else had noticed the young man sitting at the back of the theater. Livermore leaned over to ask the only woman on the team, Ann Zorn, if she had noticed the tall young man with horn-rim spectacles and the formal, professorial manner — the fellow who kept returning day after day.

"It was an impulsive, off-the-cuff exchange," remembers Livermore, "but she said she had noticed him, too. As we returned to our hotel that night, my instincts told me that I had found an ally."

Ever since their first meetings in Washington, Livermore had been studying his peers in search of a partner, an ideological cohort with whom he could form a coalition. He gathered that Zorn was a fierce advocate for strict environmental policies in her home state of Nevada. In fact, she held a permanent seat on the powerful Nevada State Environmental Commission. What he did not know was that Zorn had been studying him, too. Perhaps the gentleman from California, a Reagan appointee, would become her ally.

As the long hours of testimony came to an end on the fifth and final day of hearings in Fargo, the young man noticed by Livermore and Zorn once again stood up from his chair and approached the podium. A wing of black hair fell at an angle across his forehead. He was six foot five, and his commanding poise seemed to dominate the room. As Raymond Cross stepped up to the podium, Chairman Treen's eyes jumped. They were out of time. Treen reached for the gavel.

"Mr. Chairman, esteemed members of the commission, my name is Raymond Cross, and I am here on behalf of the Mandan, Hidatsa, and Arikara Indian nations —"

The gavel cracked sharply.

"I'm sorry, Mr. Cross," said the chairman. "We've had an awful long day here, as you well know, and we're already way past our scheduled conclusion. I'm afraid we're out of time."

"I'm not leaving," Raymond Cross replied quietly.

Ike Livermore rocked forward on his elbows. The other members of the commission were shuffling their papers, anxious to leave and get back to their hotel. Livermore glanced at Ann Zorn, who was already watching Treen. The chairman was an affable fellow, but he had shown himself to be a stickler for procedural decorum. After five days on the road and endless hours of testimony, Treen was in no mood to start bending rules.

"Well, Mr. Cross, you can suit yourself," said Treen. "But I'm afraid you'll be here talkin' to yourself, because the rest of us are finished here. It's been a long day in a long week, and it's well past time for supper."

"Mr. Chairman, with all due respect, I'm not leaving this podium until I have been heard. I have waited patiently all week. I have a right to be heard."

Treen was visibly irritated by Cross's challenge. He set down the gavel and let out a loud sigh into the microphone. By now, members of the commission had stopped whatever they were doing and were lifting their eyes to the young man.

"Let me remind you, Mr. Cross, that the questions we are seeking to answer, the reason we came to your fair state in the first place, have to do with irrigation. With all due respect, sir, there's nothing in our mandate from Congress that has anything to do with Indians."

Raymond Cross deflected Treen's calculated distinction. He had already anticipated this position, and he knew it was bulletproof if Treen wanted to make it stick. The way Treen read it, if he stuck to the letter of the charter that was drafted by Congress, the door would shut forever.

"We respectfully disagree, Mr. Chairman. We believe the questions being put to this commission are also, by implication, raised by the federal government's trust obligations to the Mandan, Hidatsa, and Arikara nations. These hearings are central to the devastating consequences that resulted from the unconstitutional taking of these tribes' homelands by the Army Corps of Engineers when the Garrison Dam was built. The lake that formed behind that dam destroyed a world they owned by aboriginal title. Nothing was left, not one home, not one community, not one school. If anyone in this state is to derive a benefit from the irrigation projects promised to the people who made a sacrifice for Garrison Dam, the compensatory legislation drafted to remedy those omissions must include the Three Affiliated Tribes."

A quiet murmur swept through the audience. Cross's well-mannered defiance seemed to have captured the attention of all the commissioners. "It was an extraordinary moment," recalls Ann Zorn. "No one who was there could possibly forget it."

Chairman Treen rocked back, as if recoiling from Cross's polite but effective challenge. Ike Livermore was busy second-guessing the chairman. He thought to himself that Treen's inner dilemma was betrayed by a little storm of confusion that seemed to hang momentarily between the governor's eyes. For the first time since the hearings began, the chairman was at a loss for words. Then a voice rang out from down the table. Treen shot a glance along the dais. It was that Livermore fellow, from California, raising his hand. Maybe he had a suggestion.

"Mr. Livermore."

"Governor, can we have a brief conference here with staff, in private?"

Treen sighed and set down the gavel. "Well, I don't see the harm, if nobody else does."

There were no objections to a conference.

"Mr. Cross, will you bear with us for a moment?" asked Treen. "As you probably know, we hadn't prepared ourselves for this eventuality."

"I'd be glad to, Mr. Chairman."

Ike Livermore; Ann Zorn; Henry Bellmon, the former governor of Oklahoma; and Patrick Noonan, the future founder of the Conservation Fund, huddled with members of their legislative support staff around Chairman Treen. The conference seemed to go on for an eternity. Almost thirty-five years to the day after his father walked out of Congress, resigned to defeat, his thirty-five-year-old son now stood with his hands at his sides and calmly waited for an answer. Was this group of strangers going to give him the opportunity to revisit a verdict that shattered his father and his family, and destroyed the world of his ancestors?

"Treen had every right to adjourn that hearing," says Cross. "There was nothing obligating the commission to hear me out. I thought I might have gotten my foot in the door, but the rest was up to them. The future for thousands of Mandan, Hidatsa, and Arikara people, unborn generations, was in Treen's hands. From where I stood, this was the last train to Yuma."

The soporific haze that had hung over the hearings all afternoon suddenly seemed to lift. Tillie Walker dashed down the aisle to remind Raymond of something, then rejoined Marie Wells at the back of the theater. While the audience stretched and milled about, a small war was being fought inside the circle of heads on the elevated stage. Treen asked their legislative support staff, Marc Messing, for a briefing on the legal issues. Messing told the commissioners that there was no problem with hearing Cross out. Cross's appeal was obviously well thought out. It was politically clever and legally on-target. Nothing prevented them from hearing an appeal from the Indians on the irrigation issues.

Treen now turned to the commissioners and invited them to present their opinions. Ann Zorn was an unknown, but Livermore's credentials carried a lot of weight with everyone on the commission. Whoever this fellow was, argued Livermore, he had come back day after day with those two Indian ladies and had patiently waited for his turn to speak. But every time he stepped up to the podium, the chairman had gaveled the hearings closed and sent him on his way. "I don't see how we can fulfill our responsibilities to resolve the institutional equity issues without hearing from the Indians," he argued. He reminded his fellow commissioners that Congress specifically instructed them to put all institutions, such as state, county, and municipal governments, on an equal footing. Contrary to Governor Treen's original interpretation of Congress' charter, the institutional equity provisions seemed to be saying that the commissioners could not *exclude* the tribes.

Institutional equity was the eye of the needle, Raymond Cross's one chance in a million. Zorn, an energetic grandmother with a salt-and-pepper hairdo and a cut-to-the-chase manner, quickly agreed, but she and Livermore were immediately challenged by two of their fellow commissioners. Nowhere, argued Commissioner John Paulson, a retired editor of the *Fargo Forum,* did the originating legislation say a word about Indians. In fact, argued his ally, Pat O'Meara, the vice president of the National Water Resources Association, "the state doesn't have to deal with the Indians in the first place. If the tribes have a problem with this, they can take it to their own advocates in Washington at the BIA. This isn't our problem, and it's not in the charter."

"Where's the harm in letting him speak?" countered Zorn.

"The state already vetted these guys," retorted Paulson. "If we were supposed to take their testimony, the tribes would be on the list."

"Besides, I've never believed any Indian I've ever talked to," blurted O'Meara.

Zorn was astounded by this slip, as were Livermore and Treen. "Let's get back to the point," said Treen, crossing visual daggers with O'Meara.

"Let's hear him out," said Henry Bellmon, the former governor and U.S. senator from Oklahoma. "Ike's got a point."

"Well, I guess this one's up to me," said Treen.

As they returned to their seats, none of the commissioners knew what Treen had decided. Chairman Treen rapped the gavel and asked the audience to return to their seats. His brow furrowed with deep creases as a hush fell over the theater.

"The Garrison Diversion Unit Commission recognizes Mr. Raymond Cross, attorney for the Three Affiliated Tribes of the Mandan, Hidatsa, and Arikara nations. Just so everybody here understands, Mr. Cross will be the final person to address this commission. Mr. Cross, the commission is granting you fifteen minutes. Please, you may begin."

⋇

Chairman Treen and members of the commission, my name is Raymond Cross, and it is my pleasure to testify on behalf of the Three Affiliated Tribes of the Fort Berthold Reservation," began Raymond. "The Three Affiliated Tribes is a federally recognized Indian tribe that resides on the Fort Berthold Reservation in northwestern North Dakota." He quickly reminded the commissioners that the aboriginal homelands of the Mandan, Hidatsa, and Arikara people were located at the center of Lake Sakakawea, which was created by the Pick-Sloan Plan. "Indeed, the Department of the Interior, from the inception of the Pick-Sloan Plan, was aware of the ethical and legal responsibilities imposed by these facts. The Bureau of Indian Affairs recognized that many of the features of the project were in part or in whole based on Indian lands and would affect Indian water rights. The BIA concluded that realization and protection of the unique Indian rights should be built into the governing principles of the Flood Control Act of 1944 at each aspect of the project's development."

But that had never happened, argued Cross, despite all the guarantees made to the tribes at the time of the bill's passage in Congress. Two generations later, the people of North Dakota were arguing that they suffered disproportionate losses of their rich, irreplaceable croplands, a fact at the heart of the state's claim that the people of the nation should now build the irrigation program they promised, four decades earlier, to mitigate the great sacrifices made by the people of North Dakota.

"The fact is," Cross concluded, "the Three Affiliated Tribes bore the brunt of the social and economic costs imposed on discrete groups for the development of these multipurpose projects that benefitted the United States as a whole. Very little account has been taken of the water development needs of the Indian tribes, developments that were promised and never delivered."

There was no time better than the present to finally make good on those promises, Cross advised the panel. The tribes had sought permission to participate in these hearings in order to ensure that the recommendations the panel made to Congress reflected the true sacrifices made by people living on the Upper Missouri River, native and nonnative alike. Unfortunately, that representation was not extended to them by the State Water Commission, so as the legal counsel for the Mandan, Hidatsa, and Arikara people, the original citizens of this High Plains country, Cross had no choice but to present their case directly to the commission.

"We would like to propose to the commission that a special study area be established to examine the North Dakota Indian tribes' water development needs, and that a portion of its report to Congress deal specifically with an assessment and recommendation as to how the tribes' unique federal water rights may be realized through development of project water from the reservoirs along the system." With that, he thanked the panel for the opportunity to speak and offered to answer any questions.

"Specifically, what promises did Congress make to the tribes regarding water development projects?" asked Livermore. "None of us have copies of those pieces of legislation, and, unless I overlooked something, there was nothing in our materials about Pick-Sloan agreements with the tribes."

"Those were outlined in House Joint Resolution 33, from the 80th Congress, and the final takings act, Public Law 437, from 1949. I can make those available, Mr. Livermore. To answer your question in a general way, there were a lot of promises made, Commissioner, ranging from irrigation to municipal and industrial water development, to the right of access to the lake to develop recreational facilities."

"So, from A to Z, so to speak . . ."

"Yes, sir."

"And . . . what is the status of those projects?" asked Governor Bellmon.

"There is no status, Commissioner, insofar as they never happened, or the guarantees, such as lakeshore development, were later denied."

"Why were they denied?" asked Zorn.

"Well, that's a good question, Commissioner. That's never been explained to us, but they never happened."

"None of them? Nothing?" asked the incredulous chairman.

"No, sir, none of them. We were awarded some settlement money by Congress at the time of the taking, but we had to use that money to build our own water system because the wells the Army engineers put in were seldom any good. The water was bad, you couldn't drink it or put it on crops or fill a stock tank with it without making your animals sick. So, the system we put in almost forty years ago is desperately inadequate, but the tribes don't have the financial resources to build a new system from scratch, so we're making do. An M and I [municipal and industrial] system was supposed to be factored into the original appropriations bills for Pick-Sloan, but we never saw it."

"How long ago was this, Mr. Cross?" asked Commissioner Patrick Noonan, the former national director of the Nature Conservancy.

"Forty years next month."

"Mr. Cross," said Zorn, "I'd just like to say that I think your idea about a special study area regarding these guarantees, and the tribes' water development needs, seeing how the tribes sacrificed so much in the first place, is an intriguing one. I think we'll be talking about this and trying to figure out the best way to pursue this with the tribes. I'm assuming you'll be available?"

"Yes, ma'am, of course, and we welcome that opportunity."

"Thank you, Mr. Cross, for being patient with us. I know you've waited a long time to speak," said Livermore.

"My pleasure. I'm grateful for the opportunity."

"Are there any other questions for Mr. Cross?" asked Treen.

"Uh, Mr. Cross, I'd like to speak with you right after the meeting, if I may," said Livermore.

"Certainly."

"Thank you, Mr. Cross," said Treen.

"Thank you, Mr. Chairman."

The gavel came down with a bang. "The Garrison Diversion Unit Commission stands adjourned."

⋇

The institutional equity clause that Raymond had found in the commission's charter was, in effect, a legal hole shaped by the bundling of the irrigation and municipal and industrial water development issues. Instead of raising questions about the "just compensation" for the Three Affiliated Tribes, a claim that would likely go nowhere, Raymond realized that he could achieve the same objective by connecting the unfulfilled promises Congress had made to his father in 1954 — to provide the tribes with municipal and agricultural water development — with the "institutional equity" clause in the Garrison Diversion Unit Commission charter. Marc Messing had immediately recognized the tactic. Raymond tailored the tribes' new appeal to fit within the narrowly defined scope of the commission's official charter.

Whoever he was, wherever he came from, the tall young Indian with the jet-black eyes had presented his case with a remarkable degree of self-assurance. The weight of his coolly delivered statement was felt immediately by the commission. "As Raymond was speaking, I could feel our entire investigation veering off in a new direction," says Zorn. "The only question in my mind, and Ike's and Henry Bellmon's, was 'How are we going to get there?' Congress had a lot of questions it wanted answered, but from that moment on, the GDUC was in Raymond Cross's hands."

Once they were finished in Fargo, the commissioners moved on to Minot and finally wrapped up their fieldwork with two days of hearings in Bismarck. Before the group left the state, the press was already noting the shift. Beneath a banner headline reading PANELISTS CONTEND INDIANS' ROLE NOT RECOGNIZED, *Fargo Forum* reporter Jim Neumann identified the maverick commissioners in the story's lead sentence and reported that Livermore and Zorn had knocked the commission off its rails. In their opinion, the Indians had paid the highest price for Missouri River development, and the tribes should be first in line when the federal government started writing checks for water projects.

"It hit me like a ton of bricks," Livermore told Neumann. "Everybody from the governor on down mentioned this great overwhelming debt owed to the state of North Dakota, and they never mentioned the Indians. The way I look at it, they're still due a couple of hundred million dollars," said Livermore, observing that the tribes may deserve one-third to one-half of all the Garrison benefits. "I know that won't fly politically, but in a court of law, I think that's what they should get."

Once the field hearings concluded, Livermore took an informal head count of his fellow commissioners. He knew that he and Zorn were within striking distance of reopening the "just compensation" issues for the tribes. Through the dauntless efforts of the staff attorney, Marc Messing, who was in charge of briefing the commissioners on legal issues related to "institutional equity," Livermore was able to slowly work his way upstream toward the legal opening that awaited them in the water development provisions of the Garrison Diversion plan.

"Certain people just come along at the right time and the right place," says Zorn. "For us, Marc was that person. We had a lot of wonderfully competent support staff, but no one was better versed in the federal issues than Marc Messing. There were turning points along the way, as there always are in these kinds of things, when I realized that he had the whole set of issues prewired before we ever got on the plane to North Dakota."

As Livermore and Zorn were entering the final negotiations for the commission's recommendations to Congress, Messing wrote them an incisive memo. "I am increasingly concerned that the commission may compound the injustices done to the Indians," he warned. There were two salient items that the commission had a legal and moral obligation to address in its final recommendations, wrote Messing. One, roughly half of the 550,000 acres the state claimed it lost to Pick-Sloan dams was owned by Indians. Two, in the category of institutional equity, indisputably the Three Affiliated Tribes had suffered the brunt of the impact of Pick-Sloan without ever receiving fair treatment or just compensation from the government. Messing concluded his sub-rosa memo by telling them:

> The history of this settlement is a tragedy from which the tribes have never recovered. The Indians can demonstrate explicit treaty language that guaranteed them rights which were violated by the inundations. The evidence I have seen regarding the construction of Garrison and Oahe Dams points to the fact that gross and fundamental injustices were done to these people, and not to reexamine this as part of the commission's mandate to consider issues of "institutional equity" would effectively close the last opportunity these tribes may have to rebuild the communities that were destroyed.

Livermore was sufficiently inspired by Messing's appeal to write a memo of his own to his fellow commissioners as they prepared to hammer out the final recommendations to Congress in the first week of December. Recapitulating the commission's findings, Livermore reminded his protégés that, if nothing else, their investigation had uncovered irrefutable evidence that the tribes "were given grossly inadequate consideration in the then-proposed Garrison Unit legislation." The Mandan, Hidatsa, and Arikara people had shouldered the full weight of Pick-Sloan. By comparison, the sacrifice made by the state of North Dakota was nominal. Forty years after the taking of the ancestral homelands, the reservation infrastructure was in shambles. The new road system promised by the Army engineers, for example, was either falling apart or never completed. Bridges over coulees and streambeds stopped in midair. Roads begun forty years earlier had yet to reach their destinations. Many simply ran for twenty miles across the prairie, then ended abruptly in the middle of nowhere. The community day schools in Nishu, Shell Creek, and Beaver Creek had disappeared. Like Indian children at the turn of the twentieth century, today's Indian children were forced to make a choice between attending white public schools, where they were not welcome, or making a long journey to BIA-sponsored boarding schools in an adjoining state. Welfare, which was all but nonexistent on the reservation before The Flood, had since increased tenfold under the "careful stewardship" of the federal government. Livermore concluded his appeal by describing the trip he and Ann Zorn took to New Town to meet with tribal leaders and elders. "The conditions we observed were enough to bring us to tears," he wrote, adding, as a historical footnote, "North Dakota's leaders had expressed little if any concern for the Indians" when the dams destroyed their world. Where were they, Livermore asked, when the Indians were starving to death and friendless?

An informal poll of the commissioners showed that Zorn and Livermore were scoring points and winning allies. As the commissioners headed toward a final showdown on formal recommendations they would make to Congress, it appeared that Zorn and Livermore's campaign had a chance of winning. "Our fingers were crossed, but we really didn't know how the vote would break until the actual votes were counted," remembers Livermore. "A number of us were playing our cards pretty close to the chest."

Undeterred by the uncertainty, Zorn and Livermore began to prepare a set of formal recommendations to Congress that would be based exclusively on unresolved "Indian issues," as Raymond Cross had suggested in his presentation in Fargo. In order to reconcile this departure from the instructions given to them by Congress, Marc Messing explained that the tribes had legal right to be included as "stakeholders who had forgone economic opportunities" as a result of the construction of Pick-Sloan dams. Since any remedy for the tribes fell outside the scope of their mandate from Congress, Zorn and Livermore recommended that Congress immediately establish a five-member Joint Tribal Advisory Committee (JTAC) under the secretary of the interior to specifically remedy the long-standing sins of omission with the tribes. The committee, they said, should address all unfulfilled promises and guarantees made to the tribes forty years earlier, including the return of excess lands, additional financial or in-kind compensation for their material losses, assessment of the potential for irrigation on reservation lands, the right to develop shoreline recreation areas, and finally, the formal establishment of the tribes' reserved water rights on the main stem of the Missouri.

When a preliminary draft of the report's recommendations reached the public, North Dakota farmers and state politicians were stunned. The first word in the press came from *Forum* reporter Jim Neumann, who warned readers that the commission was planning to "fashion a sweeping new plan for the Garrison diversion project." Neumann's story broke in late December, at the same moment Zorn and Treen were busy polishing the final draft of the report to meet their January 1 deadline. Commissioner Livermore, wrote Neumann, had been in favor of more forceful language on the Indian issues, but his fellow commissioners were concerned about the legal implications of his proposed language for the final report to Congress. Livermore gave up some of his deal points when a majority agreed to recommend that William Clark appoint a new JTAC panel to resolve the tribes' long-standing claims for compensation and "institutional equity."

In Fargo, Minot, and Washington, D.C., this was read as an enormous victory for the tribes. The commission's forthcoming report to Congress would put the tribes in the hunt for a share of the newly apportioned Garrison Diversion Unit water development funds. Those funds, long overdue to both tribes and farmers, had never been delivered. In an interview with Neumann, Cross told the *Forum*'s readers that the GDUC investigation had been prompted in the first place by the environmental issues that had brought a halt to the construction of McClusky Canal a decade earlier. The courts, he reminded Neumann, had already ruled that this phase of the Sloan Plan was in violation of the National Environmental Policy Act. If ducks and geese could get fair treatment from Congress, said Cross, perhaps it was not so far-fetched that "a tribe that was virtually destroyed by Congress has the right to raise those issues as well." Instead of eliciting a storm of protest from angry readers, Cross's remarks were answered by stony silence.

Ann Zorn told Neumann that she and her fellow commissioners were presented with indisputable evidence that the tribes had borne the brunt of the costs for Pick-Sloan. If Congress intended to make good on its commitment to farmers by bringing irrigation to 250,000 acres of prairie, she said, it could only do so after it had dealt fairly with the tribes.

Commissioners O'Meara and Paulson, the water specialist and retired newspaper editor, dug in their heels and resisted the inclusion of the "Indian recommendations" to Congress to the very end. Treen worked to find a middle ground, but it was not to be. O'Meara, an old hand at Washington politics, had nothing to lose by stonewalling. His ally Paulson would still have to look his neighbors in the eye at church and at the grocery store after the commission left town, so he held out. "Since it didn't matter how he voted in the end, and he had to live there, nobody could blame him," says Livermore.

In the end, the O'Meara-Paulson coalition never had a chance once Henry Bellmon and Patrick Noonan joined forces with Zorn and Livermore. Even Commissioner Henry Wessman — the mayor of Grand Forks, North Dakota, and a professor at the University of North Dakota School of Medicine and Health Sciences — lined up with the out of staters. "Henry was our quiet hero," says Zorn. "He took a beating in the local press for supporting me and Ike, and it ended his political career. He could have saved his skin and it wouldn't have changed the outcome, but he didn't."

In mid-January 1985, Zorn and Chairman Treen made the formal presentation of the GDUC's recommendations at a fully attended hearing of the House Interior and Insular Affairs Committee. Treen was pleased to report that the commission's work was completed on schedule and under budget. He then presented an overview of the commission's findings on municipal and industrial water development. Zorn concentrated her testimony on an explanation of the open-ended menu of unsettled Indian issues. In the commission's view, Zorn told the congressmen, nothing would ever be resolved on the Upper Missouri until the Indian people were made whole. Congress' instructions to the commission on "institutional equity" had left them with no alternative but a full airing of the Indian recommendations in their final report.

Within days of the GDUC's presentation on Capitol Hill, and at the insistence of North Dakota congressman Byron Dorgan, the committee forwarded the commission's final report to Secretary Clark. Clark requested a joint meeting with congressional committee members to identify the right people to be appointed to the new Joint Tribal Advisory Committee to resolve the "institutional equity" issues first raised by Raymond Cross. Congress and Secretary Clark needed to expedite this deal so the Bureau of Reclamation could get on with the McClusky project. Representative Dorgan suggested that Clark give North Dakota's governor a call and ask him for the names of possible chairpersons for the new committee. Governor George Sinner was certain to have a short list of qualified candidates in his shirt pocket.

Clark and Sinner were longtime political acquaintances, so the governor felt no obligation to pull punches when Clark wanted to discuss the GDUC's recommendations. More than one North Dakota governor had been sacrificed on the altar of Pick-Sloan, and as Secretary Clark began discussing the Indian issues, Sinner could see his political life passing before his eyes. As a political realist, Sinner had no choice but to cooperate in hopes that Clark could help get this McClusky Canal project back on track.

Clark assured Governor Sinner that his agency would move forward with due haste. But before another foot of irrigation canal could be built, Congress wanted its books cleared of all this unfinished business with the Indians. This thing was a real embarrassment, and it was starting to put off a bad odor on the Hill. Clark explained the nature of the investigation and the kind of man he was looking for to serve as its chairman. This was a sensitive post, but most important, the right man would know how to work fast, and he would have an extensive legislative background that included Indian law.

Governor Sinner said he had just the man Clark was looking for. "He's a retired major general, but don't let that throw you. He was the director of the state legislative council for twenty-five years. Name's Emerson Murry."

⋇

Chairman Murry, esteemed committee members, we are glad you have come here to New Town to hear our stories," began tribal councilwoman Marie Wells. "We know it is a long journey for all of you, during our coldest month of February, and you have traveled far to hear us speak. We thank you . . ."

It was February 1986, a full year after Ann Zorn and Governor Treen presented the findings of the GDUC investigation to Congress. Since then, the new five-member Joint Tribal Advisory Committee had begun to investigate the Indian issues. Emerson Murry remembers that when the JTAC's chartered plane landed at the small airport in New Town, the plane's brakes refused to hold. As they drove through town at high noon, the sign on the bank said the temperature was thirty-six below zero.

The committee had come to New Town to hear oral testimony of tribal elders who had lived through The Flood of the early 1950s. Raymond Cross, Alyce Spotted Bear, and Tillie Walker had spent six months recruiting elders willing to testify. Raymond presented the committee with a witness list that would keep the JTAC investigators in their chairs for two full days.

As a frigid ground blizzard raged outside the walls of the auditorium at the tribal community college in New Town, Emerson Murry sat relaxed and attentive at the head table between his former partner, Hans Walker, and Dr. Brent Blackwelder, the future national director of Friends of the Earth. The auditorium was filled to capacity. Hour after hour, for two days, the JTAC members looked out on a standing-room-only crowd. Councilwoman Marie Wells was the first to the lectern. She pulled a piece of paper from her pocket and smoothed it in the light. Once she began, she spoke to the end without taking her eyes off the committee.

"Many of us have waited a long, long time to tell our stories," she said. "My name is Marie Wells, and I was born in 1928. I grew up as a little child in the bottom country. It was a beautiful place, and my father was a rancher. My brother and I walked three miles to meet the school bus, and when it was really cold, like today, our dad would take us to meet the bus in our horse-drawn sled. If you look at the records of our people, you will see that my grandpa William Dean Sr. was a teacher at the school down at the Fishhook Village before we moved up to Elbowoods. Also, he was an interpreter for the bureau superintendent and the men at the trading post. He spent a lot of time chasing my dad, because my dad never wanted to go to school, and he never did learn a word of English. My father loved our place on the bottom. . . . It was a beautiful place to live, and well protected. It was so pretty there that I still dream about it, and when I wake up and remember it's gone, I have to cry.

"My father had a hundred cows. We had a big garden and we worked hard. We put up hay with horses, we shocked oats by hand. We didn't have tractors, and we worked the gardens with our arms and shoulders, and our backs. When I was little I really wanted to be an attorney, but we didn't have the money, and I didn't dare mention it. I loved school, and eventually I went off to the Indian college at Haskell, where I got two years of college. My sister is the dean of students here at the college in New Town. All of the Indians have diabetes now. I can tell you, we didn't have diabetes before we moved up here. We got diabetes right after we got electricity. Before that, it was work, work, work. We worked so hard we didn't need electricity and we didn't get diabetes. It was hard but it was better, and we lived in a beautiful place where we were all together, and people danced and sang the old songs. We picked wild grapes, chokecherries, bull berries, wild plums, buffalo berries, Juneberries — those were the ones that came down first — and we dug the wild turnips and dried them for the winter.

"My mother and grandmother dried the berries for pemmican and corn balls, the buffalo berries made good jam and jelly, and the old people pounded the chokecherries and dried them like burgers and saved them for the winter. The berries were good for us, for our kidneys and hearts and our blood, but they are all gone and now we have heart disease and kidney disease, and our blood is bad with the diabetes. Mostly, our food was corn and

Arikara squash. You can't find the seeds for that squash anymore, but it was delicious. We didn't need sugar because the food we harvested was naturally sweet. We never had sugar until we moved out of the bottom and got electricity. When I was growing up we always chopped our own wood. Some take their knowledge out of books, but me, I lived the Indian way, the Indian life, and I miss it. When The Flood came we had to leave our beautiful homes and move on top, and the Indian life ended because we had to start living the white life, but the white life is not any good for the Indian. My dad had to sell his cows and our land. He didn't die until 1982, but his life ended with The Flood. After The Flood, our life never came back. We lost our berries."

For ten hours each day, an unbroken stream of elders approached the podium and unburdened their souls of forty years of bitterness, sadness, and unanswered grief. What impressed Hans Walker was that few of the speakers blamed "the white man" for the tribes' misfortunes. Once they started speaking, it seemed, the library of stories was inexhaustible. Many elders sat quietly and wept as they listened to the stories of friends and family. Once the witnesses started speaking, the contagion of rumor quickly spread to the far corners of the reservation. Word went out that something big was afoot at the JTAC hearings in New Town. Come quickly, said the grapevine, and they did. Many would drive a hundred miles through ground blizzards to reach New Town. When Hidatsa elder Cora Baker took the podium, she asked: "When the dam produces so much cheap electricity, why have the energy costs for the three tribes soared?" Another, Dani Sue Deane, accused the government of turning the three tribes into beggars after leaving them homeless and walking away. "When our economic heartland was taken away, it left a deep poverty, the poverty of social dysfunction and broken communities," said Deane. "Many of us have never recovered from the feeling of being totally defeated. We weep before you because our stories are painful to remember. Our tears burn our eyes because they are so bitter and so real. Our tears are the only thing many of us have left."

From the moment the JTAC was formed, Raymond's strategy for winning over the committee was to put a human face on the story of the Garrison Dam. If the JTAC would come to New Town, Cross gambled, then the testimony might be enough to reopen the "just compensation" issue that was finessed by Congress in 1949. When the Garrison Diversion Unit Commission concluded its work the year before, Raymond's nature was to be skeptical until the proof was at hand. At best, he and Alyce were hoping to be awarded funding for irrigation that they could in turn divert into a much-needed municipal water project for New Town. But now, the formation of the JTAC had shifted their horizons. With Chairman Murry agreeing to bring the investigation to New Town, Alyce and Raymond suddenly realized that they had stepped onto a much larger playing field than the one they had anticipated. Cross's strategy was to put Chairman Murry, Hans Walker, and the other committee members through a wrenching ordeal of firsthand testimony.

"We had a lot of fine people break down, they just couldn't talk anymore," recalls Emerson Murry. "I have to say those two days in New Town were as deeply moving as anything I've ever experienced. I've been on a lot of commissions, and I have never heard more authentic testimony. By the end of the second day, we knew they had a very strong case on the compensation issues. Congress had blown it very badly with the takings act [in 1949]."

Murry, the two-star general and master of the legislative game, hoped his committee would agree to a democratic approach to resolving the inevitable disputes. This would be crucial in the final stages as they sorted through evidence and prepared their final report for Congress and Donald Hodel, President Reagan's new man at the Department of the Interior. All in all, Murry was encouraged by the chemistry among the members. Before they boarded the plane for New Town, the committee agreed to focus the investigation on a single question: Did the 1949 takings act properly compensate the tribes under the Fifth Amendment by making the tribes whole? In other words, did they receive compensation of equivalent value for the land and resources that were lost in The Flood? Secondarily, the JTAC asked: Did Congress make a good-faith effort to properly compensate the tribes when it passed Public Law 437?

"The real trick for me, as chairman, was to convince the committee members to accept the testimony of the Indians under the existing rules of evidence," says Murry. "I never really discussed this aspect of our investigation with anyone, and I don't think anybody but Raymond knew what I was doing. But I had to do it. Repetition from their stories was the only way I could verify their claims to Congress."

Murry decided to put the rules of evidence to a test after the first day of hearings in New Town. The committee voted unanimously to accept the oral testimony as material evidence. In other words, the oral histories they heard would carry as much evidentiary weight as a bloody knife found at the scene of a murder. "That vote was a real turning point, and the credit has to go to Ray," says Murry. "He worked his butt off to fill up that auditorium. Once the committee agreed to accept the testimony as evidence, it gave our report real weight with Congress."

While Raymond was racing around the countryside lining up witnesses for the JTAC hearings, word reached him that his world was about to become infinitely more complex. *Wold Engineering,* the case that the U.S. Supreme Court had sent back to North Dakota's highest court for further review, was back on the front burner. Raymond had flown down to the regional BIA offices in Aberdeen, South Dakota, to locate important documents for the JTAC. While waiting for his flight back home, he was paged to a phone at the airport. The call was from Kim Gottschalk, an old friend from the Native American Rights Fund in Boulder. Gottschalk had tracked him down through the tribal office in Four Bears.

"Hey, Ray!" exclaimed Gottschalk. "You'll be getting a call from the Supreme Court. They accepted cert in *Wold.*"

Certiorari, or simply *cert* in legal shorthand, is the formal process by which a superior court calls up the judicial record of a lower court to review a contested ruling. Raymond was amazed by this news. Of the thousands of cases that are sent to the U.S. Supreme Court for review each year, the court selects a few dozen. Gottschalk himself had just gotten the word from one of the clerks in the high court.

"There was so much more at stake in *Wold II,* and my own anxiety level reflected that," says Raymond, who suddenly found himself in a double bind between preparing for the JTAC and preparing for a second trip to the U.S. Supreme Court. "I'd gone through the motions of filing for cert, but it was the last thing I expected. And now the JTAC was coming to town. I couldn't let up on the JTAC, but I couldn't ignore *Wold* either."

After the U.S. Supreme Court heard what was now being called *Wold I,* the justices seemed just as confused as the state. They sent the case back to the North Dakota Supreme Court with instructions to take another look at P.L. 280, the Termination Era law that attempted to transfer power over the tribes to the states, to see if there was not a graceful way out of this dilemma. Strangely, broken water pumps in a lift station on the banks of the Missouri had brought the question of termination and the responsibilities of the "federal trust doctrine" to the country's highest court. They wanted the state to solve the riddle and clear a way to hearing the case without forcing the tribe to relinquish its sovereignty. Essentially, as Chief Justice VandeWalle recalls, the state court had "sent *Wold* up" hoping to get a "bright line" from the Supreme Court. The high court declined the offer and instructed North Dakota to resolve this at home.

"Chief Justice Erickstad read that decision, took another look at the law, and came right back to the same conclusion," says Raymond. "He said, 'Look, we appreciate your counsel, Mr. Cross, but we have no choice but to reaffirm our original finding. For us to hear this case, you will have to waive sovereign immunity.' Well, obviously we weren't going to do that. So, once again, Erickstad sent it back up to the Supremes and said, 'Nope, we don't see where we have jurisdiction.'"

In Raymond's initial arguments before the North Dakota Supreme Court, he pointed out that the jurisdictional logjam over which court could hear their case amounted to a violation of due process and equal protection. By denying the tribes access to state courts, the law effectively denied the Indians access to remedies in any civil disputes over broken contracts, whether it be the installation of water pumps or running a transit system. Then, in one of those unexpected moments of serendipity that will dazzle legal scholars for years to come, Raymond included a note about "preemption" in the brief he filed with the U.S. Supreme Court in his petition for certiorari. This was an off-the-cuff reference to amendments to P.L. 280 that Congress adopted in 1968. Those amendments corrected earlier confusion by making it clear that federal law "preempted" state law when questions of federal law were in dispute. Because Indian Country is protected by the umbrella of the "federal trust doctrine," that had to include the dispute over jurisdiction in *Wold* that had thus far confounded both courts.

Back in the early 1960s, the North Dakota state legislature adopted the recommendations of Emerson Murry and Hans Walker and agreed to apply P.L. 280 on a case-by-case basis, rather than making it a blanket law that covered all contingencies. In *Wold,* the North Dakota Supreme Court was saying that the state's "case-by-case" approach did not give the state's high court enough jurisdictional reach to overcome the "sovereign immunity" problem. In other words, the state could no more hear a tribe's complaint than it could stand in judgment of the federal government. Chief Justice Ralph Erickstad ruled that the state could not encroach on the tribes' sovereign immunity. The North Dakota court was simply honoring that protection.

"I was sitting in the law library in Grand Forks preparing for *Wold* when the 'preemption' argument came back to me. I knew the due process argument would get shredded by Brennan and Rehnquist. I suddenly remembered that clause in the brief on preemption. That's it! That's the argument! The only problem with the preemption argument was that it had never been argued in the high court. My only hope was to give enough of the justices a good reason to reverse the state supremes."

Since the preemption argument had never been tested in the high court, Raymond needed to bolster the argument with a precedent on which to base the tribes' appeal. After days of searching through federal case law at the law school in Grand Forks, he found a Montana case called *Kennerly v. District Court* with compelling parallels to *Wold*. For the purpose of securing remedy for a white businessman who had been having trouble collecting fees from his Indian clients, the Blackfoot Tribal Council had simply deferred its jurisdiction to the state district court, without waiving its sovereign immunity.

"That had to be our case," says Raymond. "*Kennerly* was a per curiam decision, meaning that there was no opinion attached. That meant that I was going to have to be very careful on just how much I pressed that issue. They were going to pressure me to give them a good reason to reverse Erickstad."

Yet as he packed his bags to return to Washington, he knew that the outcome of this battle would have as much to do with the particulars of the case as it would with the personalities and political agendas of the nine justices who would weigh its merits. For the past 150 years, the U.S. Supreme Court had been the tribes' last line of defense. Having heard more than twelve hundred Indian cases during that time, a long line of justices on the high bench had consistently reaffirmed the legal boundaries that protected tribes from the incessant encroachment of states that were jealous of their land, natural resources, and sovereign immunity. Whether the court's decisions were later enforced by Congress comprised a different set of questions with altogether different answers. The Termination Era, for example, was nothing less than a frontal assault on the court's historic and faithful defense of tribes as "domestically dependent sovereign nations."

By the mid-1980s, tribal governments were aware that in a few short years, a sea of change had taken place on the high court. Justice William Rehnquist and his ideological allies were exhibiting open hostility to tribal sovereignty and the "trust doctrine" of federal Indian law. A hundred and fifty years earlier, Rehnquist's ideological predecessors had argued that Indians were subhuman savages. In Marshall's court, Justice Baldwin had insisted that granting legal status to roving bands of forest gypsies was a calamitous mistake. Thirty years later, the ideological track pioneered by Justice Baldwin would be used to uphold the legality of slavery in the famous Dred Scott Decision. Here, a majority of justices ruled that a slave was property and therefore had no claim to legal rights guaranteed by the U.S. Constitution. Rehnquist's early Indian-law dissents telegraphed the message to Indian

Country that an ideological descendant of Justice Baldwin had taken a seat on the nation's highest court.

"By the time of *Wold II,* it was pretty obvious what was going on in the court," says Raymond. "Nixon had started a long-awaited avalanche of reform for federal Indian policy. What he and Congress had restored to the tribes in the way of rights, Rehnquist, and later Scalia, would do their level best to take away. In many respects, they've been an ideological tag team and a throwback to another century."

As an associate justice, Rehnquist wrote the lone dissent in the 1980 case *Sioux Tribes v. United States.* After a fifty-year battle in federal courts, the court agreed with the Sioux tribe's claim that the federal government had violated its treaty-protected ownership of the Black Hills in South Dakota. Justice Blackmun found Rehnquist's dissent so illogical that he refused to mention it in his opinion for the majority. With a caustic disdain seldom seen in a majority opinion, Blackmun dismissed Rehnquist's dissent in a single, terse footnote: "The dissenting opinion does not identify a single author, nonrevisionist, neo-revisionist, or otherwise, who takes the view of the history of the cession of the Black Hills that the dissent prefers to adopt." At the time of *Wold II,* Rehnquist was still an associate justice. Raymond knew from his first trip to the court that Rehnquist and Brennan would be watching for the right moment to spring their ambush.

"The question so often asked of the court by tribes today is simply this," says Cross. "Which of us gets to pass through the gates into the civilized world? A hundred and fifty years ago, the court had to answer a similar question with regard to slaves. At the heart of *Dred Scott* lay a very simple question: 'Am I, or am I not, a human being?' The court said you can't be a human being because you're property. As property, we cannot offer you protection under the Bill of Rights. Essentially, Rehnquist and Brennan were saying the same thing to the tribes. Instead of denying Indians their humanity, they accomplish the same thing by denying the tribes equal footing in the eyes of the law. This way, they get to achieve their goals by slipping under the political radar. In recent years, the message to tribes from the Rehnquist court has been pretty clear. Even if you work hard and spend lots of money and do all the right things, we're still not going to let you through the gate as an equal member of American society, not if there's any way we can stop it."

On a beautiful spring morning in March 1986, the great-great-grandson of Chief Cherry Necklace climbed the alabaster steps to the United States Supreme Court for the second time. He was prepared to challenge the nine men and women in black robes with the very questions his father had raised before members in Congress thirty years earlier. Dressed in a dark gray suit, a white button-down shirt, and a subdued blue and green tie, Raymond Cross was accompanied by Alyce Spotted Bear, all nine members of the Tribal Council, and his eighty-year-old mother, Dorothy Cross.

As he led the entourage between the soaring white columns, Raymond rehearsed his strategy one more time. He reviewed the markers he had placed in his mind. If at all possible, he hoped to force Brennan and Rehnquist into a legal box canyon where he could bog them down in tedious arguments over due process. To make his tactic work, he was counting on Brennan and Rehnquist to attack the "due process" decoys he had built into his brief. If they took the bait, he knew he could pin them into a corner. In the fleeting minutes that remained, the trick would be to identify an ally and put the answer that he was carrying in his hip pocket into his, or her, hands.

CHAPTER X

Into the Storm

⚓

"The real epic of America is the yet unwritten story of the Americaniza-
tion of the white man, the transformation of the hungry, fear-ridden,
intolerant, and greedy men that came to these shores with Columbus,
Pizarro, and John Smith into people of tolerance who value diversity . . ."

FELIX COHEN

Chief Justice Warren E. Burger gave the gavel a firm rap, then cast a sharp glance across the courtroom. Burger was a judge from the old school, with a Teutonic bearing that underscored the businesslike directness of his Midwestern upbringing. It was ten-thirty in the morning, March 24, 1986. Moments before, the black velvet curtains behind the high bench had suddenly parted as the nine justices filed into the courtroom and took their seats. Despite the imposing height of the ceiling, and the breadth of the bench, when Raymond stood to face the court, the walls crept in and the room suddenly seemed almost intimate.

The court will hear arguments this morning in Three Affiliated Tribes against Wold Engineering," announced Chief Justice Burger. "Mr. Cross, you may proceed whenever you are ready."

"Mr. Chief Justice, and may it please the court, this matter is before this court for the second time on a writ of certiorari," began Raymond, wasting no time on unnecessary flourishes. Seconds were precious. He wanted to recapitulate the facts and draw out the questions as quickly as possible. From his opening words, Sandra Day O'Connor and Thurgood Marshall appeared attentive, while Justice William Rehnquist seemed preoccupied with something on the ceiling. Raymond sped through his opening remarks, hoping to bait his trap before the questioning began. Once the justices weighed in with challenges and traps of their own, there was no way to predict where the answers would lead.

"When the North Dakota court reviewed its position," he reminded them, "it again found that it could only hear the case if the tribes waived their 'sovereign immunity'—"

"As for the waiver," broke in Chief Justice Burger, "would this then be a condition not only for this case, but for all cases?"

"That is the state's finding," said Cross. "If the tribes met the condition for this one case, the state is saying that the tribes' surrender of sovereign immunity would become a permanent condition."

Justice Sandra Day O'Connor was the first to jump in with a hypothetical question about Public Law 280. O'Connor zeroed in on the jurisdiction dilemma the law had created for the tribes and courts.

"Mr. Cross, would you have the same objection if the state conditioned its consent to use its courts to the waiver of any objection to proceedings in connection with that particular case; for example, a counterclaim by Wold that made the tribe subject to discovery orders and contempt sanctions and so forth, from the state court?"

"Justice O'Connor, the Three Affiliated Tribes would be subject to the counterclaim of the respondent, up to the extent of jurisdictional —"

Surprised by this answer, O'Connor broke back before he had finished. "I thought you said as a setoff, but not —"

"Yes, as a setoff," said Cross.

"— as a counterclaim that would result in additional liability?"

"That is right, your honor."

"What about the discovery procedures and so forth?" asked Thurgood Marshall. "How would that work?"

Marshall's probe forced the case wide open. Suddenly, questions began to fly back and forth between the justices and the tribes' attorney.

"Mr. Cross," asked Rehnquist, "are there any individual Indians who are plaintiffs, or is it just the Three Affiliated Tribes?"

"Just the tribes."

"Then these tribes have refused to consent to state court jurisdiction?"

There it was, the first step by Justice Rehnquist into the box canyon of due process. With this question, Rehnquist was also fishing for an easy way to uphold the state's high court and at the same time force the tribes to surrender their sovereign immunity.

"It was only after the state took a second look at its own statute that they declared that the intent of the statute was to completely bar tribal governments access to state courts."

Justice John Paul Stevens wanted to investigate this quandary. "Then if Wold Engineering wanted to sue the Three Tribes in the state court, it could not have done that?"

"That is correct. Requiring the tribes to waive their sovereign immunity —"

Justices Rehnquist and William Brennan had little patience for the notion of tribal sovereignty, or its correlative condition of "sovereign immunity." Both men were looking for a way to attack this issue directly. Justice Lewis Powell cut Raymond off and beat them to the question.

"Then in your view," began Powell, "the state could not dismiss the action for failure to waive the counterclaim?"

"That is correct. When a state statute bars all tribes from seeking remedies in state courts, then we would argue that the statute is overly broad. It interferes with the basic rights of due process, and it interferes with the equal protection of the law."

Cross's legal decoys were out in the open. Justice Powell had given him the opportunity to raise the issues of due process and equal protection. Justice Rehnquist pounced.

"Mr. Cross, you used the term 'overly broad.' That is something we ordinarily use in the First Amendment context. Is there any reason for this court to go any further here than in the particular application of the state statute of the facts of this case where you are not dealing with any individual Indians who are trying to sue, you are dealing with a tribe which is trying to sue, and the tribe itself has withheld its consent?"

Rehnquist was hoping to downplay the significance of tribes' potential loss of immunity in a state court.

"If this statute is allowed to stand as construed, [it] will bar all tribal Indians from access to state courts. We think that's overly broad."

"Then would you explain," shot Rehnquist, "how the tribe and non-Indian citizens are similarly situated for purposes of an equal protection analysis here? It just seems to me they are not the same because the tribe is not subject to the jurisdiction at all of the state courts under your view, not even subject to the counterclaim in this case. So, how are they similarly situated for the purpose of equal protection?"

Brennan and Rehnquist had boldly walked into the "due process" trap. If they got bogged down in this line of questioning, the other justices would leave them behind as they pursued a remedy to the "jurisdictional bar" issue that had been created by Public Law 280 thirty-five years before.

"The questions here center on whether or not a state court, or a state legislature, can pass or apply a statute that allows the enforcement of affirmative relief —"

"Well," interrupted an exasperated Justice Brennan, "if two non-Indian parties, plaintiff and defendant, were suing each other in the state court of North Dakota, the plaintiff in the case would be subject to a suit for a counterclaim in that suit by the defendant. You have told us this morning that in your view the tribes are different from everybody else. According to you, Mr. Cross, the tribes are not subject to a counterclaim . . ."

"For the purpose of equal protection, no, your honor, they are not, but I think you will encounter troublesome difficulties in comparing Indian tribes to non-Indian plaintiffs."

Thurgood Marshall smiled at Raymond's deft rejoinder as he slipped through Brennan's noose unharmed. The remaining justices seemed to make a tacit agreement at that moment that the equal protection query was going nowhere. "Mr. Cross, has the tribe now altered its laws so that a suit would be possible in tribal court today against Wold Engineering?" asked Justice Marshall.

"The tribe has altered its laws and a suit would be possible in the sense that the tribal code now recognizes jurisdiction over non-Indians. . . . The problem is that North Dakota, in a case entitled *Lowe v. Cloud,* does not recognize the enforceability of tribal court judgments that go against non-Indians."

"Could the tribes have sued Wold in federal court?"

This was the question that Raymond had been hoping to hear from the outset. His simple answer was the crux of his appeal for certiorari.

"No, your honor, they could not."

"I thought there was a special section of P.L. 280 that said that an Indian tribe, as plaintiff, can sue. Am I wrong in that?"

"Yes, sir, you are wrong in that. A contract action such as this one in question does not give the tribal government access to federal courts. Unless the tribes waive their sovereign immunity and agree to subordinate their sovereignty to the state, they have no access to the American court system, and therefore, no method of resolving a contractual dispute like *Wold.*"

Brennan and Rehnquist suddenly sobered. Simultaneously, both justices seemed to realize that their line of questioning had left them stranded in "due process" while the rest of the court headed off in another direction. The tribes' attorney, thus far, had skillfully argued that the real-world effect of applying P.L. 280 to civil disputes such as *Wold* was to bar Indian tribes from seeking redress for civil actions in the American court system. Sensing that Cross had probably already swayed his fellow justices, Justice Brennan made one more attempt to rescue the state by noting that other minorities had access to federal courts for the purpose of settling disputes over civil rights.

"Well, federal courts hear state law questions all the time in diversity cases," said Brennan.

"There is no diversity question before us, your honor," said Cross, blocking his path.

"Thank you, Mr. Cross," interrupted Chief Justice Burger. "Do you have anything further?"

"Yes, Mr. Chief Justice, simply to point out that the tribal courts are open to non-Indian plaintiffs, and many non-Indian plaintiffs take full advantage of tribal courts for debt collection and other purposes. By contrast, state courts are not open to tribal governments unless they consent [to waive sovereign immunity]. To do so would fundamentally impair how the tribes operate under federal law."

Justice O'Connor's head suddenly lifted when she heard this insight. In her mind, this was the knot that must be cut. The way P.L. 280 played out in the court system, once a tribe gave up its sovereign immunity to gain access to state courts, it could not get it back. P.L. 280 blurred the boundaries of federalism and turned the court system on its head.

"Mr. Cross, can an individual waive Indian sovereignty?" asked O'Connor.

"In the *Williams v. Lee* case, Chief Justice Marshall ruled that an individual cannot waive sovereignty. Only the tribal government can waive its sovereignty. That is why we believe this statute not only interferes with the constitutional rights of tribal members but also frustrates the exercise of federal Indian policy. Thank you, Mr. Chief Justice."

"Thank you, Mr. Cross. The case is submitted."

Back in North Dakota, Raymond's million-to-one gamble with the GDUC the year before was now beginning to pay off with the JTAC. The emotionally charged testimony heard in New Town had made a deep impression on the JTAC members. After hearing twenty-four hours of testimony in just two days, the committee reboarded its charter plane at the New Town airport and flew back to Bismarck to begin writing its final report. As the days went by, the work of sorting through the mountain of evidence seemed more and more overwhelming, yet Murry was more determined than ever to meet his spring deadline. Fortunately, both he and Hans Walker were old hands at this work. Their earlier partnership in writing the legislative report on Public Law 280 twenty years earlier proved immensely helpful when they sat down to put their findings on paper. In late May 1986, Murry and Walker hand delivered the JTAC's final report to Secretary Hodel at his office in Washington, D.C. With the JTAC work completed, and the *Wold* case submitted to the court, tribal chairwoman Alyce Spotted Bear decided not to run for reelection.

"Four years as tribal chairwoman was enough stress for one lifetime," says Alyce. "As we walked out of the Supreme Court that day, I was so proud of Raymond, and so proud of the Three Tribes, I can't begin to tell you what that felt like. As chairwoman, I had seen people face their deepest fears. Somehow, we had pooled our energies and talents and determination, and in four years we achieved things beyond our craziest hopes. When I left office, the tribes were financially sound for the first time in thirty years. The future was still a huge question mark, but Ed Lone Fight was the right guy to follow me. He brought years of administrative experience to the job."

While JTAC was being formed out in North Dakota, the tribes' future chairman, Ed Lone Fight, was startled awake by a dream on a snowy night in Washington, D.C. Lone Fight had spent twenty-five years in Washington as an administrator with the Department of the Interior. His father and grandfather had been close friends with Martin Cross and Old Dog, respectively. As a young boy, Ed had lived through The Flood before his parents sent him to off-reservation schools. Like many members of the Three Affiliated Tribes, he eventually went on to college and graduate school, where he earned a master's degree in political science from Portland State University in Portland, Oregon. On that snowy night in the nation's capital, the inspiration to return to Fort Berthold appeared to him like a burning bush.

"I sat up in bed in cold sweats. The time had come to go home. There was no doubt about it, so I resigned from my job, sold my house, and moved back to Fort Berthold. I had no idea what I was going to do when I got there."

Before he and his wife had even unpacked, Lone Fight was elected to succeed Alyce Spotted Bear as tribal chairman. He was sworn into office in a ceremony at the Four Bears tribal offices just as Chairman Murry and Walker were submitting the final JTAC report to Secretary Hodel. Murry reminded Hodel that the JTAC had been asked to investigate a broad range of issues.

The most salient and pressing of those issues had been highlighted by the Garrison Diversion Unit Commission's final report in February 1986, under its "Indian recommendations." After reviewing the work of the GDUC, Congress had directed the JTAC to answer one big question: Did the 80th Congress make a good-faith effort to meet the just compensation requirements of the U.S. Constitution and federal takings law in 1949, when the Corps built Garrison Dam?

Needless to say, said Murry, this was a sensitive question, particularly in light of the fact that the secretary had personally erased Congress' request from the JTAC charter. Nevertheless, Murry and Walker ignored the fact that Hodel had drawn a line through "the big question." They set out for North Dakota determined to return with an answer. Eventually, they succeeded. Congress, reported Murry, was clearly guilty of abdicating its trust responsibilities to the tribes in 1949. After all was said and done, JTAC determined that only an exchange of "lieu lands," as originally promised by Senator O'Mahoney's committee, could have justified the compensation package that Congress forced on the tribes "against its will" in 1949. In JTAC's view, the government's debt to the Three Affiliated Tribes ran into the hundreds of millions of dollars. What had been unjustly taken from the tribes in 1949 could never be replaced. Even though it was far too late to make the Mandan, Hidatsa, and Arikara people "whole," to restore them to their former economic and social conditions, a cash award that reflected the true value of what these people had lost would give them the wherewithal to create a future.

"I had a good idea that we were in for some rough sailing," says Murry. "Hodel didn't want to deal with just compensation, even though the GDUC had explicitly directed him to do so. So, I decided to stay loyal to the original charter from Congress and let the two of them fight it out."

Murry was warned by his friends in Washington that getting a single dime out of Congress would be next to impossible. The federal government was drowning in red ink. Congress had recently committed itself to spending no more than it took in. There was no rush in Washington to settle old scores with Indian tribes. When the report was filed and the recommendations formally presented in 1986, Secretary Hodel sat on it for more than a year.

Frustration, delays, and inertia were primary forces in Washington. Raymond had tasted enough of this life when he was working with the Pasqua Yaqui. That experience soon convinced him to apply his legal talents to other causes in other venues. But it was times like these, moments precisely like this one, when the universe offered alternative compensations. On June 16, 1986, the high court came back with its ruling in *Wold II*. Sovereign immunity had held. The chief justice of the North Dakota Supreme Court, Ralph Erickstad, now had the "bright line" he had sought from the court in the earlier go-round. Erickstad immediately reworked the procedural rules for the state courts and formally recognized the full jurisdiction of tribal courts in civil disputes.

The unsuccessful campaign Martin Cross and the National Congress of American Indians had launched thirty-five years earlier to defeat P.L. 280 had come full circle. Now, the most odious effects of that law had been successfully challenged in a case over faulty water pumps. In a single stroke, and with full cooperation from Chief Justice Erickstad, the *Wold II* decision transformed North Dakota courts into the most progressive in the United States. Erickstad personally rewrote the state code governing North Dakota's courts and formally recognized the legal efficacy of tribal courts for the purpose of resolving civil disputes with non-Indians.

"I don't mind telling you that a lot of states thought we were crazy," says Chief Justice VandeWalle. "We have never regretted it. It put us in the forefront, nationwide, with regard to tribal courts, and we have never had a single problem."

In the first two minutes of his presentation to the Supreme Court, Raymond had sensed that his principal ally on the bench would be the old ranch hand Justice Sandra Day O'Connor. The release of the court's formal six-to-three opinion reaffirmed his intuition. Justice O'Connor wrote the majority opinion. Justice Stevens, perhaps the court's most liberal judge on a broad range of issues, aligned himself with the most conservative, Rehnquist and Brennan, and dissented.

⋇

Weeks became months for the JTAC report. Legislative inertia in Washington seemed to grow more ponderous with each passing day. The new tribal chairman, Ed Lone Fight, tried pulling strings with his former colleagues at the Department of the Interior, but Secretary Hodel was showing no willingness to revisit the question of "just compensation" for the Three Affiliated Tribes. After awhile nobody at Interior returned Lone Fight's calls. The JTAC report had been dropped into the dead-letter file, where it would soon be forgotten. Finally, in November 1987, Lone Fight and Emerson Murry got a lucky break. Senator Daniel Inouye, the esteemed and knowledgeable chairman of the Senate Select Committee on Indian Affairs, sidestepped the roadblock at Interior and invited the pair to present the JTAC's report to his committee. Murry, Raymond Cross, and Lone Fight traveled to Washington on November 12, 1987. Once there, they were reacquainted with Ann Zorn, who flew in from Las Vegas to recapitulate the recommendations of the GDUC. Zorn agreed to tailor her remarks to the Fifth Amendment, taking issues highlighted in the GDUC report that she and David Treen presented to Congress two years earlier. The idea of making the tribes "whole," of restoring them to their former economic independence and self-sufficiency as required by the Fifth Amendment, was probably the most powerful tool working in the tribes' favor. Congress could abrogate a treaty, it could break a contract, it could refuse payment, but it could not ignore the Bill of Rights in the U.S. Constitution. "It became clear to all of us on the GDUC that Congress never succeeded in making the tribes whole," Zorn explained. "In our minds, there was no question whatsoever that the tribes' Fifth Amendment rights had been violated, and no good faith effort had ever been made to set things right."

Ann Zorn had again left her mark on powerful congressmen. Before the hearings had finished, her explanations for the recommendations of the GDUC were made even more dramatic in contrast to testimony presented by the Bureau of Indian Affairs and the Army Corps of Engineers. Both of these agencies declared themselves opposed to any further reviews of the "just compensation" issues raised by the attorney for the Three Affiliated Tribes.

By the time the BIA and the Corps had finished their reports, Senator Inouye was struggling to control his displeasure with both Congress and the White House. "For too long, the trustee [Congress] has acted in a strange manner. Instead of protecting the rights and resources of the tribes, it has accomplished exactly the opposite. I must apologize for my anger, but sometimes I think there is justification for anger."

"Excuse me," broke in the junior senator from Arizona, John McCain. "This seems to be a request for compensation in the range of three hundred sixty million to seven hundred sixty million dollars. Mr. Chairman, there are twenty tribes in the state of Arizona that have suffered dislocation for various reasons. Are they also eligible for compensation? I'm just wondering what's going on here?"

"This report was prepared at the request of Congress and the administration," shot Inouye. "Yet the administration has been sitting on this thing for a year now. This is unacceptable. Mr. Murry, you have worked tirelessly and without pay to produce this important document. I want to personally thank you and your committee for your excellent work and personal sacrifice."

Murry demurred. On behalf of his fellow committee members, he thanked Chairman Inouye for the opportunity to present their report. Now, said Murry, the principals had to "fish or cut bait."

With Murry's challenge as the last word, Senator Inouye adjourned the hearings.

ﱠ

After four years of ceaseless work for the tribes, the veteran Cross, and the newcomer, tribal chairman Ed Lone Fight, suddenly found themselves adrift and on their own. "Senator Inouye was very supportive," says Cross, "but he had to deal with McCain, and that was shaping up to be a bigger problem than we had anticipated."

In a few years' time, Senator John McCain's experience on this committee would transform him into a fierce defender of Native American rights. In those final days of 1987, the federal government was drowning in red ink. Deficit spending on military programs had soared during Reagan's second term in office. Cross and Lone Fight knew that the junior senator had put his finger on the budgetary impediment that would almost certainly translate into more delays. The government was hemorrhaging money. While Congress fought over ways to stop the negative cash flow, further postponements for the JTAC would be inevitable. Yet with every passing month, "just compensation" drifted farther out of reach. Under overcast skies, Cross and Lone Fight descended the Capitol steps into the gray light of dusk. Without articulating their darkest fears, both men realized that the tribes' forty-year campaign to force Congress to make them "whole," to compensate them for the abrogation of the solemn agreement they made at Horse Creek, had finally come to a dead end.

After a quick dinner, Raymond and Ed returned to their hotel room to discuss strategy. They decided to first survey the legislative landscape, the pros and cons, and assess the forces arrayed against them. When all elements had been weighed and considered, they could see only two potential pathways around Hodel's intransigence. Before they left Washington they needed to find someone who worked inside the power circuits on Capitol Hill, a professional fixer with an intimate knowledge of how things were connected behind the marble and walnut veneer. They made a number of phone calls. Oddly enough, they kept hearing the same name, which was strange, since neither Cross nor Lone Fight had ever heard it before. Alyce Spotted Bear told them that this guy was the best in the city. She had been introduced to him by Jim Bluestone, a fellow tribal member, when Bluestone was employed as a legislative intern at the Department of the Interior.

"He's a public interest lobbyist, it's right here, hold on . . . at Moss, McGee, Bradley, and Foley," said Spotted Bear. "Lee Foley. Call him tonight, and be sure to use my name."

It was too late to call Foley's office, so Lone Fight called Bluestone at home. Bluestone told him that Foley arrived on Capitol Hill in the late 1960s, fresh out of college. Since then, he had spent years working the back rooms on Capitol Hill. By sticking it out, he eventually became a highly respected journeyman, a legislative whiz kid who discovered that he had a talent for making things happen. Then, when Reagan was elected in 1980, Foley and his partners decided to open their own office. If there was anyone in Washington who could get the JTAC recommendations moving, it was Lee Foley.

The following morning they phoned the office of Moss, McGee, Bradley, and Foley at eight o'clock sharp. To their surprise, Foley invited them to come right over. "I happen to be free right now," said Foley, "but in ten minutes I could be gone for a week."

When Raymond and Lone Fight explained why they were there, Foley's initial response was short of encouraging. "I'd love to take this on, but let's face facts. The government's broke. Nobody has any money. So, on top of everything else, your timing couldn't be worse. Why didn't Alyce come to me with this three years ago?"

"Three years ago, this was a pipe dream," explained Raymond.

"You think it's too late?" asked Lone Fight.

"That's an expensive question in this town," said Foley. "I don't have an answer, but there's one way to find out. I'll make some phone calls, get the lay of the land. In the meantime, gentlemen, your job is to pray for a miracle."

The miracle would come from an unexpected source, and on another continent, on May 31, 1988. At the invitation of Soviet Prime Minister Mikhail Gorbachev, President Ronald Reagan made a visit to the Soviet Union. While he was there, he was anxious to meet with the Russian people face-to-face, so when the students at Moscow State University invited him to their school for a question-and-answer session, Reagan jumped at the chance. With the world's press there to record the event, President Reagan made an off-the-cuff response to a question regarding the federal government's mistreatment of American Indians.

"Maybe we made a mistake in trying to maintain Indian cultures," the president told them. "Maybe we should not have humored them in that, you know, into wanting to stay in that kind of primitive lifestyle."

Switchboards lit up in tribal offices across the country. Indian leaders expressed outrage on the front pages of newspapers around the world. Once the president had returned home, the White House sought to smooth the waters by inviting a dozen tribal leaders to the White House for a meeting with the president. One of those invited leaders was Ed Lone Fight, chairman of the Three Affiliated Tribes of North Dakota. After a brief photo session for the media showing the president cheerfully making amends with the Indians, the leaders were invited to join the president for an informal chat around the cabinet table. Lone Fight took the chair directly opposite the president. When the opportunity presented itself, he thanked the president for the invitation.

"So tell me, Ed, how are things on your reservation?" the president asked with genuine interest.

"I'm glad you asked that, Mr. President. As a matter of fact, we're making a lot of progress. Many of our young people are now in college, but we're stymied in the area of development . . ."

"How so?"

"Well, your administration conducted a study of our situation and found that the government had shortchanged us by a considerable amount of money when the Pick-Sloan project was built years ago. But that report, called the JTAC report, seems to be held up in a logjam at Interior."

President Reagan listened carefully to every word and detected a political opportunity. When the chairman was finished, the president turned to Secretary Hodel, who was sitting several chairs away on the same side of the table.

"What about that, Donald? What's the status on this JTAC report on Mr. Lone Fight's tribe . . ."

Hodel immediately snapped to attention, shot a glance at Lone Fight, then back to the president.

"That's been taken care of, Mr. President. In fact, it was on my desk this morning, and we'll be taking action on that report straightaway now . . ."

"Can you personally keep Mr. Lone Fight, you know, apprised . . ."

"Oh, yes, sir, he'll be the first to know."

President Reagan squared his shoulders back to Lone Fight and winked. "If you have any trouble, you call me, you put a call through to this office . . ."

"Yes, Mr. President. I'm very grateful to you. Thank you very much."

There would be four more years of committee meetings, and the endless back and forth negotiations on valuations of the actual damages the government owed to the tribes, but the president's response to the question in Moscow had produced the miracle Lee Foley had ordered. The meeting between President Reagan and Chairman Lone Fight formally took the JTAC recommendations out of the administrative purgatory where it had languished and moved it into the legislative auspices of Senator Daniel Inouye's committee. There, inching forward in a campaign carefully choreographed by Lee Foley, Lone Fight and Raymond exerted steady pressure on key members of Congress and began the long push toward a "just compensation" award for the Mandan, Hidatsa, and Arikara tribes. At a propitious moment, Senator Inouye took the matter of the three tribes into his own hands. When Raymond Cross and the tribal leaders gathered in Inouye's committee room for the final time in November 1991, Senator Inouye took the occasion to make a speech to the American people, and all the citizens of Indian Country, on the sanctity of treaties.

"During the 1940s and the 1950s, the U.S. Army Corps of Engineers flooded more than two hundred thousand acres of prime land on these reservations when it constructed a series of flood control dams on the Missouri River," began the senator, struggling to control his emotions. "The tribes were forced to sign away those lands with literally a gun to their heads, and in absolute violation of their rights as treaty signatories with the United States government. At that time, the tribes were provided with a small measure of compensation which came nowhere near the level of adequately compensating the tribes for the losses they sustained, and was even less responsive to the devastation caused to their lives by this brutal act. Senate Bill 168 is the first legislative measure to be introduced in an effort to bring this deplorable chapter in the United States' history to a close. Today, this committee calls on the rest of the United States government to live up to its trust responsibility to these tribes and join in our efforts to provide equitable and just compensation that will in some small measure help make amends for the wrongs that were done to the people of the Fort Berthold and Standing Rock Reservations.

"What you have done is to share with us part of the sad and tragic chapter of the relationship between the United States and Indian nations," continued the senator. "It is not a happy chapter. It is a chapter of deceit and deception, it is a chapter of promises and broken promises. The committee is well aware of that, and we are going to do our best to undo the damage that was wrought in those years past. It might be well that we remind ourselves at this juncture that this proud nation who maintains publicly that we keep our promises and our commitments, as President Bush so eloquently stated at the joint session of Congress, has not been honest in its dealings with the Indian nations. Throughout the years, we have had eight hundred treaties with Indian nations, treaties entered into between sovereign nations, the United

States and Indian nations. They are sovereign. As such, the U.S. Senate, our predecessors, had the responsibility of studying these treaties and acting upon them to either accept or reject. Of the eight hundred treaties, the record will show that the U.S. Senate just ignored four hundred thirty of them. . . . However, we called upon the Indian nations to live up to their promises in the treaties. The U.S. Senate did ratify three hundred seventy of them, and of the three hundred seventy treaties that this Senate, our predecessors, ratified, the United States government violated provisions in every one of them. It is a very sad chapter, and as one senator, as chairman of this committee, I can assure you that we will do our best to see that no further violations are carried out in this country."

☙

In late 1992, following another dozen trips to Washington, and dozens more hearings, a joint committee of the House of Representatives and the U.S. Senate agreed to award the Three Affiliated Tribes of North Dakota a sum of $149.2 million for the unjust taking of their reservation by an illegal act of Congress in 1949. The only remaining hitch was the mechanics of the actual funding. Bill or no bill, Congress was still handcuffed by a self-imposed spending freeze. Where would all that money come from?

"[North Dakota Senator] Kent Conrad was a real profile in courage on this," says Foley. "He was taking a lot of heat from his Norwegian constituents back home, who didn't want to see this resolved in the Indians' favor.

"You think you're so smart," says Foley, "you get these things through committee, and then reality hits you. 'Now, how are you going to find the money to pay for all this?' Remember, we were running huge deficits at the time, and Bush's people at Interior had already told us their man would kill it on sight."

Ignoring that threat as best he could, Foley pressed ahead and consulted with his connections on the Senate Finance Committee. He remembers sitting around in Senator Conrad's office one evening as he, Raymond, and the senator mulled over various ways to creatively finesse the financing package. Foley's years of experience suddenly gave him an idea, one he had never thought of before. Like most brilliant insights, this one was deceptively simple and ingeniously creative. Foley hit upon a "double accounting" scheme that, when sketched out on paper, looked like it just might work. Congress could grow the funds for a compensation package by siphoning off surplus funds that were generated each year by power receipts from Garrison Dam.

The resulting trust fund, established at the Department of the Treasury for the Three Affiliated Tribes, would generate annual interest in perpetuity. The scheme was perfectly legal, but it effectively raised the money without debiting funds from the treasury. By stretching the plan out over six years, the total deposits would reach their target of $149.2 million.

"Double accounting was the answer," says Foley. "It allowed us to explain to congressmen who had no idea of what we were talking about that the reason for the taking — the dam — would ultimately provide the solution in the compensation package. Then, by 'booting the payments over the horizon,' by putting the payoff out there beyond the five-year accounting period for the government, nobody cared whether it broke the spending freeze. It didn't take money away from any existing project or create more red ink in the current budget. Revenues from the dam would simply be counted twice by the treasury, once as receipts for power, and a second time when those surplus funds were deposited into the account for the tribes. It was poetry."

A week before the bill was to come up for a vote in early 1992, Department of the Interior deputy counsel and Bush appointee Pam Summers called Foley at his office. Summers and Foley had known each other for a long time. Summers was well informed about Senate Bill 168, which had just been sent to the full Senate by a unanimous vote in Senator Inouye's committee. Summers was calling with bad news, a professional courtesy. Foley should know going in that President Bush would never let this bill through.

"This thing is getting killed on sight," she told him. "There is no way the White House is signing off on this thing."

Foley thanked Summers for the tip, then hung up the phone. For long, pensive moments he retreated into his mind and gazed out his office window at the distant dome of the Capitol. He had not acquired this scarred-up psyche, this battered heart and soul from years of ruthless infighting and power wars just to roll over and let five years of work vanish with the stroke of President Bush's pen. No, he could not let it go down that easily. This thing was bigger than George Bush and Lee Foley. There were things about this bill that were far more important than winning, more important than power and balance sheets and kudos from colleagues and ten inches of front-page copy above the fold in the local newspaper. This fell beyond the petty skirmishes of frightened politicians and the flimsy platitudes of presidents running scared for reelection.

In the years since Lone Fight and Cross stepped into his office, Foley and Raymond had spent hundreds of hours in each other's company. Over the past three years, he and his partners had contributed more than half a million dollars of their own resources to get this bill to the floor of the Senate, and they would do it again. No, Foley had labored for too many years on the Hill, walked too many miles in the catacombs, not to have kept one trump card in reserve for just such an impasse. He reached for the phone and dialed the number for Raymond Cross's hotel room.

"Raymond, Lee here. Meet me at Congressman Miller's office, fifteen minutes."

For many years, California congressman George Miller had been ranked among the most powerful men on Capitol Hill. As the longtime chairman of the powerful House Resources Committee, Miller had ruled with political integrity and an even hand. This uncompromising environmentalist was feared, particularly by his fellow congressmen in the West, because he could spot a pork-barrel water project from across the country. The fact that he ruled the Resources Committee, the committee that held the purse strings for the Bureau of Reclamation, made him a king maker. As each election approached, dozens of political careers, on both sides of the aisle, would suddenly be riding on the backs of bills that were scheduled to come out of Miller's committee.

As Lee Foley's luck would have it, the early winter months of 1992 happened to be one of those times when congressmen were closely watching every item that appeared on the docket of Miller's committee. Foley and Cross had been working the Senate side of the aisle, where they had a powerful ally in Senator Kent Conrad. But with Bush promising to veto the Compensation Act, Senator Conrad's steadfast allegiance might mollify the folks back home, but it would not be enough legislative muscle in the Senate to override a presidential veto. Since their bill had few friends on the House side, the Senate had been the logical place to set up camp. Nevertheless, Foley had been quietly keeping an eye on Miller's docket. He knew something big was in the works. After making a few inquiries, he was told that Miller's committee was about to vote on the long-awaited Bureau of Reclamation Reform Act, an enormous bill that had taken years to work into final shape. This was a bill that held dozens of political careers hostage to final passage. Careers were on the line again. For many western politicians, passage was a must. It also just so happened that this was a presidential election year, and everyone knew that George Bush needed those western states to have any hope of winning. For Foley, a tight election was as good as a personal guarantee from the president that he would sign this bill into law as soon as it reached his desk. Once it hit the floor of both houses, the bill coming out of Miller's committee was a slam dunk.

Foley and Cross met in the hallway outside Miller's office. He told Cross about Summers's phone call, about her promise of a veto of a "just compensation" bill for the tribes. Then, in a manner of speaking, he showed him his hidden trump card, and they strolled into Miller's office together.

"Maybe it was the way the moon and the stars were lined up," says Foley. "They showed us into his office right away. That never ever happens."

Congressman Miller stood up and greeted them, shaking their hands, then invited them to sit down.

"Congressman Miller," began Foley, "we need a favor from you." He then gave the congressman an overview of Senate Bill 168, explained the double-accounting method of financing that he had concocted with Senator Conrad, and then gave him a copy of Inouye's remarks on broken treaties. "Congressman Miller, all we're asking is for you to be a hero today. We're here to ask you to attach the Three Affiliated Tribes Just Compensation Act to your Bureau of Reclamation Reform bill."

Without hesitation, Representative George Miller reached across his desk to shake Raymond's hand. "Mr. Cross, it would be my honor."

ᔐ

Ten years after Congressman George Miller made good on his handshake with Raymond Cross, the double-accounting scheme that Lee Foley devised to establish a perpetual trust fund for the Mandan, Hidatsa, and Arikara people is working precisely according to design. Every year, interest on the "corpus" of the fund is made available to the Tribal Council. The funds are deposited as a credit in the tribes' account at the Department of the Treasury. Years before the first JTAC funds arrived, in 1998, tribespeople and councilmen began arguing over how to spend the money. It is human nature, perhaps, to argue over money, to quarrel over how it should be spent, particularly when it is held in common. Properly managed, those divisions can lead to healthy struggles that help the tribes to define their common interests. As a fellow tribesman, Raymond Cross knows that those divisions can just as easily, just as quickly, turn inward and whip through a tribe like the devil's wind, destroying clans and communities from the inside out.

"After so many years of abuse, bad court decisions, cultural disintegration, and the systemic dysfunction of both societies, white and Indian, our tribal governments have evolved into Indian Country surrogates for these television survival shows that just seem to go on and on," says Raymond. "For my people, I worry that our modern-day version of the smallpox epidemic is the

JTAC money. The trick for the tribal leaders will be to turn the viral qualities of money into a positive inoculation. My greatest fear is the tribe will miss this opportunity to re-create itself."

As for the farmers of North Dakota, fifty years after their grandfathers threw their political weight behind the Pick-Sloan project, they are still waiting. While water released through the power tunnels of Garrison Dam has kept barges floating between St. Louis and Sioux City, South Dakota, for more than fifty years, not a drop of water has moved down the McClusky Canal. Of the 1 million acres of irrigation promised by Sloan's original plan, fewer than 9,000 have been irrigated, yet the federal government has spent more than $20 billion, ten times the original estimate, on Pick-Sloan projects. After drought-stricken farmers on the Great Plains watched millions of acre-feet of water flow out of Garrison Dam to fill shipping channels on the lower river, in January of 2004 the state of North Dakota appealed to the U.S. Supreme Court to bring the fifty years of economic and environmental devastation that have resulted from Pick-Sloan to a merciful end.

"You want to give everybody the benefit of the doubt," says North Dakota chief justice VandeWalle. "I'm afraid it's [Pick-Sloan's] all been one huge scam, an economic and environmental disaster, from beginning to end."

Raymond's brothers and sisters make it a point to return to the shores of Lake Sakakawea as often as possible. It is a beautiful day in late spring of 2002, and Bucky is standing beside a small, meandering stream called the Knife River, about a mile northeast of the small county seat of Stanton, North Dakota. Bucky has found the spot, the very spot, where George Catlin was standing when he painted one of his famous landscapes of the Hidatsa Village, with the Knife River in the foreground. On that same piece of muddy bank, beneath the overhanging limbs of the sheltering oaks, Catlin struggled with brush and pen to capture the scene before him for posterity before it had vanished entirely.

"There are dwellings all about me, and they are purely unique," wrote Catlin, when he lived at the Knife River Villages in 1832. "They are all covered with dirt, the people are all red, and yet distinct from all other red folks I have seen. The horses are wild, every dog is a wolf, the whole moving mass are strangers to me, and the living, in everything, carry an air of intractable wildness about them, and the dead are not buried, but dried upon scaffolds. . . . The groups of lodges around me present a very curious and pleasing appearance, resembling in shape so many potash kettles inverted, and on the tops of these are to be seen groups standing and reclining, whose wild and picturesque appearance it would be difficult to describe. . . . stern warriors, like statues, standing in dignified groups, wrapped in their painted quills of the war eagle, extending their long arms to the east or to the west, pointing to the scenes of their battles, which they are recounting to each other . . ."

"This was our village," says Bucky, smiling to himself as he takes in the landscape from the spot where Catlin set his easel. "This is where we come from."

ᴧᴧ

On the trip back to Parshall on Old State Road Number Eight, Bucky and Crusoe carry on in the backseat of the van like schoolboys reliving the pranks of summer camp. Marilyn turns off the road to Stanton at Pick City, just west of Sakakawea Park, and drives up onto the crown of the dam. As if on cue, the voices in the van suddenly go quiet, and the cheerful, sibling banter does not resume until the van is skirting past the town of Riverdale, half a mile east of the dam. Marilyn has promised to take Phyllis and Bucky on a quick side trip up to the lake, to a spot called Indian Point. When we arrive at their favorite lookout, it is immediately obvious why they enjoy coming here. Far below, a light breeze has picked up and corrugated the surface of the lake. The high white clouds overhead hurry off toward evening. Spokes of silver light wheel through the western clouds and skip over the moody surface of the inland sea that spreads beneath us for miles in all directions. Bucky lifts his nose to the wind and fills his lungs. A hawk soars overhead, getting a free ride on the steady currents. Crusoe switches his eyeglasses and squints to the far side. Then, he lifts his arm and points.

"You see where that light's moving, way over there, in that valley . . . oops, there it went. That was Red Butte. And over there," he says, swinging his arm fifteen degrees toward the south, "that was Beaver Creek, right between those two low hills."

"That spot on the water, look at where the light's hitting . . ." says Phyllis. She's pointing at something in the middle of the lake, where a medallion of sunlight has burst across the gray surface.

"That's right where our place was," says Marilyn.

"That's what I thought," says Phyllis.

"Sure is," says Bucky. He points, too. "Look, it's moving right across the horse pasture, up toward the house."

The four of them stand there, side by side, and gaze out across the water from this promontory. Tired and cold, Phyllis turns first and heads back to the van, then Marilyn and Crusoe, with Crusoe helping his older sister up onto the seat. Bucky cannot quite tear himself away. "I'll just be a minute," he says. Then, after another moment of reflection, Bucky begins talking, as though he is sorting things out by telling himself a story.

"Our experience of the dam was violent," he begins. "It tore families apart behind a thousand doors. It had the effect of disassimilating people from their origin, and ripping up their identities, and tossing them to the winds of fate and misfortune like so much confetti. In Elbowoods, we still had the old relationships that were very much like the villages on the Knife River. And at Nishu and Shell Creek, Red Butte and Independence, these communities were the last connection we had to the Knife River Villages, to a world that was defined by a beautiful web of relationships, of relatedness. Today, when my brothers and sisters and I look out across this lake to where our communities once thrived and sustained us, we don't only lament the loss of the physical place. Surely, we loved that land more than any other. But what was taken away was more than the land. We look out across that water today and we are reminded that as a people, we were whole once. We sang and we danced. We have to live with that loss every day. What the Allotment Era started in the 1800s, the Garrison Dam finished. Now, it is up to us, to this generation, to start dancing again."

✤

If the people of the Mandan, Hidatsa, and Arikara nations are to begin dancing again, in earnest, Raymond Cross believes the arduous process of re-creation will have to begin with a reaffirmation of the spiritual laws that sustained their ancestors through the mortal trials endured by countless generations. Among the tribes that met 150 years ago at the confluence of the Platte and Horse Creek, this spiritual law was called the *wouncage*. Translated from Crow, Mandan, or Sioux, *wouncage* is today known as the Sacred Trust. Put simply, that trust is an expression of the communal reverence shown by the people of a tribe or community for the originating force that makes the wind, that brings the clouds, that carries the rain, that falls to the grass, that feeds the buffalo to nourish the man. For millennia, from the Arctic Circle to the tip of Chile, the native people of the western hemisphere have seen themselves living inside this circle as its guardians, as have all the great spiritual leaders of the world's great religions. The *wouncage* tells them that no good has ever come from leaving that circle, or breaking the trust.

Raymond Cross sees this circle enclosing his own life, for it is now the first winter in a new millennium, and once again, a federal commission convened by the Army Corps of Engineers has come to Missoula, Montana, to find out what people here think about salmon, the Snake River dams, and the economic future of this vast region of the American outback. Missoula, a railroad, logging, and university town of seventy thousand citizens, is one of ten stops in what will be remembered for years to come as a rolling-thunder road show of white men in blue suits and funny hats. At every venue thus far, the commission has drawn angry, standing-room-only crowds of farmers and ranchers, businessmen and railroaders, commercial fishermen, barge operators and environmentalists, grandmothers in hiking boots and secretaries in heels, college professors and housewives burping babies — a widely divergent constituency accustomed to sweet water, "poverty with a view" under the big skies, and packing protein off the land. Crossing all socioeconomic, age, cultural, and gender boundaries, the testimony of citizens thus far has tended to address two dominant themes: one, the threatened extinction of native salmon in the Columbia River Basin, a geographic area the size of France, is the leading edge of an unprecedented environmental crisis; and two, any realistic solutions to meeting this crisis will be economically excruciating.

Agreements tend to end there. The capacity mob that thronged the convention center in Boise, Idaho, a few days earlier was ready to light a fuse under the Snake River dams before the sun went down. Why wait another day, was the overwhelming consensus of the crowd. Emotions ran high. Voices rang out in fervid pitch. A brave young wheat farmer from Lewiston, Idaho, took the microphone and accused the "dam breachers" of willfully destroying three generations of his family's hard-won livelihood. The farmer was followed by Nez Percé elder Carla HighEagle, who stepped up to the microphone and scanned the eyes of each member of the commission. The auditorium fell silent. She then addressed the commission, and the farmer from Lewiston, without a trace of rancor or a note of bitterness.

"Sirs," she began, "no one empathizes with you and your family more than the Nez Percé people, the Umatilla people, the Yakima people, and all the members of the Columbia River tribes. It is a terrible thing to see three generations of work wiped out, just like that. We empathize with you. We ask the commission to consider that in one generation, just one, the five federal dams on the lower Snake River have virtually destroyed a salmon legacy among my people that goes back five hundred generations. It is all but gone. We have watched it vanish in less than one lifetime. For five hundred generations, my people have been subsisting on salmon. We and the salmon people are one. If you kill the last of them, if you allow them to go extinct, we will go away with them, for there will be nothing left to keep us here. That is all I have to say."

A week later, at a large conference room at the Doubletree hotel in Missoula, those same commissioners have taken a break for lunch. They are due back any moment. How things will go here in Missoula, a wild card in a region of wild cards, is anybody's guess. The task before the commission is formidable, and the protestors have already lined up outside to meet them when they arrive. A colorful coalition of activists has arrived in costume, masquerading in the parking lot as spawning salmon. Most of the young people from the university are on bicycles, wearing T-shirts and shorts. There are the usual banners, placards, and dreadlocked activists with rings around their toes and through their noses. The year's most popular bumper sticker reads: WILD SEX FOR WILD SALMON.

Like the Missouri River watershed, which begins less than a hundred miles from Missoula on the eastern front of the Rocky Mountains, marine scientists have testified in Congress that the Columbia River watershed is dying. Many people have come here because they believe this may be their final opportunity to avoid that looming, yet unimaginable, catastrophe.

The wild white-water rivers that boil through narrow canyons at the head of the Columbia River Basin have been traveled by oceangoing salmon and steelhead trout for tens of thousands of years. For all of its hydraulic bravado, this finely tuned ecosystem depends on thousands of independent performers to make it work. At the turn of the twentieth century, the Columbia River accounted for more salmon than all the rest of the world's anadromous fish runs put together. If an eighteenth-century hat fetish led to the near demise of the beaver, then the invention of the tin can initiated the long downward spiral of the salmon. When William Clark first saw the run of fall chinook on the Columbia River in October of 1805, he exclaimed that he could get from one shore to the other without a boat. He said he could walk across on the backs of the fish and reach the far side without getting wet.

In 1991, only one sockeye salmon returned to Redfish Lake, an alpine jewel set among snowy crags in Idaho's Sawtooth Range. This lone sockeye, having made the three-year journey to Japan and back, has since been nicknamed Lonesome Larry. After his sperm was collected by marine biologists, Lonesome Larry was stuffed, shellacked, and mounted on a pine board and hung in the governor's office in the Idaho statehouse in Boise. In the entire river basin, the 5 million salmon of Lewis and Clark's day had dropped to fewer than 50,000.

The lecture hall is abuzz with human energy and packed to overflowing with all the usual suspects. Apart, alone, keenly observant, a man with short-cropped hair and penetrating black eyes sits quietly at the back of the room. His legs are crossed, his fingertips pressed together in a prayerful shape as he surveys the milling crowd. Once again, Raymond Cross finds himself at the center of a storm, a national debate over how to rescue native fish stocks on thousands of miles of dying streams and rivers, and how to ensure the cultural survival of the dozen regional tribes that depend on that resource for their survival. And once again, he finds himself sitting at the back of a room, waiting patiently for his opening to address a commission. His own circle, it seems, continually brings him back to a point of origin that is very familiar, another face-to-face encounter with the Army Corps of Engineers.

What marine and aquatic scientists are telling us about the salmon in the Columbia River Basin is a perfect illustration of the Cartesian conflict for which Cross sees no easy political solution. As the health of our environment becomes increasingly stressed by man-made processes, politicians will be forced to confront dilemmas they have historically directed to the courts. "From the beginning, the Man versus Nature argument was a contrived dichotomy," argues Cross. "Yet the post-Renaissance Europeans bought it lock, stock, and barrel. It played right into a disaffected culture that was swept up by Luther's Reformation. In America, the mythology spawned by Cartesian dualism told the immigrants, 'Now, this is your chance to claw your way back to Redemption, back to the Garden of Eden, by bringing nature to heel, by taming it.' The minute you tame nature, you've destroyed the garden you idealized. So I find myself outside that conversation. It doesn't reflect the world, or the laws, that I was taught by my father, or he by his. He taught me that human culture is a project of nature, one of many projects in a network of ongoing, unfinished, never-to-be-finished projects, and that man is a part of that work, not apart from it. The failure of the mythology to explain how the Garden of Eden came to be destroyed poses a troublesome question for the dominant society: 'Now what?' Our experience with the natural world tells us that the unfolding tragedy with the salmon, this looming extinction, is not a failure of science. The salmon's failure to return to the rivers and streams and high mountain lakes is not a crisis of biology or hydrology. It is a crisis of the human spirit."

Raymond Cross predicts that the dialogue between "Europeans" and "Native Americans" in coming years will be very tense, up and down, potentially heartbreaking. There will be the occasional, but brief, celebrations of mutual understanding and reconciliation. But with the last great deposits of natural resources locked up in Indian Country reserves, no one is fooling anyone about what is at stake. How the nation's dwindling natural resources will be managed in the twenty-first century is an unanswered question that is pushing both sides toward a colossal train wreck of economic ideologies and spiritual world views. Raymond Cross is ready. He will have a seat at that table where the future is divided. His voice will be heard in the courtrooms when difficult questions are asked. He issues a gentle warning to those who will join in this conflict.

"Non-Indians will never have western eyes so long as they cling to the Man versus Nature dichotomy. Four hundred years of this thinking gets you a civilization of people lost in shopping malls, coast-to-coast take-out windows, a culture that has lost its connection to the natural world. That is the ultimate poverty for all men, and no amount of money can ransom that sadness."

The gavel cracks. Members of the Army engineers' commission have taken their seats at a long table. The room, overflowing with a standing-room-only crowd, falls silent. Tall and deliberate, the Mandan/Hidatsa attorney with the long eyes who has journeyed across a nation that most Americans will never know, rises to his feet and steps forward to the open microphone. A door closes in another part of the building. A car horn blares on the street. A binder snaps shut across the room as one thousand eyes swivel, yielding the ticking silence to the lone coyote.

"Mr. Chairman," he begins, "my name is Raymond Cross, and I am here to testify on behalf of the salmon, and the American Indian nations . . ."

Indian Law
An Evolutionary Time Line

❧

No field of American jurisprudence has enjoyed a greater surge of popularity among students and public-service law firms in the past twenty years than the topsy-turvy, often counterintuitive world of Indian law. Compared to more conventional and well-traveled disciplines of the law, Indian law is the Wild West, a territory so wide open and fluid that it is still possible for bright young lawyers to strike out and make names for themselves on unclaimed terrain.

"Indian law has emerged in the past ten to fifteen years as the hottest place to be if you've got the intellectual horsepower," says Houston mediator Douglas Sandage. "It's devilishly complex and exciting. There is nothing else quite like it in our legal system."

What follows is a cursory listing of important precursors to American Indian law and the subsequent cases heard in American courts that have played a leading role in shaping the law as we know it today. Some of the more recent cases, such as the 1998 case *Isleta Pueblo v. City of Albuquerque* and the 1999 decision in *Minnesota v. Mille Lacs Band of Chippewa Indians,* are leading indicators of the battles that will be fought over natural resources in the decades to come.

PRECURSORS

Innocent III and IV — Midway through the thirteenth century, Pope Innocent IV, an intellectual pontiff known as the Lawyer Pope, wrote a commentary on Innocent III's papal decree of 1204, *Quod super his,* distinguishing the legal status and rights of non-Christian societies against the emerging background of legal scholarship known as natural law. Innocent IV would ask: "Is it licit to invade a land that infidels possess, or which belongs to them?" He went on to construct a broad-based defense of the Crusades and the conditions justifying Christian warfare against infidel peoples occupying the Holy Lands. Innocent's underlying legal premise was that Christ's life and death had consecrated the Holy Land. Therefore, Christ's followers, not Muhammad's, should dwell there.

Turning Aristotle's humanism on its head, Innocent IV reasoned that infidels indeed had a natural law right to the ownership of land, but there was a catch. Pagan worship of idols and other rites constituted an unpardonable breach of natural law, said Innocent, and these blasphemous practices required Christ's supreme representative on earth, the pope, to intervene and set things right. At the heart of his argument was the premise that every rational creature was bound by the dictates of Christian and Eurocentric precepts of natural law, standards of conduct that the pope was required to enforce by the mantle of responsibility transferred to him by divine law. Furthermore, the pope's privileged authority on divine law made obedience to him the only means of salvation. Today's lawyers would call this a "bright line."

Innocent IV's commentary midway through the thirteenth century would profoundly influence the thinking of kings and conquistadors in discovery-era Europe two centuries hence.

Legal scholar Robert Williams explains how Innocent's commentaries successfully rooted themselves in the ensuing discourses on conquest: "Secular power could be invoked to suppress ecclesiastically defined evil in a world governed by the divinely constructed precepts of natural law. . . . Secular authority in and of itself possessed no inherent function or aspect. . . . It was only an auxiliary power to be used by the pope in appropriate circumstances and at his sole, divinely inspired discretion. This, needless to say, suited the ambitions of the medieval popes. By abstracting the principles of divine justice and remitting them in an earthly form of crusading armies, the feudal-era papacy was fulfilling its divinely ordained responsibility to establish the Christian church as the dominant reality on earth."

Sepulveda v. Bartolomé de Las Casas — After spending twentysome years among the Caribbean Indians on the island of Hispaniola, the humanistic Dominican friar Bartolomé de Las Casas returned in 1555 to the University of Salamanca, Spain, to defend the natural law rights of the natives. The battle between the prelate, arguing Innocentian law, and the dogmatic Sepulveda became the most celebrated debate in discovery-era Europe. Sepulveda argued that the law of nature was honored and understood only by the wisest and most prudent of the higher races. Therefore, heathen Indians could not possibly live by the law of nature. The Dominican priest countered with the argument that the Indians had demonstrated the rational capacity to comprehend the gospel (Las Casas estimated that 20 million Indians had been slaughtered by the Spanish in less than half a century). Despite his passion and logic, Las Casas's appeal to the crown failed to convince the king or his lawyers that the Indians had a legitimate claim to rights and privileges.

Lord Coke and Robert Calvin — In 1608, a decision in a case tried in Elizabethan England would have consequences for Indians in the New World for the next three centuries. A Scotsman named Robert Calvin filed a suit to recover land that he claimed had been taken from him unjustly. The opposing attorney argued that the claimant Calvin was "an alien born," and therefore, since he was out of allegiance to the king of England, his claim on English turf was specious.

In considering this argument, Lord Coke, who had for the first time systematized English common law, attempted to play Solomon by making fine distinctions under the broad category of aliens: "A perpetual enemy, as distinguished from friendly aliens, cannot maintain any action or get anything within this realm. All infidels are in law *perpetui inimici,* perpetual enemies [of the enlightened people], and between them, as with devils whose subjects they be, and the Christian people of the European states, there is perpetual hostility, and there can be no peace."

Once the New World was claimed by the discoverer (the English crown), the land and everything and everyone on it fell under the province of the king. Therefore, the legal status of "savages and infidels" in the New World had already been decided in an English court before the first colony was established at Jamestown.

Lord Coke, in fact, would help draw up the official royal charter for Sir Walter Raleigh's new Virginia Company in 1606. As agents of the king, Raleigh's company had the responsibility for the propagation of "Christian religion to such people as yet living in darkness and miserable ignorance of the true knowledge and worship of God, and may in time bring the infidels and savages to living civility." The king and his agents had not only a right but a responsibility to be at war with infidels who refused conversion. Thanks to Lord Coke, explains Robert Williams, Innocent IV's thirteenth-century commentaries on natural law had become the invisible hand that wrote the official royal charter for the first English colony in the New World.

Federal Indian Law

Marshall Trilogy — The following cases, *Johnson v. McIntosh* (1823), *Cherokee Nation v. Georgia* (1831), and *Worcester v. Georgia* (1832), comprise what is known today as the Marshall Trilogy. In these pivotal early cases, the great chief justice John Marshall laid down the foundation of Indian law, and laid out the boundaries of the federal trust relationship with the tribes, by explicating the legal meaning of the term *sovereignty.*

Marshall explained that treaties protect Native American *sovereignty* as a preexisting condition to the ratification of any contract with the federal government. To complicate this state of affairs for their descendants (namely us), James Madison and James Wilson had insisted that the constitutional convention adopt treaties in Article VI of the U.S. Constitution as the "'supreme law of the land." The founding fathers spread the jaws of a trap that their descendants would step into two hundred years later. In the 1990s, the waste industry was only too happy to embrace sovereignty when it attempted to build landfills in Indian Country that were out of reach of federal regulators. When the tribes began to use sovereignty as a legal tool to withhold resources and coerce tough deals with extraction companies, sovereignty suddenly ceased to be a wonderful thing in the eyes of non-Indians.

Lone Wolf v. Hitchcock — In this watershed case from 1903, the high court ruled that the United States Congress had "plenary power" over the tribes. Legal scholars have reminded Congress ever since that those powers are balanced against their ongoing responsibilities to treaty tribes to act in their best interests as legal trustee. Finding themselves in conflict with the will of Congress, tribes such as the Mandan, Hidatsa, and Arikara commonly encounter a Congress anxious to exercise its "plenary power" but reluctant to balance that power against its responsibilities as trustee for Indian lands, resources, and self-governance.

Winters Doctrine — Foundational Indian law has evolved in roughly seventy-year cycles. In the first decade of the twentieth century, the U.S. Supreme Court heard a case now referred to simply as *Winters* that built on the Marshall Trilogy. In *Winters,* the court ruled that by entering into a treaty with the United States government some years prior, the Gros Ventre tribe in Montana had reserved unto itself and its tribal members all the natural rights of nationhood. The court further explained that one of these reserved rights, which did not have to be stipulated in the treaty to exist but rather existed as a precondition to the treaty, was the tribe's right to sufficient water to conduct its affairs, engage in commerce, and raise crops or harvest fish. The water in question flowed from the Milk River in Montana. White farmers and ranchers were seeking to divert the Milk for their own economic purposes. To their astonishment, they lost.

Canons of Construction — A *canon of construction* is a term of art used by the courts to identify a legal principle that has become axiomatic — a legal guidepost ensuring continuity of interpretation from one generation to the next. These legal aids to navigation, so to speak, illuminate what would otherwise be a murky world. Two canons of construction cited regularly in both the federal courts and the Supreme Court are *Hagen v. Utah* and *Washington v. Washington State Commercial Passenger Fishing Vessel Ass'n.*

In *Hagen,* the court established the idea that ambiguities and conflicts that arise in the interpretation of statutes "are to be resolved in favor of the Indians." In other words, a draw goes to the tribes. This is a crucial distinction and a deciding factor in many cases at the lower court level. Nevertheless, *Hagen* is seldom cited in news stories.

Similarly, in *Washington v. Washington State Commercial Passenger Fishing Vessel Ass'n,* the

U.S. Supreme Court laid down a powerful guiding principle when it ruled that the terms of treaties and agreements with Indian tribes must be construed and interpreted "in the sense in which they would naturally be understood by the Indians." Justice O'Connor cited both of these canons in the majority opinion in the high court's controversial 1999 decision in *Minnesota v. Mille Lacs Band of Chippewa Indians.*

Minnesota v. Mille Lacs Band of Chippewa Indians — In this classic case of pitting a tribe against a state over the disposition of treaty-protected "usufructuary rights," the court upheld the Mille Lacs Chippewa tribe's claim to treaty rights guaranteeing it "reserved rights" to fish in Mille Lacs Lake in central Minnesota. Non-Indian sports fishing groups, supported by the state, fought the tribe's claim. The typical five-to-four decision favoring the tribe in *Mille Lacs* is an important reaffirmation of earlier "usufructuary rights" cases, such as the infamous Boldt Decision of 1974. What was interesting about this case was the fact that the lake in question lies outside the modern boundaries of the Chippewa reservation. Usufructuary rights agreed upon in their nineteenth-century treaty with the federal government guaranteed the tribe perpetual rights to fish, gather, and hunt in their accustomed forests and lakes.

A few weeks later, the high court let stand a lower court ruling in a case in Washington state that ruled in favor of seventeen Puget Sound tribes who asserted their rights of access to traditional shellfish beds. In a decision that mirrored *Mille Lacs* in many respects, the 9th Circuit Court of Appeals ruled that neither the state of Washington nor private property owners could deny tribal members the right to cross private land in order to harvest shellfish in their "traditional and accustomed" manner.

Boldt Decision — About seventy years after *Winters,* the 9th Circuit Court of Appeals was asked to rule on a case that challenged the foundations of Indian law. Treaty tribes on the West Coast, and in Puget Sound in particular, began to assert their treaty rights over the storied salmon runs. Clearly, salmon were already a dwindling resource. In 1974, Judge George Boldt wrote a landmark opinion for the court — one that the Supreme Court let stand on appeal — that remains as controversial today as it was thirty years ago. Building on both Marshall's Trilogy and *Winters,* the 9th Circuit Court then ruled that the reserved rights of West Coast tribes guaranteed the Indians fully half of the annual catch of the prized fish. White legislators and fishermen were stunned.

The losing attorney in that case, Slade Gorton, went on to become a U.S. senator. As a national legislator, Gorton would repeatedly attempt to introduce legislation or budget riders that would undermine tribal sovereignty or that would disband tribes altogether. The downstream effect of the Boldt Decision will be felt profoundly in the Northwest as states, tribes, and the Endangered Species Act converge on an almost imponderable high noon confrontation that pits treaty rights against the displacement of enormous economic power and states' rights.

United States v. Michigan — In the 1979 case of *United States v. Michigan,* Judge Noel P. Fox was asked to determine whether the twentieth-century descendants of nineteenth-century Chippewa treaty signatories had retained fishing rights under the treaties. Further, if those rights were indeed present, the suit asked how many and what kind of fish could the Indians take?

In a powerful postscript to Boldt (and precursor to the Voigt Decision), Judge Fox strongly affirmed in a very wide-ranging decision the Indians' rights as secured to them by the treaties of 1836 and 1854. Judge Fox wrote: "The mere passage of time has not eroded, and cannot erode, the rights guaranteed by solemn treaties that both sides pledged on their honor to uphold. The Indians have a right to fish today wherever fish are to be found within the area of cession, a right established by aboriginal right and confirmed by the Treaty of Ghent and the Treaty of 1836."

Fox further emphasized the basis of these rights as being grounded in treaties: "Because the right of the . . . tribes to fish in ceded waters of the Great Lakes is protected by treaties . . . , that right is preserved and protected under the supreme law of the land, does not depend on state law, is distinct from the rights and privileges held by non-Indians, and may not be qualified by an action of the state. . . ."

The Voigt Decision — Nearly ten years after Boldt, states' rights activists in Washington and in state capitals took another hit from a federal appeals court, one that expanded on Boldt in ways no one had anticipated. Oddly, Boldt centered on salmon while the Voigt Decision focused on walleye perch.

In the early 1980s, Wisconsin's Chippewa tribe claimed a treaty right to spear walleye in their ancestral lakes. Year after year, Indian spearfishing provoked violent protests from white sports-fishing groups. Year after year, Indians and whites spilled each other's blood on regional boat landings. Initially, in *Lac Courte Oreilles v. Voigt*, Judge James Doyle decided against aboriginal fishing claims. But on appeal, the 7th Circuit reversed Doyle, and though the 7th Circuit had the final word, the controversial case is still referred to as *Voigt*. At that time, Lester Voigt was the director of the Wisconsin Department of Natural Resources. The "Final Judgment" in this contentious case was written by Judge Barbara Crabb. Crabb's ruling was issued in March 1991. White/Indian relations in the Upper Midwest have never been the same since.

Judge Crabb ruled that the usufructuary rights of the tribes arising from the Treaties of 1837 and 1842 included "rights to those forms of animal life, fish, vegetation, and so on that they utilized at treaty time . . . on their ancestral land, lakes, and rivers, regardless of modern-day reservation boundaries." Once again, non-Indians were stunned. Wisconsin appealed. Six months later the U.S. Supreme Court denied certiorari and refused to retry the case. Wisconsin Governor Tommy Thompson was so angry that he tried to buy out the Chippewa's treaty rights. The Indians refused to sell. As with Boldt, Crabb's ruling has held.

Isleta Pueblo v. City of Albuquerque — After fighting its way through the court system for nearly ten years, the Isleta Pueblo tribe of New Mexico won a landmark case in a federal court of appeals that upheld the tribe's right to establish its own water-quality standards. Those standards, fiercely contested by their upstream neighbor, the city of Albuquerque, would force the city to spend $300 million in upgrading its water-treatment facilities in order to come into compliance with the Indians' standards. The tribe was the first in the nation to act on a little known provision in the federal Clean Water Act of 1976 that allowed tribal governments to establish water-quality standards independently of the state in which they reside. In 1998, the U.S. Supreme Court upheld a lower court that had ruled in favor of the Pueblo. Since that victory, dozens more tribes have followed the Isleta's lead in a rush to protect their resources from off-reservation polluters. This avalanche of regulatory freelancing by the tribes is viewed somewhat dimly by state governments, developers, city planners, and mining-industry lobbyists.

Elbowoods, North Dakota: Final Roll Call of Relocation and Dispossession — 1953

The following is a list of Mandan, Hidatsa, and Arikara families who lost their homes and ancestral lands on the river bottoms of the Upper Missouri River in 1954. While the three tribes' membership suffered the highest percentage of loss of any of the tribes in the Missouri River Basin (approximately 95 percent), they were by no means the only tribes impacted by Pick-Sloan projects. Before the agencies were finished "taming" the wild Missouri, twenty-three different tribes would suffer similar fates. Where particulars differed for the Sioux, the Crow, and the Northern Cheyenne, the results were invariably the same. The Crow, led by their legendary tribal chairman Robert Yellowtail, would be the last to lose the fight. Rubbing salt in the wound, the Bureau of Reclamation, upon erecting a massive impoundment on the Bighorn River, named the structure Yellowtail Dam.

RESIDENTS OF ELBOWOODS

Rita Abe
Mr. and Mrs. Philip Atkins
Lillian Bad Brave
Serena Bad Brave
Mr. and Mrs. Anson Baker
Christine Bear
Mr. and Mrs. Nathan Bear
Mr. and Mrs. Charles Bearstail
Mr. and Mrs. John Bearstail
Minnie Bearstail
Patrick Bearstail
Vincent Bearstail
William Bearstail
Mr. and Mrs. Karmen Blake
Frances Boyd
Mr. and Mrs. Evan Burr, Sr.
Mr. and Mrs. Arnold Charging
Anna Chase
Emerson Chase
Mr. and Mrs. John Chase
Joseph Chase, Jr.

Inez Coffee
Mr. and Mrs. Peter Coffee
James Conklin
William Conklin
Alfred Cross
Carol Cross
Dorothy Cross
Marilyn Cross
Martin Cross, Jr.
Mr. and Mrs. Martin Cross, Sr.
Michael Cross
Phyllis Cross
Raymond Cross
Mr. and Mrs. Burr Crowsbreast
Polly Dalby
Clara Danks
Edward S. Danks
James Danks
John Danks
Francis Deane
Mr. and Mrs. Joseph Deane

Peter Deane
Mr. and Mrs. William Deane
Cecelia Drags Wolf
Bertha Driver
Eugene Eagle
Mr. and Mrs. Frank Eagle
Mr. and Mrs. Tom Eagle
Joseph Face
Mr. and Mrs. Walter Face
Jerine Fox
Leon Fox
Lloyd Fox
Mr. and Mrs. Ted Gillette
Mary Goodreau
Cecilia Grinnell
Dorothy Grinnell
Mr. and Mrs. John Grinnell
Luther Grinnell
Maggie Grinnell
Perpetua Grinnell
Richard Grinnell
Virginia Grinnell
Wilbur Grinnell
Celeste Hall
Edward Hall, Jr.
Ina Hall
Mr. and Mrs. Jim Hall
Margie Hall
Mervel Hall
Mr. and Mrs. Lloyd Howard
Myra Howard
Mr. and Mrs. Charles Huber
Ernestine Huber
Mr. and Mrs. Fred Huber
Mr. and Mrs. Gordon Huber
Mr. and Mrs. John Hunts Along
Rollo Jones
Zona Kills Thunder
Marcia Kirkaldie
Jeannette Little Crow
Elizabeth Little Owl
Raymond Little Owl
Mr. and Mrs. Wilfred Lockwood
Mr. and Mrs. Charles Malnourie
Mr. and Mrs. Patrick Malnourie
Mr. and Mrs. Jim Martin
Cecelia Mason
Medicine Crow
Floyd Montclair

Margaret Necklace
August Newman
Sam Newman
Lucy Old Dog
Elizabeth Packineau
Katie Packineau
Mr. and Mrs. Lambert Packineau
Melda Packineau
Mr. and Mrs. Tracy Packineau
Josephine Paetz
Mr. and Mrs. Clarence Perkins
Fannie Perkins
Rudolph Perkins
Tony Perkins
Angela Plante
Mr. and Mrs. Paul Reed
Inez Huber Reidhead
Bryan Rogers
Mr. and Mrs. Tom Rogers
Ermel Rush
Larry Rush
Mr. and Mrs. Wilbur Schettler
Mr. and Mrs. Lawrence Sears
Miriam Sears
Mr. and Mrs. Frank Sherwood
Mr. and Mrs. John Sitting Crow
Ben and Margie Slocum
Emma Smells
Mr. and Mrs. Carroll Smith
Jefferson Smith, Jr.
Jefferson Smith, Sr.
Lillian Smith
Ruth Smith
Frank Spotted Bear
Julia Spotted Bear
Nora Mae Spotted Bear
Theodore Spotted Bear
Mr. and Mrs. Peter Sterud
Germaine Swift Eagle
Jerome Tomhave
Mr. and Mrs. Mason Two Crow
Mr. and Mrs. Willis Two Crow
Martha Voigt
Delphine Wheeler
Mr. and Mrs. Joseph Wheeler
Mr. and Mrs. Albert Whitman
Mr. and Mrs. Carl Whitman, Jr.
Mr. and Mrs. Clay Whitney
Mr. and Mrs. Ernest Wilkinson

Mr. and Mrs. John Wilkinson
Margaret Wilkinson
Mr. and Mrs. William Wilkinson
Lillie Wolf
Elizabeth Wounded Face
Mr. and Mrs. Francis Young

RESIDENTS OF BEAVER CREEK

Mr. and Mrs. Adolph Bell, Sr.
Burton Bell, Sr.
Joseph Bell
Mary Bell
Rose Bell
Ophelia Black Hawk
Frieda Duckett
Irene Duckett
Mr. and Mrs. Alfred Fox
Mr. and Mrs. George Gillette
Mr. and Mrs. Russell Gillette
Thelma Hunter
Emma Jones
Mr. and Mrs. August Little Soldier
Mr. and Mrs. Nathan Little Soldier
Willena Little Soldier
Edward Lockwood, Jr.
Mr. and Mrs. Wilfred Lockwood
Mr. and Mrs. Isaac Price
Jonathan Price
Mr. and Mrs. Stephen Price
Glenn Snow Bird
Mr. and Mrs. Gilbert Starr
Mr. and Mrs. John Starr
Mr. and Mrs. Peter Starr
Wilson Starr
Aileen Whitman
Mr. and Mrs. Carl Whitman, Sr.
Clarine Whitman

RESIDENTS OF SHELL CREEK

John Bad Brave
Nora Baker
Sarah Baker
Veronica Baker
Mr. and Mrs. Harry Beaks
Mr. and Mrs. Jacob Bird
Steven Bird
Frank Birdsbill
Rosie Birdsbill
Mr. and Mrs. Joe Black Bear

Alvin Black Hawk
Georgeline Black Hawk
Mr. and Mrs. Charles Blake
Annie Brown
Mr. and Mrs. Louis Brown
Mr. and Mrs. George Bruce, Sr.
Miriam Bullseye
Robert Cherries
Agnes Conklin
Norma Marie Cummings
Felix Dancing Bull
Josephine Dancing Bull
Mr. and Mrs. Raymond Dancing Bull
Mr. and Mrs. Maurice Danks, Jr.
George Drags Wolf, Jr.
Mr. and Mrs. George Drags Wolf, Sr.
Grace Drags Wolf
Mr. and Mrs. Louis Drags Wolf
Mr. and Mrs. Alfred Driver, Sr.
Mr. and Mrs. Jim Driver
Mr. and Mrs. Joe Driver
Paul Driver
Bessie Elk
Myrtle Elk
Spencer Elk
Victor Elk
Mr. and Mrs. George Fast Dog
Naomi Foolish Bear
Mr. and Mrs. Albert Fox
Mr. and Mrs. Charles Fox
Mr. and Mrs. Clark Fox
Cuthbert Fox
Mr. and Mrs. George Fox, Jr.
Mr. and Mrs. George Fox, Sr.
Mr. and Mrs. Glen Fox
Mr. and Mrs. Guy Fox
Mr. and Mrs. Lee Fox
Mr. and Mrs. Thomas Fox
Vincent Fox
Wanda Fox
Mr. and Mrs. Lawrence Good Bear
Charles Grady, Sr.
Harry Grady
Mary Grady
Benedict Grant
Charles Grant
David Grant
Agnes Gray Wolf
Savina Gullickson

Adelbert Gun
Aline Gun
Austin Gun
Benjamin Gun
Fred Gun, Jr.
Mr. and Mrs. Fred Gun, Sr.
Martha Gun
Edward O. Hale
Eleanor Hale
Leona Hale
Aline Horn
Bernice Mandan
Mr. and Mrs. Ben Many Ribs
Mr. and Mrs. Michael Mason
Mr. and Mrs. Mark Necklace
Wilson Packineau
Charles Parshall
Delores Parshall
Paul Parshall
Ruby Parshall
Alice Prue
Mr. and Mrs. Percy Rush
Belle Smith
Mr. and Mrs. Cecil Smith
Dell Smith
Dora Smith
John Smith, Sr.
Phoebe Smith
Mr. and Mrs. Sam Smith
Wayne Smith
Mr. and Mrs. William Smith
Mr. and Mrs. George Spotted Wolf
Pete Spotted Wolf
Sterling Spotted Wolf
Adlai Stevenson
Caroline Stevenson
Mr. and Mrs. Rufus Stevenson
Wilbur Stevenson
Mary Two Crow
Sadie Two Shields
Ira Waters
Mr. and Mrs. Herbert White Owl
George Wolf, Sr.
Margaret Wolf
Rachel Wolf
Warren Wolf
Fannie Young Bird
Joseph Young Bird
Frank Young Wolf
Leo Young Wolf

RESIDENTS OF RED BUTTE

Minnie BearGhost
Blanche Benson
Mr. and Mrs. Phillip Benson
Clayton Bull
Duane Bull
Jessie Bull
Julia Bull
Mildred Bull
Miriam Bull
Mr. and Mrs. Bernard Chase
Frank Chase
Mr. and Mrs. Gilbert Eagle
Joseph Eagle
Rose Fournier
Adolph Fox
Mr. and Mrs. Lawrence Fox
Mr. and Mrs. Ben Fredericks
Mr. and Mrs. Emory Fredericks
Lorraine Gayton
Mattie Grinnell
Mr. and Mrs. Amos Holding Eagle
Anna Holding Eagle
Mr. and Mrs. James Holding Eagle
Mr. and Mrs. Matthew Holding Eagle
Naomi Holding Eagle
Agnes Holen
Eloise Johnson
Albert Little Owl
Ralph Little Owl
Mr. and Mrs. David Little Swallow, Sr.
Mark Mahto
Mr. and Mrs. Ernest Medicine Stone
Mr. and Mrs. Delbert Nagle
John Nagle, Jr.
John Nagle, Sr.
Caroline Pleets
Mr. and Mrs. Sylvan Sage
Herbert Sitting Crow
Mr. and Mrs. John Sitting Crow
Sally Sitting Crow
Joanna Stops
Viola Wilson

RESIDENTS OF CHARGING EAGLE

Mr. and Mrs. Sam Bad Gun
Charity Benson
Christine Benson
Edwin Benson
Frank Benson, Jr.

Mr. and Mrs. Frank Benson, Sr.
Mr. and Mrs. John Benson
Charles Burr
Mr. and Mrs. Richard Crows Heart
Mr. and Mrs. Roy Crows Heart
Flora Demaray
Gabriella DuBois
Annie Eagle
John Fredericks, Jr.
Mr. and Mrs. John Fredericks, Sr.
Kenneth Fredericks
Wilhelmina Fredericks
Ailsa Gwin
Duveen Keene
Mr. and Mrs. Sam Lincoln
Gertrude Sillitti
Mr. and Mrs. John Stone
Mary Whiteman
Oscar Whiteman
Quentin Whiteman, Jr.
Lois Whitman
Mr. and Mrs. Alonzo Young Bear
Frank Young Bear
Mr. and Mrs. Ivan Young Bear
Vivian Young Bear

Residents of Nishu District

Mary Bateman
Robert Bear, Sr.
Pete Beauchamp
Lizzie Bedell
Josephine Blue Earth
Bernard Breuer
Margaret Breuer
Peter Breuer
Mr. and Mrs. Sam Dancing Bull
Delores Deane
Kenneth Deane
Mr. and Mrs. William Deane, Jr.
Dora Deegan
Gardner Deegan
Marmie Deegan
Mr. and Mrs. Felix Dickens
Mr. and Mrs. Clair Everett
Mr. and Mrs. Lloyd Everett
Mr. and Mrs. Theodore Everett
Elizabeth Felix
Mr. and Mrs. Louis Felix
Grace Flute
Alfreda Fox

Ernest Fox
Esther Fox
Frank Fox, Sr.
Fred Fox
George Fox
Hannah Fox
Isaac Fox
Mr. and Mrs. John Fox
Mr. and Mrs. Joseph Fox
Mr. and Mrs. Matthew Fox
Mr. and Mrs. Nick Fox
Redmond Fox
Mr. and Mrs. Robert Fox
Sidney Fox
Wilbert Fox, Jr.
Mr. and Mrs. Evan Gillette
Mary Gillette
Larry Goodall
Arlene Gullickson
Mr. and Mrs. Phillip Hand
Mr. and Mrs. Wallace Hand
Mr. and Mrs. Ben Heart
Frank Heart
Mr. and Mrs. Archie Hopkins
Mr. and Mrs. Dan Hopkins
Mr. and Mrs. Harvey Hopkins
Mildred Hopkins
Susie Hopkins
Mr. and Mrs. Ambrose Hosie
Mr. and Mrs. Everett Hosie
Lottie Hosie
Mr. and Mrs. Franklin Howard
George Howard, Jr.
Carroll Howling Wolf
Mr. and Mrs. Dan Howling Wolf
Terry Howling Wolf
George Lewis, Jr.
Lena Malnourie
Mr. and Mrs. Vincent Malnourie
Clara Packineau
Alice Painte
Mr. and Mrs. Davis Painte
Marvin Painte
Nora Painte
Mr. and Mrs. Orville Painte
Robert Painte
Elizabeth Perkins
Esther Perkins
Mr. and Mrs. Gilbert Perkins
Lorraine Perkins

Regina Perkins
Mr. and Mrs. Sybert Perkins
Rose Pfliger
Mr. and Mrs. Clyde Plenty Chief
Mr. and Mrs. Walter Plenty Chief
Helen Price
Andrew Reed
Mr. and Mrs. Joseph Reed
Ella Ripley
Gladys Ripley
Jackson Ripley
Mr. and Mrs. Perry Ross
Mr. and Mrs. Philip Ross
Winnie Seminole
Abbie Shell
Roger Shell
Albert Simpson
Quentin Simpson, Jr.
Eugene Spotted Horse
Mamie Spotted Horse
Esther Star
McRoy Star
Mr. and Mrs. Phillip Star
Theresa Star
Woodrow Star
Ruth Taylor
Mr. and Mrs. Levi Waters
Mr. and Mrs. Thomas Wells
Mr. and Mrs. Eugene White, Jr.
Mr. and Mrs. Eugene White, Sr.
Mr. and Mrs. John White
Lena White
Rhoda White
Robert White
Cynthia White Arm
Alton White Bear
Donald White Bear
Mr. and Mrs. Matthew White Bear, Jr.
Mr. and Mrs. Matthew White Bear, Sr.
Myron White Bear
Pauline White Bear
William White Bear
Albert White Calf, Jr.
Albert White Calf, Sr.
Lois White Calf
Mr. and Mrs. Oscar White Calf
Mr. and Mrs. Byron Wilde
John Wilkinson, Jr.
Ignatius Winans

Nellie Yellow Bird
Mr. and Mrs. Willard Yellow Bird
Mr. and Mrs. Delancy Yellow Face
Mr. and Mrs. Thomas Yellow Face
Mr. and Mrs. Ben Young Bird

RESIDENTS OF INDEPENDENCE

Clement Baker
Mr. and Mrs. Clyde Baker
Ellen Baker
Gail Baker
Lawrence Baker
Mr. and Mrs. Philip Baker
Ted Baker
Mr. and Mrs. Owen Beaks
Martha Bell
Maureen Bell
Nora Bell
Mr. and Mrs. William Bell
Mr. and Mrs. Robert Bird Bear
Mr. and Mrs. Solomon Bird Bear
Mr. and Mrs. Theodore Bird Bear
Priscilla Bird Day
Mr. and Mrs. Edward Black Hawk
Frederick Black Hawk
Geraldine Black Hawk
Mr. and Mrs. Kingdon Black Hawk
Rita Black Hawk
George Buffalo
Mr. and Mrs. Ted Buffalo
Christine Burr
Mr. and Mrs. Newton Burr
Mr. and Mrs. Oscar Burr
Albert Charging
Mr. and Mrs. David Charging
Mr. and Mrs. Ernest Charging
Mr. and Mrs. Francis Charging
Susie Charging
Mr. and Mrs. Evan Finley
Mr. and Mrs. Charles Fredericks
Mr. and Mrs. Ben Good Bird
Donald Good Bird
Mr. and Mrs. Emory Good Bird
Isabelle Good Bird
Mr. and Mrs. John Good Bird
Marcella Good Bird
Mildred Good Bird
Patricia Good Bird
Mr. and Mrs. Raymond Good Bird

Benjamin Grinnell
Sarah Gwin
Mr. and Mrs. Anthony Hale
Maggie Hale
Trilby Hale
Freida Hall
Mr. and Mrs. William Hall
Basil Hunts Along
Mr. and Mrs. Vincent Hunts Along
Martin Levings
Jack Lone Fight, Jr.
Lois Lone Fight
Mary Lone Fight
Roderick Lone Fight
Mr. and Mrs. Ted Lone Fight
Thad Mason
Primrose Morgan
Elmer Rush
Mr. and Mrs. Robert Rush
Mr. and Mrs. James Smith
May Smith
Mildred Smith
Phillip Snow
Mr. and Mrs. Alton Standish
Mr. and Mrs. Douglas Standish
Mr. and Mrs. Leo Standish
Polly Standish
Gladys Turner
Mr. and Mrs. Hans Walker
Melvin Walker
Reba Walker
Tillie Walker
Robert Walks
Job White Calf
Mr. and Mrs. Arnold White Eagle
Mr. and Mrs. Frank White Owl
Jessie White Owl
Josephine White Owl
Mabel White Owl
Mr. and Mrs. Richard White Owl
Mr. and Mrs. Simon White Owl
Geraldine Wounded Face
Joseph Wounded Face, Jr.
William Wounded Face
Julia Wound Face
George Yellow Wolf
Mr. and Mrs. John Yellow Wolf
Celina Young Bear
Clifford Young Bear

Mr. and Mrs. Curtis Young Bear
David Young Bear
George Young Bear
Pearl Young Bear
Victor Young Bear
Lucy Young Bird
Mr. and Mrs. Matt Young Bird

RESIDENTS OF LUCKY MOUND

Fred Baker
Gerard Baker
Paige Baker
Mr. and Mrs. Paige Baker
Mr. and Mrs. Phillip Bear
Florence Berryhill
Austin Beston
Francis Beston
Gertrude Beston
Ida Beston
John Beston
Mr. and Mrs. Finley Blake
Julia Bluestone
Mr. and Mrs. Tom Bluestone
Mr. and Mrs. Charles Bracklin
Mr. and Mrs. Eugene Brugh
Margaret Brugh
Duane Charging
Grace Charging
Kenneth Charging
Rose Charging
Adrian Foote
George Foote, Jr.
Mr. and Mrs. George Foote, Sr.
Mr. and Mrs. Jim Foote
Alfreda Goodiron
Charles Grinnell
Mr. and Mrs. David Grinnell
Grace Grinnell
Mr. and Mrs. Lee Hall
Margaret Harney
Flora Irwin
Mr. and Mrs. John Irwin
Laura Irwin
Louis Irwin
Mr. and Mrs. Jack Lone Fight
Adam Mandan
Anna Mandan
Richard Mandan
Rita Mandan

RoseMarie Mandan
May Packineau
Mr. and Mrs. John Rabbithead
Mr. and Mrs. Melvin Rabbithead
Stephen Rabbithead
Richard Smith
Mr. and Mrs. Charles Snow
Dennis Snow
Mr. and Mrs. Tom Spotted Wolf
Mr. and Mrs. Bill Wells
Mr. and Mrs. Leslie Wells
Mr. and Mrs. Ralph Wells, Jr.
Ralph Wells, Sr.
Reginald Wells
Mr. and Mrs. Valentine Wells

Bertha White Body
Izora White Body
Mr. and Mrs. John White Body, Jr.
John White Body, Sr.
Malcolm White Body
Mamie White Body
Mary White Body
Sidney White Body
Mr. and Mrs. Timothy White Body
Henry Young Bird
Mr. and Mrs. Herman Young Bird
Leroy Young Bird
Philomena Young Bird
Mr. and Mrs. Tom Young Bird

1851 Treaty of Fort Laramie (Horse Creek)

Articles of a treaty made and concluded at Fort Laramie, in the Indian Territory, between D. D. Mitchell, superintendent of Indian affairs, and Thomas Fitzpatrick, Indian agent, commissioners specially appointed and authorized by the President of the United States, of the first part, and the chiefs, headmen, and braves of the following Indian nations, residing south of the Missouri River, east of the Rocky Mountains, and north of the lines of Texas and New Mexico, viz, the Sioux or Dahcotahs, Cheyennes, Arrapahoes, Crows, Assinaboines, Blackfoot, Piegans, Gros-Ventre [Hidatsa], Mandans, and Arrickaras, parties of the second part, on the seventeenth day of September, A.D., one thousand eight hundred and fifty-one.

This treaty, as signed (with an amendment changing the annuity from fifty to ten years), was ratified by the United States Senate in 1853. In all subsequent agreements "this treaty has been recognized [by the United States Supreme] Court as in force."

ARTICLE 1. The aforesaid nations, parties to this treaty, having assembled for the purpose of establishing and confirming peaceful relations amongst themselves, do hereby covenant and agree to abstain in future from all hostilities whatever against each other, to maintain good faith and friendship in all their mutual intercourse, and to make an effective and lasting peace.

ARTICLE 2. The aforesaid nations do hereby recognize the right of the United States Government to establish roads, military and other posts, within their respective territories.

ARTICLE 3. In consideration of the rights and privileges acknowledged in the preceding article, the United States bind themselves to protect the aforesaid Indian nations against the commission of all depredations by the people of the said United States, after the ratification of this treaty.

ARTICLE 4. The aforesaid Indian nations do hereby agree and bind themselves to make restitution or satisfaction for any wrongs committed, after the ratification of this treaty, by any band or individual of their people, on the people of the United States, whilst lawfully residing in or passing through their respective territories.

ARTICLE 5. The aforesaid Indian nations do hereby recognize and acknowledge the following tracts of country, included within the metes and boundaries hereinafter designated, as their respective territories, viz:

The territory of the Sioux or Dahcotah Nation, commencing the mouth of the White Earth River, on the Missouri River; thence in a southwesterly direction to the forks of the Platte River; thence up the north fork of the Platte River to a point known as the Red Butte, or where the road leaves the river; thence along the range of mountains known as the Black Hills, to the head-waters of Heart River; thence down the Heart River to its mouth; and thence down the Missouri River to the place of beginning.

The territory of the Gros Ventre, Mandans, and Arrickaras Nations, commencing at the mouth of Heart River; thence up the Missouri River to the mouth of the Yellowstone River; thence up the Yellowstone River to the mouth of Powder River in a southeasterly direction, to the head-waters of the Little Missouri River; thence along the Black Hills to the head of Heart River, and thence down Heart River to the place of beginning.

The territory of the Assinaboin Nation, commencing at the mouth of Yellowstone River; thence up the Missouri River to the mouth of the Muscle-shell River; thence from the mouth of the Muscle-shell River in a southeasterly direction until it strikes the head-waters of Big Dry Creek; thence down that creek to where it empties into the Yellowstone River, nearly opposite the mouth of Powder River, and thence down the Yellowstone River to the place of beginning.

The territory of the Blackfoot Nation, commencing at the mouth of Muscle-shell River; thence up the Missouri River to its source; thence along the main range of the Rocky Mountains, in a southerly direction, to the head-waters of the northern source of the Yellowstone River; thence down the Yellowstone River to the mouth of Twenty-five Yard Creek; thence across to the head-waters of the Muscle-shell River, and thence down the Muscle-shell River to the place of beginning.

The territory of the Crow Nation, commencing at the mouth of Powder River on the Yellowstone; thence up Powder River to its source; thence along the main range of the Black Hills and Wind River Mountains to the head-waters of the Yellowstone River; thence down the Yellowstone River to the mouth of Twenty-five Yard Creek; thence to the head waters of the Muscle-shell River; thence down the Muscle-shell River to its mouth; thence to the head-waters of Big Dry Creek, and thence to its mouth.

The territory of the Cheyennes and Arrapahoes, commencing at the Red Bute, or the place where the road leaves the north fork of the Platte River; thence up the north fork of the Platte River to its source; thence along the main range of the Rocky Mountains to the head-waters of the Arkansas River; thence down the Arkansas River to the crossing of the Santa Fé road; thence in a northwesterly direction to the forks of the Platte River, and thence up the Platte River to the place of beginning.

It is, however, understood that, in making this recognition and acknowledgement, the aforesaid Indian nations do not hereby abandon or prejudice any rights or claims they may have to other lands; and further, that they do not surrender the privilege of hunting, fishing, or passing over any of the tracts of country heretofore described.

ARTICLE 6. The parties to the second part of this treaty having selected principals or head-chiefs for their respective nations, through whom all national business will hereafter be conducted, do hereby bind themselves to sustain said chiefs and their successors during good behavior.

ARTICLE 7. In consideration of the treaty stipulations, and for the damages which have or may occur by reason thereof to the Indian nations, parties hereto, and for their maintenance and the improvement of their moral and social customs, the United States bind themselves to deliver to the said Indian nations the sum of fifty thousand dollars per annum for the term of ten years, with the right to continue the same at the discretion of the President of the United States for a period not exceeding five years thereafter, in provisions, merchandise, domestic animals, and agricultural implements, in such proportions as may be deemed best adapted to their condition by the President of the United States, to be distributed in proportion to the population of the aforesaid Indian nations.

ARTICLE 8. It is understood and agreed that should any of the Indian nations, parties to this treaty, violate any of the provisions thereof, the United States may withhold the whole or a portion of the annuities mentioned in the preceding article from the nation so offending, until, in the opinion of the President of the United States, proper satisfaction shall have been made.

In testimony whereof the said D. D. Mitchell and Thomas Fitzpatrick commissioners as aforesaid, and the chiefs, headmen, and braves, parties hereto, have set their hands and affixed their marks, on the day and at the place first above written.

Notes

INTRODUCTION

Interviews: *James Abourezk, Elizabeth Bell, John Carter, Raymond Cross, Tom Goldtooth, Lori Goodman, Verna Teller.*

4   pressure on tribal governments: In May of 1996, just months after human rights activist Ken Saro-Wiwa was executed by Nigerian strongman Sani Abacha, the World Council of Churches (WCC) and Mine Watch International hosted a ten-day conference in London of leaders of indigenous groups from around the world engaged in battles against multinational mineral conglomerates. Typical of the strategy employed by most, Royal Dutch/ Shell formed an informal partnership with General Abacha and gained unhindered access to the oil fields in the Ogoni people's homelands. When Saro-Wiwa took the Ogoni's complaints to the world, a kangaroo court set up by General Abacha found him guilty of treason and executed him on a public square in Lagos. At the WCC conference in London, indigenous leaders reported that the situation in Nigeria was commonplace. In 1998 Amnesty International reported that in Myanmar, formerly Burma, the Mitsubishi and Unocal corporations were funneling money to the military junta to build a gas pipeline with "the slave labor of children." Unocal has since been sued for its alleged collusion with the junta. For a full discussion of this, see Gedicks, *The New Resource Wars.*

4   in August 1999 . . . federal district: Although it has enormous implications for future relations between Indian and white governments, *Eloise Pepion Cobell, et al., v. Bruce Babbitt, Lawrence Summers, Kevin Gover* has been ignored by the mainstream public. After twice citing Secretary of the Interior Gale Norton for "contempt of court," Judge Lamberth called the agency "a blight on the Government of the United States."

5   By the mid-1990s, the IEN had: Through its contacts with indigenous groups in the International Indian Treaty Council — the largest nongovernmental organization (NGO) at the United Nations — the IEN joined a global network of indigenous and non-indigenous groups that monitor industry and governments.

5   Dateline: Isleta, New Mexico: The Isleta Pueblo were the first to use Section 517 of the federal Clean Water Act for the purpose of establishing their own water standards on the Rio Grande. Their rights to the river predate claims by the city. The Isleta case was soon followed to the high court by a similar case brought against the Salish and Kootenai tribes of Montana by the state's governor, Marc Racicot. Here, the tribes were claiming jurisdiction over white residents on the reservation. The Salish and Kootenai also won their appeal to the United States Supreme Court.

6   what lurks behind the details: In 1987, the Strategic Minerals Task Force urged President Ronald Reagan to declare Indian country a "national sacrifice zone." The task force, made up entirely of representatives from the extraction industry and right-wing "think

tanks" such as the Heritage Foundation, reasoned that the nation's reservation Indians could be forcibly relocated to America's large urban centers. For a full discussion of the SMTF's agenda under the Reagan administration, see Gedicks, *The New Resource Wars,* pp. 41, 110.

6   Dateline: Missoula: With national elections hanging in the balance, and with the Pacific Northwest states holding deciding votes, the Clinton administration finessed the "breaching" question by postponing the decision for another five years.

7   in October of 1804 . . . five: Lewis and Clark, *The Journals of Lewis and Clark,* Nicholas Biddle, ed., pp. 168–174.

7   In his seminal work: Rhonda, *Lewis and Clark Among the Indians,* pp. 67–70.

7   the artist George Catlin: In 1832, the elderly Clark met with George Catlin before the young artist boarded the steamboat *Yellowstone,* then set to embark on its maiden voyage up the Missouri to Fort Union. See Catlin, *North American Indians,* p. 32.

8   the Papal See was asserting: Williams, *The American Indian in Western Legal Thought,* pp. 23–40.

Chapter I: Heart of the World

Interviews: *Everett Albers, Dorothy Atkinson, Al (Bucky) Cross, Martin (Crusoe) Cross, Michael Cross, Calvin Grinnell, Marilyn Hudson, Ed Lone Fight, Dr. Monica Mayer, Phyllis Old Dog Cross, Ray Quinn, Jr., Dr. Herbert Wilson, Professor W. Raymond Wood.*

11   Martin and 9 million other people: For a firsthand account of "The War of the Worlds" broadcast on the night of October 30, 1938, see Bogdanovich, *This Is Orson Welles,* pp. 18–20, 346, and Callow, *Orson Welles,* pp. 398–408.

11   It was October 30, 1938: Ibid.

11   In the CBS studio in New York: Ibid.

11   Out in the great beyond: Ibid.

12   The young couple's home lacked any: Many memorable works have chronicled the life of the homesteader. Several first-rate accounts are: Sandoz, *Old Jules;* Rolvaag, *Giants in the Earth;* and, more recently, Raban, *Bad Land.*

12   Temperatures in Elbowoods: Fitzharris, *The Wild Prairie,* pp. 7–10. In *Short Grass Country,* p. 190, Stanley Vestal tells of a four-month period in Dodge City when the wind blew for 1,420 hours and was calm for 27.

13   A team of government surveyors: Meyer, "Fort Berthold and the Garrison Dam," pp. 239–40.

15   Old State Road Number Eight: This highway has since been renamed North Dakota Highway 37. On its north-south axis, it makes a ninety-degree turn just shy of Lake Sakakawea and runs due east, along the old section lines, to the town of Garrison.

16   To the dismay of many: For a more detailed account of the life of the homesteaders, see Raban, *Bad Land,* pp. 195–223, or, perhaps the most important novel ever written about immigrant life on the High Plains, Rolvaag, *Giants in the Earth.*

17   Like their newly arrived neighbors: Meyer, *The Village Indians of the Upper Missouri,* pp. 5–9. Meyer's terminology differs slightly from that of W. Raymond Wood and Preston Holder, but he draws similar conclusions from archaeological data collected in recent decades. Meyer's "archaic Mandan" were already semisedentary when they began moving up the Missouri River in the tenth century A.D. Evidence from excavations in the Middle Missouri region, in modern-day South Dakota, show that the Mandan were trading for dentalium shell beads in the 1300s. These shells, which were a form of trading currency

in pre-Columbian America, are known to have only one source: the seabed surrounding the Queen Charlotte Islands, sixty miles off the coast of British Columbia.

Also see Holder, *The Hoe and the Horse on the Plains,* pp. 29–42. This is a little-known but excellent analysis of the migration of the prehistoric Village Indians and their interaction with the historic nomads of the plains.

17 Two centuries before the first French: Wood and Thiessen, *Early Fur Trade on the Northern Plains,* pp. 1–3.

17 Comanche of the Southwest brought: Ibid. The first documented contact between the villagers of the Upper Missouri and Europeans came in 1738, but evidence suggests that there may have been earlier encounters (Holder, *The Hoe and the Horse on the Plains,* p. 9). La Salle's men mapped the Mississippi River from its mouth, at the Gulf of Mexico, to Minnesota in the mid-1600s. That map was so accurate that today it is almost indistinguishable from a map drawn from satellite photos. Maps drawn in Paris in 1719 from data gathered by surveyors show the location of the Mandan Villages twenty years before the arrival of La Vérendrye.

18 When the French explorer Sieur de La Vérendrye: Ibid., and Smith, *The Explorations of the La Vérendryes in the Northern Plains,* pp. 26, 33, 51.

18 and Spain: Adorno, *Álvar Núñez Cabeza de Vaca,* and DeVoto, *The Course of Empire,* pp. 11–18. He writes: "The story of Cabeza de Vaca is incredible and would have to be considered myth except that it is true." The fantastic stories that grew from de Vaca's seven-year adventure prompted Coronado to mount his fabled search for the Seven Cities of Cibola.

18 Winter would come early: What anthropologists call the Little Ice Age spanned a period of four centuries, beginning in the mid-1400s and lasting into the mid-1800s. At the time of the Lewis and Clark expedition, average winter temperatures on the Upper Missouri were fifteen degrees colder than in the late twentieth century. In 1804, subzero temperatures lingered for months and dropped as low as minus fifty. Clark marveled at the physical resilience of his native hosts, who would often sleep out on the plains with nothing more than a buffalo robe to keep them warm. Clark also notes that the women in the village bathed in the river every morning, even when they had to break the ice. See Lewis and Clark, *The Journals of Lewis and Clark,* Nicholas Biddle, ed., pp. 172–205.

18 A single village was commonly home to a thousand: Thompson, *David Thompson's Narrative,* Richard Glover, ed., pp. 171–177. In their survey of early expeditions, Wood and Thiessen (*Early Fur Trade on the Northern Plains*) relied on both La Vérendrye's estimates and those of David Thompson, who visited the villages at the Knife River in December 1797. He was intent on ascertaining their latitude for the purpose of mapping the region. Wood and Thiessen found that Thompson's population estimates were the most reliable of all the early explorers.

19 To the good fortune of: Rhonda, *Lewis and Clark Among the Indians,* pp. 67–112, is the most authoritative source, though there is general agreement among modern historians that Lewis and Clark owed whatever successes that came from their adventure to the generosity of the Mandan people, whose extensive caches of food got the Corps of Discovery through the severe winter of 1804. Also see Ambrose, *Undaunted Courage,* and Peters, *Women of the Earth Lodges.*

19 Corps of Discovery: Wood and Thiessen, *Early Fur Trade on the Northern Plains.* In Table I of the appendix, Wood and Thiessen include a chronological list of twenty-five French, Spanish, and English expeditions that preceded the Corps of Discovery to the Mandan Villages.

19   the sexual hospitality: Although a number of historians have written on this subject, no one has done a better job of framing the cultural perspective than Rhonda, *Lewis and Clark Among the Indians,* pp. 62–66.

20   Bird Woman was adopted: From interviews with Marilyn Hudson, tribal historian, and from the Cross family lineage. Bowers, *Hidatsa Social and Ceremonial Organization,* also contains a number of interesting reminiscences about Cherry Necklace that Bowers collected from interviews with elders in the 1920s.

20   feudal Europe was languishing: Erbstosser, *The Crusades,* pp. 43–49. Writer Charles Mann asked five anthropologists where they would have preferred to live in 1491, Europe or the Americas. They all answered . . . the Americas. Mann, "1491."

21   Disease and famine ravaged: Ibid., and Riley-Smith, *The Oxford History of the Crusades.* Also, Cox, *The Crusades,* or Treece, *The Crusades.*

21   Centuries of favorable: Dobyns, *Their Number Become Thinned.* For a full discussion of this debate, see Mann, "1491." While social scientists will probably never agree on specific population numbers in the pre-Columbian Americas, ethnographers do agree that material conditions in the Americas were significantly better than those found in Europe at the same time.

21   Sometime around the beginning: From an interview with professor W. Raymond Wood on the early migration of the Mandan up the Missouri River. Also, Will and Spinden, *The Mandans,* and Schlesier, *Plains Indians, A.D. 500–1500.*

22   a dispute between the Hidatsa leaders: Meyer, *The Village Indians of the Upper Missouri,* p. 10, and Wilson, *Notes on the Hidatsa Indians.*

22   The continent's central lowlands: Holder, *The Hoe and the Horse on the Plains,* pp. 2–10.

22   The Mandan had learned to exploit: The Mandan's gradual migration up the Missouri during the mild neo-Atlantic period allowed the horticulturists to get established in their settlements before the Little Ice Age set in.

22   This narrow geologic niche: Holder, *The Hoe and the Horse on the Plains,* pp. 2–3. Also see Webb, "The American West," pp. 25–31. Webb breaks the North American continent into three contiguous regions . . . north, south, and west. The west itself is broken into three subregions: plains, mountains, and Pacific slope. "If we do not understand the West," writes Webb, "it is because we perversely refused to recognize this fact; we do not want the desert to be there."

23   Little could they imagine: Diamond, *Guns, Germs, and Steel,* pp. 104–114, and Mann, "1491," p. 13.

23   By the twenty-first century: Mann, "1491," pp. 13–15. Mann examines the most current scientific explanations for how crops first cultivated in the pre-Columbian Americas transformed cultures around the world.

23   In hopes of bringing order: Williams, *The American Indian in Western Legal Thought,* pp. 62–64.

24   The Vatican's discovery-era conquests: Ibid., pp. 74–86. Also, for an intimate encounter with the thinking of the Spanish scholastics of the sixteenth century, see Suarez, *Selections from Three Works of Francisco Suarez.*

24   historic debates in the great ecclesiastical universities: White, *Hispanic Philosophy in the Age of Discovery.* For a critical examination of the debates that arose in Valladolid between Victoria and Las Casas, see Williams, *The American Indian in Western Legal Thought,* pp. 93–108.

     Williams makes the following observation about the links between discovery-era international law and federal Indian policy: "While Victoria's extensive contribution to European international law's conception of American Indian rights and status is not in controversy, a lively scholarly debate has long raged over the Dominican's [Las Casas] sometimes asserted status as 'the real founder of modern international law.'" Felix Cohen, the leading twentieth-century scholar on Indian rights and status in United States law, has cemented permanently in the minds of United States Indian law scholars the notion that Victoria was principally responsible for providing "a humane and rational basis for an American law of Indian affairs."

What is not debated, however, is that international law took shape in the minds of the scholastic thinkers of Spain. Williams explains Cohen's deference to Victoria as the father of international law based on the work of the "unimpeachable" legal scholarship of James Brown Scott, who served as the director of the Carnegie Endowment for International Peace foundation's Division of International Law and was the editor of its publication, *The American Journal of International Law*. He was also editor of a series of tests entitled *Classics of International Law*. Williams cites Scott's caveat on Victoria's preeminence in the founding of modern international law:

> The general editor is unwilling to allow the volume to get to press without a tribute in passing to the broad-minded and generous-hearted Dominican, justly regarded as one of the founders of International Law, and whose two tractates here reproduced are, as Thucydides would say, a perpetual possession to the international lawyer. Victoria's claims as a founder of the Law of Nations must unfortunately be based upon these two readings taken down by a pupil and published after his death, without the professor's revision and in a very summary form. They are sufficient, however, to show that International Law is not a thing of our day . . . nor indeed the creation of Grotius, but that the system is almost as old as the New World. In the lecture by Victoria on the Indians, and in his smaller tractate on War, we have before our eyes, and at hand, a summary of the modern Law of Nations (Williams, *The American Indian in Western Legal Thought*, pp. 114–115).

24 "preserved the legacy of 1,000 years": Ibid., p. 317.

24 "Doctrine of Discovery": Ibid., pp. 325–326.

26 by enacting the Flood Control Act of 1944: *Flood Control Act of 1944*, U.S. Public Law 534. This law is fully explored in Lawson, *Dammed Indians,* and, Morgan, *Dams and Other Disasters.*

27 In less than five years: Though the true figures of the dust bowl exodus can never be known, this is a conservative estimate. See Thornthwaite, "Climate and Settlement in the Great Plains," p. 179.

27 During the dry months of summer: Ibid.

29 Old Dog and his half brother, White Duck: Curtis, *The North American Indian.* Curtis's photos of Old Dog and White Duck are in the appendix, where he compiled the biographies of individual tribal members.

31 Psychologists studying the long-term effects: Duran, with Duran and Yellow Horse Brave Heart, "Native Americans and the Trauma of History." Also Friesema and Matzke, "Socio-Economic and Cultural Effects."

Chapter II: Savages and Infidels

Interviews: *Scott Bosse, Marilyn Cross, Raymond Cross, Philip Key, Jesus O'Suna, Charlie Rae, Bud Ullman, Wendy Wilson.*

36 While the Columbia Basin accounts: For a current discussion of the Columbia River Basin dams, see Grossman, *Watershed.* Also, for a remarkable "white paper" prepared by the *Idaho Statesman* newspaper in Boise, Idaho, see "Dollars, Sense, and Salmon," *Idaho Statesman.*

37   After completing a three-year round-trip to Japan: Each of the native salmon stocks makes its own journey. Some spend a full year in the river before heading for the ocean, where they will spend as many as six years growing to full size before returning to their stream of origin.

37   Millions of dollars and decades later, marine biologists: By 2003, two decades on salmon restoration had cost more than $3.5 billion. Annually, the BPA spends $12 million on rearing Redfish Lake sockeye, only to see fewer than a dozen return to the Sawtooth Mountains. Wendy Wilson, founder of Idaho Rivers, calculates that every sockeye returning to Redfish Lake costs American taxpayers and electricity rate payers more than $1 million. Also see Barcott, "Blow Up."

37   But as soon as the Army Corps of Engineers: Ice Harbor, 1962; Lower Monumental, 1969; Little Goose, 1970; Lower Granite, 1975. Salmonid populations in the Snake River drainage "crashed" dramatically when Lower Granite was completed. The trip that once took salmon four days from lake to ocean now took five to six weeks. Each dam accounted for 8 percent mortality of the descending smolts. A 2 percent return is needed to maintain existing populations, a figure that has not been reached since the Snake River dams were built.

37   The Snake was also the main corridor: Marine biologist Scott Bosse testified before the Senate Committee on Environment and Public Works on September 14, 2000: "While most tributary habitat in the Columbia has been severely degraded by logging, mining, grazing, urbanization, and agricultural development, the Snake River stocks still have available to them nearly four thousand miles of prime spawning and rearing habitat . . . capable of producing millions of wild smolts." Bosse told the panel that with five dams in the way, the fish have no access to their prime spawning ground.

37   The moment these stocks: Most of the treaties affected by this declaration were negotiated in 1855 by future Washington governor Isaac Stevens, who spent two years in the region negotiating treaties with dozens of tribes. Most recently, these treaties came into play in the famous Boldt Decision in 1974. Boldt awarded West Coast tribes 50 percent of the catch of all native salmon stocks, from northern California rivers to Puget Sound. The ruling has weathered many challenges.

38   This *supremacy clause,* relating specifically to treaties: The *supremacy clause* was brought to the floor of the Constitutional Convention on June 1, 1787, by James Madison and Benjamin Franklin. This principle, which would eventually be built into Article VI of the U.S. Constitution, was a subtle way of finessing the states' rights position being advanced by Patrick Henry of Virginia, who wanted nothing to do with a central government. The *supremacy clause* accorded to the central government the exclusive right to make treaties, a power that indirectly suborned the states' rights argument calling for "equal footing" with the federal government. Ketcham, *James Madison,* pp. 196–206.

39   By September 2002, seventy thousand young Indians: Boyer, *Tribal Colleges.*

40   Barring a dramatic and unforeseeable turnabout: From biologist Scott Bosse's testimony in the U.S. Senate Committee on Environment and Public Works: Subcommittee on Fisheries, Wildlife, and Water. On September 14, 2000, Bosse told senators that the National Marine and Fisheries Service extinction models showed several of the endangered stocks going extinct by 2017.

40   Author David James Duncan: Duncan, "Salmon's Second Coming," p. 39.

42   this case, now a textbook study in water law: *United States v. Adair,* 478 Fed. Supp. 336, and *United States v. Adair II,* 723 Fed. 2nd 1394.

42   Their challenge proved: *United States v. Adair* [also known as *Adair II*], Fed. Supp. 2nd 1273.

42   formally terminated by the U.S. Congress: An excellent overview of the Termination Era

is included in Josephy, *Now That the Buffalo's Gone,* and Tyler, *A History of Indian Policy,* pp. 172–181.

45 In 1800, the young republic had grown to sixteen states: Carruth, *The Encyclopedia of American Facts and Dates.*

45 In Adams's view, the Marshall nomination: Henry, *The Lives and Times of the Chief Justices of the Supreme Court,* pp. 404–407. The praise for Marshall in his own time, and since, is perhaps without equal among the nation's founders.

45 The great lawyer and orator: Ibid., p. 410. Marshall's biographer and future Supreme Court associate justice Joseph Storey wrote:

> If we except Washington, it may be safely asserted that no American citizen, either in public or private life, has been so universally beloved and esteemed. He occupied the post of chief justice during the long period of thirty-four years, and thirty-two volumes of reports, in which his decisions are collected and preserved, attest the extent, variety, and importance of his labors. In all coming time, the student of international and constitutional jurisprudence will there discover that intellectual power, that depth of investigation, and wisdom of decision . . . a mind which no sophistry or subtlety could mislead; a firmness that nothing could shake, untiring patience, and spotless integrity (Ibid., p. 411).

46 To the end of his life: Thayer, *John Marshall,* pp. 151–155.

48 this was the same "natural law" justification: Williams, *The American Indian in Western Legal Thought,* pp. 315–317. Williams explains that "The Doctrine of Discovery assumed that the European discoverer would eventually establish its feudal prerogative rights of conquest over the infidel-held lands, either by wars of expulsion or by treaties of cession contracting the limits of the tribes" (p. 315). This meant that within the body of federal Indian policy, "the primordial mythic icon of Europe's medieval, feudal past, had been preserved and brought to readability in a modern form that spoke with reassuring continuity to a nation that was about to embark on its own colonizing crusade against the American Indians. . . ." (p. 317). By incorporating the Doctrine of Discovery into foundational law, Williams concludes that the chief justice inadvertently "ensured that future acts of genocide would proceed on a rationalized, legal basis" (p. 317.)

48 on the native people of North America: Each academic inquiry into this subject contributes important information to the story of the decline of the native populations in the Americas. Dobyns, in *Their Number Become Thinned,* speculated that the native population in the western hemisphere reached 100 million by the time Columbus landed in the Bahamas. Scientists at the Smithsonian Institution have documented ninety-three widespread epidemics among native peoples in the post-Columbian Americas. Smallpox is believed to have come ashore in the Americas in 1519, carried by a sailor in the Cortés expedition. See Verano and Ubelaker, *Disease and Demography in the Americas.*

48 Law of Nations: Modern legal scholars credit the seventeenth-century Swiss jurist Emmerich de Vattel as the first to codify international law. By then, the earlier work of the Spanish scholastics, notably Victoria and Suarez, and Elizabethan-era lawyers had formalized discovery-era laws governing nations.

48 In 1776, John Adams commented: Williams, *The American Indian in Western Legal Thought,* p. 290.

49 In his examination of Revolutionary War–era: Ibid., p. 288.

51 The American people, wrote William Gilpin: Reisner, *Cadillac Desert,* pp. 39–41.

51 "So long as a tribe exists and remains": Prucha, *American Indian Treaties,* pp. 165–166. Attorney General Wirt's uncompromising counsel to Congress on the constitutionally derived power of Indian treaties is a landmark in the history of American federalism.

52   Fitzpatrick's wagon tracks: There are numerous accounts of Fitzpatrick's contributions to the "opening" of the West to white settlement. Hafen, *Broken Hand.* Also see Limerick, *The Legacy of Conquest.*

52   When gold was discovered: Authoritative accounts of James Marshall's discovery of gold at the sawmill that he and his compatriots had built for Mr. Sutter on the American River fill entire shelves in libraries. Limerick, *The Legacy of Conquest,* p. 105.

52   a region of prairie and plains: Webb, "The American West," pp. 25–31.

53   The second era of treaty making: Prucha, *American Indian Treaties,* p. 236.

54   "If you can find one man in Washington": Miller, *From the Heart,* p. 243.

55   As long as Congress secured: Brown, Letters to the *Missouri Republican.* Not long after Mitchell's wagon train departed St. Joseph, Missouri, his secretary and future governor of the state B. Gratz Brown made an entry in his journal that bordered on clairvoyance:

> Even now, along her whole southern boundary, [the Missouri River] is a pent-up crowd, impatiently awaiting the action of the United States government to let them pass the barrier of the state line into the territory of Nebraska, now occupied by a large number of Indians. How long the restraint of law and the guardianship of the general government may be able to keep the whites from the occupancy of these lands, remains to be seen. It cannot be long . . . and with it will arise questions of deep import, both of policy and humanity, as to the rights and disposition of the Indians now occupying these lands (Ibid., p. 3).

55   With visions of white women's scalps dangling: Wischmann, *Frontier Diplomats,* p. 191.

55   Fortunately for David Mitchell: Margaret, *Father DeSmet,* pp. 225–228. In his dispatch of September 26, 1951, Brown writes of Fitzpatrick:

> He is a real mountain man, and adapts himself completely to the habits and mode of life of the Indians. I have seen no man in the country who seems to have so entirely and implicitly the confidence of the various tribes. What he says passes for law with them, and even where they may not agree with him, they respect him and pay great deference to his opinion.

56   DeSmet had recently returned to the city: Ibid., pp. 20–24.

Chapter III: Miracle at Horse Creek

Interviews: *Mike Cross, Susan Dingle, Marilyn Hudson, Luther Grinnell.*

57   two weeks into the voyage: Wischmann, *Frontier Diplomats,* pp. 188–190, and Margaret, *Father DeSmet,* pp. 232–236. Helene Margaret's account is written like a travelogue, compiled from DeSmet's journals and a variety of other contemporary sources.

58   word of the cholera: Brown, Letters to the *Missouri Republican.* A dispatch printed by the *Missouri Republican* newspaper on October 14 begins: "We regret to learn that the cholera is again raging among some tribes of the Rocky Mountain Indians . . . to wit: Fort Berthold and Fort Clark, the former situated about two hundred and twenty-five miles, and the latter about three hundred miles, below the mouth of the Yellowstone" (Ibid., p. 29).

58   By 1851, the Mandan: Meyer, *The Village Indians of the Upper Missouri,* pp. 101–104.

58   leaders such as Cherry Necklace: By the midpoint of the nineteenth century, the Village Indians had learned bitter lessons resulting from their associations with whites. Their societies had suffered great losses, while the more bellicose Sioux and Cheyenne seemed to flourish around them. Ibid., pp. 105–106.

58   Though the origin: Chardon, *Chardon's Journal at Fort Clark,* pp. xiv–xlvi.

58   On July 14, the white trader: Ibid., p. 121.

59 "killed her two children, one a fine boy of eight": Ibid., p. 133.

59 "My youngest son died today": Ibid., p. 137.

59 the epidemic of 1837: Meyer, *The Village Indians of the Upper Missouri*, pp. 94–97. Fearing that a new outbreak of the pox would devastate the western tribes, William Clark sent a doctor up the Missouri to inoculate as many Indians as he could find. Clark's humanitarian act was quickly undone by Congress' refusal to appropriate the funds necessary to accomplish the task. The doctor ran out of inoculations before he reached the tribes of the Middle and Upper Missouri.

59 claimed half a million Indian lives: Ibid., pp. 97–98. Though Chardon's account of the 1837 epidemic at the Mandan Villages is the only eyewitness record known to exist, enough traders and trappers were working in remote western settlements at the time to piece together a larger picture of how this epidemic struck the western tribes. Fragments have filtered down through the diaries of traders, such as that of Alexander Culbertson and James Audubon, and that of artist George Catlin.

59 A previous outbreak, in 1781: Schlesier, *Plains Indians*. Most information about the first epidemic of smallpox is anecdotal and derived from the stories that accumulated around the adventures of early explorers such as David Thompson, McKay, and others. Professor W. Raymond Wood believes the scourge broke out among southwestern tribes in 1780 and traveled north to the Mandan Villages with a party of Comanche in 1781. The following summer, in 1782, it swept through Canada.

None of the deadly European diseases, such as bubonic plague, smallpox, measles, influenza, diphtheria, scarlet fever, typhus, malaria, and cholera, had existed on the North American continent prior to the age of discovery. Disease swirled around the Spaniards wherever they went. By the time La Salle laid claim to the territory of Louisiana in the 1650s, much of the continent had been swept clear of inhabitants by diseases that ran before them.

60 "We get no help at all": Meyer, *The Village Indians of the Upper Missouri*, pp. 105–106.

60 Culbertson translated: Wischmann, *Frontier Diplomats*, pp. 192–194.

60 After a journey of eight hundred miles: Ibid., pp. 194–195.

61 Mitchell's promise: Ibid., pp. 191–192.

61 Fifty thousand Indian ponies ranged loose: Hill, "The Great Indian Treaty Council of 1851," pp. 90–95. Hill provides a richly detailed description of the scene at Fort Laramie when Mitchell arrived. The actual number of horses present was an estimate, though likely an accurate one. When traveling, tribes of the West always made a great show of their horses, which were their most prized form of personal wealth. A nomadic band of a thousand Sioux or Cheyenne would often have six to seven thousand horses. A herd of fifty thousand would have quickly reduced to dust the grassland surrounding the fort.

63 news awaited them that the Apache: Wischmann, *Frontier Diplomats*, p. 196.

63 both had identified: Brown, Letters to the *Missouri Republican*, and Wischmann, *Frontier Diplomats*, pp. 195–196. Brown makes numerous references to the Crow in his dispatches while en route to Fort Laramie. When Mitchell first hears of the cholera outbreak, he begins preparing himself for the fact that the Crow and other tribes in the North and West will not make the trip.

63 surrounded on every side by fierce enemies: For an excellent oral history of the Crow, as told to Frank Linderman by the Crow's last hereditary chief, Plenty Coups, see Linderman, *American*.

63 The council's secretary: Hill, "The Great Indian Treaty Council of 1851," p. 90.

63 "the cannon gave forth its thunder": Brown, Letters to the *Missouri Republican*, p. 36.

64 As he surveyed the faces: Margaret, *Father DeSmet,* p. 235.

64 "For quietness, decorum": Brown, Letters to the *Missouri Republican,* p. 36. In his dispatch to the *Missouri Republican* newspaper printed on October 24, 1851, Brown describes a remarkable scene that took place shortly after the council convened. A Shoshone woman entered the circle, leading a horse with a boy on its back. She approached a Cheyenne chief who had killed her husband in battle years earlier, and now presented the boy to the Cheyenne chief as his new son. By Indian custom, it now fell to him to raise the boy as though he were his own. After this delay, the treaty proceedings resumed.

64 "The Great Spirit sees it all and knows it all": Ibid., pp. 39–43.

65 "I am glad we have all smoked together like brothers": Ibid.

65 "I have heard you were coming": Ibid.

66 "The ears of my people have not been on the ground": Ibid.

66 Shortly before noon on September 11: Ibid., p. 55.

67 "The Crow were all mounted and their horses": Ibid., pp. 49–50. When the artist George Catlin traveled in this country in the 1830s, he, like B. Gratz Brown, noted that the Crow were the most "resplendent horsemen on the plains," a reputation they maintain to this day.

67 "The White Father does not understand": Ibid., p. 50.

67 "We have moved around": Ibid., p. 51.

68 "I thank the Great Spirit": Ibid., p. 56. The Crow's spokesman, Big Robber, told the commissioners that he was a stand-in for the tribe's next chief, who was then only a boy. He was referring to Plenty Coups, who was only eight at the time of the Treaty of Horse Creek. The boy would grow up to be the last hereditary chief of the Crow people and would live well into the twentieth century.

68 "Father," he began, "we live a great way off": Ibid.

69 "Tomorrow begins the most important task": Ibid.

69 "There is no man living so extensively and correctly": Ibid., p. 57.

70 After devising a new strategy over lunch: Wischmann, *Frontier Diplomats,* pp. 204–206.

71 The text of the final agreement: Prucha, *American Indian Treaties,* pp. 238–239.

72 Since they were now living as one tribal people: Brown, Letters to the *Missouri Republican,* p. 65.

72 After the official treaty signing concluded: Eighteen handwritten copies of the treaty were made. One returned to Like-a-Fishhook with Four Bears. Four Bears was killed by a Sioux raiding party in 1861, when he was swimming in the river, undefended and unarmed.

72 "Glad or satisfied, but always so quiet": Wischmann, *Frontier Diplomats,* p. 208.

73 Less than two years later, it would: Prucha, *American Indian Treaties,* pp. 239–240.

73 Tribal leaders expressed bitter resignation: Meyer, *The Village Indians of the Upper Missouri,* pp. 108–110. Wischmann makes a very interesting observation regarding Culbertson's postconference change of heart, noting that he came around to sharing DeSmet's preconference reservations: "What will become of the aborigines, who have possessed this land from time immemorial? This is indeed a thorny question awakening gloomy ideas in the observer's mind, if he has followed the encroaching policy of the States in regard to the Indians." Killoren, *Come Blackrobe,* pp. 179–193.

74 While Fitzpatrick was circulating the revised treaty: Prucha, *American Indian Treaties,* pp. 239–240. Also, a rare account of the treaty council can be found in Hafen, *Broken Hand,* pp. 281–301.

74 When the ice broke on the Upper Missouri: Meyer, *The Village Indians of the Upper Missouri,* pp. 103–108.

74   Ten years after Horse Creek: Ibid., p. 107.

74   their isolation forced them to live like prisoners: Ibid., pp. 107–109.

75   Washington's lax attention to their: Ibid., pp. 107–108, and Prucha, *American Indian Treaties*, pp. 237–238.

75   the baby girl was called Many Dances: From interviews with Marilyn Hudson and Phyllis and Crusoe Cross.

76   At the age of twenty-one, the grandson of Cherry Necklace: Curtis, *The North American Indian.*

76   "What shall be done about the Indian as an obstacle": Drinnon, *Keeper of Concentration Camps.*

77   Frederick Jackson Turner: For a critical discussion of Turner's hypothesis, see Limerick, *The Legacy of Conquest.*

77   In 1885, the new agent at Fort Berthold: Curtis, "The Last Lodges of the Mandans."

77   lived alone in his earth lodge in the company: Ibid.

CHAPTER IV: GREAT WHITE FATHERS

Interviews: *Bucky Cross, Crusoe Cross, Phyllis Old Dog Cross, Luther Grinnell, Louise Holding Eagle, Marilyn Hudson, Roger Johnson, Emerson Murry, Ken Rogers, Alyce Spotted Bear, W. Raymond Wood.*

79   What followed, rather hastily: Lewis and Clark, *Original Journals of the Lewis and Clark Expedition*, pp. 200–203, and Lewis and Clark, *The Journals of the Expedition Under the Command of Capts. Lewis and Clark*, pp. 70–71. Also Lewis and Clark, *The Journals of Lewis and Clark*, Gary Moulton, ed.

80   "Everybody else wanted to secure a trading monopoly": Wood and Thiessen, *Early Fur Trade on the Northern Plains.* Also see Botkin, *Our Natural History*, and Rhonda, *Lewis and Clark Among the Indians*, pp. 67–80.

81   It seldom slept in the same bed and was forever jumping its banks: Hart, *The Dark Missouri*, p. 120.

82   when the first of three large floods inundated Omaha: Ibid., pp. 122–128.

82   But in the spring of 1943, the nation's attention was focused: "British Pursue Rommel North from Sfax: Allies Push Through Mountains on Flank," *New York Times.*

82   While researching her now classic study: Hunt with Huser, *Down by the River.*

83   The river's unpredictable upstream behavior: Reisner, *Cadillac Desert*, pp. 182–183. Also, for a comprehensive hydrological report on the river before the building of the Pick-Sloan dams, see *Missouri River: A Letter from the Secretary of War.*

83   When Congress created the Army Corps of Engineers: Morgan, *Dams and Other Disasters.*

84   Unable to compete with the railroads: For the story on the demise of the Missouri River steamboat, see Lass, *A History of Steamboating on the Upper Missouri River.*

84   At the same time the Army Corps of Engineers: Reisner, *Cadillac Desert*, pp. 183–184.

84   The river, it seemed, was a living thing: Ibid., pp. 181–182.

84   Against its better judgment, the agency yielded: Ibid., p. 183. For a comprehensive report on the Corps' history on the Missouri, see Hart, *The Dark Missouri*, pp. 120–128.

85   By 1930, farmers: These figures came from a report compiled on the entire Missouri River Basin region by the Department of the Interior; see *Missouri River: A Letter from the Secretary of War.* This is a comprehensive profile of the river and the terrain it drains, from the headwaters in the Rocky Mountains to its confluence with the Mississippi above St. Louis, Missouri. For extensive data on the dust bowl exodus, see Hill, "Rural Migration and Farm Abandonment."

85 After mapping the West's great river systems: For the comprehensive story on John Wesley Powell, see Stegner, *Beyond the Hundredth Meridian.*

86 In the *Atlantic Monthly:* Smalley, "The Isolation of Life on Prairie Farms." Also see Thornthwaite, "Climate and Settlement in the Great Plains."

87 For its part, the Army Corps of Engineers: *Missouri River: A Letter from the Secretary of War.*

88 This site, in view of field engineers, was "entirely impracticable": Ibid.

91 Many of the Mandan, Hidatsa, and Arikara: Meyer, "Fort Berthold and the Garrison Dam," pp. 241–245.

91 In addition to bountiful crops and material well-being: Ibid., pp. 223–228.

92 Instead, the Merriam Report found: Tyler, *A History of Indian Policy,* pp. 162–163, and Meyer, *The Village Indians of the Upper Missouri,* pp. 150–155.

93 Materially and economically: *Fort Berthold Agency Report of 1943.* It is quite extraordinary that the BIA happened to choose the year 1943 to compile data for this profile of the Three Affiliated Tribes. Particularly striking is the medical portion, which found that most of the Indians still lived on a traditional diet, few had any serious medical problems, and the budget for medical care for all two thousand members of the tribe was $29,000. For that amount, they got a well-equipped hospital, a doctor and two nurses, a cook, a laundress, and a part-time ambulance driver. There were 45 births and 6 deaths, 25 minor surgical cases, 59 typhoid inoculations, and 427 smallpox vaccinations given over the course of the year. The most common complaint was generally related to eyesight and eye infections, a vulnerability that was noted by Lewis and Clark a century and a half earlier.

 Dr. Herbert Wilson moved to Elbowoods in 1951 and took over the medical practice at the hospital. Wilson retired to Bismarck some fifty years later. He remembers that the 1943 BIA report reflected the overall state of health of members of the three tribes in 1951. "They were remarkably healthy, robust people, and of course, they were still self-sufficient for the most part. They grew their own food, gathered wild fruits and berries, and ate wild game. Diabetes was unknown, kidney problems were unknown, and heart disease was very rare, as was cancer." After the valley was flooded by Garrison Dam, and the tribal members were forced to eat government commodities and processed foods, the medical profile of the tribes changed dramatically in two generations. When Wilson left his practice in New Town in 1998, diabetes among the three tribes was twelve times the national average. The chance that a tribal member would die of heart disease, diabetes, kidney failure, or cancer had climbed from less than 3 percent in 1951 to higher than 80 percent in 1995. In 2002, life expectancy for an Indian male on the Fort Berthold Reservation was forty-eight, and dropping.

95 Beneath a headline: Meyer, "Fort Berthold and the Garrison Dam," p. 240.

96 Madison and his chief ally in Philadelphia: Ketcham, *James Madison,* pp. 196–207, 228–229. Ketcham re-creates the alliance between Madison, Franklin, and James Wilson and the conditions under which the *supremacy clause* became a crucial element of the Constitution. (See n. for p. 61.)

  The clause empowering Congress to "negate" state laws, long thought by Madison to be the only effective way to prevent state encroachment on national authority, had been dropped in favor of the less explicit supreme-law clause. Persuaded by [James] Wilson's brilliant arguments, Madison came gradually to see the virtue of this change (Ibid., p. 228).

96 For more than a generation: Williams, *The American Indian in Western Legal Thought,* pp. 256–309.

96 With the full support of President Washington: Ibid., pp. 229–230, 251–263.

98 When the floods of 1943: All three of the following books present different aspects of the 1943 flood story: Reisner, *Cadillac Desert*, p. 183; Morgan, *Dams and Other Disasters;* and Lawson, *Dammed Indians.*

99 "I want to control the Missouri!": Reisner, *Cadillac Desert*, pp. 183–188. Reisner states that Pick actually spied on all his top officers during this period. Those who were not devoting themselves to this project "around the clock" were dismissed from duty.

99 General Wheeler rushed his subordinate's master plan: Ibid., pp. 182–186.

100 The President had serious problems with the plan: Ibid., and Roosevelt, Letter to Congress on desirability of Missouri Valley Authority. Also Reisner, *Cadillac Desert*, p. 146.

100 Harold Ickes, was fearless in his official rebuke: U.S. Senate Committee on Indian Affairs, *Missouri River Basin.*

In years to come, Ickes accused the Corps of being a "willful . . . self-serving clique in contempt of the public welfare." To a degree that was unimaginable, said Ickes, the Corps' wanton waste of money surpassed any agency in the history of the country. "No more lawless or irresponsible group than the Army Corps of Engineers has ever attempted to operate in the United States either outside of, or within, the law. . . . It is truly beyond imagination." Reisner, *Cadillac Desert*, p. 181.

100 "windshield reconnaissance": Ibid., p. 185.

101 Sloan, in turn, told Congress: U.S. Senate Committee on Indian Affairs, *Missouri River Basin.* This report was the most openly critical of the Corps' plan for the large dams on the Missouri. Ickes echoed Glenn Sloan's argument that the largest of the Corps' proposed dams were unnecessary for effective flood control. The "loveless, shotgun marriage" between the two made the point moot.

102 everybody engaged in the Pick-Sloan debate: Reisner, *Cadillac Desert*, pp. 182–188. See also "Golden River: What's to Be Done About the Missouri?"

102 The editor of the *Sanish Sentinel:* Meyer, "Fort Berthold and the Garrison Dam," p. 249.

103 "A dam below the Fort Berthold Reservation": Ibid., p. 250–251. This initial protest was widely supported in white communities and by many white civic organizations and churches.

103 the O'Mahoney-Millikin Amendment: Ridgeway, *The Missouri Basin's Pick-Sloan Plan.* Also see Meyer, *The Village Indians of the Upper Missouri.*

104 Farmers Union president James Patton: Ibid., p. 240.

105 In a follow-up letter, Governor Aandahl: Aandahl, Letter to Martin Cross.

105 "We Indians on the Fort Berthold Reservation": Meyer, "Fort Berthold and the Garrison Dam," p. 232.

Chapter V: Hell and High Water

Interviews: *Everett Albers, Dorothy Atkinson, Fred Baker, Jim Bear, Bucky Cross, Crusoe Cross, Mike Cross, Phyllis Old Dog Cross, Luther Grinnell, Marilyn Hudson, Roger Johnson.*

110 all but 6: During World War II, Indians had the highest percentage of enlistees of any ethnic group. For the vast majority of these, the war was the first time most of them had spent more than a few days off the reservation. Meyer, *The Village Indians of the Upper Missouri.*

110 In Old Dog's view: In Old Dog's lifetime, a series of executive orders and Homestead Acts had reduced the three tribes' landholdings from 12 million acres to just over half a million acres. The last came in the great Homestead Act of 1910, as a final installment of the Allotment Era resulting from the Dawes Act of 1887.

110 Religious Crimes Code: It was under the pretext of this law that Indian agents on the Great Plains called for federal troop reinforcements when the Paiute holy man Wovoka

brought the Ghost Dance to the reservation Indians in the late 1880s. For all practical purposes, the massacre at Wounded Knee was the end of the American Indian Wars that had paralleled the westward migration of Europeans in the second half of the century. *General Allotment Act* [also known as the *Dawes Act*], *U.S. Statutes at Large*.

110 as an adjunct to the Dawes Act during President Harrison's: The Allotment Era became an indirect way for the federal government to emancipate itself from its responsibilities as the trustee of Indian lands by privatizing the tribal commons.

111 The first missionary to live among the Mandan, Hidatsa, and Arikara: Hall, *The Fort Berthold Mission.*

111 "The people of these tribes turned the tables on me": Ibid.

111 By 1945, Hall's half century of activism was bearing latent fruit: *Fort Berthold Agency Report of 1943.*

112 Yet the tribe had very little money: Ibid.

114 The historic meeting between Martin Cross and members: U.S. Senate Committee on Indian Affairs. *Protesting the Construction of Garrison Dam.*

114 "Garrison Dam, the construction of which is embodied": "The Indians and the Pick-Sloan Plan," Missouri River Basin Investigations 67.

114 Congress' joint resolution: Portions of SJ Res. 79 that apply to this hearing are reprinted in the official transcript from Senator O'Mahoney's committee.

114 "To investigate the administration of Indian affairs": Ibid.

115 Chairman Cross immediately sent a telegram to Commissioner Brophy: Meyer, "Fort Berthold and the Garrison Dam," p. 243.

115 Department of the Interior warned Brophy: Ibid.

116 "Mr. Chairman, senators": U.S. Senate Committee on Indian Affairs, *Protesting the Construction of Garrison Dam.* The transcript of this hearing clearly reflects the confusion on the part of the committee members regarding application of treaty rights and federal Indian law to a "checkerboarded" reservation.

116 "Mr. Cross," said Senator O'Mahoney: Ibid.

118 "Of course, nothing can be done to dispossess": Ibid.

118 "contain some records relative to the treaties of 1851": Ibid.

119 "These Indians were at their present location one hundred forty years ago": Ibid. Felix Cohen's memorandum to the committee on the legal questions regarding bifurcated Indian lands is attached as an appendix to the official transcript of the hearing.

120 The Dawes Act effectively divided: *General Allotment Act* [also known as the *Dawes Act*], *U.S. Statutes at Large.*

120 Congress, explained Cohen: Ibid.

120 "Did Congress recognize specific boundaries": U.S. Senate Committee on Indian Affairs, *Protesting the Construction of Garrison Dam.*

121 "has always been sacred and can never be disturbed": Ibid. In his memorandum to the Select Committee on Indian Affairs, Cohen reintroduces Attorney General William Wirt's famous declaration on the sanctity of treaties entered into between the federal government and the tribes.

122 attach a rider to a deficiency appropriations bill: Meyer, "Fort Berthold and the Garrison Dam," p. 246.

123 Pick rallied his allies: Meyer, Ibid., p. 245.

123 War Department Civil Appropriations Act for 1947: *Lieu Lands Act for Fort Berthold* [also *Civil Functions of the War Department*], U.S. Public Law 374.

123 Oscar Chapman, sent a letter to Case: Fogarty, "New Indian 'War' May Slow Development of MVA." Fogarty reported that

Congress authorized construction of the Garrison Dam . . . for harnessing river basin sources in ten states. . . . The Project will make possible irrigation of a large semi-arid region. But the dam designed to improve the lot of millions will dispossess the Three Affiliated Tribes now living in the area. The Fort Berthold Reservation has been their home since they signed a treaty of friendship in 1851. Their spokesmen insist it is a "perpetual treaty."

124 Locally, the *Sanish Sentinel* explained: Meyer, "Fort Berthold and the Garrison Dam," p. 247.

124 "Several conferences have been held with you": Pick, Transcript of meeting at Elbowoods High School on Garrison Dam.

125 "I hear that you have come here to ask us": Ibid.

127 the *Hazen Star* newspaper: Meyer, "Fort Berthold and the Garrison Dam," p. 248. The editor, F. J. Froeschle, quoted a local supporter of the dam as saying that the government was not about to walk away from that much money after it had already been spent.

127 The fact that no money had been allocated: Ibid., pp. 254–255.

128 a "willful and expensive Corps" that made up its own rules: Morgan, *Dams and Other Disasters.*

128 "The quickest and most merciful way": Ibid.

129 "acquisition of the lands and rights therein": Ibid.

130 Phyllis Old Dog Cross turned: Biographical material in this section was compiled from interviews with the Cross children, their friends, and their acquaintants.

132 "I will not accept any money from the sale of the tribal land": Meyer, "Fort Berthold and the Garrison Dam," p. 277.

132 "As everyone knows": Ibid., p. 259.

134 "We are again violating a treaty solemnly entered into": U.S. House, Congressman William Lemke speaking on the injustice of the Fort Berthold takings act.

134 guarantee of irrigation: Ibid.

135 For years, Watkins and Mormon politicians had tried: Drinnon, *Keeper of Concentration Camps.* Drinnon's work is a devastating indictment of the Truman administration's laissez-faire approach to federal Indian policy. Also, for more on the history of the Ute and white men in Utah, see Wilkinson, *Fire on the Plateau.*

137 "The only thing we've ever been able to figure": Details of this and other sporting events were reconstructed from newspaper accounts and interviews with Arnie Charging and Bucky Cross.

138 was named White Duck: Old Dog, Letter to Phyllis Old Dog Cross.

Chapter VI: Leaving Elbowoods

Interviews: *Fred Baker, Arnie Charging, Bucky Cross, Crusoe Cross, Michael Cross, Phyllis Old Dog Cross, Raymond Cross, Calvin Grinnell, Luther Grinnell, Louise Holding Eagle, Emerson Murry, Byron Sneva, Chief Justice Gerald VandeWalle, Marie Wells.*

141 Pick's widely published accusations: Meyer, *Fort Berthold and the Garrison Dam.* And for details on the floods, see U.S. Weather Bureau, *Kansas-Missouri Floods of June–July 1951.* Also "Truman Says G.O.P. in Kansas Blocked Key Flood Control," *New York Times.*

141 "stampede tactics": Lawson, *Dammed Indians*, p. 114.

141 "senseless competition": Miller, "The Battle That Squanders Billions."

141 Both were guilty: Ibid. Former president Herbert Hoover, himself an engineer, had been asked by the Truman administration to make a study of the government's public works. Hoover asked former Wyoming governor Leslie Miller, a man well versed in western resource issues, to head up the Natural Resources Committee.

Miller and his seven colleagues were "dismayed to learn how bad the situation really is, how billions of dollars are being squandered on duplicating badly engineered projects. Both agencies are guilty of brazen and pernicious lobbying," charged Miller.

Members of the commission recommended that a review board be established at the executive level so future "boondoggles, frills, and duplicating activities are chopped off before they sprout."

Word of these charges leaked out before Hoover had the opportunity to present the report to President Truman. Lawmakers were deluged by tens of thousands of identically worded telegrams from farmers all over the Midwest. The Corps had not lost a minute in mobilizing its civilian troops. Though Hoover and Miller ignored the criticism, the press gleefully milked the venom of disgruntled lawmakers. Ibid.

141 The Pick-Sloan Plan . . . was "a conscienceless": Ibid.

141 "Do you want to pay a fifty-two-billion-dollar water bill?": Miller, "The Battle That Squanders Billions."

142 The bill Congress wrote: Ibid., and Maass, "Congress and Water Resources."

142 As a feat of engineering: Meyer, "Fort Berthold and the Garrison Dam," p. 275, and Seybold, "Constructors Roll Nearly One Million Yards a Week into Garrison Dam."

145 "Native Indian leadership is what the Indians need": Yellowtail, Letter to Martin Cross, April 4, 1953.

146 "try and control the whims and fancies of the starry-eyed politicians": Cross, Letter to Sioux tribes on termination.

146 Myer, who told the *New York Times*: "Two Congress Bills on Indians Scored." Myer told the press that the intention of the new bills was not to give anyone the broad powers suggested in the resolution, and that the measures had been written by an Indian and approved by the legal departments at the Department of the Interior. In an op-ed piece published on December 3, 1950, in the *New York Times,* Collier charged Myer with launching a "grave attack upon the corporate liberties of all Indians," arguing that "the predatory pressures against Indians are not sated yet, and 'liquidation' and 'assimilation' are stereotypes appealing to many minds," including that of the commissioner.

147 "Indians with their tax-free land holdings as a thorn": Yellowtail, Letter to Martin Cross, April 7, 1953.

147 "Felix's death has shattered me as no death": Drinnon, *Keeper of Concentration Camps,* p. 319, endnotes on chapter XI. Collier wrote the following in a letter of condolence to Cohen's wife, Lucy Kramer Cohen, on October 20, 1953: "The agony is on account of all the Indians — and of you and your children — but it is yet more. . . . I daren't come to the funeral tomorrow — no more. Felix is my highest experience of power and thought united with disinterested power of action."

148 "from stomping on Indians": Ibid., pp. 193–195. The former secretary found himself coaching the new secretary on how to manage the unseemly affairs being orchestrated right under his nose by his own Indian commissioner. "So far as American Indians are concerned, Commissioner Dillon Myer of the Bureau of Indian Affairs is a Hitler and Mussolini rolled into one," wrote Ickes. Ickes, Column on Dillon Myer.

148 Myer's career with the Japanese: Ibid., p. 265. Myer had a natural talent for enemies. Truman's secretary of the interior, Oscar Chapman, whose professional disregard for Myer rivaled Ickes's, was in the "unfortunate position of relying upon an Indian commissioner who is a reckless, bullheaded fool, and a Solicitor who does not scruple to cheat you when you ask for an opinion on Indian law." Drinnon, *Keeper of Concentration Camps,* p. 195.

148 "blundering and dictatorial tin-Hitler": Leviero, "Antagonisms Rife over Indian Policy."

148 Myer shrugged off his critics: "Two Congress Bills on Indians Scored," *New York Times.*

149 The *New York Times'* opening story: "Indian War Whoop Marks Hearings," *New York Times.* Also Drinnon, *Keeper of Concentration Camps,* p. 196.

149 "wily Indians and their champertous attorneys": Ibid., p. 189. Myer's campaign against the tribes' right to select their attorneys was every bit as rancorous as the McCarthy hearings on "un-American" activities. Three decades after Cohen's death, documents secured by author Drinnon through the Freedom of Information Act revealed that Myer had solicited help from the director of the FBI, J. Edgar Hoover, to gather information on Cohen. Ibid., p. 229, and Cohen, "Colonialism."

150 Reporters such as Ruth Mulvey Harmer: Harmer, "Uprooting the Indians," pp. 54–55.

150 "form an inseparable unit": Macgregor, "Social and Economic Impacts of Garrison Dam on the Indians of the Fort Berthold Reservation." Also see Macgregor, "Attitudes of the Fort Berthold Indians Regarding Removal from the Garrison Reservoir Site and Future Administration of Their Reservation." Macgregor helped write and edit a series of excellent reports to Congress, known as the Missouri River Basin Investigation reports, over a period of seven years. These accounts detail what life looked like in the Mandan, Hidatsa, and Arikara world, and the Upper Missouri River Valley, before it was flooded by Garrison Dam.

151 Cherokee philosopher John Ross's: Rogin, *Fathers and Children,* p. 231.

152 "Federal responsibility for administering": Lewis, Letter to Senator Arthur Watkins.

153 "dispose of tribal lands, tribal funds, tribal water rights": George, Letter to NCAI tribal chairmen.

153 "The Government of the United States first dealt with": Cross, Telegram to Associated Press.

154 "Could it be that those who propose": Commissioner Myer seriously misread the media's willingness to weigh in on this issue. Drinnon, *Keeper of Concentration Camps,* pp. 127–128.

154 "forced atomization, cultural prescription, and": "Plot on U.S. Indians Charged by Collier," *New York Times.* Also see Korey, "The Genocide Treaty." For a complete account of Cohen and Collier's charges of genocide, see Drinnon, *Keeper of Concentration Camps,* pp. 243–244.

155 Curry and Anderson had locked horns: The deaths of Felix Cohen and Harold Ickes left James Curry exposed on either flank. I am indebted to Drinnon for his extraordinary scholarship in assembling the many pieces that went into this mosaic. He notes that Curry wrote a searching and desperate letter to his old friend, John Collier, on June 29, 1952, in which he stated with great insight: "Chapman is still holding our arms while Myer, Anderson, and McCarran slit our throats." On August 30 of the same year, Curry defended his record in an article published by the *Washington Post* entitled "Speaking for the Indians." After explaining that he was being investigated to death by the Indian bureau, he finished with a foreboding note: "I expect that I, a single mouthpiece of the Indian, can and will be destroyed. But the voice of the national conscience will not thereby be permanently stilled."

155 "Frankly, sir, we'd like to have an answer": U.S. House Committee on Interior and Insular Affairs. *Hearing with BIA Director Dillon Myer on Indian Attorneys and Per Capita Payments to Enrolled Members of Three Affiliated Tribes.*

161 President Eisenhower: In a speech he delivered a year earlier at Lowery Air Force Base in Denver, CO, in August 1953 (Eisenhower, Speech made on Public Law 280), President Eisenhower declared that he had serious questions as to the legality of termination but did nothing to stop it. See Tyler, *Indian Affairs: A Work Paper.*

Chapter VII: Hitting Bottom On Top

Interviews: *Fred Baker, Bucky Cross, Crusoe Cross, Mike Cross, Phyllis Old Dog Cross, Raymond Cross, Luther Grinnell, Emerson Murry, Hans Walker, Dr. Herbert Wilson, Marie Wells.*

163   Thus far, no one in Washington: For a full discussion of this period in regard to federal Indian law and policy, see Tyler, *A History of Indian Policy,* and Washburn, *Red Man's Land/White Man's Law.*

   Martin knew the tribe was at a turning point and had to make a decision. His private correspondence suggests that he was inclined to take the entire matter to federal court. This was the last thing Congress, or the Army Corps of Engineers, wanted to see happen. What probably swung his decision, or lack of one, to pursue legal remedies was the fact that he had championed the large faction of tribal members who were anxious to receive per capita payments — checks to individuals — rather than a lump-sum payment to the tribal government. Crusoe believes Martin always regretted not taking it to court.

   The dilemma was made more cruel by the fact that Watkins told the tribe the settlement offered was a "take-it-or-leave-it" proposition. If the tribe refused it, they could take their chances in court, but that might mean they would get nothing if they lost. The tribal leaders had watched the original offer of $18 million spiral downward. By 1948, the tribe had no reason to think Watkins, Anderson, and Pick would not make good on this implied threat to leave them homeless and penniless. I have come to believe that Martin would have preferred to go to court, but the "prisoner's dilemma" he found himself in prompted him to opt for the bird in the hands of his fellow tribal members rather than the pair he saw in the bush.

163   Public Law 280: Much of the history of P.L. 280 in North Dakota derived from interviews with Emerson Murry, Hans Walker, Chief Justice Gerald VandeWalle, and the correspondence of Martin Cross.

164   Legislative Research Committee: This history comes from the committee itself, which is now called the Legislative Council. Two directors preceded Murry, who would hold the post for twenty-five years.

165   Congress was busy: Tyler, *Indian Affairs: A Work Paper.* Also Drinnon's chapter entitled "Terminator" examines the role of Congresswoman Reva Beck, Senators Arthur Watkins and Clinton Anderson, and Dillon Myer in the formation of Termination Era legislation. Drinnon, *Keeper of Concentration Camps,* pp. 233–267.

   The vice president of the NCAI, Frank George, a Nez Percé, wrote member tribes as early as September 1952 that "Commissioner Myer now has fifteen bills all ready to introduce in the next Congress asking for the abandonment of federal trusteeship responsibilities over Indian property and the withdrawal of Indian bureau services such as schools, hospitals, and social welfare from various Indian tribes." George, Letter to NCAI tribal chairmen.

   For his part, former Indian commissioner John Collier called Myer's strategy a "hoax" in which the commissioner was pursuing "as a new policy those social genocides of the earlier generations of dishonor toward Indians (Drinnon, *Keeper of Concentration Camps,* p. 236). Also see Drinnon's endnotes on p. 308 for the legislative evolution of Reva Beck Bosone's original termination bill in the second session of the 82nd Congress.

165   "all Federal supervision": U.S. Senate Committee on Indian Affairs, *Hearings on Termination of Federal Trust Responsibility over Indian Lands.*

165   existing policy was out of step: Tyler, *A History of Indian Policy,* p. 163. Tyler's overview of the Termination Era, and his analysis of legislative initiatives instigated by Dillon Myer and Senator Arthur Watkins, are as unsettling as they are sober and insightful. William

Zimmerman replaced William Brophy as acting commissioner until President Truman nominated Dillon Myer for the post. Congress asked Zimmerman to compile a set of standards that Congress could use to determine whether a tribe was ready for termination. On November 3, 1951, the *New York Times* reported that Zimmerman, regarded by many as the greatest living expert on Indian affairs, left the field on the day that Dillon Myer became commissioner in May 1950. At that point, Congress was already moving toward a "final solution" for the Indian bureau.

Myer's right hand at the bureau would be the same man who designed his relocation strategy for interned Japanese at the end of World War II. H. Rex Lee, wrote Ickes, was a man "who feels perfectly at home in a puppet show." Ickes, Column on Indian bureau.

Not to be outdone, former commissioner John Collier also chimed in after a face-to-face confrontation with Lee at a congressional hearing on termination.

> Lee was asked if he had any idea how many treaties there were between the Federal Government and the Indians. Lee said that he did not have any idea. However, he did feel that many of the existing treaties could be adjusted in some way in order to terminate the Federal obligations. . . . Lee also said several times that the object was to sit down, get to work, and get this thing wound up fast (Drinnon, *Keeper of Concentration Camps,* p. 171).

All these years later, policies applied by Myer to the Japanese and the American Indian are now recognized for what they were. Author David Abram writes:

> The massive relocation or transmigration projects underway in numerous parts of the world today in the name of progress (for example, the forced relocation of oral peoples in Indonesia and Malaysia in order to make way for the commercial clear-cutting of their forests) must be understood as instances of cultural genocide. . . . The local earth is, for them, the very matrix of discursive meaning; to force them from their native ecology is to render them speechless — or to render their speech meaningless — to dislodge them from the very ground of coherence. It is, quite simply, to force them out of their mind (Abram, *The Spell of the Sensuous,* p. 178).

166 soon to be followed by the Three Affiliated Tribes: U.S. Senate Committee on Indian Affairs, *Hearings on Termination of Federal Trust Responsibility over Indian Lands.* In his remarks to the Tribal Council in 1948, acting commissioner William Zimmerman told them:

> Your home in North Dakota along the Missouri River was established by a solemn treaty of your ancestors with the United States in 1851, almost a hundred years ago. When the government proposes to move you in the public interest, you have every right to insist that the special overall costs, which attach to moving you as a group, shall be defrayed (see Zimmerman, Acting Indian commissioner's statement and remarks).

166 "complete termination of wardship status": U.S. Senate Committee on Indian Affairs, *Hearings on Termination of Federal Trust Responsibility over Indian Lands,* and Tyler, *A History of Indian Policy,* pp. 172–173.

166 "We only oppose their interference in the management": Meyer, "Fort Berthold and the Garrison Dam." It is noteworthy that the position Cross staked out in this response to termination was the very principle Richard Nixon would reiterate in his speech to Congress in July 1970, when he told lawmakers that just because the federal treasury paid Indian tribes money it owed them, and provided assistance, it did not give the government the right to meddle in tribal affairs or dictate how the money was managed.

166 "The tribes are now enjoying the highest level of resources in their history": U.S. House, *Report on House Resolution 108 Authorizing the Committee on Interior and Insular Affairs.*

This report is remarkable for the fictions it masquerades as facts for the purpose of moving the Three Affiliated Tribes closer to termination. The Department of the Interior compiled a report on the Three Affiliated Tribes at the same time and concluded: "Less than 50 percent of the approximately 650 Fort Berthold Indian families have demonstrated the ability to support themselves by their own efforts." Just ten years earlier, the BIA's report of 1943 found that *all* the Fort Berthold families were self-sufficient. With the tribe now fully enveloped in dislocation, the 1954 report concludes:

It is the conclusion of the Bureau of Indian Affairs field staff, and this conclusion is supported by anthropologists independently of Federal personnel, that to a considerable extent a substantial percentage of Fort Berthold Indians suffer from the mental conflicts which develop in the process of transition from the earlier Indian cultural environment to the environment now being imposed on these people by a dominant non-Indian culture with its differing social and economic system of values. As a result of this situation it is probable that any program under which the great majority of Fort Berthold Indians were permitted to assume full responsibility for independent management of their own affairs, would result in rapid depletion of existing assets followed by widespread dependence upon welfare assistance. "Background Data Relating to the Three Affiliated Tribes of the Fort Berthold Reservation Located in the State of North Dakota."

166 the Three Affiliated Tribes: Ibid.

166 "We can see no particular gain": Ibid.

167 "I am packing some resolutions": U.S. Department of the Interior, *Conference with Delegation from Fort Berthold Tribal Council on March 20, 1953.*

170 "recent court decisions": Indian Claims Commission case, n. 350, "The Three Affiliated Tribes of the Fort Berthold Reservation v. The United States of America."

170 "A government attorney reported": "Indians Seek Pay for 70 Pct. of Nation's Land," *Indianapolis Star.*

170 Robert Yellowtail and Martin Cross: Yellowtail, Letter to Martin Cross, April 7, 1953. Yellowtail also wrote a public challenge to the BIA that was distributed to members of Congress and all tribal leaders in the NCAI.

The United States courts have repeatedly pointed out that on account of the greed, avarice, and rapacity of the white race toward the Indians, and their constant eagerness to take advantage of them through sharp practices, it has become necessary to protect them, to set up safeguards to prevent such wrongs. The Indian bureau sprang into being because of this fact.

Now, said Yellowtail, the bureau, through people such as Myer and Watkins, had closed ranks with the very forces they were obligated by law to hold at bay.

170 painful experiences of the previous decade: U.S. Congress, *Declaration of Indian Rights.*

171 "There is no satisfaction in our record": U.S. House, Congressman Lee Metcalf speaking on proposed revision. Congressman James Murray called for a complete revision of federal Indian policy and P.L. 280. For Goldwater's speech decrying Termination Era objectives, see U.S. Congress, Senator Barry Goldwater speaking against termination legislation. For an analysis of Senators Goldwater and Metcalf's challenges to Termination Era legislators, see Tyler, *A History of Indian Policy,* pp. 176–178.

172 "WASPs [white Anglo-Saxon Protestants] assume that the value system": Drinnon, *Keeper of Concentration Camps,* p. 266.

172 "I have been to Washington to see the Great White Father": Cross, Letter to Marilyn and Kent Hudson.

173 "Their poverty, coupled with the isolation of many": U.S. House, *Report on House Resolution 108 Authorizing the Committee on Interior and Insular Affairs.*

173 The authors concluded that the forced relocation: Ibid.

173 "Since I have time on my hands": Ibid.

176 "Indian kids were dying of hunger and exposure": Meyer, "Fort Berthold and the Garrison Dam," p. 344.

176 Bureau of Reclamation: When Congress set up this civilian water agency in 1902, projects were supposed to be financed through a reclamation fund. This fund would initially be charged with taxpayer dollars that would later be repaid through receipts collected from the farmers who derived the benefit from the projects. But by 1924, not all was well with this plan. Reisner explains that in passing the act, Congress ignored much of John Wesley Powell's advice and made things worse. By building so many projects in a rush, the bureau was repeating its mistakes before it had a chance to learn from them. The bureau was in financial trouble almost before it had a chance to open its doors for business.

Every congressman wanted a reclamation project approved for his state or district, regardless of whether it made economic sense. By 1924, less than 10 percent of the money loaned out by the bureau had been repaid. Sixty percent of the irrigators were in default. Congress simply extended the repayment period from twenty to forty years, which only created a new problem: crop surpluses. Despite the financial woes with the fund, the "psychic value of the Reclamation farms" remained high. A "preproject" acre that was worth no more than ten dollars was suddenly worth fifty times as much to speculators. At least one out of three Reclamation farmers sold out just in time, creating a fluidity in population and regional economics that the Reclamation Act was attempting to curtail. "Despite official declarations from more sensitive administrators that 'Reclamation is measured not in engineering units but in homes and agricultural values' . . . the Service [bureau] regarded itself as an 'engineering outfit.'" Robinson, "Water for the West," as quoted by Reisner, *Cadillac Desert,* pp. 118–119. An astonished Reisner reported that "No one seemed bothered by a government creating expensive farmland out of deserts in the West" at the same time as it was "drowning millions of acres of perfect farmland in the east. . . . The entire business was like a giant pyramid scheme," and American taxpayers were picking up the tab. Ibid., p. 141.

177 could not have secured congressional approval: U.S. Congress, Representative Usher Burdick charges the Army Corps of Engineers with unconstitutional taking of Fort Berthold.

177 the first drop of irrigation water had yet to fall: Between 1957 and 1964, Congress held three different sets of hearings in North Dakota. U.S. House Committee on Interior and Insular Affairs, *Hearing on HR 7068;* U.S. House Committee on Interior and Insular Affairs, *Hearing on Provisions in Connection with the Construction of the Garrison Diversion Unit,* 86th Cong.; and U.S. House Committee on Interior and Insular Affairs, *Hearing on Provisions in Connection with the Construction of the Garrison Diversion Unit,* 88th Cong.

178 "This would be a good time for the governors and senators and representatives": Limvere and Madsen, "Rumblings from the Ditch." This special report is a "must-read" document for anyone interested in the history of Pick-Sloan.

CHAPTER VIII: RETURN OF THE NATIVES

Interviews: *Raymond Cross, Louise Holding Eagle, Dr. Monica Mayer, Emerson Murry, Jesus O'Suna, Chief Justice Gerald VandeWalle, Hans Walker, Marie Wells, Dr. Herbert Wilson.*

186 Nixon's message: Nixon, *The Public Papers of the Presidents of the United States,* pp. 223–224.

186 "The American Indians have been oppressed": Ibid., p. 564. Declaring that "the policy of forced termination is wrong," Richard Nixon let it be known that his position on this

matter was nonnegotiable. To its credit, Congress not only responded by passing the Self-Determination Act but followed later with the Indian Education Act of 1972 and the Indian Health Care Improvement Act of 1976. Unlike many social remedies attempted by lawmakers, these laws have had beneficial effects on the residents of Indian Country that far exceeded Congress' greatest hopes. Funding made education available to many thousands of Indian students, who have earned degrees in science, law, the arts, and social sciences.

187   After his dramatic victory in the *Adair* case: *United States v. Adair*, 478 Fed. Supp. 336; *United States v. Adair II*, 723 Fed. 2nd 1394; and *United States v. Adair* [also known as *Adair II*], Fed. Supp. 2nd 1273.

187   help the Yaqui people: What made this a particularly difficult challenge was the fact that there were two different tribes of Pasqua Yaqui in Arizona by the late 1970s. Jesus O'Suna, a veteran tribal councilman for the Yaqui, credits Cross's effort with bringing the tribes into the twentieth century. The tribes' casinos have given the Yaqui people the opportunity to live in real homes, operate their own schools and medical facilities, and become a political force in Arizona politics.

188   Fragments of Public Law 280: *Establishing State Jurisdiction over Indian Nations in Civil Disputes,* U.S. Public Law 280. For a full discussion of P.L. 280, see Josephy, *Red Power.*

188   "it was the *Wold Engineering* case": *Three Affiliated Tribes v. Wold Engineering,* 463 U.S. 1248, and *Three Affiliated Tribes v. Wold Engineering,* 476 U.S. 877.

189   "routine disputes over the ordinary": A case in Alaska arose between a small tribe and a subcontractor over an unpaid bill for twelve hundred dollars. By the time the case reached the U.S. Supreme Court, what was at stake was the ownership of millions of square miles of Alaskan wilderness and resources resulting from the Alaska Native Claims Settlement Act.

191   The unemployment rate at Fort Berthold had risen: Spotted Bear recalls this period as the tribe's post-dam nadir of social disintegration.

191   Life expectancy for men: These and other current medical statistics were taken from interviews with Dr. Monica Mayer and Dr. Herbert Wilson. It is noteworthy that the profile of the Mandan, Hidatsa, and Arikara in 2003 is not dissimilar from that of hundreds of other tribes.

192   The accounts were in such disarray: From interviews with Alyce Spotted Bear and members of the Three Affiliated Tribes Tribal Council. Of her many achievements during four years in office, Spotted Bear is most proud of leaving the tribal government in a state of solvency. "I had to practically beg the people at Interior to give me one more month to get the books in order. Frankly, I don't believe they thought we had a chance in the world of turning it around, but somehow we did."

192   "Hiring Ray was your classic no-brainer": Interviews with Alyce Spotted Bear.

193   "The Supremes asked us to take another look": Interviews with Chief Justice VandeWalle and Raymond Cross.

193   North Dakota State Water Commission: The state agency responsible for acting as liaison between federal water programs, such as the Garrison Diversion Unit, and the state legislature.

195   almost forty years after: Russell, *Promise of Water.*

195   Pick-Sloan's original price tag: The current price for Pick-Sloan is $20 billion and counting. Accountants and investigators for organizations such as the North Dakota Farmers Union believe this figure is very conservative, though it is the one most commonly cited.

196   "the kind of working alliance": Limvere and Madsen, "Rumblings from the Ditch."

196   "The reason people killed this idea when it first came up": Ibid.

Chapter IX: The Last Train to Yuma

Interviews: *Raymond Cross, Marilyn Hudson, Roger Johnson, Ike Livermore, Emerson Murry, Alyce Spotted Bear, Governor David Treen, Chief Justice Gerald VandeWalle, Hans Walker, Marie Wells, Ann Zorn.*

201 Congress' requirements: *Establishing Garrison Diversion Unit Commission,* U.S. Public Law 360.

201 municipal and industrial water systems: Ibid. In separate interviews, Ann Zorn and Ike Livermore, two of the eleven members of the Garrison Diversion Unit Commission, explained that the "institutional equity" issues they were asked to look at in the implementation of the Pick-Sloan Plan eventually dominated all other factors Congress asked them to investigate.

203 Yet this lawless practice: Reisner, *Cadillac Desert,* pp. 114, 382–383.

203 Others aligned themselves: Russell, *Promise of Water.* These alliances would soon harden into a kind of trench warfare, a phenomenon not at all uncommon in the West, where water is prized. This is particularly true at the local level, when state and local governments bump up against the sovereign immunity of tribal governments that have first claim to diminishing water resources. At the Washington State Republican Convention in 2000, a motion was put on the floor calling for the "abolition of all Indian tribes." That same year, the legendary "Indian fighter" from Washington, Slade Gorton, lost his bid for a fourth term in the U.S. Senate to Maria Cantwell. In a very close election that required a recount, votes turned out by the state's Indian tribes swung the election to the newcomer Cantwell.

206 Institutional equity was the eye of the needle: *Establishing Garrison Diversion Unit Commission,* U.S. Public Law 360.

207 "Chairman Treen and members of the commission": Cross, Statement to the Garrison Diversion Unit Commission.

209 Instead of raising questions about the "just compensation": Cross, Recommended changes to recommendations.

210 PANELISTS CONTEND INDIANS' ROLE NOT RECOGNIZED: Neumann, "Panelists Contend Indians' Role Not Recognized."

211 "Marc Messing": In a private note to Zorn and Livermore, Messing wrote: "I am increasingly concerned that the commission may compound the injustices." Messing, Memorandum to Ike Livermore and Ann Zorn on fundamental Indian issues.

211 "The history of this settlement is a tragedy": Ibid.

211 Livermore reminded his protégés: Livermore and Zorn, "Observations on Visits to Fort Berthold and Standing Rock."

212 Zorn and Livermore began to prepare: GDUC, Final recommendations regarding Indian claims. See a complete manifest of final recommendations in U.S. House Subcommittee on Water and Power Resources of the Committee on Interior and Insular Affairs, *Hearings on the Final Recommendations of the Garrison Diversion Unit Commission.*

213 in late December, at the same moment Zorn and Treen: GDUC, Transcripts of final meeting with Treen, Zorn, and O'Meara on recommendations to Congress.

214 In mid-January 1985: U.S. House Subcommittee on Water and Power Resources of the Committee on Interior and Insular Affairs, *Hearings on the Final Recommendations of the Garrison Diversion Unit Commission.*

214 unsettled Indian issues: The report to Congress stated in unequivocal terms that the commission had found *"the tribes were entitled to additional awards"* (Ibid).

216 "Many of us have waited a long, long time": Marie Wells was still on the Tribal Council

when the JTAC arrived in New Town to hear testimony. Her testimony, re-created from interviews with Wells herself and others who were there, was very typical of the statements the committee members heard from the tribal elders.

216 "We picked wild grapes, chokecherries": The loss of these natural foods to the Indians' diet would have a profound impact on their general health over the next two generations. Emerson Murry told me that the challenge for the JTAC was to find a way to put a valuation on sources of food and sustenance that were lost to The Flood, such as the chokecherry bushes. The loss of the chokecherry, in particular, seems to have left its mark. Researchers have recently discovered that antioxidants in the chokecherry are nature's perfect antidote for heart disease. Prior to The Flood, less than 1 percent of the Indian population was afflicted with heart disease. Today, it is a leading cause of death.

217 Hidatsa elder Cora Baker: Some of the testimony heard by the JTAC has been taken from abbreviated transcripts and posted on the Three Affiliated Tribes' Internet home page (www.threeaffiliatedtribes.org). Many of the original records from these hearings were lost in a fire that destroyed several tribal records. Alyce Spotted Bear's records were also lost when her home burned down many years after the hearings. Chairman Murry was able to provide me with boxes of bound reports compiled by staff, with the assistance of Raymond Cross, as the committee prepared its final report for Secretary Hodel and Congress.

217 "When our economic heartland was taken away": Ibid.

218 Alyce and Raymond suddenly realized: From the beginning their strategy was to secure federal funds to develop water projects, then divert some of those funds to other projects such as feeding schoolchildren and heating the homes of the elders in winter.

218 "We had a lot of fine people break down": Chairman Murry and Hans Walker both told me they believed the oral testimony was the single most important factor in determining the direction of their report. In the opening hours, Murry knew that the JTAC investigation would produce a report condemning the actions of Congress in 1949.

218 "Congress had blown it very badly": As a lawyer with twenty-five years of experience as the director of the state's legislative council, Murry was in a unique position to assess both the mistakes made by Congress and the means of reconciling them to existing laws. Early in the process, Murry recognized that they would be talking about monetary compensation. Congress went astray when it dismissed Felix Cohen's warning that serious consequences would result if lawmakers ignored their responsibilities as trustees to the tribes.

218 "I never really discussed this aspect of our investigation": Murry said he did not feel the need to discuss the fine points of the "rules of evidence" with the nonlawyers on the committee, but the outcome hinged on the committee's willingness to take the oral testimony at face value, as though it were actual "evidence." Chairman Murry: "This was the only way we could eventually put some kind of value on all the things that were lost, such as the timber, the wild fruit and berries, all the things that had gone into making their world what it was."

219 "There was so much more at stake": The efficacy of P.L. 280 was more clearly at stake in the second appeal than it had been the first time. This was a result of Erickstad's insistence that the state had no right to hear the case without the tribe surrendering its "sovereign immunity."

CHAPTER X: INTO THE STORM

Interviews: *Bucky Cross, Crusoe Cross, Raymond Cross, Lee Foley, Marilyn Hudson, Roger Johnson, Ed Lone Fight, Emerson Murry, Alyce Spotted Bear, Governor David Treen, Chief Justice Gerald VandeWalle, Hans Walker, Marie Wells, Ann Zorn.*

225 Chief Justice Warren Burger gave the gavel a firm rap: *Three Affiliated Tribes v. Wold Engineering,* 476 U.S. 877. The courtroom scene is taken from the transcript and from interviews with Raymond Cross and Alyce Spotted Bear. While trained lawyers will have no trouble following the arguments, those unfamiliar with the arcane vernacular of the law will likely find some of the arguments difficult to follow. Nevertheless, I felt that it was important to accurately portray the intellectual challenge of the exchange and the specialized training it required. In some places, for the sake of brevity or clarity, I have paraphrased the actual exchanges between Cross and the justices.

231 What had been unjustly taken from the tribes: U.S. Senate and House, Joint hearing of the Senate Select Committee on Indian Affairs, the Senate Committee on Energy and Natural Resources, and the House Committee on Interior and Insular Affairs, *Final Report and Recommendations of the Garrison Unit Joint Tribal Advisory Committee.*

231 a cash award that reflected the true value: U.S. House Subcommittees on Indian Affairs of the Committee on Public Lands, *Providing for the Ratification by Congress of a Contract for the Purchase of Certain Indian Lands Under HJ Res. 33.* A similar, more comprehensive report was compiled by the Missouri River Basin investigation team headed by Gordon Macgregor, which produced a number of excellent "white papers" on the effects of Pick-Sloan on the Missouri River tribes in the years prior to the actual flooding. Macgregor, "Social and Economic Impacts of Garrison Dam on the Indians of the Fort Berthold Reservation."

231 On June 16, 1986, the high court came back with its ruling in *Wold II: Three Affiliated Tribes v. Wold Engineering,* 476 U.S. 877.

233 Zorn agreed to tailor her remarks: U.S. Senate and House, Joint hearing of the Senate Select Committee on Indian Affairs, the Senate Committee on Energy and Natural Resources, and the House Committee on Interior and Insular Affairs, *Final Report and Recommendations of the Garrison Unit Joint Tribal Advisory Committee.*

233 "the tribes' Fifth Amendment rights had been violated": Ibid.

Zorn was invited to join Hans Walker, Raymond Cross, and Emerson Murry to make this presentation. Senator Daniel Inouye presided. Ronald Reagan's secretary of the interior, Donald Hodel, shelved the entire investigation. Inouye summarizes Hodel's position in a question to Zorn (p. 5):

"The Department of the Interior has suggested that the report of the Tribal Advisory Committee does not provide adequate documentation to justify and establish that the tribes are entitled to additional financial compensation in the form of substitute or replacement value of the economic basis lost, as a result of the action taken. Do you believe there is adequate documentation to establish this claim?"

Zorn: "I think we fully thought so at the time we were bringing the issues forth. We expected more documentation to come from the JTAC examinations."

Murry answered this question directly: "There was no question in our minds that the construction of the two dams and the impoundment of waters destroyed the major economic base of both the Standing Rock and the Fort Berthold Reservations. . . . In the case of the Fort Berthold Reservation, these activities made it one of the few, possibly even the only, economically self-sufficient reservation in the country. . . . The emotional impact, and we found it to be material, of this abrupt and radical change, could not be quantified, but it certainly was major, and its effects last until this day. The committee found that the tribes are entitled to be made whole for their specific losses."

Hodel's strategy was to shelve the entire report, which he did for nearly two years. JTAC member Brent Blackwelder tells Congress that "the Department of the Interior never initiated any discussion with the Tribal Advisory Committee members to ask us questions, if they had any, about the report. . . . The question here is more a matter of right and just compensation. The Indians were deprived in a most unfair manner of resources vital to their livelihood, to their self-sufficiency, and we as a matter of right, ought to make that compensation and not delay further after decades. So, it's not a question of can we afford it, but there is a right and an entitlement here, and in a nation as wealthy as we are, we ought to be able to make that budgetary commitment and fulfill this entitlement."

Zorn recalled the moment Inouye lost his patience during this hearing with the intentionally indirect testimony of the Army engineers' General Dominy, who tried to lay the entire blame for Pick-Sloan at the feet of Congress. Inouye asks Dominy if he thinks the 1949 compensation package was fair. Dominy sidesteps the question.

Senator Inouye: "I'm not in a position to decide whether it's appropriate or not, because if I apply my experience from Hawaii, I would say that this was not even robbery. It was murder."

233　The junior senator from Arizona: U.S. Senate Select Committee on Indian Affairs, *Hearing on the Final Report of the Garrison Unit Joint Tribal Advisory Committee.* "This was back in John's anti-Indian days," reflects Raymond. "He's come a long way since then. There aren't many politicians in Washington who command more respect from Indian leaders than John McCain."

235　President Reagan made an off-the-cuff: University of Wisconsin professor Al Gedicks has explored the Reagan administration's failed attempts to create a "neo–Termination Era" (Gedicks, *The New Resource Wars*). Gedicks shows how Secretary Watt relied on the support of right-wing think tanks in Washington to roll back recent court victories that secured rights to the tribes. One of the strongest arguments for turning parts of Indian Country into national "sacrifice zones" was the fact that uranium exploration in Indian Country over the past three decades had left thousands of test holes venting radon into Indian homes and schools. It seemed to administrators in Washington that it would be cheaper and easier to move the Indians into the cities than to clean up the messes left behind by the mining companies. In the end, the government neither filled in the test holes nor moved the Indians to urban centers. Lori Goodman, the founder and director of Diné CARE, was still trying in 2003 to secure monetary compensation from the federal government for the families of hundreds of Navajo uranium miners who have died of cancers linked directly to uranium poisoning.

Gedicks is particularly informative on the subject of Wisconsin's Chippewa, Potawatomi, and Oneida tribes' battles against former governor Tommy Thompson and the Exxon Corporation. For nearly twenty years, Exxon tried to open a copper mine near Crandon Lake but was thwarted by tribal environmental standards that were supported by the National Environmental Policy Act, or NEPA. Eventually, the Wisconsin legislature passed a law forbidding the cyanide-leech mining for copper or zinc. Exxon finally pulled out of the fight and left the state when white sports-fishing groups closed ranks with the tribes.

235　"Maybe we made a mistake": "Remarks on 'Humoring Indians' Bring Protest from Tribal Leaders," *New York Times.*

236　the White House sought to smooth the waters: "Indians Confer with President and Top Aides," *New York Times.*

237　During the 1940s and the 1950s: U.S. Senate Select Committee on Indian Affairs, *Hearing on the Three Affiliated Tribes and Standing Rock Sioux Tribal Equitable Compensation Act of 1991.* Senator Inouye opened the hearings with the summary of the taking of the Mandan, Hidatsa, and Arikara lands, then concluded the hearings with his statement on

the "deceit and deception" used by Congress to abrogate hundreds of treaties. After Inouye finished, North Dakota senator Kent Conrad put his cards on the table in a forceful speech: "All the people of Fort Berthold and Standing Rock want is a chance to
rebuild. They pray for a better life for their children, and they demand justice from the
government that has treated them with brutality and indifference."

237 "What you have done is to share": Ibid.

241 overview of Senate Bill 168: U.S. Senate Select Committee on Indian Affairs, *Implementing Recommendations of the Garrison Unit Joint Tribal Advisory Committee.*

242 they are still waiting: "Sakakawea Levels Worry North Dakota," *Bismarck Tribune.* Following the GDUC hearings in the mid-1980s, Governor Guy and Sinner organized more
meetings between congressional delegations and farmers in the Pick-Sloan irrigation district, but they only succeeded in creating frustration in a new generation of farmers.

242 Of the 1 million acres of irrigation: Russell, *Promise of Water.* Author Michael Lawson
manages to introduce a note of humor to this bitter situation.

> Navigation, Pick's pet project on the lower Missouri, has become a bad, very
> bad, joke. Taxpayers have spent untold millions to float no more than 2.6 mil-
> lion tons of commercial freight up the river each year. The Corps admitted that
> commercial navigation would no longer be viable after 2000, and in 1973 they
> admitted that there would not be sufficient water by then to maintain a nav-
> igation channel, so they proposed a new plan, with a cost of $60 billion, to
> constantly dredge the river and extend navigation to Yankton, South Dakota.
> Congress is still laughing (Lawson, *Dammed Indians,* p. 187).

242 drought-stricken farmers: After drought devastated a thousand square miles of crops in
the Upper Missouri River Valley in the spring and summer of 2002, the region's farmers
turned to Congress, seeking $5 billion in relief. Throughout the ordeal, North Dakota
farmers watched helplessly as water levels in Lake Sakakawea were drawn down to keep
downstream barge traffic moving without interruption between St. Louis and Sioux City,
Iowa.

242 in January of 2004: In an earlier ruling over the best use of upstream water, the 8th Circuit Court of Appeals held that in a contest for water impounded on the Upper Missouri,
barge traffic should take precedence over recreational uses upstream. As far as the upstream states were concerned, "recreational uses" was a red herring that allowed lower
states to finesse the real issue. In January 2004, North Dakota's attorney general, Wayne
Stenehjem, petitioned the U.S. Supreme Court to review the management plan of the
Army Corps of Engineers in light of the original O'Mahoney-Millikin Amendment to
the Flood Control Act of 1944.

242 "I'm afraid it's [Pick-Sloan's] all been one huge scam": Farmers on the Upper Missouri have
learned that falling water levels always result in unforeseeable trouble. As water levels drop,
industrial and agricultural toxins become more concentrated and, consequently, more lethal
to fish and migratory bird life. Dozens of species that once flourished on the Missouri River
bottoms are now on the federal government's endangered species list. In late 2002, the non-
partisan watchdog group American Rivers declared the Missouri the most endangered river
in America.

242 "There are dwellings all about me": Catlin, *George Catlin.*

245 At every venue thus far: "Dollars, Sense, and Salmon," *Idaho Statesman.* Also see Whitelaw,
"Breaching Dam Myths." "Between 1988 and 1997, logging in Oregon and Washington
fell 87 percent on federal lands and 47 percent overall, and the timber-industry employment dropped 21 percent," writes Whitelaw, "but total employment actually increased 32
percent, and real per capita income grew 21 percent. When politicians like George Bush

and Gordon Smith claim that breaching the dams will hurt the region's economy, the hard numbers tell a different story." The numbers, in fact, argue that those claims are political nonsense. "In the case of the dams the most conservative estimates show that dam breaching will actually result in a $200 million annual windfall."

246 In 1991, only one sockeye salmon returned to Redfish Lake: "Dollars, Sense, and Salmon," *Idaho Statesman,* and Barcott, "Blow Up."

In 1892, commercial fishermen on the Columbia netted 873,106 sockeye salmon heading upstream into the high mountains of Idaho and Montana. When the Ice Harbor Dam was built on the Snake in 1962, sockeye counts "crashed" to 1,118. By 1981, with all four dams in place, the counts were down to 218, and in 1991, only one fish made it home.

Reporters for the *Idaho Statesman* newspaper have documented recent efforts by state and federal fisheries' biologists to reintroduce the sockeye to Redfish Lake. Tens of millions of dollars have been spent on the effort. To date, fewer than sixty fish have returned.

Bibliography

٭

This book stands on the broad shoulders of skilled and dedicated predecessors. Roy Meyer's *The Village Indians of the Upper Missouri* is a journeyman's monument to the craft of the academic historian. Not to be overshadowed, James Rhonda's *Lewis and Clark Among the Indians* is a work from which all other writings on Lewis and Clark are measured. Similarly, Marc Reisner's exhaustive investigation of the Bureau of Reclamation and the Army Corps of Engineers, *Cadillac Desert;* Henry C. Hart's *The Dark Missouri;* and Michael Lawson's *Dammed Indians* gave me firm footing for the water wars that have been waged for the past fifty years on the Upper Missouri River. Reisner's bibliography could be published under its own title: "Anatomy of an American Paradox."

Alfred Bowers's twin volumes, *Hidatsa Social and Ceremonial Organization* and *Mandan Social and Ceremonial Organization,* were indispensable for shaping the background of this story. Bernard DeVoto's *The Course of Empire;* Walter Prescott Webb's timeless study, *The Great Plains;* and the extraordinary journals of the Spanish adventurer Cabeza de Vaca, *Álvar Núñez Cabeza de Vaca,* framed the larger boundaries of the discovery-era Americas. Both DeVoto and Webb were indebted to Hiram Martin Chittenden's three-volume work, *The American Fur Trade of the Far West.* In the decades since the publication of these academic landmarks, renowned archaeologists W. Raymond Wood and Thomas Thiessen, in *Early Fur Trade on the Northern Plains: Canadian Traders Among the Mandan and Hidatsa Indians, 1738–1818,* have systematically exposed mythologies about Lewis and Clark that have been masquerading as historical fact in school classrooms for generations.

The American Indian in Western Legal Thought: The Discourses of Conquest, Robert Williams's investigation into the evolution of Western legal thought from the twelfth-century Crusades to the Marshall Court, belongs on a shelf all by itself. David Getches's reductive analysis of the Rehnquist Court, "Conquering the Cultural Frontier," from the *California Law Review,* and Raymond Cross's penetrating analysis of John Marshall in two major law-review monographs, "Sovereign Bargains" and "Tribes as Rich Nations," join Wilcomb Washburn's and Francis Paul Prucha's works, *Red Man's Land/White Man's Law* and *The Great Father,* respectively, to contribute fresh insights into Marshall and the intellectual big bang that resulted in the formulation of federalism and the United States of America.

Books

Abourezk, James. *Advise and Dissent.* Chicago: Lawrence Hill Books, 1989.
Abram, David. *The Spell of the Sensuous.* New York: Vintage, 1998.
Adorno, Rolena. *Álvar Núñez Cabeza de Vaca: His Account, His Life, and the Expedition of Panfilo de Narvaez.* Lincoln: University of Nebraska Press, 1999.

Ambrose, Stephen. *Undaunted Courage: Meriwether Lewis, Thomas Jefferson, and the Opening of the American West.* New York: Simon and Schuster, 1997.

Beckwith, Martha Warren. *Myths and Ceremonies of the Mandan and Hidatsa.* Poughkeepsie, NY: Vassar College, 1932.

Bogdanovich, Peter. *This Is Orson Welles.* Edited by Jonathan Rosenbaum, with an introduction by Peter Bogdanovich. New York: DaCapo Press, 1998.

Botkin, Daniel B. *Our Natural History: The Lessons of Lewis and Clark.* New York: Penguin Books, 1995.

Bowers, Alfred W. *Hidatsa Social and Ceremonial Organization.* Lincoln: University of Nebraska Press, 1992.

———. *Mandan Social and Ceremonial Organization.* Chicago: University of Chicago Press, 1950.

Boyer, Ernest L. *Tribal Colleges: Shaping the Future of Native America.* Princeton: The Carnegie Foundation for the Advancement of Teaching, 1989.

Brophy, William A., and Sophie D. Aberle. *The Indian: America's Unfinished Business.* Norman: University of Oklahoma Press, 1966.

Buenker, John D., and Lorman A. Ratner. *Multiculturalism in the United States: A Comparative Guide to Acculturation and Ethnicity.* New York: Greenwood Press, 1992.

Callow, Simon. *Orson Welles: The Road to Xanadu.* New York: Viking, 1996.

Carruth, Gorton. *The Encyclopedia of American Facts and Dates.* 9th ed. New York: Harper-Collins, 1993.

Catlin, George. *George Catlin: Letters and Notes on the North American Indians.* Edited by Michael MacDonald Mooney. New York: Clarkson N. Potter, distributed by Crown, 1975.

———. *North American Indians: Being Letters and Notes on Their Manners, Customs, and Conditions.* 2 vols. Edinburgh: John Grant, 1926.

Chardon, Francis A. *Chardon's Journal at Fort Clark, 1834-1837.* Edited by Annie Heloise Abel. Pierre, SD: Department of History, State of South Dakota, 1932.

Chittenden, Hiram Martin. *The American Fur Trade of the Far West.* 3 vols. New York: FP Harper, 1902.

Clarke, Charles. *The Men of the Lewis and Clark Expedition: A Biographical Roster of the Fifty-One Members and a Composite Diary of Their Activities from All Known Sources.* Glendale, CA: Arthur H. Clark, 1970.

Clark, Robert. *River of the West: A Chronicle of the Columbia.* New York: Picador, 1995.

Cohen, Felix. *Handbook of Federal Indian Law.* 1st ed. Washington, D.C.: United States Department of the Interior, Washington, D.C.: GPO, 1941.

———. *Handbook of Federal Indian Law.* 1982 ed. Edited by Rennard Strickland et al. Charlottesville: Bobbs-Merrill, 1982.

———. *The Legal Conscience: Selected Papers of Felix S. Cohen.* Edited by Lucy Kramer Cohen, with a foreword by Felix Frankfurter. New Haven: Yale University Press, 1960.

Cohen, Lucy Kramer, ed. *The Legal Conscience: Selected Papers of Felix S. Cohen.* New Haven, CT: Yale University Press, 1960.

Collier, John. *From Every Zenith.* Denver: Sage Books, 1963.

———. *Indians of the Americas.* New York: W. W. Norton, 1947.

Costello, David. *The Prairie World.* New York: Thomas Crowell, 1969.

Cox, George. *The Crusades.* New York: Charles Scribner's Sons, 1886.

Curtis, Edward. *The North American Indian.* Vols. 4 and 5. Seattle: Curtis Publishing, 1970.

Damon, Charles Ripley. *The American Dictionary of Dates.* Vols. 1 and 2. Boston: The Gorham Press, 1921.

Deloria, Vine Jr., ed. *American Indian Policy in the Twentieth Century.* Norman: University of Oklahoma Press, 1985.

Deloria, Vine Jr., and Raymond J. Demallie, eds. *Documents of American Indian Diplomacy: Treaties, Agreements, and Conventions, 1775–1979.* Norman: University of Oklahoma Press, 1999.

DeVoto, Bernard. *Across the Wide Missouri.* Boston: Houghton Mifflin, 1947.

———. *The Course of Empire.* Boston: Houghton Mifflin, 1952.

Diamond, Jared. *Guns, Germs, and Steel: The Fates of Human Societies.* New York: W. W. Norton, 1999.

Dobyns, Henry F. *Their Number Become Thinned: Native American Population Dynamics in Eastern North America.* Knoxville, TN: University of Tennessee Press, 1983.

Drinnon, Richard. *Keeper of Concentration Camps: Dillon S. Myer and American Racism.* Berkeley: University of California Press, 1987.

Duncan, Dayton. *Out West: An American Journey.* New York: Viking Press, 1987.

Durant, Will. *Adventures in Genius.* New York: Simon and Schuster, 1931.

Erbstosser, Martin. *The Crusades.* New York: Universe Books, 1979.

Fite, Emerson, and Archibald Freeman. *A Book of Old Maps: Delineating American History from the Earliest Days Down to the Close of the Revolutionary War.* Cambridge: Harvard University Press, 1926.

Fitzharris, Tim. *The Wild Prairie: A Natural History of the Western Plains.* New York: Oxford Press, 1983.

Flanders, Henry. *The Lives and Times of the Chief Justices of the Supreme Court of the United States.* Vol. 2. New York: James Cockcroft, 1875.

Frey, Rodney, ed. *Stories That Make the World: Oral Literature of the Indian Peoples of the Inland Northwest.* Norman: University of Oklahoma Press, 1995.

Gass, Sergeant Patrick. *Gass's Journal of the Lewis and Clark Expedition.* Chicago: AC McClurg, 1904.

Gedicks, Al. *The New Resource Wars: Native and Environmental Struggles Against Multinational Corporations.* Boston: South End Press, 1993.

Getches, David et al., eds. *Handbook of Federal Indian Law.* 4th ed. New York: Bobbs-Merrill, 1988.

Gilman, Carolyn, and Mary Jane Schneider. *The Way to Independence: Memories of a Hidatsa Family.* St. Paul: Minnesota Historical Society Press, 1987.

Goetzmann, William. *Exploration and Empire: The Explorer and the Scientist in the Winning of the American West.* New York: Knopf, 1966.

Gray, Arthur Amos. *Men Who Built the West.* New York: Books for Libraries Press, 1945.

Grossman, Elizabeth. *Watershed: The Undamming of America.* New York: Counterpoint, 2002.

Hafen, LeRoy R. *Broken Hand: The Life of Thomas Fitzpatrick — Mountain Man, Guide, and Indian Agent.* Denver: Old West Publishing, 1973.

Hall, Charles L. *The Fort Berthold Mission.* New York: The American Missionary Association, 1924.

Hart, Henry Cowles. *The Dark Missouri.* Madison: University of Wisconsin Press, 1957.

Henry, Alexander, and David Thompson. *The Manuscript Journals of Alexander Henry and of David Thompson.* Vol. 1. Edited by Elliott Coues. New York: Francis P. Harper, 1897.

Hobson, Charles F. *The Great Chief Justice: John Marshall and the Rule of Law.* Lawrence: University of Kansas Press, 1996.

Holder, Preston. *The Hoe and the Horse on the Plains: A Study of Cultural Development Among North American Indians.* Lincoln: University of Nebraska Press, 1970.

Holt, P. M., ed. *The Age of the Crusades: The Near East from the Eleventh Century to 1517.* London: Longman, 1986.

Hunt, Constance, with Verne Huser. *Down by the River: The Impact of Federal Water Projects and Policies on Biological Diversity.* Foreword by Jay D. Hair. Washington, D.C.: Island Press, 1988.

Ivison, Duncan, Paul Patton, and William Sanders, eds. *Political Theory and the Rights of Indigenous Peoples*. London: Cambridge University Press, 2000.

Jackson, Donald. *Voyages of the Steamboat Yellowstone*. Norman: University of Oklahoma Press, 1984.

Jackson, Donald Dale. *Golddust*. New York: Knopf, 1980.

Josephy, Alvin J. *The American Heritage History of the Congress of the United States*. New York: McGraw Hill, 1975.

——. *Now That the Buffalo's Gone: A Study of Today's American Indians*. New York: Knopf, 1982.

——. *Red Power: The American Indian's Fight for Freedom*. New York: American Heritage Press, 1971.

Kappler, Charles, ed. *Indian Treaties, 1778–1883*. New York: Interland Publishing, 1972.

Kelly, Lawrence C. *The Assault on Assimilation: John Collier and the Origins of Indian Policy Reform*. Albuquerque: University of New Mexico Press, 1983.

Ketcham, Ralph. *James Madison*. New York: Macmillan, 1971.

Killoren, John J. *Come Blackrobe*. Norman: University of Oklahoma Press, 1994.

Kreyche, Gerla. *Vision of the American West*. Lexington: University of Kentucky Press, 1989.

Lass, William E. *A History of Steamboating on the Upper Missouri River*. Lincoln: University of Nebraska Press, 1962.

Lawson, Michael. *Dammed Indians: The Pick-Sloan Plan and the Missouri River Sioux*. Norman: University of Oklahoma Press, 1982.

Lazarus, Edward. *Black Hills, White Justice: The Sioux Nation Versus the United States, 1775 to the Present*. New York: HarperCollins, 1991.

Lewis, Meriwether, and William Clark. *The Journals of the Expedition Under the Command of Capts. Lewis and Clark*. Vol. 1. Edited by Nicholas Biddle, with an introduction by John Bakeless. New York: Heritage Press, 1962.

——. *The Journals of Lewis and Clark*. Edited by Nicholas Biddle, with an introduction by Rev. John Bach McMaster. New York: Allerton Book Co., 1922.

——. *The Journals of Lewis and Clark*. Edited by Bernard DeVoto. Boston: Houghton Mifflin, 1953.

——. *The Journals of Lewis and Clark*. 2 vols. Edited by Gary Moulton. Lincoln: University of Nebraska Press, 2001.

——. *Original Journals of the Lewis and Clark Expedition*. Edited by Reuben Gold Thwaites. New York: Dodd, Mead, 1904.

Limerick, Patricia Nelson. *The Legacy of Conquest: The Unbroken Past of the American West*. New York: W. W. Norton, 1986.

Linderman, Frank. *American: The Life Story of a Great Indian, Plenty-Coups, Chief of the Crows*. New York: John Day Company, 1930.

——. *Pretty-Shield, Medicine Woman of the Crows*. Lincoln: University of Nebraska Press, 1932.

Lowie, Robert H. *Myths and Traditions of the Crow Indians*. Lincoln: University of Nebraska Press, 1993.

Margaret, Helene. *Father DeSmet: Pioneer Priest of the Rockies*. New York: Farrar and Reinhart, 1940.

Matthews, Richard K. *If Men Were Angels: James Madison and the Heartless Empire of Reason*. Lawrence: University of Kansas Press, 1995.

Matthiessen, Peter. *Indian Country*. New York: Viking Press, 1984.

Maxfield, Christyann Ranck. *Goodbye to Elbowoods: The Story of Harold and Eva Case*. Bismarck, ND: State Historical Society of North Dakota, 1986.

Mayer, Hans Eberhard. *The Crusades*. London: Oxford University Press, 1965.

McCabe, Joseph. *Crises in the History of the Papacy.* New York: G. P. Putnam's Sons, 1916.

McNickle, D'Arcy. *Indian Man.* Bloomington, IN: Indiana University Press, 1971.

Meyer, Roy. "Fort Berthold and the Garrison Dam." In *North Dakota History.* Vol. 35, nos. 3 and 4. Bismarck, ND: State Historical Society of North Dakota, 1968.

———. *The Village Indians of the Upper Missouri.* Norman: University of Oklahoma Press, 1972.

Miller, Lee, ed. *From the Heart: Voices of the American Indian.* New York: Knopf, 1995.

Morgan, Arthur E. *Dams and Other Disasters: A Century of the Army Corps of Engineers in Civil Works.* Boston: Porter Sargent, 1972.

Munroe, James P. *A Life of Francis Amasa Walker.* New York: Henry Holt, 1923.

Nabakov, Peter. *Native American Testimony: A Chronicle of Indian-White Relations from Prophesy to the Present.* New York: Penguin, 1991.

Neihardt, John G. *Black Elk Speaks.* Introduction by Vine Deloria Jr. Lincoln: University of Nebraska Press, 1979.

Nesbitt, Jack. *Sources of the River.* Seattle: Sasquatch Books, 1994.

Newlands, Francis G. *The Public Papers of Francis G. Newlands.* Edited by Arthur B. Darling. New York: Houghton Mifflin, 1932.

Nies, Judith. *Native American History: A Chronology of a Culture's Vast Achievements and Their Links to World Events.* New York: Ballantine Books, 1996.

Nixon, Richard. *The Public Papers of the Presidents of the United States.* Washington, D.C.: Federal Register Division, National Archives and Records Service, General Services Administration, 1975.

Papanikolas, Zeese. *Trickster in the Land of Dreams.* Lincoln: University of Nebraska Press, 1995.

Peters, Virginia Bergman. *Women of the Earth Lodges: Tribal Life on the Plains.* Norman: University of Oklahoma Press, 1995.

Prucha, Francis Paul. *American Indian Policy in Crisis: Christian Reformers and the Indian, 1865–1900.* Norman: University of Oklahoma Press, 1976.

———. *American Indian Treaties: The History of a Political Anomaly.* Berkeley: University of California Press, 1994.

———. *The Great Father: The United States Government and the American Indians.* Lincoln: University of Nebraska Press, 1984.

Raban, Jonathan. *Bad Land: An American Romance.* New York: Vintage, 1996.

Read, James H. *Power Versus Liberty: Madison, Hamilton, Wilson, and Jefferson.* Charlottesville: University Press of Virginia, 2000.

Reisner, Marc. *Cadillac Desert.* New York: Penguin, 1986.

Rhonda, James. *Lewis and Clark Among the Indians.* Lincoln: University of Nebraska Press, 1984.

Ridgeway, Marian. *The Missouri Basin's Pick-Sloan Plan: A Case Study.* Champagne-Urbana: University of Illinois Press, 1955.

Riemer, Neal. *James Madison: Creating the American Constitution.* Washington, D.C.: Congressional Quarterly, 1986.

Riley-Smith, Jonathan. *The Oxford History of the Crusades.* New York: Oxford Press, 1995.

Rogin, Michael Paul. *Fathers and Children: Andrew Jackson and the Subjugation of the American Indian.* New York: Knopf, 1975.

Rolvaag, Ole E. *Giants in the Earth.* New York: Harper and Brothers, 1929.

Roosevelt, Franklin D. *The Public Papers and Addresses of Franklin D. Roosevelt.* New York: Random House, 1938.

Sandoz, Mari. *The Beaver Men.* Lincoln: University of Nebraska Press, 1964.

———. *Old Jules.* Boston: Little, Brown, 1935.

Schlesier, Karl H. *Plains Indians, A.D. 500–1500: The Archaeological Past of Historic Groups.* Norman: University of Oklahoma Press, 1994.

Schwartz, Herman. *The Burger Years: Rights and Wrongs in the Supreme Court, 1969–1986.* New York: Viking, 1987.

Skarsten, M. O. *George Drouillard: Hunter and Interpreter for Lewis and Clark.* Glendale, CA: Arthur H. Clark, 1964.

Smith, Hubert. *The Explorations of the La Vérendryes in the Northern Plains, 1738–43.* Edited by W. Raymond Wood. Lincoln: University of Nebraska Press, 1980.

Stegner, Wallace. *Beyond the Hundredth Meridian.* Boston: Houghton Mifflin, 1953.

———. *Where the Bluebird Sings to the Lemonade Springs.* New York: Random House, 1992.

Suarez, Francisco S. J. *Selections from Three Works of Francisco Suarez: On Laws and God the Lawgiver.* Introduction by James Brown Scott. New York: Oceana Publications, 1964.

Sunder, John. *Joshua Pilcher: Fur Trader and Indian Agent.* Norman: University of Oklahoma Press, 1968.

Takaki, Ronald T. *Iron Cages: Race and Culture in Nineteenth-Century America.* New York: Knopf, 1979.

Thayer, James Bradley. *John Marshall.* New York: DaCapo, 1974.

Thompson, David. *David Thompson's Narrative of His Explorations in Western America 1784–1812.* Edited by J. B. Tyrrell. Toronto: Champlain Society, 1916.

———. *David Thompson's Narrative of His Explorations in Western America 1784–1812.* Edited by Richard Glover. Toronto: Champlain Society, 1962.

Treece, Henry. *The Crusades.* New York: Random House, 1963.

Tyler, S. Lyman. *A History of Indian Policy.* Washington, D.C.: U.S. Department of the Interior, 1973.

Verano, John W., and Douglas H. Ubelaker, eds. *Disease and Demography in the Americas.* Washington, D.C.: Smithsonian Institution Press, 1992.

Vestal, Stanley. *Short Grass Country.* Westport, CT: Greenwood Press, 1941.

Washburn, Wilcomb E. *The American Indian and the United States: A Documentary History.* Vol. 3. New York: Random House, 1973.

———. *Red Man's Land/White Man's Law: A Study of the Past and Present Status of the American Indian.* New York: Charles Scribner's Sons, 1971.

Weatherford, Jack. *Native Roots: How the Indians Enriched America.* New York: Crown, 1991.

Webb, Walter Prescott. *The Great Plains.* New York: Ginn, 1931.

Wheat, Carl I. *Mapping the Trans-Mississippi West, 1540–1861.* Vol. 2, *From Lewis and Clark to Fremont: 1804–1845.* San Francisco: Institute of Historical Typography, 1958.

White, Kevin, ed. *Hispanic Philosophy in the Age of Discovery.* In *Studies in Philosophy and the History of Philosophy.* Vol. 29. Washington, D.C.: The Catholic University Press, 1997.

Wied, Prince Maximilian zu. *People of the First Man: Life Among the Plains Indians in Their Final Days of Glory.* Edited by Davis Thomas and Karin Ronnefeldt. New York: E. P. Dutton, 1976.

Wilkinson, Charles F. *Crossing the Next Meridian: Land, Water, and the Future of the West.* Washington, D.C.: Island Press, 1992.

———. *The Eagle Bird: Mapping a New West.* Boulder: Johnson Books, 1999.

———. *Fire on the Plateau: Conflict and Endurance in the American Southwest.* Washington, D.C.: Island Press, 1999.

Will, George, and J. J. Spinden. *The Mandans: A Study of Their Culture, Archaeology, and Language.* Cambridge: Peabody Museum, 1906.

Williams, Robert. *The American Indian in Western Legal Thought: The Discourses of Conquest.* New York: Oxford University Press, 1990.

Wills, Gary. *James Madison.* New York: Times Books, 2002.

Wilson, Gilbert L. *Notes on the Hidatsa Indians*. Edited by Bella Weitzner. Vol. 56, part 2, Anthropological Papers. New York: The American Museum of Natural History, 1979.

Wischmann, Lesley. *Frontier Diplomats: The Life and Times of Alexander Culbertson and Natoyistsiksina*. Glendale, CA: Arthur H. Clark, 2000.

Wolf, Edward C., and Seth Zuckerman, eds. *Salmon Nation: People and Fish at the Edge*. Portland, OR: Ecotrust, 1999.

Wood, W. Raymond. *Historical Overview of the Fort Clark State Historic Site*. Bismarck, ND: State Historical Society of North Dakota, 1999.

Wood, W. Raymond, and Thomas Thiessen. *Early Fur Trade on the Northern Plains: Canadian Traders Among the Mandan and Hidatsa Indians, 1738–1818*. Norman: University of Oklahoma Press, 1985.

PERIODICALS

"Advocates of MVA Assail Its Critics." *New York Times*, March 26, 1949.

"Announcement of Missouri River Changes Delayed Indefinitely." *Minot Daily News*, June 15, 2002.

Barcott, Bruce. "Blow Up." *Outside*, February 1999.

"British Pursue Rommel North from Sfax: Allies Push Through Mountains on Flank." *New York Times*, April 11, 1943.

Cohen, Felix. "Colonialism: U.S. Style." *Progressive* 15 (February 1951).

Collier, John. "Our Indian Population." *New York Times*, December 3, 1950.

"Costs Rise in Plan for Missouri Basin: New Estimates Up $2 Billion in Six Months." *New York Times*, July 30, 1950.

Cross, Mike. "Listen to All Sides." *Minot Daily News*, April 2, 1994.

Curtis, George Louis. "The Last Lodges of the Mandans." *Harper's Weekly* 33, no. 1684 (March 1889).

"Debate on Indians in Senate Likely." *New York Times*, December 17, 1950.

DeVoto, Bernard. "The Anxious West." *Harper's Magazine*, December 1946.

———. "The West Against Itself." *Harper's Magazine*, January 1947.

"Dollars, Sense, and Salmon: An Argument for Breaching Four Dams on the Lower Snake River (A Special Series)." *Idaho Statesman*, July 20, 21, and 22, 1997.

Duncan, David James. "Salmon's Second Coming." *Sierra*, March 2000.

"Emancipation Seen Far Off for Indians: Commissioner Under Fire." *New York Times*, November 1, 1951.

Fey, Harold E. "The Indian and the Law." *Christian Century*, March 9, 1955.

———. "Indian Winter." *Christian Century*, March 2, 1955.

———. "What Indians Want." *Christian Century*, September 21, 1955.

"First Power Generated at Garrison." *Minot Daily News*, January 21, 1956.

"Five Concerns to Get Initial Power from Garrison Dam." *Minot Daily News*, January 21, 1956.

Fogarty, Hugh A. "New Indian 'War' May Slow Development of MVA." *New York Times*, December 28, 1946.

"Forced Assimilation of Indians Decried." *New York Times*, May 10, 1952.

"$4,480,000 Asked for MVA Program." *New York Times*, March 20, 1945.

"Four Missouri Dams Speed Basin Plan." *New York Times*, August 16, 1953.

"Garrison Dam Closure Ceremonies." *Bismarck Tribune*, June 10, 1953.

"Gauges and Dials Will Keep Record of Every Phase of Power Generation at Garrison Dam." *Minot Daily News*, January 21, 1956.

"Golden River: What's to Be Done About the Missouri?" *Harper's Magazine*, May 1945.

Harmer, Ruth Mulvey. "Uprooting the Indians." *Atlantic Monthly*, March 1956.

Hill, Burton S. "The Great Indian Treaty Council of 1851." *Nebraska History*, 1956.

"House Votes to Facilitate Citizenship for Indians." *New York Times,* July 22, 1947.

Ickes, Harold. Column on Dillon Myer. *New Republic* 124 (May 1951).

————. Column on Indian bureau. *New Republic* 125 (September 1951).

"Indian Claims Total Billions." *Omaha World-Herald,* January 4, 1956.

"Indians in Canada Farm Prime Lands." *New York Times,* August 16, 1953.

"Indians Confer with President and Top Aides." *New York Times,* December 13, 1988.

"Indians Seek Pay for 70 Pct. of Nation's Land." *Indianapolis Star,* January 4, 1956.

"Indian Trails Familiar Paths to Father of Whapeton Resident." *Richland County Farmer,* July 5, 1929.

"Indian War Whoop Marks Hearings." *New York Times,* January 4, 1952.

Korey, William. "The Genocide Treaty: Unratified 35 Years, Comments by Chief Justice Warren." *New York Times,* June 23, 1984.

LaFarge, Oliver. "The Indian Frontier: An Appraisal." *Association of American Indian Affairs,* June 1963.

————. "Not an Indian, but a White-Man Problem." *New York Times,* April 30, 1950.

Leviero, Anthony. "Antagonisms Rife over Indian Policy." *New York Times,* November 2, 1951.

Liebling, A. J. "The Lake of the Cui-Ui Eaters." Four-part exposé on the plight of the Pyramid Lake Paiute. *The New Yorker,* January 1, 8, 15, and 22, 1955.

Limvere, Karl, and Rich Madsen. "Rumblings from the Ditch: A Special Report." *North Dakota Union Farmer,* Summer 1972.

Mann, Charles C. "1491." *Atlantic Monthly,* March 2002.

Miles, Jonathan. "The Eco Warriors." *Men's Journal,* November 2002.

Miller, Leslie A. "The Battle That Squanders Billions." *Saturday Evening Post,* May 14, 1949.

"Myer Out as Head of Indian Bureau." *New York Times,* March 20, 1953.

Neumann, Jim. "Panelists Contend Indians' Role Not Recognized." *Fargo Forum,* December 23, 1984.

"Officials Say Indian Claims Ruling Could Cost U.S. Billions." *Lewiston Tribune,* January 4, 1956.

Old Dog Cross, Phyllis. "Do We Want Old Systems or Better Government?" *New Town News,* February 4, 1999.

————. "Remembering Winter in Elbowoods." *Mountrail County Record,* January 23, 1997.

"Pick-Sloan Transforms Missouri River Area." *New York Times,* June 12, 1948.

"Pick's Pyke to China." *New York Times,* January 17, 1945.

"Pick Uses Floods to Back Dam Plea: General Asserts 'Billion Dollar' Disaster Could Have Been Prevented by Projects." *New York Times,* July 21, 1951.

"Plot on U.S. Indians Charged by Collier." *New York Times,* December 30, 1950.

"Policy on Indians Scored: Ex-Official Says Bureau Head Views Affairs as Patronage." *New York Times,* December 2, 1951.

"Remarks on 'Humoring Indians' Bring Protest from Tribal Leaders." *New York Times,* June 1, 1988.

"Republican West Urges State Rule." *New York Times,* November 4, 1953.

"Residential and Industrial Areas in Omaha Inundated." *New York Times,* April 13, 1943.

"Rivers on Rampage." *New York Times,* July 22, 1951.

"Sakakawea Levels Worry North Dakota." *Bismarck Tribune,* October 29, 2000.

"Senate Unit Scores Lawyer for Indians." *New York Times,* January 4, 1953.

Seybold, J. S. "Constructors Roll Nearly One Million Yards a Week into Garrison Dam." *Civil Engineering,* October 1949.

"Six Jobs Accomplished by Garrison Dam and Reservoir." *Minot Daily News,* January 21, 1956.

Smalley, E. V. "The Isolation of Life on Prairie Farms." *Atlantic Monthly,* December 1893.

"Three Indian Tribes Sell Land for Dam, but Reluctantly." *New York Times,* March 17, 1950.

"Truman Asks Fund of $4,000,000,000 for Flood Control." *New York Times,* July 17, 1947.

"Truman Says G.O.P. in Kansas Blocked Key Flood Control." *New York Times,* August 7, 1951.

"$12.6 Million for Indians' Land." *New York Times,* November 1, 1949.

"Two Congress Bills on Indians Scored: Measures to Widen the Police Powers of the U.S. Bureau Called Un-American." *New York Times,* March 27, 1952.

"U.S. Indians Seen Going Downgrade." *New York Times,* April 26, 1950.

Van de Mark, Dorothy. "The Raid on the Reservations." *Harper's Magazine,* March 1956.

"Varied Plans Seek Indians' Welfare." *New York Times,* November 3, 1951.

"Venerable Pastor, Dr. C. L. Hall, Dies." *Bismarck Tribune,* November 1939.

Watkins, T. H. "Beyond Mile Zero." *Wilderness,* Spring 1995.

Webb, Walter Prescott. "The American West: Perpetual Mirage." *Harper's Magazine,* May 1954.

Whitelaw, Ed. "Breaching Dam Myths." *Oregon Quarterly,* Autumn 2000.

"World Commission on Dams Says Woes Outweigh Benefits for Many Large Dams." *Knoxville News-Sentinel,* November 24, 2000.

LETTERS, MEMORANDUMS, MISCELLANEOUS

Aandahl, Fred G. Letter to Martin Cross, April 2, 1946.

Archdale, James. Letter to Martin Cross, November 24, 1947.

Bearce, Franklin. Letter to Martin Cross and Floyd Montclair, April 25, 1948.

Bosse, Scott. Testimony before the Senate Committee on Environment and Public Works: Subcommittee on Fisheries, Wildlife, and Water, September 14, 2000.

Brown, B. Gratz. Letters to the *Missouri Republican,* August 8, 1851, to November 30, 1851. Columbia, MO: Missouri Historical Society, September 1956.

Burdick, Usher L. Letter to Martin Cross, May 4, 1953.

Case, Ralph. Expense account. Tribal Delegation in Washington, January 17, 1947.

———. Letter to George Gillette and Tribal Council, January 21, 1947.

———. Letter to Martin Cross, December 27, 1945.

Cohen, Felix. Letter to Amos Lamson. Omaha Tribal Council, May 12, 1950.

Cross, Martin. February 12, 1964.

———. July 22, 1963.

———. Letter to *Harper's Magazine,* April 25, 1956.

———. Letter to John Shaw, June 23, 1954.

———. Letter to Marilyn and Kent Hudson, March 25, 1963.

———. Letter to Mrs. Alfred Zuger, January 21, 1947.

———. Letter to Robert Yellowtail, May 1953.

———. Letter to Sioux tribes on termination, December 22, 1951.

———. Letter to sister Alice, December 26, 1923.

———. Letter to sister Alice from Wahpeton School, January 15, 1924.

———. Letter to son Crusoe, July 10, 1951.

———. Letter to son Crusoe, September 24, 1951.

———. Letter to W. W. Short, February 24, 1953.

———. March 2, 1964.

———. Memo to NCAI members, June 19, 1963.

———. October 9, 1963.

———. Report on Governor's Interstate Indian Council, October 29, 1962.

———. Telegram to Associated Press. Bismarck, ND, June 26, 1952.

———. Telegram to Senator William Langer, March 13, 1950.

Curry, James E. Letter to Senator Zales N. Ecton, October 1, 1952.

Department of the Interior. Lieu lands press release, December 4, 1946.

Dickinson, Mrs. LaFell. Letter from Federation of Women's Clubs supporting the Three Affiliated Tribes, July 10, 1946.

Fort Berthold Bulletins [biweekly newsletters], January 1950–August 1954.

Fort Berthold Superintendent's personal log, 1907–1912.

Fort Berthold Tribal Court. Minutes of hearings, December 4, 1946.

Foster, W.G. Letter to Martin Cross and Senator Milton Young, March 11, 1950.

Garner, Warner. Letter to Mr. De Lacy on Fort Berthold, July 30, 1946.

Garrison Dam Closure Ceremony. Guest list and agenda, June 10, 1953.

Garry, Joseph. Letter to member tribes of the NCAI, January 2, 1956.

George, Frank. Letter to NCAI tribal chairmen, September 26, 1952.

Kirk, Seldon. Letter to the BIA superintendent of the Klamath reservation, February 20, 1947.

Krueger, Representative Otto. Letter to Martin Cross, December 28, 1953.

Lewis, Orme. Letter to Senator Arthur Watkins, March 13, 1953.

McNickle, D'Arcy. Letter to Martin Cross, May 1946.

———. Letter to Martin Cross, November 20, 1945.

Missionary Herald. Notes on the Fort Berthold Mission, June 1877.

Montclair, Floyd. Pamphlet by Montclair on Fort Berthold Indians. Minot, 1946.

Myer, Dillon. Letter on termination to all regional BIA superintendents, August 1952.

NCAI. Agenda of annual meeting. Billings, MT, November 1952.

———. Letter of appeal to modify P.L. 280, 1953.

———. Telegram to Martin Cross, January 7, 1956.

New Ebbitt Hotel. Receipt for hotel room, January 15, 1947.

Old Dog, Alice. Letter to Phyllis Old Dog Cross, May 14, 1966.

Pick, Lewis. Transcript of meeting at Elbowoods High School with Three Affiliated Tribes on Garrison Dam. Archives, Four Bears Museum, Three Affiliated Tribes, May 27, 1946.

Quinn, R. W. Letter to Warren Spaulding, BIA, September 21, 1951.

Schulte, Q. R. Letter to Martin Cross, October 14, 1954.

Shane, Ralph M. Letter to Colonel H. Hille, Army engineers, March 16, 1955.

Short, W. W. Letter to Martin Cross, March 5, 1953.

Three Affiliated Tribes. Constitution and bylaws, approved June 29, 1936.

———. Corporate charter, ratified April 24, 1937.

———. Report on meeting with BIA in Washington, March 15–28, 1953.

Wheeler, General R. A. Letter to George Gillette, December 3, 1947.

Whitman, Carl. Telegram to Floyd Montclair and Martin Cross, January 15, 1950.

Yellowtail, Robert. Letter to Martin Cross, April 4, 1953.

———. Letter to Martin Cross, April 7, 1953.

———. Newsletter on the BIA, November 1952.

———. Newsletter on Termination, October 9, 1952.

———. Open letter to Indian tribes, May 1952.

Young, Senator Milton R. Letter to Martin Cross, January 20, 1947.

———. Letter to Martin Cross, May 7, 1953.

———. Letter to Martin Cross, May 27, 1953.

Zimmerman, William. Acting Indian commissioner's statement and remarks to the Tribal Business Council of the Three Affiliated Tribes, Washington, D.C., January 21, 1948.

Garrison Diversion Unit Commission

Cross, Raymond. Recommended changes to recommendations. Letter to Ike Livermore, December 14, 1984 (on file with author).

———. Statement to the Garrison Diversion Unit Commission, October 1984 (on file with author).

Establishing Garrison Diversion Unit Commission. U.S. Public Law 360. 98th Cong., 2nd sess., July 16, 1984.

GDUC. Commission members and biographical information (on file with author).

———. Congressional charter for commission, May 1984 (on file with author).

———. Final recommendations regarding Indian claims. Department of the Interior, 1985 (on file with author).

———. Summary of technical recommendations to Congress (on file with author).

———. Synopsis of final plan, December 14, 1984 (on file with author).

———. Transcripts of final meeting with Treen, Zorn, and O'Meara on recommendations to Congress, December 19, 1984 (on file with author).

Livermore, Ike. "A Plea for Economic and Social Justice for the Fort Berthold and Standing Rock Indian Tribes and Reservations of North Dakota." To Representative George Miller, House Resources Committee, March 31, 1987 (on file with author).

Livermore, Ike, and Ann Zorn. Itinerary for trips to reservations, December 12, 1984 (on file with author).

———. "Observations on Visits to Fort Berthold and Standing Rock." Report to members of GDUC, December 1984 (on file with author).

Messing, Marc. Memorandum to Ike Livermore and Ann Zorn on fundamental Indian issues, December 10, 1984 (on file with author).

———. Memorandum to Ike Livermore and Ann Zorn regarding trips to reservations, December 6, 1984 (on file with author).

U.S. House Committee on Interior and Insular Affairs. *Hearing on the Garrison Diversion Unit Reformulation Act of 1986.* 99th Cong., 2nd sess., April 9, 1986.

U.S. House Subcommittee on Water and Power Resources of the Committee on Interior and Insular Affairs. *Hearings on the Final Recommendations of the Garrison Diversion Unit Commission.* 99th Cong., 1st sess., February 28, 1985.

REPORTS, JOURNALS, MONOGRAPHS

Case, Harold. "100 Years at Fort Berthold." Bismarck, ND: State Historical Society of North Dakota, 1978.

Cohen, Felix S. "Americanizing the White Man." *American Scholar* 21 (Spring 1952).

———. "Erosion of Indian Rights." *Yale Law Journal* 62 (February 1953): 348–390.

Cross, Raymond. "Sovereign Bargains, Indian Takings, and the Preservation of Indian Country in the Twenty-First Century." *Arizona Law Review* 40, no. 2 (Summer 1998).

———. "Tribes as Rich Nations." *Oregon Law Review* 79, no. 4 (Summer 2001).

———. *"Twice-Born from the Waters."* From a collection of essays edited by Mark Spence. Berkeley: University of California Press, 2002.

Deloria, Vine Jr. *A Brief History of the Federal Responsibility to the American Indian, Based on the Report "Legislative Analysis of the Federal Role in Indian Education."* Department of Health, Education, and Welfare [Education Division]. Office of Education. Washington, D.C.: GPO, 1979.

Deloria, Vine Jr., and Raymond J. Demallie. *Documents of American Indian Diplomacy: Treaties, Agreements, and Conventions, 1775–1979.* Norman: University of Oklahoma Press, 1984.

Duran, Bonnie, with Eduardo Duran, and Maria Yellow Horse Brave Heart. "Native Americans and the Trauma of History." In *Studying Native American Problems and Prospects.* Edited by Russell Thorton. Madison, WI: University of Wisconsin Press, 1998.

Durning, Alan. "Guardians of the Land: Indigenous Peoples and the Health of the Earth." *World Watch* 112 (1992).

Fort Berthold Agency Report of 1943. Aberdeen, SD: Bureau of Indian Affairs, Regional Office, 1944.

Friesema, H. Paul, and Charles S. Matzke. "Socio-Economic and Cultural Effects of the Garrison Dam upon Members of the Three Affiliated Tribes of Fort Berthold Indian Reservation: A Report to the Joint Tribal Advisory Commission," May 1986 (on file with the author).

Getches, David H. "Conquering the Cultural Frontier: The New Subjectivism of the Supreme Court in Indian Law." *California Law Review* 84, no. 6 (December 1996).

Grijalva, James. "Tribal Governmental Regulation on Non-Indian Polluters of Reservation Waters." *North Dakota Law Review* 71, no. 2 (1995).

Grijalva, James, with Richard A. DuBey. "The Assertion of Natural Resource Damage Claims by Indian Tribal Trustees." *Environmental Claims Journal* 4, no. 2 (Winter 1991–1992).

Hill, George W. "Rural Migration and Farm Abandonment." Washington, D.C.: Federal Relief Administration, 1935.

"The Indians and the Pick-Sloan Plan." Missouri River Basin Investigations 67. Department of the Interior. Washington, D.C.: GPO, November 1948.

Jenkinson, Clay Straus. *"The West of Jefferson's Imagination." Halcyon: Journal of the Humanities 13 (1991).*

Johnson, Jerome E., and Richard J. Goodman. "Negative Impacts of Garrison and Oahe Reservoirs on the North Dakota Economy." Department of Agricultural Economics. Fargo, ND: North Dakota State University of Agriculture and Applied Science, April 1962.

Lemkin, Raphael. "Axis Rule in Occupied Europe." Washington, D.C.: Carnegie Endowment for International Peace, 1944.

Maass, Arthur A. "Congress and Water Resources." *American Political Science Review* 44 (1950).

Macgregor, Gordon, ed. "Attitudes of the Fort Berthold Indians Regarding Removal from the Garrison Reservoir Site and Future Administration of Their Reservation." Missouri River Basin Investigations. Department of the Interior. Washington D.C.: GPO, August 1947.

McLaughlin, Castle, and Tracy J. Andrews. "Nation, Tribe, and Class: The Dynamics of Agrarian Transformation on the Fort Berthold Reservation." *American Indian Culture and Research Journal* 22, no. 101 (1998).

"McLean County Heritage." Washburn, ND: McLean County Historical Society, 1978.

Merriam, Lewis et al. "The Problem of Indian Administration" [also known as the Merriam Report]. Baltimore: Johns Hopkins University Press, 1928.

Meyer, Roy. "Fort Berthold and the Garrison Dam." *North Dakota History* 35, no. 215 (1968).

———. "The Resources, People, and Administration of Fort Berthold Reservation." Missouri River Basin Investigations 60. Department of the Interior. Washington, D.C.: GPO, August 1948.

Robinson, Michael. "Water for the West." Chicago: Public Works Historical Society, 1979.

Russell, Brian Keith. *Promise of Water: The Legacy of Pick-Sloan and the Irrigation of North Dakota.* North Dakota Humanities Council, 2002.

"Seeking a Re-study and Investigation and Due Consideration of Treaty Rights for the Three Affiliated Tribes on the Fort Berthold Indian Reservation; Opposing the Garrison Dam Project and Urging Relocation of the Dam." Three Affiliated Tribes Fight Eviction. Fort Berthold Indian Defense Association. Elbowoods, ND, 1945.

———. "Social and Economic Impacts of Garrison Dam on the Indians of the Fort Berthold Reservation." Missouri River Basin Investigations 2. Department of the Interior. Washington, D.C.: GPO, 1949.

Thornthwaite, C. Warren. "Climate and Settlement in the Great Plains." In *Climate and Man: Yearbook of Agriculture.* Washington, D.C., 1941.

Tsosie, Rebecca. "Tribal Environmental Policy in an Era of Self-Determination." *Vermont Law Review* 21 (1996).

Tyler, S. Lyman. *Indian Affairs: A Study of the Changes in Policy of the United States Toward Indians.* Provo: Institute of American Indian Studies, 1964.

———. *Indian Affairs: A Work Paper on Termination with an Attempt to Show its Antecedents.* Provo: Institute of American Indian Studies, 1964.

Zimmerman, William Jr. "The Role of the Bureau of Indian Affairs since 1933." *Annals of the American Academy of Political and Social Science* 311 (May 1957).

GOVERNMENT DOCUMENTS (REPORTS, HEARINGS, LEGISLATION, SPEECHES)

"Background Data Relating to the Three Affiliated Tribes of the Fort Berthold Reservation Located in the State of North Dakota." Bureau of Indian Affairs Report. Washington, D.C.: GPO, 1954.

Black Hills Settlement Act. U.S. Public Law 243. 95th Cong., 2nd sess. *U.S. Statutes at Large* 92, pt. 1, March 10, 1978.

Chapman, Oscar. Transcript of "lieu lands" meeting between BIA, Martin Cross, Army engineers, Bureau of Reclamation, and Felix Cohen in Chapman's Office on December 16, 1946. Washington, D.C.: Department of the Interior, 1946.

Eisenhower, Dwight. Speech made on Public Law 280 and termination at Lowery Air Force Base in Denver, CO, in August 1953. Reprinted in the Pine Ridge news bulletin, September 1, 1953.

Establishing Garrison Diversion Unit Commission. U.S. Public Law 360. 98th Cong., 2nd sess., July 16, 1984.

Establishing the Indian Claims Commission. U.S. Public Law 726. 79th Cong., 2nd sess. *U.S. Statutes at Large* 60, pt. 1, August 13, 1946.

Establishing State Jurisdiction over Indian Nations in Civil Disputes. U.S. Public Law 280. 83rd Cong., 1st sess. *U.S. Statutes at Large* 67, August 15, 1953.

Flood Control Act of 1944. U.S. Public Law 534. 78th Cong., 2nd sess. *U.S. Statutes at Large* 58, pt. 1, December 14, 1944.

The Fort Berthold Taking Act. U.S. Public Law 437. 81st Cong., 1st. sess. *U.S. Statutes at Large* 63, pt. 1, October 29, 1949.

General Allotment Act [also known as the *Dawes Act*]. *U.S. Statutes at Large* 24 (1887): 388.

Indian Appropriations Act of 1892. U.S. Public Law 478. In *Documents of American Indian Diplomacy: Treaties, Agreements, and Conventions, 1775–1979.* Edited by Vine Deloria Jr. and Raymond J. Demallie. Norman: University of Oklahoma Press, 1999.

Lieu Lands Act for Fort Berthold [also *Civil Functions of the War Department*]. U.S. Public Law 374. 79th Cong., 2nd sess. *U.S. Statutes at Large* 60, pt. 1, May 2, 1946.

Missouri Basin Inter-Agency Committee. *Report on Adequacy of Flows in the Missouri River.* Department of the Interior. Omaha, 1951

Missouri River: A Letter from the Secretary of War: Referred to the Committee on Rivers and Harbors, February 5, 1934. 73rd Cong., 2nd sess. As ordered by the *Flood Control Act* of January 21, 1927. Washington, D.C.: GPO, 1935.

Myer, Dillon. Speech on termination to the western governor's conference at Phoenix, AZ, December 9, 1952.

National Environmental Policy Act. U.S. Public Law 91-190. 91st Cong., 2nd sess., January 1, 1970.

Reclamation Act of 1939. U.S. Public Law 76-260. 76th Cong., 1st sess. *U.S. Statutes at Large* 53, pt. 2, August 4, 1939.

Replacing Lieu Lands Conditions with Cash Settlement. U.S. Public Law 296. 80th Cong., 1st sess. *U.S. Statutes at Large* 61, pt. 1, July 31, 1947.

Roosevelt, Franklin. Letter to Congress on desirability of Missouri Valley Authority. *Congressional Record,* September 21, 1944. Washington, D.C.: GPO, 1945.

U.S. Congress. *Declaration of Indian Rights.* 83rd Cong., 2nd sess. *Congressional Record,* March 11, 1954. Washington, D.C.: GPO, 1954.

———. *Northwest Ordinance of 1787.* 2nd Cong., 1st sess. *U.S. Statutes at Large* 50. Adopted on August 7, 1789.

————. Representative Usher Burdick charges the Army Corps of Engineers with unconstitutional taking of Fort Berthold, and violating treaties. 83rd Cong., 1st sess. *Congressional Record* 99, pt. 3 (April 20, 1953). Washington, D.C.: GPO, 1954.

————. Senator Barry Goldwater speaking against termination legislation. 86th Cong., 1st sess. *Congressional Record,* March 9, 1959. Washington, D.C.: GPO.

U.S. Department of the Interior. *Conference with Delegation from Fort Berthold Tribal Council on March 20, 1953.* From the files of Homer Jenkins, Program Officer, and Ross Landon, Program Counsel. Meeting chaired by Warren Spaulding, Deputy Commissioner of the Bureau of Indian Affairs.

U.S. General Accounting Office. *Descriptive Data on Garrison Diversion Unit and Other Reclamation Projects, RED-76-80,* March 5, 1976. Washington, D.C.: GPO, 1976.

U.S. House. Congressman James Murray speaking on the need for a complete revision of federal Indian policy. 85th Cong., 2nd sess. *Congressional Record,* April 17, 1958. Washington, D.C.: GPO, 1958.

————. Congressman Lee Metcalf speaking on proposed revision of federal Indian policy and P.L. 280. 85th Cong., 2nd sess. *Congressional Record,* April 17, 1958. Washington, D.C.: GPO, 1958.

————. Congressman William Lemke speaking on the injustice of the Fort Berthold takings act. 81st Cong., 1st sess. *Congressional Record,* October 20, 1949. Washington, D.C.: GPO, 1950.

————. *The Pick Plan.* 78th Cong., 2nd sess. House Doc. no. 475, 1944.

————. *Report on House Resolution 108 Authorizing the Committee on Interior and Insular Affairs to Conduct an Investigation of the Bureau of Indian Affairs.* HR 2680, September 20, 1954. Washington, D.C.: GPO.

U.S. House Committee on Interior and Insular Affairs. *Garrison Diversion Unit Reformulation Act of 1986, Accompanying HR 1116.* 99th Cong., 2nd sess., April 9, 1986. H. Rept. 525.

————. *Garrison Unit Joint Tribal Advisory Committee: Hearings on HR 2414 to Implement Certain Recommendations.* 102nd Cong., 1st sess., October 30, 1991, November 4, 1991.

————. *Hearing with BIA Director Dillon Myer on Indian Attorneys and Per Capita Payments to Enrolled Members of Three Affiliated Tribes.* 82nd Cong., 2nd sess., April 5, 1952.

————. *Hearing on the Garrison Diversion Unit Reformulation Act of 1986.* 99th Cong., 2nd sess., April 9, 1986.

————. *Hearing on HR 7068: Provisions in Connection with the Construction of the Garrison Diversion Unit.* 85th Cong., 1st. sess., October 30, 1957.

————. *Hearing on Provisions in Connection with the Construction of the Garrison Diversion Unit.* 86th Cong., 2nd sess., June 10, 1960.

————. *Hearing on Provisions in Connection with the Construction of the Garrison Diversion Unit.* 88th Cong., 2nd sess., February 20, 1964.

U.S. House Committee on Public Lands. *Providing for the Ratification by Congress of a Contract for the Purchase of Certain Indian Lands.* 81st Cong., 1st sess., May 9, 1949. H. Rept. 544.

U.S. House Subcommittee of the Committee on Indian Affairs. *Congressional Investigation of Indian Bureau: Hearings on HR 166.* 78th Cong., 1st sess., July 22 to August 8, 1944.

U.S. House Subcommittee on Water and Power Resources of the Committee on Interior and Insular Affairs. *Hearings on the Final Recommendations of the Garrison Diversion Unit Commission.* 99th Cong., 1st sess., February 28, 1985.

U.S. House Subcommittees on Indian Affairs of the Committee on Public Lands. *Providing for the Ratification by Congress of a Contract for the Purchase of Certain Indian Lands Under HJ Res. 33.* 81st Cong., 1st sess., April 29–30, May 2–3, 1949.

U.S. Senate Committee on Appropriations. *Hearing on War Department Civil Functions Appropriation Bill of 1948.* 80th Cong., 1st sess., July 16, 1947.

U.S. Senate Committee on Indian Affairs. *Hearings on Termination of Federal Trust Responsibility over Indian Lands, and HR 108.* 83rd Cong., 1st sess., July 18 to August 1, 1953 (Transcripts reprinted in *The American Indian and the United States.* Edited by Wilcomb E. Washburn. Smithsonian Institution. New York: Random House, 1973).

——. *Missouri River Basin: Conservation, Control, and Use of Water Resources of the Missouri River Basin in Montana, Wyoming, Colorado, North Dakota, South Dakota, Nebraska, Kansas, Iowa, and Missouri, with Full Report by Secretary of the Interior Harold L. Ickes on Bureau of Reclamation Plan for Basin Development.* 78th Cong., 2nd sess., May 5, 1944. S. Rept. 191.

——. *Protesting the Construction of Garrison Dam: Hearing on SJ Res. 79 to Establish a Joint Committee to Study Claims of Indian Tribes and to Investigate the Administration of Indian Affairs.* 79th Cong., 1st sess., October 9, 1945.

——. *Survey of Conditions Among the Indians of the United States.* 78th Cong., 1st sess., June 11, 1943. S. Rept. 310.

U.S. Senate Committee on Interior and Insular Affairs. *Hearing on S 1830 and 2424, and to Hear Claims to Mineral Rights by Three Affiliated Tribes of North Dakota.* 82nd Cong., 2nd sess., April 9, 1952.

——. *Presentation of Final Report of the Garrison Unit Joint Tribal Advisory Committee (JTAC).* 100th Cong., 1st sess., November 19, 1987.

——. *To Provide for the Return to the Former Owners of Certain Lands Acquired in Connection with the Garrison Dam Project of Mineral Interests in Such Lands: Hearing on S 536 and S 746.* 84th Cong., 1st sess., March 28, 1955.

U.S. Senate Committee on Irrigation and Reclamation. *Hearing to Establish a Missouri Valley Authority.* 79th Cong., 1st sess., 1945. 109.

U.S. Senate and House. Joint hearing of the Senate Select Committee on Indian Affairs, the Senate Committee on Energy and Natural Resources, and the House Committee on Interior and Insular Affairs. *Final Report and Recommendations of the Garrison Unit Joint Tribal Advisory Committee.* 100th Cong., 1st sess., March 30, 1987.

U.S. Senate Select Committee on Indian Affairs. *Authorizing the Three Affiliated Tribes of Fort Berthold to File Claim for Damages in the Delay of Payment for Lands Claimed to Have Been Taken in Violation of the U.S. Constitution.* 96th Cong., 2nd sess., June 25, 1980. S. Rept. 833.

——. *Hearing on the Final Report of the Garrison Unit Joint Tribal Advisory Committee.* 100th Cong., 1st sess., November 19, 1987.

——. *Hearing on the Three Affiliated Tribes and Standing Rock Sioux Tribal Equitable Compensation Act of 1991.* 102nd Cong., 1st sess., April 12, 1991.

——. *Implementing Recommendations of the Garrison Unit Joint Tribal Advisory Committee.* 102nd Cong., 1st sess., November 26, 1991. S. Rept. 102-250.

——. *Three Affiliated Tribes and Standing Rock Sioux Just Compensation Act.* 100th Cong., 1st sess., March 30, 1987. S. Rept. 249.

U.S. Senate Subcommittee on Water and Power of the Committee on Energy and Natural Resources. *Hearings in the Field to Ascertain the Impact of Garrison Dam and Lake Sakakawea on Local Communities.* 101st Cong., 1st sess., August 25, 1989, October 9, 1989.

U.S. Weather Bureau. *Kansas-Missouri Floods of June–July 1951.* Technical paper no. 17. Washington, D.C.: GPO, 1952.

COURTS AND CASES

Arizona v. California, 373 U.S. 546 (1953).

Brendale v. Confederated Tribes and Bands of Yakima Indian Nation, 109 S. Ct. 2994, 3008 (1989).

Cherokee Nation v. Georgia, 31 U.S. 1 (1831).

Fletcher v. Peck, 11 U.S. 164 (1810).

Indian Claims Commission case, n. 350, *"The Three Affiliated Tribes of the Fort Berthold Reservation v. The United States of America."* Filed with the ICC, November 7, 1952.

Johnson v. McIntosh, 21 U.S. 543 (1823).

Lone Wolf v. Hitchcock, 187 U.S. 553 (1903).

Oliphant v. Squamish Indian Tribe, 435 U.S. 191 (1984).

Oregon v. United States, 467 U.S. 1252 (1984).

Tee-Hit-Ton Indians v. United States, 358 U.S. 272 (1954).

Three Affiliated Tribes v. Wold Engineering, 476 U.S. 877. Alderson Reporting. Washington, D.C. (1986). Transcripts of oral arguments in the U.S. Supreme Court, March 24, 1986 (on file with author).

———, 463 U.S. 1248 (1983).

———, 476 U.S. 877 (1986).

United States v. Adair, 478 Fed. Supp. 336, Dist. of Oregon (1979).

United States v. Adair [also known as *Adair II*], Fed. Supp. 2nd 1273, Dist. Of Oregon (2002).

United States v. Adair II, 723 Fed. 2nd 1394, 9th Cir. Court of Appeals (1984).

Winters v. United States, 207 U.S. 364 (1908).

Worcester v. Georgia, 31 U.S. 515 (1832).

Acknowledgments

❦

A nd then at long last, in the final breath of gratitude to a book's many midwives, we learn the name of the one person without whom the project "could not have happened." In gratitude for her singular support, everything from hundreds of tuna fish sandwiches to the thousands of miles we ran together in the coastal mountains to "decompress" at the end of innumerable days, I'll cheerfully break with tradition. Brenda Jean, my loving refuge and faithful beacon, belongs at the head of this parade, where I can accord her the same prominence she so selflessly conferred on this project from its conception. Words of thanks cannot redeem the gazillion sacrifices she made along the way, both large and small, nor begin to reward her unflinching dedication to its telling. There are angels among us.

Alas, the list of generous spirits who have contributed to the making of this book is long, and, by its finite nature, incomplete. As with most great adventures, it began with those teachers whose own imaginations were fired by the power of story. For this legacy I am indebted to Mrs. Hall and Professor Harry Fritz, the late K. Ross Toole, Craig Carlson, and Jean Fields, and to Robert McGiffert and Nathaniel Blumberg, paragons who taught a generation of journalists that courage is unwavering devotion in the pursuit of that which is true. I thank you.

Preparing to tell this story required schooling in parallel educations, particularly in federal Indian law. I am very grateful to Vine Deloria Jr. for orienting me to "the spiders at the center of this vast web." Mr. Deloria joined Senator James Abourezk, Raymond Cross, General Emerson Murry, Professor Ron Manuto, and Chief Justice Gerald VandeWalle in bringing generosity, enthusiasm, and insights to this education that I will never be able to repay. I am also indebted to Indian law professors James Grijalva, Charles Wilkinson, Robert Williams, and David H. Getches for their invaluable insights and indispensable precursory work. My investigation was informed and advanced by dozens of generous Indian law experts, including John Echohawk at the Native American Rights Fund in Boulder, Colorado; Philip Key at the Bonneville Power Administration; Wes Martell of Martell and Associates at Fort Washikie; Leigh Price at the Environmental Protection Agency; Judith Espinosa of the attorney general's office for the state of New Mexico; Liz Bell, counsel to Kevin Grover, former commissioner of the Bureau of Indian Affairs; Eric Eberhard of Dorsey and Whitney; Hans Walker and Lee Foley; and not last by any stretch, John Carter and Dan Decker, with the Confederated Salish and Kootenai Tribes, who have always been willing to share their experiences from the trenches. Many thanks go to Bud Ullman, NARF attorney for the Klamath tribe, for all those timely (and crucial) faxes.

The words of gratitude somehow seem manageable until I get to this spot, to Indian Country. How is it possible that a little boy born in Charlie Russell's last house, Trail's End, and who spent his childhood with the Aymara on the Altiplano of Bolivia and in Mexico City, would come to have so many good friends in Indian Country, from the Penobscot River in Maine to the Cahuilla of the Anza Valley? You have made me laugh and weep, and have enriched my life in ways for which there is no telling: Tom Goldtooth of the Indigenous Environmental Network; Christine Benally and Lori Goodman of Diné CARE; Ben Winton, Preston Singletary, and Verna Teller, former governor of the Isleta Pueblo tribe; Jim Welch; Northern Cheyenne attorney Gail Small, mother of four and *Ms.* magazine's Woman of the Year; former EPA administrator Bill Yellowtail; Karl Humphrey, Steve Lopez, Christine Hansen, Steve Dodge, Arnie Charging, the late Walt Bressette, the Old Elk clan, Louise Holding Eagle, Neshune Heredia, Rose and Jim Main, Marie Wells, Ed Lone Fight, Luther Grinnell, Bradley Angel, Andrea Carmen, Janine Pease, Fred Baker, Jesus O'Suna, Charles and Clarise Hudson, Jim Bear, Early Tulley, Paul De Main, Leslie Logan, Calvin Grinnell, Dr. Monica Mayer, Sherry Meddick, and Julene Woods, and Tiny Man Heavy Runner. Your invaluable contributions are all over these pages.

With the generous help of Alyce Spotted Bear, Ike Livermore, Ann Zorn, Governor David Treen, and Marie Wells, the story of the Garrison Diversion Unit Commission came alive. Likewise, thanks for the accounts of the Joint Tribal Advisory Committee go to General Emerson Murry, Hans Walker, Lee Foley, and Marilyn Hudson. Also, blessings are sent to research librarians everywhere, particularly those who quietly go about their work at Oregon State University — Dave Johnson and Carrie Ottow; and at the North Dakota Heritage Center, where Susan Dingle worked on weekends bird-dogging semitrivial pursuits when I was a thousand miles away canoeing in the Cascades. Also, a heap of gratitude to Pam Musland at the North Dakota Farmers Union and to Professor W. Raymond Wood, both of whom were so helpful in directing me to primary source material.

Everett Albers, director of the North Dakota Humanities Council, Dr. Herbert Wilson, and Roger Johnson, North Dakota's commissioner of agriculture, all gave me important directions at various forks in the road, as did Ted Quanrud and Ken Rogers. Similarly, Scott Bosse, Kathy Krist, Wendy Wilson, and Charlie Rae honored me with their time and unique insights into the plight of the Columbia River salmon.

Once in the trenches, I could always look to special friends whose intangible contributions and steadfast support somehow held my doubts at bay when the sun went down. I am grateful for your ideas, insights, and suggestions, and for suffering through early drafts of this story before it had grown edges: John Byrne, Raymond Chavez, Melissa Hartley, Natasha Kern, Evalyn Lee, John Nichols, Ronna Pomeroy, and my very own Merlins, David Bella and Blake Rodman, whose tuning forks were faultless, and whose capacity for worry so often spared me the burden; and Paul Lynn and Douglas Sandage, whose loyalty across decades has been a light in the forest. The contributions of my agent, Joe Vallely, and publisher, Michael Pietsch, were indispensable from beginning to end, as were the contributions of Deborah Baker, my tireless editor at Little, Brown, whose exacting commitment to this family and their story never wavered, despite the length of the trail and the height of the mountain. While we were busy discerning that trail, Allison Markin Powell lent us both her certain ear and her steady voice, and on numerous occasions kept both of us from tumbling off the earth. Then, in the nick of time, Reagan Arthur, Michael Mezzo, and Karen Landry caught us when we did.

To the grandchildren of Old Dog and Many Dances, Phyllis, Crusoe, Bucky, Marilyn, Michael, Uppy, Milton, Carol, and Raymond, I speak for many when I thank you for your courageous generosity, and your willingness to bring your private stories forward. You have pulled a bright thread through the tapestry of our nation's story, one that will continue to remind generations to come that we are all immeasurably richer for the indomitability of the human spirit of America's first citizens.

And finally, to my father and mother, Frank and Mary VanDevelder, who pored over every line of this book, and made invaluable contributions. Their unwavering devotion to decency, justice, and the invincible power of love never flickered in the storms. I was blessed to have been included on the remarkable journey they have made together.

Index

※

About the Author

Paul VanDevelder has been an investigative reporter, photojournalist, and documentary filmmaker for more than twenty years. He has written extensively about the law and the role of natural resources in emergent twenty-first-century conflicts between competing cultures and political economies. His award-winning work has appeared in newspapers and magazines around the world, including the *New York Times, Native Americas, National Geographic Traveler, Paris Match, Esquire,* and the *Seattle Times.* He lives with his family in the Pacific Northwest. Drawn from a decade of research, this book is his first.

ZZ	SINGLE Mo	S

Customer:

James S Downey

L WED AM

Coyote Warrior: One Man, Three Tribes, and the Trial That Forged a Nation

Paul VanDevelder

W1-S006-14-21

No CD

Used - Very Good

W3-DPD-521

9780316896894

Picker Notes:

M _____ '2 _____

WT _____ 2 _____

CC _____

68674876

1 Item

1068842343

Monday Singles HD

Ship. Created: 11/10/2019 11:44:00 AM